SHIFTING GEARS

TECHNOLOGY, LITERATURE,

CULTURE IN MODERNIST AMERICA

BY CECELIA TICHI

SHIFTING GEARS

The University of North Carolina Press Chapel Hill and London

© 1987 The University of North Carolina Press

Manufactured in the United States of America

92 91 90 89 88 5 4 3 2

Library of Congress Cataloging-in-Publication Data

Tichi, Cecelia, 1942–
  Shifting gears.

  Bibliography: p.
  Includes index.
  1. American literature—20th century—History
and criticism. 2. Literature and technology—
United States. 3. United States—Popular culture.
I. Title.
PS228.T42T5 1987 810'.9'005 86-16161
ISBN 0-8078-1715-5
ISBN 0-8078-4167-6 (pbk.)

The author is grateful for permission to
reproduce the following:

From *The Waste Land* by T. S. Eliot. Copyright
1958, 1962. Reprinted by permission of Harcourt
Brace Jovanovich and Faber and Faber, Ltd.,
London.

From *Earlier Poems* by William Carlos Williams:
"Rapid Transit"; "The Red Wheelbarrow" and
excerpts from "Homage"; "The House"; "First
Praise"; "Good Night"; "To Wish Myself Courage";
"Pastoral"; "The Flower." Copyright 1938 by New
Directions Publishing Corporation. Reprinted by
permission of New Directions Publishing
Corporation.

From *Pictures from Brueghel* by William Carlos
Williams: "Children's Games II." Copyright 1962
by William Carlos Williams. Reprinted by permission of New Directions Publishing Corporation.

For Bill
and for Claire and Julia

CONTENTS

*Machinery will tend to lose its
sensational glamour ... for ...
the wonderment experienced in
watching [airplane] nose dives
is of less immediate creative
promise to poetry than the
familiar gesture of a motorist in
the modest act of shifting gears.*
Hart Crane, "Modern Poetry," 1930

PREFACE

"Bessemer" was a good name, smelt of money and mighty rolling mills and great executives stepping out of limousines.... "Bessemer."

John Dos Passos, *The 42nd Parallel*, 1930

An American born before, say, 1960 can probably recall the personal incident that crystallized his or her knowledge of the current technological revolution. Mine occurred on a 1985 visit to Pittsburgh's Station Square, a recycled riverfront railroad station with restaurants and shops. On a fine spring day the crowd gathered at a crafts fair set up near a hulking structure that had been moved to the riverfront site from a shut-down steel mill. I approached and stood before it, a towering, 1930 Bessemer converter bearing the brass plaque of a historical commission.

You stare hard at that plaque if you are a native Pittsburgher born during World War II, your earliest memories those of the wartime night sky blazing from the steel mills. You stare because you realize that the Bessemer converter has now become an official symbol of your past and America's as well. The steel retort essential to steelmaking from the 1890s through the better part of this century has now become the focus of tourist curiosity and nostalgia. Economically, of course, it represents a bygone industrial era, one grimly echoed in the abandoned steelworks up and down the Monongahela Valley.

But the industrial relic signifies something else as well. Mounted for exhibition in the era of the digital computer, the Bessemer converter represents a superseded technology. It is the technology we associate with eighteenth- and nineteenth-century inventions like boilers and gear wheels, ball bearings, pistons, and the like. It is the technology of interconnected component parts, many of them visible to the naked eye in traditional machines and structures. In operation, this technology became familiar in the last century in steam locomotives whose rods and wheels pushed and rotated before the eyes of bystanders on railroad station platforms. It is a technology still with us in the automobile engine and in steel-frame building construction. It is the technology of girders and gears.

It is no longer, however, the dominant or defining technology. That position belongs to the computer. Even popular slang underscores the change. An eccentric or crazy individual formerly had a "screw loose"; he or she now has a "bad chip." Mental effort is now the work of a "computer mind"; no longer do the "wheels go around." These images mark the transition from one dominant technology to another. The change involves much more than the adaptation of language to new material conditions. Behind the shift of images are new, technological definitions of the human relation to the world.

Twentieth-century science, of course, is also reconceiving the material world. In quantum mechanics it is a statistically probable set of circumstances at any given moment, in nuclear physics fluctuating energy levels. The functioning of higher organisms, biochemists argue, may depend upon chemical information systems far more sophisticated than the computer's binary model allows. Within technology, however, it is the computer which provides the powerful new metaphor for the human mind and brain. The classicist and student of the computer, J. David Bolter, explains this power on a historical basis. In any given era, he argues, there exists a technology which defines or redefines man's role in relation to nature. Currently, Bolter argues, the computer is giving us a new definition of man as an "information processor" and of nature as "information to be processed" (13). Accordingly, a contemporary magazine cover portrays the human brain as a mass of digital microcircuitry.

The now-eclipsed technology of gears and girders defined human beings and their relation to nature differently. Its central conception was that of an energy-transforming machine. True, some of its machine terms are still in use. "Systems" and "components," for instance, continue from the Bessemer era into the computer age, where they are newly defined in a context of information processing. But when used in the era of gear-and-girder technology, these terms meant something very different. In fact, they referred to a different world view. The gear-and-girder era, powerful through the late nineteenth century and well into the twentieth, fostered a conception of the human being as a machine for the consumption and production of energy. And it defined nature similarly as a congeries of machines and stuctures comprised of interworking component parts, meaning structural and mechanical members (gears, crankshafts, sprocket arms, armatures, belts, etc.). According to this technological outlook, each machine or combination structure-machine produced energy with greater or lesser efficiency, depending upon its design.

The human role in such a world was to formulate new designs. It was to engineer the structures and machines able to function with maximal efficiency and minimal waste. Under the aegis of this technology human beings intellectually understood the material world as dynamic, integrated assemblies of component parts. Studied analytically, the parts and the wholes could be reconceived in new relations to each other. They could be improved upon by redesign, making the systems stronger and more efficient. New, better designs were possible with redesigned, reconstituted components. The emphasis was always upon the component parts and the human role in design.[1]

1. The reader will notice that throughout this study writers and other nontechnical commentators mix up technical terminology, some of it more appropriate to machinery with

This machine world of the gear-and-girder technology had vast implications for all of American culture during the late nineteenth and earlier twentieth centuries. Until recently we have been simply too involved in it to see it, too much a part of its assumptions to gain the necessary analytical perspective. Now its decline in importance in the computer age opens up that perspective. The assumptions of the gear-and-girder technology can emerge clearly as just that—a set of assumptions. These can be seen as formulations of reality and not as reality itself. When we study these assumptions, therefore, we essentially study an era's perception. We investigate an outlook on the world and recognize that certain imaginative forms are necessarily cognate with it. In this instance I will approach that once-definitive technology of gears and girders in order to see how its assumptions affected diverse areas of American culture, from skyscrapers and autos to popular media and the arts of the written word.

We must bear in mind, all the while, that the gear-and-girder technology pushed aside certain cherished assumptions about the material world in its own day. Its ascendance brought about new conceptions of art because it posed a radical challenge to the existing order. Specifically, the machine world of gears and girders displaced the dominant Romantic view of a holistic, spiritual world of vegetative and bodily being. When the twentieth-century poet, William Carlos Williams, called the poem a machine made of words, he presumed a very different world from that of Henry David Thoreau, who wrote in the *Dial* that "poetry . . . is a natural fruit" and that "man bears a poem . . . as naturally as the oak bears an acorn and the vine a gourd" (4:290–91). This nineteenth-century belief that nature, the human imagination, and art were unitary, fertile, maternal, and co-generative changed radically under the the gear-and-girder assumptions of the twentieth.

Even Edgar Allan Poe, the Romantic writer fascinated by the machinery of works of art, repudiated a machine-based aesthetic of visible component parts and design. "To see distinctly the machinery—the wheels and pinions—of any work of Art is, unquestionably, of itself, a pleasure," he began. But in the next breath Poe made it clear that to emphasize the artist's design is to deform the work of art. To reveal the anatomy of form is to destroy aesthetics (1464). In a holistic and spiritually unitary world, the mechanisms and structures of the poem, like those of the

---

moving parts and the rest better suited to static structures like bridges and buildings. The sometimes-confusing mingling of terms is evidently a problem extending to professional engineers. As Dr. David Billington, a civil engineer concerned about engineering aesthetics, remarks in a letter concerning this study, "A major part of the problem lies in the ambiguous use of such language even within the engineering community [and] is another example of how engineering differs from natural science; in the latter terms are more carefully used."

Clarifying the distinction between the function of gears and girders, Dr. Billington remarks, "In mechanical engineering a gear is certainly part of a mechanism but in civil engineering a girder becomes a mechanism only when it fails (as when girders freely spanning between two walks are loaded so greatly that a hinge forms at midspan). The gear does transmit energy although the engineer speaks of transmitting motions (kinetics) or transmitting power (which signifies force times distance per unit of time). Energy is usually the term used for fuel capacity (14,000 British Thermal Units in one pound of coal, for example)."

Bessemer converter decorated for holiday season at Station Square, Pittsburgh

acorn or gourd, must remain concealed. Artifice must suit the world to which it refers. Even Walt Whitman, who sometimes carpentered the poem ("jointing, squaring, sawing, mortising, / The hoist-up of beams, the push of them in their places, laying / Them regular") was responding to a hand-crafts tradition and referred solely to static forms, not to energy-producing machines. He sings to a locomotive, but essentially to compel that "fierce-throated beauty" to "merge" into the organically holistic song-poem (186, 472).

Cracked, worn-out gear wheels illustrate a magazine cover story in the 1980s (Copyright 1984, by Newsweek, Inc. All rights reserved. Reprinted by permission.)

Human brain modeled as electronic microcircuitry (Courtesy Science 85)

Approaching the world of gears and girders, therefore, we enter into a world very different from that of the Romantics. It is a world whose sociopolitical difficulties have been addressed by numerous scholars and critics of culture. In this century its premises have precipitated a crisis of the liberal imagination by repudiating the Romantic concept of organic wholeness which gave the individual and society their integrity. Modernist thought lent itself to contemporary crises ranging from spiritual anomie to social fragmentation and even the political atrocities of fascism. In imaginative literature and criticism its presumptions have conceptually dislocated the word and the text in a crisis continuing from the late Victorians to the deconstructionists. The modernist world view, in addition, has left us disturbing paradoxes. It is ironic, for instance, that William Carlos Williams, a man of deeply liberal social sympathies, would nonetheless define the poem impersonally as a machine made of words.

Yet Williams and others could not sustain the terms of an older world. They saw signs of its exhaustion in sentimental, fey, and precious literature, and they rejected it. This study, then, is not a reiteration of the spiritual and political crises of twentieth-century modernism, but the story of American writers' efforts to reinvigorate imaginative literature in accordance with the terms of a new world. Materially, that world appeared to them to be a system of component parts, and human beings its designers. It is the world of Archimedes come to fulfillment, and one likely to remain with us in life and art insofar as it legitimately represents the visual and the kinetic. Now it is time to see how the principles of that technology emerged in the forms of language, art, and popular culture from the 1890s through the 1920s.

ACKNOWLEDGMENTS

The issues in this study were apparent to me several years before the argument took shape. A number of friends and colleagues validated my work and helped me formulate the lines of argument. I wish to thank Myra Jehlen, Amy Lang, Michael T. Gilmore, John Stilgoe, and Emily Wallace, each of whom contributed time and expertise so generously that I learned from them how helpful friends and colleagues can be to one's own work.

Along the way friends, scholars, and informal consultants made helpful suggestions or engaged in the informal discussions that proved most valuable to my thinking. In this regard I am thankful to Burton Cooper, Bonnie Costello, Eugene Green, Jeffrey Halprin, Ron Mistratta, William Newman, Mary Panzer, Mary Ann Stilgoe, William Vance, Helen Vendler, Sam Bass Warner, Jr., and Marjorie Wekselman.

The work of this book was supported by a generous research grant from the Humanities, Science, and Technology Program of the National Endowment for the Humanities. The project officer, Dr. David Wright, provided excellent advice, as did Dr. David Berndt of Boston University's Office of Sponsored Programs. Professor David Billington, Department of Civil Engineering, Princeton University, agreed to serve as consultant to the project and provided a number of helpful suggestions in response to a draft of the manuscript. The research itself proceeded expeditiously and thoroughly because of my good fortune in having Diana Kleiner and John Pearson work on it. Robert Vogel and Anne Golovin of the Smithsonian Institution were most generous and helpful during my research there. As the manuscript took shape, Iris Tillman Hill, editor-in-chief of the University of North Carolina Press, undertook its direction with care and dispatch, for which I am grateful, and Sandra Eisdorfer, senior editor, scrutinized the text with an astute eye and keen ear. I thank Townsend Ludington for his appraisal of the manuscript and John Seelye for his continual help and suggestions. Two manuscript-preparation grants from the Graduate School of Boston University were helpful at timely moments. Portions of this material have appeared in somewhat different form in *Prospects: The Annual Journal of American Cultural Studies* 7 (1982); *William Carlos Williams Review* 9, nos. 1 and 2 (1983); *Essays from the Lowell Conference on Industrial History 1982 and 1983* (1985); *When Information Counts: Grading the Media*, ed. Bernard Rubin (1985).

Long-term projects inevitably become a part of personal life. On the home front, therefore, I want to thank Bill Tichi, to whom this book is oral history.

SHIFTING GEARS

INTRODUCTION

"I wanted to design."

Frank Lloyd Wright, *A Testament*, 1957

At the United States Centennial Exposition in Philadelphia in 1876, the mother of a five-year-old boy paused before an exhibition of educational blocks. Designed in 1830 by the German educator, Friedrich Froebal, the "Froebal Gifts," as they were called, consisted of smooth cardboard and maplewood cubes, cylinders, triangles, spheres. They were intended for programmed play. This mother determined that her son must have a set.

Whether Frank Lloyd Wright's mother knew it or not, her decision to educate young Wright with the Froebal blocks fit with the industrial age into which the boy was born. Post–Civil War America increasingly presented a landscape of machines and structures whose component parts were visible to the naked eye. The era of handicrafts was rapidly giving way to an age of manufacture from prefabricated component parts. The parts were integrated into the total design. Gear-and-girder technology was in ascendance, and prefabricated parts were the order of the day. Wright's mother somehow recognized that the multiform blocks were appropriate to that order.

For the blocks, factory milled, were components of design. Each smooth shape, an abstract solid, was nonetheless a prefabricated part to be integrated into a larger design system of the child's invention. Programmed play with the wood components perfectly suited the new industrial age. Wright recalled, "I sat at the little kindergarten table top and played with the cube, the sphere and the triangle. . . . I soon became susceptible to constructive pattern evolving in everything I saw. I learned to see this way, and when I did, I did not care to draw casual incidentals of nature. I wanted to design" (*Testament* 19–20).

The American industrial-age passion for component-part design continued. Few children had the opportunity to experience the esoteric Froebal blocks, but the vernacular version reached millions in the form of the Erector Set. By the early 1910s American boys were hard at work designing structures and machines with the steel components of the phenomenally successful Erector. Its component parts of stamped-out steel could be assembled into numerous designs. The Erector rewarded boys' ingenuity by awarding dazzling prizes for original models. Operating manuals otherwise guided boys in the component-part construction of a range

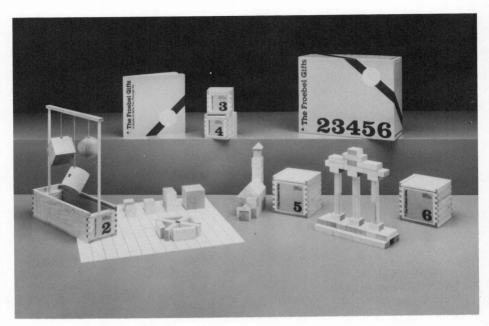

The Froebal blocks, Frank Lloyd Wright's toys
(Courtesy Korver/Thorpe Ltd., Boulder, Colorado)

of designs from bridges to skyscrapers and Ferris wheels. Powered by small electric motors, the girders and gears became moving parts of machines.

The toys and the industrial culture mirrored each other. Steel-girder bridges and buildings were rising on the landscape by the late nineteenth century, and electric motors and internal combustion engines soon powered a variety of machines. Americans found themselves living in a gear-and-girder world. The New Yorkers walking the concourses of Penn Station experienced much the same environment as the San Franciscans who swam at the steel-girdered indoor pools of the Sutro baths. The railway passengers routed over bridges routinely saw the same girdered trusses which World's Fair visitors to Chicago or St. Louis marveled at as they rode the steam-powered, original Ferris wheel. People found themselves in an "Erector" world.

That world was remarkable for visual accessibility. To scan photographs of the machines and structures between the 1890s and the 1920s—or to look, really look, at them and at their counterparts today—is to be visually involved. An onlooker has immediate access to the construction, to the design decisions of the engineers and architects. Open to view, so obviously *designed*, the world of girders and gears invites the onlooker to see its internal workings, its component parts. It insists upon the recognition that it is, in fact, an assembly. It demands that the viewer notice the design in and of itself and acknowledge its constructed

Baby puts aside other toys to make block constructions in Thomas Eakins, Baby at Play,
1876. (Courtesy National Gallery of Art, John Hay Whitney Collection)

reality. In turn it redirects the eye to the natural world, teaching by example that all
forms, including nature's own, can be perceived in this way. Nature may be the
engineer, but the energy-producing acorns and gourds must be made to reveal
their "gears" and "girders" too.

This world of component-part design is visually compelling. Gears go round,
bearings roll, pistons push, girders support. The foremost traits of this world are its
visuality and its kinetics. They arrest onlookers' attention. Not surprisingly, schools
of visual artists engaged the new technology. The American Precisionist painters
and photographers were defined in the 1920s by their visual enactments of the
gear-and-girder world. Other industrialized nations similarly produced schools of
artists committed to machine aesthetics. Pictures and sculptural constructions
were the clear and obvious response to the new technological landscape.

The pictorial quality of machines and structures was easily transferred into
fiction and poetry. The novelist Frank Norris painted word-pictures of locomotives
and harvesters, while in verse Carl Sandburg represented the skyscraper, its girders
and rivets. Hart Crane, of course, comes immediately to mind because *The Bridge*
(1930) bases the whole American experience on symbolic possibilities in the
engineering-aesthetic triumph, the Brooklyn Bridge. All these writers freely developed symbolic meanings from pictorially vivid machines and structures, knowing
that their readers were as familiar with these forms as they themselves were. Thus

Toy truss bridge of wire, cardboard, and blocks. St. Nicholas Magazine, *1897*

Erector set, 1913 (Courtesy National Museum of American History, Smithsonian Institution)

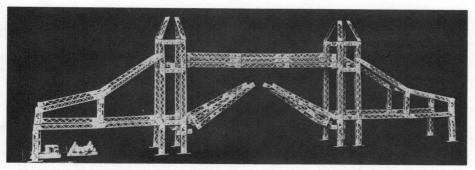

Erector bridge with draw spans powered by electric motor (Courtesy National Museum of American History, Smithsonian Institution)

Main Concourse, Penn Station, New York, ca. 1900 (Courtesy Library of Congress)

Swimming pool, Sutro baths, San Francisco, 1900 (Courtesy Library of Congress)

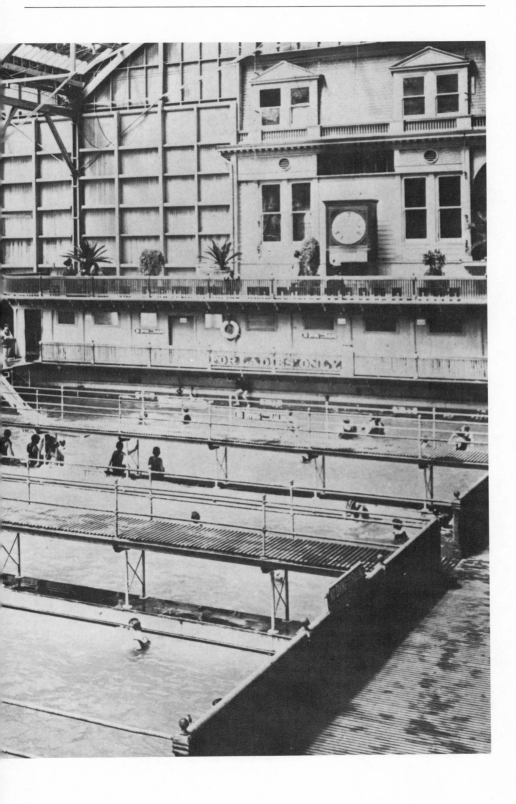

Lobby of The Rookery, Chicago, Burnham and Root, 1895–96; remodeled by Frank Lloyd
Wright, 1905 (Courtesy Chicago Historical Society)

Railroad truss bridge (Courtesy National Museum of American History,
Smithsonian Institution)

FURNISHED AND ERECTED
BY THE
AMERICAN
BRIDGE
COMPANY
OF
NEW YORK
1909

Brochure for automobile touring in Pacific Northwest (Courtesy National Museum of American History, Smithsonian Institution)

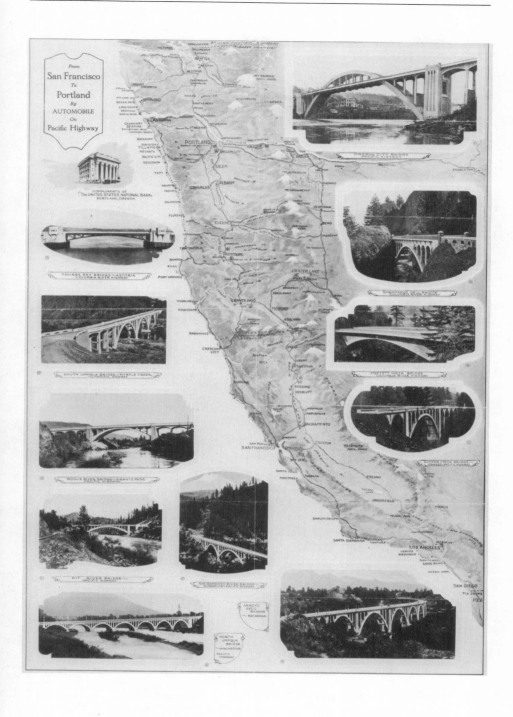

Postcard showing machinery at Panama Canal, ca. 1914 (Courtesy National Museum of American History, Smithsonian Institution)

nama Canal.

the writers exploited the idea that culture is a bridge into history, that the sky-scraper began in a smelter of human blood and so signifies human vitality, that the harvester in operation represents dangerous energies. The symbolic meanings vary, but the machines and the engineered structures remain as original points of reference. They remain, that is, pictorially vivid. They are pictorial representations set inside the texts in which they appear. The poems and novels are, so to speak, the galleries hung with pictures of machines and structures.

Yet pictures of machines and of machine parts are not the point here. Form is. We must return to the notion that a dominant technology defines or redefines the human role in relation to nature. Thus the gear-and-girder technology summoned new literary forms suited to its perceptual values. The novel and poem, like the automobile and bridge (and gourd and acorn), exhibited formal traits of this technology. Fiction and poetry became recognizable as designed assemblies of component parts, including prefabricated parts. By this logic a poem or novel containing machine images was not necessarily a work of the gear-and-girder world. Yet fiction and poetry about flowers or fishing or chilled plums or a red wheelbarrow could enact the defining technology in its very form. The author's role in this technology was to design, even engineer, the arts of the written word.

In fact, three prominent early-twentieth-century American writers did just that—as John Dos Passos indicated when he called himself an architect and as William Carlos Williams showed when he called the poem a machine and put himself in the role of engineer. In American literature their work, together with that of Ernest Hemingway, is the achievement of the gear-and-girder technology. Their fiction and poetry introduced a radically new conception to the arts of the written word. As we shall see, their poems and fiction were not the contexts in which machines could be pictorially represented. Their written texts were not galleries featuring pictorial representations of machines and structures. In that sense their works are not *about* machines. Their fiction and poetry, instead, *is* the machine.

The machine-age text does not contain *representations* of the machine—it too *is* the machine. It is the functional system of component parts designed to trans-mit energy. As such, it can be shown to obey the design rules for sound structures and efficient machines. The components must all function systematically. There must be no unnecessary parts to lessen efficiency. The poet or novelist, as designer, must labor with those objectives in mind. Dos Passos, Hemingway, and Williams did so, and their work endures largely because of it. These writers benefited, while some others, notably Willa Cather and Sherwood Anderson, failed to recognize the opportunities intrinsic to the gear-and-girder technology and consequently suf-fered artistically. Grasping the creative potential of the dominant technology, Dos Passos, Hemingway, and Williams exploited its possibilities and vivified the national literature. Their work shows that the culture of the gear-and-girder technology was a collaborative effort of the engineer, the architect, the fiction writer, and the poet. It demonstrates that a technological revolution is a revolution not only of science and technology but of language, of fiction, and ultimately of poetry.

CHAPTER ONE

TREES, ANIMALS, ENGINES

*There are no sagas—only trees now, animals, engines:
There's that.*

William Carlos Williams, *Notes in Diary Form*, 1927

William Carlos Williams voiced a new worldview when he wrote that his was an age of "trees, animals, engines." For one thing, he acknowledged the proliferation of machines and structures in contemporary life. Trolleys, telephones, and automobiles, etc., were everywhere on the landscape. Sheer numbers made a claim for their recognition. Williams's statement is a concession to a new reality. It suggests a new outlook in which the bridge and the engine would be equal in status to animals and plants.

Two relevant issues underlie Williams's statement. The first, as we see, is logistical. The trees, animals, and engines could be listed as equal items in a series simply because technology was so pervasive in American life. It impinged on consciousness everywhere in the home and on the street. The traditional natural world of flora and fauna now included machines and structures.

Williams's observation, however, goes much further in its assumptions about the relation of technology to nature. As we shall see, it makes an important statement about contemporary perception. Quite simply, Williams joins trees, animals, and engines together because he, like many of his contemporaries, presumes that the structural principles of these phenomena are identical. For Williams, trees and animals, like machines and structures, were integrated systems of component parts. He sees them as categorical equals because they are anatomical analogues of each other. Perceiving in this way, Williams had every reason to join organism with mechanism. Both, in his view, were comprised of functional, integrated components. The body's skeletal and digestive systems had their counterparts in the structures of the tree and the automobile. Structurally they belonged together. When Frank Lloyd Wright proposed that "an entire building might grow up out of conditions as a plant grows up out of soil" and added that the tree is the "*ideal* for the architecture of the machine age," he only elaborated Williams's position. He, like Williams, saw the structural similarity between organic and inorganic forms. Both he and Williams recognized a similarity between nature's mechanisms and man's (*Autobiography* 147).

The perception of trees, animals, and engines as structural analogues had far-reaching implications for imaginative literature, as we shall see. It eventuated in a new conception of the novel as a designed structure of component parts, of the sentence as a structuring component of fiction, and of the poem as a mechanism comprised of constituent word-objects. This perception is the basis on which the technological revolution of late-nineteenth- and early-twentieth-century America was really a revolution in language as well as in engineering.

These matters, however, must await further discussion. For the moment we begin with the logistical side of Williams's remark, with his assumption that technology is as omnipresent in modern America as its flora and fauna. Briefly we must survey an America of trees, animals, engines. To do so is to see a nation that perceives technology mixing freely with nature both in the external environment and in the popular media. Middle-class periodicals presented this America both in visual and verbal texts from journalism to advertisements. Popular magazines are a valuable source showing how many Americans of the late nineteenth and early twentieth centuries were encouraged to think about machine technology in con-temporary life.

This opening discussion will also reveal the development of a new machine-age consciousness. The proliferation of machines and structures in American life between the 1890s and the 1920s began to make itself felt in popular and serious fiction. Novels of commercial and artistic intent showed a new consciousness of a world of "trees, animals, engines." Mixed metaphors of nature and machines abutted each other even in novels whose themes were antitechnological. Fiction offered a good opportunity to see this cultural amalgamation of technology and nature, especially in the work of Frank Norris, Jack London, and Edna Ferber.

As we shall see, this process of amalgamation occurred with such rapidity that it often had the appearance of discontinuity. Suddenly loosed from their separate categories, technological and organic figures of speech seemed to jostle each other, suggesting the tensions that invariably arise in times of rapid sociocultural change, when the old order seems to vanish in the onrush of the new. The novelist Edith Wharton (1862–1937) summarized the pace of this change. Born in an America that still adhered to Old World traditions, Wharton lived to see them repudiated in modernist America materially characterized by "telephones, motors, electric light, central heating, X-rays, cinemas, radium, aeroplanes, and wireless telegraphy [which] were not only unknown but still mostly unforeseen" (*Backward Glance* 6–7).

Wharton refers to a culture of discontinuities, one wrenched in the process by which values and material circumstances undergo rapid change. It is important to examine the enactment of those discontinuities in the very texture of imaginative writing. Of course not all writers experienced tortuous change. Williams and Wright, men trained in technological disciplines (in medicine and engineering-architecture, respectively), were comfortable with their perceptually unified world of trees, animals, and engines. They had reason to be, having learned to see the objects in the material world as designed assemblies of integrated component parts. Writers further away, however, from immediate sources of such perception felt caught between tradition and change in a post-Darwinian world that seemed above all unstable. It is perhaps surprising to find that their writings, nevertheless, prepared the way for technology's new prestige and its formal enactment in fiction and poetry.

MAGAZINE MACHINESCAPES

Logistically speaking, technology was everywhere on the American landscape by the turn of the twentieth century. Rail and telegraph lines were a commonplace, and citizens even of smaller towns saw their dusty streets dug up for water, gas, and sewer lines, and poles sunk for the new telephone wires. Those living along the major river valleys of the Ohio and Mississippi had seen, and continued to see, mammoth bridge construction, and every medium-sized city could boast a tall, metal-frame building of the kind to be known as skyscrapers. For middle-class families the automobile and home electrification were just in the offing.

Personal knowledge of technology, however, exceeded the experience of one's family or hometown, whether in the metropolis or the heartland. The burgeoning, successful American magazines like *Cosmopolitan*, *Harper's Weekly*, *Collier's*, *The Saturday Evening Post*, *The Ladies Home Journal*, and *Literary Digest* brought images of technological values and accomplishments into middle-class American living rooms weekly and monthly. A subscription to a mainstream magazine, even one specialized for children, for homemakers, or for businessmen, was a guarantee that the reader would be made constantly aware of the national and worldwide presence of machines and structures. Journalism and advertising saw to it. To scan some of these periodicals is to see that Americans from the 1890s to the 1920s were systematically taught that technology was no longer confined to the factory grounds. Virtually all readers learned that they now inhabited a world of "trees, animals, engines."

The home provides a good example of the magazines' role in technological consciousness-raising. A subscriber to the *Ladies Home Journal* (*LHJ*) was offered, via advertisements, a range of technological equipment including cameras, bicycles, furnaces, electric dishwashers, irons, waffle irons, phonographs, automobiles. These objects were unified in the concept of the home as factory, and the lady of the house as engineer. *Good Housekeeping* (*GH*) (1910) said that "a house is nothing more than a factory for the production of happiness" and urged that it be equipped accordingly, with machinery" (58:525). The magazine's famous institute offered a booklet entitled *Household Engineering*, which promised that the technical ability heretofore applied to the factory and business world would now be devoted to "a housekeeper's engineering problems" (67 [Oct. 1918]: 45). Similar articles in *Technical World* and *Woman's Home Companion* included "Running the Home Like a Factory" and "Training the Home Engineer" (23 [July 1915]: 589–92; 53 [Feb. 1926]: 42). One 1920 article presented a young bride aghast at the first sight of her new mechanized kitchen. She exclaims to her husband, "You know I did not have a course in machinery at the finishing school!," only to hear him say that a happy marriage will result from these labor-saving machines, those which the Hotpoint Corporation vowed originated with "a *housekeeping* engineer—not in some casual workshop" (*LHJ* 37 [Sept. 1920]: 3; 39 [Apr. 22]: 173). If such articles show the extent to which disempowered women were co-opted in an industrial age, they also mark the deep incursion of technology into the domestic sphere.

In one respect, in fact, the homemaker was crucial to the encouragement of technological activity, since advertisers bought space in women's magazines to promote such toys as steam engines, electrical sets, motorboats, and construction kits for boys, most of them appealing on the basis of education, motivation, and character development. (Erector, typically, promised mothers to "help prepare [their boys] for the business world by developing ambition" and promised to "encourage imagination, concentration, ingenuity and skill—and increase chances for success as a man") (*LHJ* 33 [Dec. 1916]: 85; *Collier's* 58 [Dec. 9, 1916]: 22–23).

Boys themselves could alternate hands-on play with forays into encyclopedic literature intended to explain the new world of machine processes. One good example, *The Book of Wonders* (1916), shows precisely how the young (or adults for that matter) would understand the era as one of trees, animals, and engines. Typically the book tells the "story" of some item in daily use, such as a suit of clothes or rubber tires, moving from photographs of pastured sheep and plantation rubber trees to a pictorial display of the complicated machinery that completes the story by turning wool and sap into cloth and tires. The world's "wonders" are both natural ("Why the Moon Travels with Us") and technological ("The Story in a Submarine Boat"). The book's cover sends that very message, displaying the double image of a wise old owl whose head and eyes also become the world rotated, Archimidean-fashion, by belts and pulleys.

Middle-class youngsters with access to wonder books would probably also enjoy subscriptions to a children's magazine like *St. Nicholas*, which relegated the sewing machine and the camera to little girls, but offered boys a world of adventure in the realm of the engineer and inventor. To turn the pages of *St. Nicholas* from the turn of the century is to see it define an interesting, worthwhile life as one of adventure and ingenuity. The publisher spared no effort to involve boys in contemporary machine and structural technology. One illustrated series—"Nature Giants that Man Has Conquered"—portrayed human triumph over natural forces via steam, waterpower, electricity, chemistry. There were also inspirational feature stories on prominent inventors like Edison ("The Boyhood of Edison"), George Westinghouse, and the explosives wizard Hudson Maxim (whose book on literary criticism, as we shall see, made Ezra Pound conscious of the technological values inherent in language). One *St. Nicholas* series, entitled "With Men Who Do Things,"

Illustrations of precise food measurement and of efficient and wasteful vacuuming.
Good Housekeeping, *1919*

Mechanized home laundry. Good Housekeeping, *1913*

Household Enginee

Beginning a Series of Articles on the Technic of Homem

The kitchen cabinet space is sufficient to enable us to keep the routine supplies and utensils concentrated in the one place.

The kitchen curtains are of oilcloth in a s

RE you a household engineer? Have you learned that there are ways of taking at least some of the drudgery out of the old, familiar household routine? Long ago I became interested enough to study out new and easier ways, perhaps because I first learned household tasks under the hardest of conditions—in a New England town, where was cherished the wholly unconscious feeling that any work that was agreeable, that one did because one loved it, *must* be wrong. Not that anyone voiced such an idea; but nevertheless its stultifying effect was there. And it must have had some influence in preventing the overworked housekeeper from accepting as her due the new tools and methods of progressive housekeeping as readily as competition forced her husband to meet new conditions in his business.

Frankly, women are not without a very

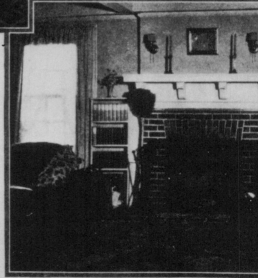

Bookshelves on either side of the fireplace fill unused space an

The well-engineered household.
Ladies Home Journal, *1925*

Applied

By Mildred Maddocks Bentley

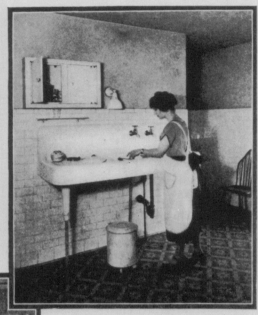

It has been proved without a doubt that the sink set at a convenient height ranks highest of all as a kitchen labor saver.

s of old friends.

I do know that as much business judgment and ability as I could offer were demanded of my business day, because a budget and its management loom large in any business. But not one whit less is required of my home day. The budget is much smaller, but it is no less important that grocery and butcher bills be paid, and that both routine and occasional expenditures be thoughtfully plotted. Add to this the task of food selection and purchase, to secure the very best conditions for all the different ages to be found in the average family, those who are growing into maturity as well as those who are leaving that maturity behind them, and you have a task that matches any business assignment. Indeed, Uncle Sam calls it the commissariat, and it is a job in itself. Certainly there never was a time when so much could be done by "preventive" feeding to maintain the health and happi-

NATURE GIANTS THAT MAN HAS CONQUERED

BY RAYMOND PERRY

GIANT NO. 4—THE EXPLOSIVE

THE fairy story of a large and powerful genie confined in a small jar, is no more wonderful than is the true story of a bit of powder packed in a cartridge; when the powder is exploded, it propels the bullet far and with terrific speed. A Chinaman first discovered the power of explosives when he invented gunpowder, and it has proved to be the greatest of all the forces that have changed the maps of nations. Explosives so powerful have been discovered now that no gun can be made strong enough to be discharged more than a comparatively small number of times; and there are machine-guns, submarine mines, and torpedoes—engines of destruction so powerful that no battle, either on land or sea, could last more than a few hours. Indeed, it is predicted that soon no two nations will dare to go to war, so terrible would be the consequences to themselves and to the rest of the world.

While explosives are needed less and less for war than formerly, they are used more and more in the victories of peace. When the genie was let out of the jar, he built great palaces for his master and transported him great distances by land, by sea, and in the air; and that is just what the Giant Explosive is doing to-day for man, his master. The power of dynamite is blasting rock for the foundations of sky-scrapers and bridge piers, and boring tunnels through the solid mountain; while gasolene, the new explosive, is used for transportation, in automobiles on land, in motor-boats in the water, and in aëroplanes in the air; thus finally accomplishing the dream that man has cherished for centuries,—the marvel of human flight.

Technological exploitation of explosives. St. Nicholas Magazine, *1911*

invited young readers to identify with the boy-narrator and his friend, both transported to major civil engineering sites, where they work and learn the design
principles of elevators, suspension bridges, tunnels, dams, explosives, submarines,
electrical power stations, skyscrapers, the Panama Canal locks and excavations,
waterway diversions, and industrial machinery. Photographs, illustrations, and
diagrams vividly enhanced the text, doubtless increasing the attraction to young
readers.

"With Men Who Do Things" was evidently so successful a series that *St. Nicholas* followed it up in 1916–17 with another entitled "On the Battle-Front of
Engineering," emphasizing that ingenuity can triumph over natural and man-made
perils, including floe ice and tunnel collapse. The heroic modern life in this
periodical was clearly that of the engineer or inventor, and boys were encouraged
to think of their place in the technological future, whether as builders of bridges or
architects of airships (38 [Apr., May, June, 1911]: 499, 593, 700; 40 [Mar., Apr., May,
June, July, Aug., Sept., Oct., 1913]: 402–9, 533–40, 638–44, 735–40, 822–27,
927–33, 1023–30, 1126–33; 41 [Jan., Feb., Mar., Apr., May, July, Aug., Sept., Oct.]:
237–43, 333–39, 421–27, 526–31, 621–27, 837–41, 893–99, 1006–12, 1094–1100).

The husbands and fathers of these same middle-class families also imbibed a
steady stream of technological messages from magazines, prominent among them
the *Literary Digest* (*LD*), forerunner of Henry Luce's *Time*. The *Digest*, as its title
implies, distilled stories from a wide range of American periodicals, including
journals like *Engineering-News*, *Iron Age*, and *Cassier's*, all periodicals of professional engineers, as well as *Popular Science Monthly* and the *Scientific American*.
A reader would have found *Digest* articles on "The Development of American
Industries since Columbus," "New York's Great Underground Railroad," "Some
Wonderful Calculating Machines," "America at the Paris Fair," "Achievements of
Electricity in Human Progress," and "American Mechanical Supremacy and Ameri-
can Character" (2, no. 7 [Dec. 13, 1899]: 9–10; 20, no. 6 [Feb. 10, 1900]: 183; no. 8
[Feb. 24, 1900]: 247; no. 17 [Apr. 28, 1900]: 505–6; no. 19 [May 12, 1900]: 577; 21
[Oct. 6, 1900]: 402).

Engineering and its achievement was a recurrent emphasis in the *Digest* and in
other magazines like *Collier's* and the *Saturday Evening Post*. The middle-class
male reader heard his magazines tell him that "in this country we have gone
further in engineering than any other people," that "in the progress of engineering
we are contributing more than our share," and that "civil engineers have supplied
the grand arches and ribs of steel which made it possible thus to excel in vastness
every building enterprise which earth in its unnumbered centuries has borne upon
its bosom" (*LD* 24, no. 6 [Feb. 8, 1902]: 182; no. 11 [Mar. 15, 1902]: 357; *Scientific
American* 71 [Aug. 11, 1894]: 87).

Many articles emphasized the power and resourcefulness of engineering. "The
Greatest Bridge in America," "Seventy Years of Civil Engineering," and "Character
in the Engineering Profession" were typical and went hand in glove with articles
like "The Mighty River of Wheat" in *Munsey* and "Gigantic Labor Savers" in
Collier's, whose text and large-format photographs extolled the wonders of power-

Postcard view of Queensboro Bridge, New York

ful machines from reapers to conveyer belts. All such articles endorsed the ingenuity of those conceiving, building, and using machinery. They invited the reader to
enter a state of informed awe. The American middle-class man, like his son,
learned that modern progress was the result of ingenuity and the development and
application of machines and structures all over the world. The family parlor magazine rack held constant reminders that the old American agrarian world was
transforming itself into one in which machines and structures took a proper place
in the field, on the farm, and even in the forest (*Collier's* 32 [Dec. 19, 1903]: 7–8;
Scientific American 112 [June 5, 1915]: 527–33; 71 [Aug. 11, 1894]: 87; *Munsey* 25
[Apr. 1901]: 17–30; *Collier's* 58 [Nov. 11, 1916]: 12–13).

WOLVES, WHEELS, PISTONS, PETUNIAS

Magazines reflect contemporary consciousness; so does fiction. Between the 1890s and the 1920s American writers and journalists were quick to
reflect their awareness of the new integrated world of nature and machines. It was
not, for instance, unusual to see that *Country Life in America*, a magazine devoted
to articles on fruits and nuts, gardens, and sporting dogs, would include an essay
on "The Rise of the Aluminum Piston" without editorial acknowledgment that
anything incongruous was going on (31 [Nov. 1916]: 84). Indications are that from
the viewpoint of the editors and the readers, nothing was. The new world of inte-

Postcard view of Panama Canal construction (Courtesy National Museum of American History, Smithsonian Institution)

grated organism and mechanism was firmly established by the 1910s. And if the magazines make this point abundantly clear, it is nonetheless important to search beyond them to find the record of this new world in the texts of imaginative writers.

Novels, in particular, provide a good source for inquiry. Novelists have the task of encoding culture in word choices that represent the vanguard of contemporary consciousness. The world of "trees, animals, engines" could be validated or denied in the very texture of prose fiction of the era. For the novelist is by definition the figure acutely sensitive to the nuances of language. The coarse-minded mass-magazine editor might juxtapose images of the forest glade against the automobile factory floor, but we expect the novelist to keep the two qualitatively separate—or to join them if perception so warrants. It is therefore helpful to look for the world of "trees, animals, engines" in the fiction of prominent contemporary novelists.

We begin with the commercially successful fiction of Edna Ferber, whose early novels make an excellent case study. As a newspaper reporter for local midwestern papers and for the *Chicago Tribune*, Ferber had a shrewd sense of the timely, the practical, the middle-class slant on her subjects. Although she is best remembered for such later novels as *Show-Boat*, *Saratoga Trunk*, and *Giant*, Ferber's earlier, so-called "Emma McChesney" novels of 1914–15 interest us here. Under the improbable titles of *Roast Beef, Medium*, *Personality Plus*, and *Emma McChesney & Co.*, Ferber created a popular new heroine. She is the spirited divorcée "Mrs. Mac," a traveling saleswoman guiding her son through the perils of young manhood as she outwits all her business competitors.

The "Limited" passing through the Orange Groves, California.

Postcard view of passenger train passing through irrigated groves in southern California

Of interest here, of course, is the range of machine images to be found in these novels, whose audience probably included the same women who subscribed to *Good Housekeeping* and the *Ladies Home Journal*. For instance, when Mrs. Mac's son interviews for a job in advertising, he feels his prospective employer send a warning "from that wireless station located in his subconscious mind." Soon we hear the man speak in similar figures: "Let me tell you something, young 'un. I've got what you might call a thirty-horse-power mind. I keep it running on high all the time, with the muffler cut out, and you can hear me coming for miles." Later on, the young man pays tribute to his mother's child-rearing skill. "If I've got this far," he says, "it's all because of you. I've been thinking all along that I was the original self-starter, when you've really had to get out and crank me every few miles" (*Personality Plus* 21, 35–36).

Not all Ferber's images come from the automobile. Nor do they belong only to a man's world. A stenographer compliments Mrs. Mac (and herself) in these terms: "some people are just bound to—well, to manufacture, because they just can't help it. Dynamos—that's what the technical book would call 'em. You're one—a great big one. I'm one. Just a little tiny one. But it's sparking away there all the time." Even business days can be described in technological images. Ferber writes that "the machinery of [Mrs. Mac's] day, ordinarily as noiseless and well-ordered as a thing on ball bearings, now rasped, creaked, jerked, stood still, jolted on again" (*Emma McChesney & Co.* 135, 143–44).

In Ferber we have an impressive lot of figures from machine technology, from rolling stock to the automobile to the dynamo. These images serve the fictional techniques of characterization, of description, of evocation of mood. In these novels no character scoffs to hear such terms used. Nor does Ferber duck responsibility for them. Not once are these images set inside the apologetic punctuation of quotation marks. As a journalist and commercial writer with her eye on the novelist's marketplace, Edna Ferber would be unlikely to take any stylistic risks that might alienate her audience. Her use of images from machine technology suggests a middle-class receptivity to such language. It signals its acceptability among respectable people. Ferber's readiness to use images from machine technology indicates how thoroughly assimilated technology had become in American middle-class culture.

Contemporary readers of artistic fiction also found technology making inroads in the prose of Frank Norris, Jack London, Willa Cather, and Edith Wharton—none of them enthusiasts of the new machine age of gears and girders. To see the mixture of nature and technology in their writings is to appreciate the depth of the new consciousness.

It is, we notice immediately, a consciousness reflective of cultural discontinuities. Edith Wharton shows both sides. She hates the incursion of machine values into traditional social life, identifying a character as "an appalling woman who runs a roaring dinner-factory that used to catch [a person] in its wheels" (*The Reef* 74). Yet elsewhere contemporary technology provides Wharton the analogy she seeks to define a character's relation to self and home: "It was as though in leaving his home he took his whole self with him, like a telephone receiver unhooked and carried on a long cord into another room" (*Hudson River Bracketed* 190). The literary critic, Fred Lewis Pattee, shows Wharton's kind of ambivalence. First he scorns a too-prolific writer as a novel factory, then approves the belated discovery of Emily Dickinson's poems in terms dear to Edison's heart: "she was brought like a phonograph record into the period that needed a poet" (155, 199). These writers instance the alternating attitudes of people whose culture is in rapid transition. On the one hand, technology intrudes into a traditional world and feels invasive. On the other, the machine defines the new age, providing the writer a wealth of new and vivifying terms.

In clustered images one early twentieth-century novelist, Robert Herrick, explored these discontinuities between preindustrial American values and the new technologies seeming to threaten them. Herrick called the novel *Together* (1908) his "colossus of marriage" because he had trouble writing an exposé of such a hallowed institution. Numerous passages in *Together* reveal Herrick's up-to-the-minute awareness that technology was making its impress in American social intercourse and in turn revealing new social values. One woman taunts her lover for his reputation as "a calculating machine—one of those things they have in banks to do arithmetic stunts." And a railroad executive is "an Industrial Flywheel of society" (216, 84).

Herrick's critique of technological America emerges in images drawn from familiar contemporary machinery. His dialogue is riddled with electrical-mechanical figures when his most engaging character, the wife of a railroad executive, consults family and physicians about her psychological problems. The woman worries whether "we are just machines, with the need to be oiled now and then" and is skeptical when the nerve doctor promises to be "your temporary dynamo." But she listens closely when her brother warns about exertion: "You may shift the batteries, Belle, but you are burning up the wires, all the same." And she confesses to her physician, "I never thought before what it means to be tired. I have worked the machine foolishly. But one must travel fast—be geared up as you say—or fall behind and become dull and uninteresting" (232, 234, 375, 243).

Herrick deliberately uses images that double back on themselves to express his alarm at the emotional and physical consequences of this new fast-paced modern life. Not surprisingly, he sends his exhausted matron into the country, which is to say into preindustrial America, to a sanitorium directed by a physician who is himself an urban emigré. The true healer at the sanitorium is the blacksmith. This symbol of preindustrial America embodies spiritual and neural health and has the power to confer it on those around him. The smith, whose forge and house are principal buildings of the sanitorium, is the man of "vision, of something inward and sustaining . . . something that expressed itself in the slow speech, the peaceful manner." At suppertime his "ripest wisdom" emerges (446–47). Relaxed, he gazes at his wife and finds the world good.

Herrick's blacksmith exists as a totemic figure in this realistic novel drawn from contemporary America of the 1910s. The novelist virtually exhumes Longfellow's village smithy and makes his forge a shrine of miracles from a vanished, preindustrial era. Modern urbanites, their nerves so many burned-out wires, can visit the forge and somehow be neurologically restored and spiritually revived. Blessed by the benedictory wave of the smithy's glowing bar of iron, the urbanite reenters modern life inwardly aglow himself. In this novel the matron returns to the city to find her estranged husband, renews the marriage, and ultimately moves west with him to found a new railroad—and thus by an implication Herrick failed to see, begins again the very technological cycle that keeps people "geared up" and overloads the electrical circuits (491).

It is clear that in *Together* Herrick grappled unsuccessfully with the meaning of cultural change. He struggled with problems he suspected evaded solution. On the one hand, he identified humane life with the preindustrial America of the farmer and the artisan. Yet he acknowledged the disappearance of that world, for the stock ticker now penetrated the forested mountains which, in this century, are but pleasant views the city people see through plate glass. The images of electrical and mechanical power, moreover, indicate that speed and movement were becoming new values in contemporary America. As one character remarks, "The merest backwoodsman in Iowa is living faster in a sense than Cicero or [Daniel] Webster" (356). One may visit preindustrial America in a theme park of a sanitorium, but one lives fast and powerfully in a world of dynamos and gears.

The texture of the novelists' prose tells the same story. Writings that date from the turn of the century through the 1910s show that "the machine culture," to use

Thorstein Veblen's phrase, had pervaded novelists' imaginations just as it had captured journalists' energies. It is startling, nevertheless, to see machine-based figures of thought appear abruptly in texts of writers known to be hostile to technology, writers devoted to the natural world of field and farm. For instance, in *Winesburg, Ohio* (1919), Sherwood Anderson describes the endearing rural eccentric, Wing Biddlebaum, as a man whose "slender expressive fingers, forever active, . . . came forth and became the piston rods of his machinery of expression" (28). And in *Song of the Lark* (1915), Willa Cather describes her Colorado "Lark," Thea Kronborg, as a girl who lies awake at night by her window "vibrating with excitement, as a machine vibrates from speed" (177). Here, ingrained in prose, we see the inadvertent acceptance of machine technology by two writers overtly hostile to it.

Jack London's *Call of the Wild* (1903) is an excellent case study in the covert assimilation of machine values in fiction. London's dog-hero, Buck, reared in civilization, answers the wilderness call to the northern "uncharted vastness" which London portrays all at once as edenic, pastoral, and primitive. This dog has the wild nobility of London's beloved free spirit, the wolf, for Buck is at the "high tide of his life, overspilling with vigor and virility." Into these organic phrases, however, London suddenly interjects an image direct from machine technology when we hear that every part of the dog, "brain and body, nerve tissue and fibre, was keyed to the most exquisite pitch," that "between all the parts there was a perfect equilibrium or adjustment." As a result of this perfect synchrony of machine parts, the animal responds to stimuli with "lightning-like rapidity." Electrically charged, the dog's muscles snap into play "like steel springs." Giving no sign whatever that these images are different from those of the natural world, London tells us that the dog is lithe as wild cats and covert as the snake (130–31).

London repeats the pattern in a subsequent novel, *White Fang* (1906), which chronicles the wild wolf-dog's gradual accommodation to civilization. White Fang, like Buck, is a consummately efficient fighter whose neural calculations are "automatic," his parts being in "better adjustment" than those of the other dogs. "Body and brain," says London, "his was a more perfect mechanism" (303–4). Following these phrases, however, London hastens on to describe summer in the Rockies, as if unaware of the incongruity, the very incongruity which Mark Twain deliberately exploited for humor in "The Damned Human Race," in which the Machine is tried in a court of law along with its putative peers, the animals. It is especially ironic for London to be unaware of his discontinuity, since he was vehemently opposed to industrial society, having parodied Milton's Satan: "Better to reign among booze-fighters a prince, than to toil twelve hours a day at a machine at ten cents an hour" (qtd. in Pattee 125).

London is by no means singular. The same covert assimilation of machine technology in American fiction occurs in the writings of Frank Norris. His fiction is interesting because he tries so hard, and so unsuccessfully, to keep the world of "trees and animals" separate from that of the "engines." His *The Octopus* (1901) is plotted on the hostility between California ranchers and the corporate railroad whose tentacles reach out to strangle everything. Essentially Norris portrays two worlds in the novel, one romantic and mystical and the other reflective of brutal socio-cultural-economic realities. The novelist-poet's self-appointed task is to fuse these two, somehow, in order to create a modern American epic. In *The Octopus* Norris's ranchers are agribusiness corporate men who farm vast tracts of wheat with the aid of farm machinery, the telephone, the telegraph, tickertape (connecting them with international markets), and ranch hands who, at plowing time, form a military echelon in machine-like discipline. One of the ranchers is a civil engineer, and another thinks of the ranch as a machine ultimately to be automated. In the meantime, because "the machine would not yet run of itself, he must still feel his hand upon the lever" (48).

Norris intermingles these many machine motifs with those of the Homeric epic. But he keeps machine-age images essentially separate from the romantic, mystical passages on the spirit inherent in the California land. In the course of *The Octopus* readers come to expect that distinction to be preserved. The mystical landscape is separate and distinct from the modern machine culture. Yet Norris, like Jack London, allows a miscellany of machine figures to enter, apparently without awareness of the discontinuity. In an early scene, for instance, Norris's aspirant poet, Presley, climbs a mystical California mountaintop, about to recognize that the titanic struggle in the wheatlands of the San Joaquin Valley is the true subject for his American epic poem. Before the would-be poet can have his revelation, however, he must first calm himself and enter a receptive frame of mind. But what language does Norris use for the transition?—that of a machine coming to a stop. "By degrees . . . the little wheels and cogs of thought [moved] slower and slower." Then "the animal in him stretched itself, purring" (37). Shifting his images from machine to cat, Norris gives no sign that he recognizes the stunning discontinuity.

Once again Norris reveals his unconscious assimilation of machine technology in the scene of a turbulent barn dance. Trouble starts when a messenger arrives with a wire announcing the railroad's public sale of the very acreage the ranchers have been working and improving on lease options. Instantly, festivity turns to tumult. To describe it, Norris first uses images from nature. The scene is a "whirlwind," and the people's shouts sound like "thunder." In Hobbesian terms that echo Alexander Hamilton, Norris calls the crowd a "great beast" and a "brute . . . baring its teeth." But these organic-natural terms of intensifying, monstrous energy evidently left the novelist unsatisfied. So he sought an additional term to express an exponential increase in power. This brute mob, Norris writes, "imposes its will with the abrupt, resistless pressure of the relaxed piston," a piston "inexorable, knowing no pity" (199–200). The transition from the organic to the technological is instantaneous and never acknowledged by the author.

Norris's mixing of the machine with nature continues in his sequel to *The Octopus*. *The Pit* (1903), set in Chicago, concerns the stock market manipulations of a wheat financier who drives a team of horses impressive even to men who know good stock. The team moves with "heads up, the check rein swinging loose, ears all alert, eyes all alight, the breath deep, strong, and slow, *and the stride machine-like, even as the swing of a metronome*" [emphasis added] (153). In this passage, of course, the synchrony and rhythm of the machine is the standard against which the movement of the horses can be measured. The equine ideal is not organic, but mechanical. Norris, as usual, shows no self-consciousness about his craft or about the underlying assumptions of his language.

Pistons, cogs, wheels, steel springs, telephone cords, a metronome—what are we, the readers, to make of this odd lot of machine parts? It is tempting at first to find nothing new in these tailings from a Newtonian universe. (Did not Ralph Waldo Emerson, moreover, deliberately invoke images direct from the New England textile industry?) It may even seem petty of a reader virtually to tweezer these images from texts which otherwise yield rich language patterns far more consenting to literary interpretation. Why not be satisfied, for instance, to verify the Darwinian world of Theodore Dreiser from his many animal figures? In *The Titan*, the financier Frank Cowperwood is described as leonine, wolfish, and canine (a "sort of bounding collie"); so why should readers take notice of the remark that "Cowperwood's brain had been reciprocating like a well-oiled engine" (432, 343 532)? When Edith Wharton, in *The House of Mirth* (1905), exploits the tension between aesthetics and commerce, why ought readers to notice that a desperate Lily Bart, ever a figure of "loveliness in distress," suddenly invokes phrases from a world utterly foreign to her experience? "I can hardly be said to have an independent existence," says the fragile flower, Lily. "I was just a screw or a cog in the great machine I called life" (319–20). And further, when the romantic F. Scott Fitzgerald turns an automobile into a symbolic garden and writes seriously of Jay Gatsby's "tuning fork struck upon a star," why should readers pause to notice that his West Egg is of "spectroscopic brilliance" (25)? Or, for that matter, why heed Sinclair Lewis, a writer so consistently scornful of American technology throughout *Babbitt*, when in *Dodsworth* he dispenses with irony to say that "it was raining, and the street looked like the inside of a polished steel cylinder" (224)?

Most of these technological figures are striking precisely because they are desultory and seem, for the most part, to enter the texts without awareness by their authors that they are inconsistent—or that they create problems. For they change the narrative tone of voice abruptly. Or they insinuate a new realm of imaginative possibility, but fail to develop it. Appearing infrequently in lengthy novels, these images seem aberrant, as if indicative of authors' momentary inattention or of their failure to edit their own work.

And yet this evident lack of self-consciousness on the part of these American writers is itself important. It provides a clue to the basis for a changing worldview in twentieth-century American literature and culture. For it is clear that the artistic strategies of Norris, London, Dreiser, etc., are not like the metaphysical poets' yoking of disparate images for poetic wit. The authorial self-consciousness of John Donne's lovers-as-compasses forms no part of the imagination of these American authors. Nor (closer to home) do they seem to have been moved to use technological images, as Whitman did, to enhance themes of democracy and national vitality. Nor is it useful to repeat old charges of "clumsiness" in the craftsmanship, for instance, of Dreiser or London.

The crux of the issue lies precisely in the authors' obliviousness to the discrepancy between themselves and the machine image. In fact, the abruptness, the very instantaneous appearance of the technological figures in these earlier twentieth-century writings suggests that the authors have begun to think of it as natural (at least unexceptional) to move back and forth from the organic to the technological, from the "trees and animals" to the "engines." This enmeshment of images really signals a new worldview in the twentieth century. For the mix of American flora and fauna with pistons, gears, and engines indicates that the perceptual boundary between what is considered to be natural, and what technological, is disappearing. The world of the pastoral, the primitive, the edenic, the agrarian is fusing with that of machine technology. This is the new outlook to which Williams gave expression when he described the contemporary world of "trees, animals, engines."

NATURE'S MECHANISMS

At this point we can acknowledge what the novelists only hint. The world of trees and animals, like that of engines, is by definition a world of component-part constructions. Some are static, some dynamic, depending upon whether they are structures (for example, bridges) or mechanisms. And some intermix the two, the structural "skeleton" giving overall form while moving parts within transmit motion or power. But whether the construction is static, dynamic, or a combination of both, it is presumed to be an assembly of component parts. The world to which it refers is a gear-and-girder world. Its components are integrated into innumerable structures and into the machines which function to transmit energy. In this world the human being is perceived in mechanistic terms, as are flora and fauna everywhere. Whether the object is a tree, a dog, the human ear, or the earth itself, the underlying assumption about it is the same. It is a mechanism. It is a construction. Whatever its category, animal, mineral, or vegetable, it is presumed to be mechanical in its form and operation. The novelists' various images of the piston-rod fingers, of the reciprocating engine of a heart, of the machine vibration of an excited individual—all point to the presumption of this world.

Nor is it strictly a Newtonian one, for Darwinism brought into play the notion of nature itself as an engineer of increasingly sophisticated mechanisms. The survival and endurance of adaptive species testify to nature's ingenuity. By this logic the successful species are the well-engineered ones. In turn, nature's evolutionary role in design implies a parallel human role. Humankind's function is to expedite progress, wherever necessary, by redesigning sociocultural parts of the material world ranging from the kitchen to the government. It is not unusual to come upon figures of speech which presume that human progress is a function of mechanical advances in design. "The time is coming," wrote a feminist in 1922, "when we are going to be as proud of our political machine as we would be of any piece of industrial machinery, when that machine is directed by men and women in the interest of . . . cordial equality" (*LHJ* 39 [Oct. 1922]: 123).

As we shall see, presumptions about human ingenuity in design had a major impact on American imaginative writing of the 1920s. That impact was felt on popular literature, which made the engineer a modern hero. And it was felt with equal power in serious fiction and poetry, in which words or sentences were viewed as component parts by authors self-identified as designers. But before examining the development of engineering aesthetics in the arts of the written word, we must take another look at some machine images. The novelists whose work we have just glimpsed refer to a perceived world of machines and structures. Swirling around them, however, are contemporary texts that so clearly define that world, so explicitly set it forth, that we must stop to listen to the figures of speech and to grasp their perceptual implications.

A typical example of such explicit discourse reached readers of *Everybody's Magazine* in 1911. An article on "Our Human Misfits" indicates that the human body is an energy-consuming-and-producing machine comprised of numerous component parts. The passage is worth seeing in its entirety:

> Is it any wonder that in the making of that exquisitely balanced and wonder-fully complicated machine which we call the human body—body, mind, and soul—here and there one should be turned out with a flaw in its castings, with a twist in its transmission, with a balance wheel badly hung, or a bearing ill fitted, or a leak in its cylinder, or a twist in the spoke of its driving wheel?
>
> We are beginning to be able to construct a sort of table . . . for the probable percentage of defects in the different cogs and wheels of our human machine. (25 [Oct. 1911]: 519)

The journalist and his readers knew, of course, that the human body was not comprised, literally speaking, of these automotive parts. But the word choices were not arbitrary either. The writer, like his audience, understood that body and machine were alike in one important way. Both were dynamic systems of integrated, functional component parts. On that basis, the language of the automotive machine was appropriate to a description of the human body. The concept of the machine, in fact, helped readers better understand the issues being discussed. The use of the machine images presumed that the readers could understand the human issue better if they saw it presented in machine terms. The accuracy of the analogy lay in the presumption that the two objects, the body and the machine, could be discussed in a language of component parts. The journalist's language presumes that both referents, body and machine, are structural analogues of each other and that the writer and his readers would grasp the validity of that connection immediately.

This same presumption is at work in many similar statements in a variety of texts. Some deal explicitly with the body. An educator noted a medical theory that

156   *The Ladies'* HOME JOURNAL   December, 1921

Fine Fuel
for Young Engines!

THOSE young human engines—with their healthy, hundred horse-power appetites—what heaps of Aunt Jemima Pancakes they do consume!

Everybody likes these pancakes. But children—they "love" 'em.

And it's well that they do, for their ever-active little bodies need just such breakfast nourishment as they get in this famous food. It warms them and satisfies them—gives them an abundant store of energy to start the day with.

Aunt Jemima Pancakes are always light and fluffy and tender because Aunt Jemima Pancake Flour is always exactly right. It's ready-mixed, with everything perfectly proportioned, with even the sweet milk in it.

So easy to prepare! So inexpensive!

Just a little water stirred into Aunt Jemima Pancake Flour, then a hot griddle—

—in two minutes you have a big, inviting plate of golden-brown pancakes on the table. Pancakes wonderfully light and fluffy, rich and satisfying, too—perfect pancakes!

And they're so inexpensive—just a few cents for the whole family's breakfast!

Order from your grocer today a package of Aunt Jemima Pancake Flour—and, for a change-off pancake treat, a package of Aunt Jemima Buckwheat Flour. That's the yellow package, you know.

Aunt Jemima Mills Company, St. Joseph, Mo.

Try Aunt Jemima Pancake Flour for waffles, muffins and breadsticks. They're mighty good!—and economical

AUNT JEMIMA PANCAKE FLOUR
REG. U.S. PAT. OFF.

"I'se in town, Honey!"

Aunt Jemima Pancake Flour
in the red package
Aunt Jemima Buckwheat Flour
in the yellow package

**For the kiddies' Christmas
Aunt Jemima Rag Dolls**

With any package of Aunt Jemima Pancake or Aunt Jemima Buckwheat Flour you will receive instructions (printed on the top or on slip enclosed) telling just how to get the jolly Aunt Jemima Rag Dolls. These dolls come in bright colors, ready to cut and stuff—and top off gaily the little Christmas stockings.

Copyright, 1921, Aunt Jemima Mills Company, St. Joseph, Mo.

Pancake flour advertisement. Ladies Home Journal, *1921 (Courtesy Quaker Oats Co.)*

toxins are "packed away in the interstices of our physical machine to clog the wheels and make trouble" (Wild 348). The eminent physician, William Osler, wrote that to remove the thyroid gland is to "deprive man of the lubricants which enable his thought-engines to work—it is as if you cut off the oil supply of a motor" (17). Ezra Pound called the mind of a mature man "a heavier and heavier machine, a constantly more complicated structure [requiring] a greater voltage of emotional energy to set it in harmonious motion" (*Literary Essays* 52). And in Dos Passos's *The Big Money* a weary executive is urged to visit the Mayo Clinic for "a little overhauling, valves ground, carburetor adjusted, that sort of thing" (569). In innumerable texts the image of the "human engine" is virtually a cliché, presumed to be as true as it is commonplace.

Still other texts show the same outlook on a range of subjects. In Wharton's *The Fruit of the Tree* a well-managed household is "a perfectly adjusted machine," while a children's book describes earthquake geology in terms of a boiler that can burst if its safety valve clogs and malfunctions ("In a way the volcanoes are the safety valves of the earth") (Wharton 380; Appleton, *Motion-Picture Boys* 88). One writer explained that "the bodily structure of a tree is a machine, because it provides for the life processes of the tree suitable channels, just as the steel structure of the steam-engine provides for the flow of steam suitable channels in which by its pressure and expansion it can do useful work" (Pupin 62–63). Each of these statements refers to the same world. From the earth-boiler to the tree and the household each presumes an engineered world in nature and culture. Each insists upon a material world of interworking systems of component parts.

Even those clinging to the romantic perception of an earlier age, those hostile to the idea of a mechanized world, found themselves acknowledging its authenticity. "The body rusts, clogs, and weakens, the mind dulls, the spirit goes out of you, and you are scrapped" under the influence of the machine, one critic complained (O'Brien 60–61). The novelist William Faulkner argued a similar point. The unimaginative mind, he suggests, is the one that conceives of thought in purely mechanistic terms. Faulkner's example is the character who consoles himself that the Lord intended human beings "not to spend too much time thinking, because his brain it's like a piece of machinery . . . it's best when it all runs along the same . . . and not no one part used more than needful" (*As I Lay Dying* 68).The writers detest the machine age, but we see at once that their terms presume the existence of a mechanized world. It is fair to say that machine-based values were so pervasive in American thought of the early twentieth century that even efforts to reject or evade them could result in inadvertent compliance with them.

One writer understood this dilemma, yet went on to argue that the twentieth-century moderns could have no valid alternative perception of the material world. Those who try, he suggests, are schizoid or hypocritical. His statement, too, deserves attention because it argues so conclusively that to be alive in the twentieth century is to see the world for what it is, a complex of mechanized systems. The writer, a Columbia University professor of science, insists that every person confront the inescapable fact that the individual is comprised of machines:

Energy
for youthful engines

"ORDER...*please!*"...
And whether this *midget-miss* chooses by color, by name, or just at random, doesn't matter. For bottled carbonated beverages are delicious, are wholesome, and contain highest quality sugar which, through natural action with the other elements in these drinks, is *pre-digested* .... supplying instant energy for youthful "machines" . . . .

Besides Sugar, these drinks contain pure water and wholesome flavors. Carbonation adds that tangy taste and prevents germs that may lurk in even what seems to be pure water. The bottles are scientifically sterilized and hermetically sealed.

There's a
BOTTLER
in your town!

COLD DRINKS

Kerb Service

SPONSORED BY

Bottled Carbonated Beverages
These taste-tempting drinks also are known by less formal names . . . *tonics* in New England . . . *soda water* in Dixie . . . *soda pop* in the Mid West . . . *soft drinks* in the Far West and we all know the *ginger ales*. Call them what you will, but drink your fill—they're good and good for you!

Send for
this Helpful Book
A.B.C.B.. 822 Bond Bldg.
Washington, D. C.
Enclosed find 10c. Send me your illustrated book "Recipes for Housewife and Hostess."

Recipes

NAME
ADDRESS
CITY   STATE

Soft-drink advertisement. Good Housekeeping, *1927*

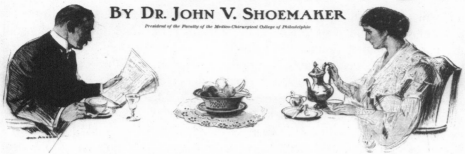

THE SATURDAY EVENING POST · 17

Fuel for the Human Engine

By Dr. John V. Shoemaker

President of the Faculty of the Medico-Chirurgical College of Philadelphia

Magazine illustration for article on nutrition. Saturday Evening Post, *1906*

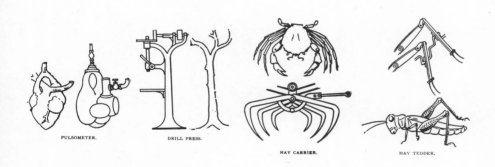

PULSOMETER.   DRILL PRESS.   HAY CARRIER.   HAY TEDDER.

Drawings showing analogues in nature and technology. Literary Digest, *1898*

Let him remember that an incomparably larger number of machines are set in motion whenever a message of our sensations is transmitted from a part of our body to the brain. . . . When the organs [of sight, hearing, taste, smell, and touch] are busy transmitting our sensations, each one of their functional units is busy contributing its share to the performance of the organ. Each one of them is a machine and works at the expense of the energy supplied by the foodstuffs, just as ordinary machines work at the expense of the energy of wood, coal, gas, and oil. We speak of feeding the fires under the boilers of our steam-engines just as we speak of feeding an organic body. This mode of speech expresses the similarity between the two processes. . . . When the word "machine" is used in this connection it is not used as a mere figure of speech. (Pupin 62–63, 17)

It is fitting to close this part of our discussion with this passage. For it really makes a definitive perceptual statement on the dominant gear-and-girder technology of the earlier twentieth century. Its implications are profound. Knowledge of the workings of nature is, it argues, knowledge of machines. By this logic there is no escape from, say, the mechanized city to the bucolic countryside. Perception itself has abolished the distinction between them. Nostalgic yearning for a pastoral world is, therefore, not only futile but impossible, even for "the aesthete who avoids employing machines, or even speaking of them . . . [who] longs for the simplicity of the classical civilization, and considers the employment of a great multiplicity of machines an artificiality, and therefore objectionable" (62–63). Like it or not, the statement says, contemporary knowledge brings cognizance of a world of mechanisms. This, then, is the world with which intellectuals and artists must contend. This is the world in which their opportunities lie.

CHAPTER TWO

INSTABILITY, WASTE, EFFICIENCY

ear-and-girder technology defined human be-
ings as designers in a world of machines. It
fostered belief that the material world was a
congeries of machines and structures made
up of component parts. The structures and
machines, whether products of nature or of
humankind, were thought to function with
varying degrees of efficiency. This dominant
technology encouraged the idea that human beings, as designers, could improve
the strength and efficiency of the material world.

On the face of it, this technology is one of unfettered optimism. It supports the
idea of continual progress, at least in the material world. It implies the potential for
progressive improvement in human affairs. To achieve this progress, it suggests,
human beings need only press on in their role as designers. Their ingenuity can
achieve new and better machinery in every area of nature and culture.

But so optimistic an outlook rested on—in fact, apparently sprang from—a far
more somber worldview. For the gear-and-girder world existed in a dialectic relation to another, much darker world in which nature and civilization were subject to
flux and upheaval. This was the world of instability, proclaimed by novelists,
psychologists, and sociologists. This world was defined by the constant changes,
shiftings, destabilizing movements of the material world, including those in the
realm of civilization and of the human organism itself. Thus the gear-and-girder
world was thought to cohabit another domain, one which presupposed sudden,
dreadful fluctuations and changes.

This world of instability, too, was Darwinian, for evolution, of course, cut two
ways. As we noticed, the adaptation and survival of higher species indicated that
nature itself was a designer whose ingenuity brought progress to the material
world. Evolutionary design, from this perspective, showed nature in the process of
solving its problems. Evolutionary change, by this definition, was change for the
better.

Yet an evolving world, on the other hand, was constantly unstable. Undergoing
relentless change, it was continually in a state of disequilibrium brought on by
geologic, biologic, sociologic, and psychologic forces. At any given moment this
world could prove to be the undoing of constructive effort of every kind. It threatened all human effort, from dams and bridges to governments and families.

This world of instability, as we shall see, ultimately gave special urgency to the
utilitarian gear-and-girder technology. It did so when Americans recast the very

concept of instability in utilitarian terms which lay at the heart of the gear-and-girder world. Before examining that utilitarian effort, however, we must venture into the world of instability. Paradoxically, that world both threatened and fostered Americans' recourse to technology.

INSTABILITY

And what is stable? find one boon
That is not lackey to the moon
Of Fate. The flood ebbs out—the ebb
Floods back; the incessant shuttle shifts
And flies, and wears and tears the webb.

Herman Melville, *Clarel*, 1876

Brooks [Adams] had discovered or developed a law of history. . . .
Everything American, as well as most things European and Asiatic,
became unstable by this law, seeking new equilibrium and
compelled to find it. . . . The instability was greater than he
calculated.

Henry Adams, *The Education of Henry Adams*, 1907

Calculating instability was a major occupation of American writers and intellectuals living in a Darwinian world. In texts of all sorts, from fiction to philosophy, Americans of the 1890s–1920s ratified their fearful convictions on instability in every area of life from the home to the workplace. Major writers chronicled the inevitable crack-up of communities, families, individuals in an unstable world, while the "lightning lines" of the news-service wires brought the public instantaneous evidence of instability in reports on disasters like the Johnstown Flood (1889) and the great Galveston Hurricane (1900).

Technology was not exempted from the calculus of instability. As we shall see, machines, their users, and their designers drew fire for abetting the destabilization of culture and society. Ironically, it was precisely this anxiety about a global state of instability that fostered an intense appreciation for the power of technology and its exponents, the engineers. It was anxiety over instability that evidently thrust technology into prestige and prominence, both for its actual and its potential power. By an intricate intellectual route through a realm of waste and efficiency, it was instability that led to the incorporation of technology and its values in the written word.

In some ways it seems odd that instability should be a source of anxiety to Americans of the late nineteenth and early twentieth centuries. Back in 1830 the precocious observer of American civilization, Alexis de Tocqueville, foresaw an America long accustomed to it. Tocqueville was struck by the instability that seemed essentially to define American culture. His classic *Democracy in America* describes "everyone in motion" in a "universal tumult." He asked, "How can the mind dwell on any single point when everything whirls around it?" And he concluded that Americans, lacking ancient traditions, sprang from a "heterogeneous and agitated mass" and live "in a state of incessant change of place, feelings, and fortunes" (334–35, 341, 344, 351, 369). Tocqueville anticipates the virtually identical observations of the philosopher George Santayana who, one century later in 1922, observed that Americans incessantly abandon their traditions, that "every house is always being pulled down for rebuilding," that no commonwealth of culture can be nourished, in short that "nothing can take root" (141–42).

The America of Santayana's observation, however, differed fundamentally from that of Tocqueville, whose assumptions were those of a preindustrial and pre-Darwinian world. Subject to the spasms of revolution and war, Tocqueville's world, including the New World, was nonetheless presumed to be physically and biologically constant or stable. Such was its nature. That presumption, of course, had vanished by the 1880s–1910s, when writers as diverse in form and outlook as Hamlin Garland and William James, as Robert Herrick and Henry Adams all resorted to one word—instability—to characterize America and the modern world. Inevitably, the premises of social thought in their era of Darwin, of his proponent Herbert Spencer, and of Auguste Comte, asserted the truth of continuous change in biological, social, and political life. Emphasis on process supplanted outworn Enlightenment views on categorical fixity. (This was also the period in which the great process technologies of electrical power, petroleum refining, and automobile manufacturing first arose.) Instability thus became the modern term which designated the constantly changeful state of the organism, its environment, and the interrelation of the two. Thus the term "instability" was uttered recurrently by novelists, physicians, and psychologists—and uttered most often in tones of anxiety.

Novels, once again, provide a useful record. Applied to New York City of the 1910s, Robert Herrick's phrase, "unstable flux," was intended to characterize modern America. "All the world that could move," in Herrick's New York, is "in unstable flux" (*Together* 221). Many writers saw the modern world in precisely that term. The written record from the 1890s reveals, to an astonishing degree, qualities of agitation, restlessness, frenzy—in short, of undisciplined, destabilizing energies loosed throughout American life. Whether one reads categorically in the literature of naturalism, realism, or in that of the muckraking school, the emphasis is the same. From the unflinching nihilism of Stephen Crane to the zealous reformism of Upton Sinclair to the Christian Socialism of the later William Dean Howells, contemporary American life is represented as unstable. Family and community life, personal relationships, experiences in the workplace—all are shown to be fluctuant, frenzied, dissolute.

Hamlin Garland said it outright: "Nothing is stable, nothing absolute, all changes, all is relative" (qtd. in Pizer 39). Garland, like most late-nineteenth-century writers, went on to affirm the ultimate improvement this evolutionary instability would bring about in life and in literature. But his best work, like that of his fellow writers, represents the present as grimly, wretchedly unstable. Years before W. B. Yeats wrote that "things fall apart; the centre cannot hold" American writers were busy demonstrating that view (184). "Willy nilly," said Stephen Crane, "the firm fails, the army loses, the ship goes down," while Dreiser wrote of the "unheralded storms . . . that so often brought ruin and disaster to so many" (*What Was Naturalism* [*WWN*] 92; *Titan* 551). Dreiser sets the modern agenda of "jails, diseases, failures, and wrecks" (*WWN* 154), while Frank Norris closes *The Octopus*, the first volume of his American epic, with the summary of his story line of disintegration and destruction: "Men—motes in the sunshine—perished, were shot down in the very noon of life; hearts were broken; little children started in life lamentably handicapped; young girls were brought to a life of shame; old women died in the heart of life for lack of food. In that little, isolated group of human insects, misery, death, and anguish spun like a wheel of fire" (458).

No locale, be it small town, hamlet, city, or pristine nature, affords rest or respite from flux and instability, according to the major writings of this period. Dreiser called man "an infinitesimal speck of energy . . . blown here or there by larger forces," and Jack London's *Cruise of the Snark* says that great natural forces —cyclones and tornados, lightning and riptides, earthquakes and volcanos—are apt to crush humans to a pulp (R. Martin 220, 191–92). In *The Open Boat* Stephen Crane's shipwrecked sailors can see cottages and trees and vacationers on the Florida shoreline even as they cower in their dinghy betwixt the heaving, deadly walls of water. Nature menaces them at night as a "monstrous knife" of a shark stalks these "babes of the sea" cradled in their open boat. A "flatly indifferent" Nature at last proves ironically fatal to the strongest of these men, the oiler, who drowns just as he reaches the sandy beach where men offer help and women brew coffee for the survivors (277–302).

Rural life of American agrarian traditions affords no protection against destabilizing forces. Edith Wharton's midwesterner, Undine Spragg, recalls the tornados that flatten the towns and villages of her "native state" (*Custom of the Country* 123). Such force in the natural world squanders farmers' lives in the stories of Hamlin Garland, whose premise of instability explodes the myth of agrarian bounty and stability. The stories in *Main-Travelled Roads* (1891) show farm families destroyed both by usurious mortgages and by natural disasters of drought and pestilence.

As an agent of human ruin, moreover, nature's energies are as deadly in the city as in the country. In *Sister Carrie* Dreiser shows the great extent to which the destitute Hurstwood's death is attributable to the severity of the winter, to the relentless cold that culminates in a blizzard which swirls "great clouds of snow along the streets, sweeping it down from the roofs and up from the pavements until the faces of pedestrians tingled and burned as from a thousand needle pricks" (415). Similarly, Upton Sinclair exploited the mortal threat of Chicago winters. In *The Jungle* a boy sees his workmate, also a child, run screaming into the packing plant in winter, his extremities so frozen that, when chafed, his ears snap off. On winter nights in their flimsy Chicago Packingtown house Sinclair's principal characters, a Lithuanian family, crouch and cower, trying in vain to escape the cold, "a grisly thing, a specter born in the black caverns of terror; a power primeval, cosmic . . . cruel, iron-hard. . . . Hour after hour they would cringe in its grasp, alone, alone" (83–86).

Natural and other disasters loomed large in a world that telegraphic communication was beginning to shrink. Readers of serious literature were by no means the only group to absorb the message of global instability. Journalism and other media of popular culture made the point constantly. News of disaster and catastrophe could be carried along the "lightning lines" of Western Union in a network of Associated Press wires in use since the 1870s (Czitrom 3–29). No story of havoc or destruction need be local or go unreported. The fire and explosion, for instance, of a boxcar of dynamite in a Boulder, Colorado, freight yard in August 1907, resulting in four deaths, could become an event of national reportage. Such national disasters as the Johnstown Flood (1889), the San Francisco Earthquake and fire (1906), the Homestead Strike (1892), the great Galveston Hurricane (1900), the sinking of the *Titanic* (1912) all signaled human helplessness against destabilizing energies. All were presented to the public both in vivid prose texts and in dramatic visual images. These included newspaper and magazine illustrations and photographs, moving pictures (*The Johnstown Flood* was a film of 1926), three-dimensional stereographic views, and even postcards. Multiplied, such sensational stories of disasters reinforced the sense of a dangerously unstable world.

One emphatic point pervades all these texts, popular and literary, in which "indifferent nature" squanders human life and the structures of civilization. The fire and ice, the snow, the waves, infestation of insects, cyclones, etc., all represent uncontrolled, undisciplined, destabilizing energy. They embody raw power against which people cannot defend themselves. It is especially significant to see this catastrophic natural energy in the civil settings. Nature overwhelms even in modern "fireproof" Baltimore, as well as in the novelists' middle landscape and the city. The furrowed field and the habitat of stone and masonry are no match for it.

The naturalist writers extend this worldview to personal, family, and community life, in which chaotic energies exceed all human efforts at order or discipline. Instability, shown in war, sudden hardship, industrial accidents, economic privation, corporate action—all corrupt and dissolve the family. Edith Wharton presents a disturbing world in which "couples were unpairing and pairing again with . . . ease and rapidity" (*Custom of the Country* 287). And Dreiser offers a searching analysis of familial disintegration in *Jennie Gerhardt* (1911), the novel in which he presents a young woman who is loyal and responsible to her large working-class family. She undertakes personal and financial responsibility for the clan in the aftermath of her father's injuries at a glassworks, toiling alongside her mother as a domestic worker. Yet by the end of the novel all the Gerhardt children are scattered and out of touch with one another. There is no scene of fraternal reconciliation, only a relentless process of dissolution, the same dissolution which Garland, Norris, Sinclair, and others make graphic in their fiction. The family tree is blasted in a world of instability.

Stereograph showing aftermath of Baltimore fire (Courtesy Library of Congress)

Great Baltimore Fire—On North St., looking S. W. of B. & O. Office
Bldgs., Balto., Md.

*Stereograph showing wreckage of Galveston Hurricane, 1900
(Courtesy Library of Congress)*

*Stereograph showing damage in Homestead Strike, 1892
(Courtesy Carnegie Library of Pittsburgh)*

Postcard view of aftermath of San Francisco Earthquake and fire, 1906

Destruction of the community correlates with the breakdown of family life. It is true that in many naturalistic works the principal characters are on the move or on the run and that community life is a secondary subject. Yet these writers address that subject, if only to repudiate the possibilities of community stability. Garland's farmers, even those well-intentioned toward one another, are too self-absorbed in toil and too certain to be uprooted by default on their impossibly heavy mortgages to develop a sense of community. As transient tenant farmers, they become isolates. The city scene is no better. In the immigrant novel, *The Rise of David Levinsky* (1917), an elderly Jew recalls that in Russia "people go to the same synagogue all their lives," while in America "people are together for a day and then, behold! they have flown apart. Where to? Nobody knows" (214).

Of all the American writers of this era Frank Norris perhaps worked hardest to explore the basis for the failure of community. In *McTeague* the young dentist and his wife live a pleasant neighborhood life on San Francisco's Polk Street. Yet behind the daily scenes of trade and personal interchange Norris warns that brutal, animal drives are at work to undermine the attractive surface, ultimately to reveal it as a sham. Similarly, in *The Octopus* the San Joaquin wheat ranchers, all of them strike-it-rich 'Forty-niners, join together to make common cause against the railroad. Yet their efforts at communal celebration, a barn dance and a rabbit shoot, both end in violence. And after the massacre of principal figures the "community" turns into a defecting crowd moved by cowardice and fear. The population is not communal but dissolute. Again Dreiser: "The sea is ever dancing or raging" (*Titan* 551).

We notice that the workplace, too, is a theater of instability, precarious at the top and ruinous at the bottom. Possibilities of injury haunt workmen daily. Dreiser's Gerhardt falls victim to injury, as do numerous characters in *The Jungle*, in which

Composite photograph showing Johnstown Flood damage, 1889
(Courtesy Carnegie Library of Pittsburgh)

New York newspaper report of the sinking of the Titanic, *1912*
(Courtesy Library of Congress)

the beef boners' hands are "criss-crossed with cuts," mutilated, eaten with pickling acids, swollen with arthritis in the damp chill (101). These are men jeopardized by infection, every moment at risk of the mortal mistake like a tumble into the rendering vats.

Yet life in the executive suite, physically less brutal, is apt to be just as ruinous even though it runs on paper symbols. The stock certificates, banknotes, and bonds, together with the vellum of social invitations and calling cards prove to be as powerful as the hammer and the boning knife. At this level, too, life is precariously fluctuant. Edith Wharton's *The House of Mirth* (1905) suggests a troubled Wall Street background of reversals and setbacks that intermittently curtail the stylish life of the Fifth Avenue rich.

Dreiser probes what Wharton only hints. *The Financier* is a business novel played out against the historical background of the financial house of Jay Cooke. Chaos perpetually threatens. "It was useless . . . to try to figure out exactly why stocks rose and fell. . . . Anything can make or break a market . . . from the failure of a bank to the rumor that your second cousin's grandmother has a cold" (34, 40–41). It is a financial world filled with "sudden and almost unheard-of changes" (65). Dreiser plays out Cowperwood's story against a background of financial panic—"those inexplicable stock panics, those strange American depressions which had so much to do with the temperament of the people, and so little to do with the basic conditions of the country" (155). Throughout the text Dreiser sprinkles the historically memorable name of Jay Cooke, which many readers of the 1910s would remember from the years leading to his ruin in the financial panic of 1873. As if to emphasize the instability at the very power center of American business, Dreiser closes *The Financier* with a summary of the fall of the man whose name once had been synonymous with wealth. From the *Philadelphia Press* the novelist found the apt metaphor—"a financial thunderclap in a clear sky" (491).

A brief foray into the developing social sciences shows instability to be a major concern of the sociologist and psychologist. Robert Ezra Park, a leading figure in the Chicago school of sociology, made a clear statement in one of the school's landmark publications, *The City* (1925). In a culture dominated economically by the stock exchange, Park says, individuals live in "a condition of instability that corresponds to . . . crisis." He echoed Georg Simmel's essay, "The Metropolis and Mental Life" (1903), and the 1880s writings of the American neurologist, George Beard, who blamed "American nervousness" on the sensory demands made by urban, technological life. The burden of instantaneous change troubled Park as it had worried Beard nearly a half century earlier. "Cities, and particularly the great cities," Park writes, "are in unstable equilibrium. The result is that the vast casual and mobile aggregations which constitute our urban populations are in a state of perpetual agitation . . . in a constant condition of crisis" (22). He writes, "We are living in such a period of individualization and social disorganization. Everything is in a state of agitation" (107). In the newer technologies of automobiles and flying machines Park saw further validation of Americans' "mental instability"

(118). (One can only guess at Park's probable response to Sinclair Lewis's novel, *Main Street* [1920], which thrusts instability to the center of small-town life. The sociologist who proclaimed it an urban crisis stood challenged by the novelist of small-town America, whose Gopher Prairie characters charge each other with "instability" as a major personality flaw [248, 352].)

William James, too, joined this chorus on instability, though from a different point of view. Unlike Park and the naturalist writers, James did not concur with the presumption that burgeoning urban, technological stimuli were psychologically harmful or neurologically detrimental, or morally or physically incapacitating.

Yet on the subject of fluctuant neural energies, James presumes that instability is the defining state of the human organism. In *The Principles of Psychology* (1890) James asks what "are the defects of the nervous system in those animals whose consciousness seems most highly developed?" His answer: "*instability.*" Though it works *for* the animal by making minute degrees of adaptation possible, this "brain tension shifts from one relative state of equilibrium to another, like the gyrations of a kaleidoscope. . . . [A]s in a kaleidoscope revolving at a uniform rate, although the figures are always rearranging themselves, there are instants during which the transformations seem minute . . . followed by others when it shoots with magical rapidity." James asserts that the brain is "an organ whose internal equilibrium is always in a state of change . . . the pulses doubtless more violent in one place than in another" (139, 235, 246). James's viewpoint on neural instability is pertinent here because he, like the sociologist Park and like the novelists, presumes it to be fundamental to the human condition. His optimism may not be shared by the others, but James is in full accord with them in his neurological theory.

It is not surprising to find that machine technology, like the forces of nature, sometimes comes to represent uncontrolled, destabilizing power. From the Colonial period Americans had worked at "civilizing the machine," but in the 1880s and 1890s machine symbols of anxiety and menace become prominent in American texts (Kasson). One social critic asked scornfully whether "that fatally fascinating sky-line of Manhattan . . . will ever assume the attribute of stability" (Huneker 39). He thought civilization was best symbolized in the traditional church steeples which got lost amid the new New York skyscrapers like "stone needles in metallic haystacks" (40). Such a negative image of modern technology eroded the reassurance implicit in figures of the civilized machine. Modern writers sought new terms in which to express their alarm that structures and machines, like nature, manifested the horrific, destabilizing energies loosed in the universe.

In fiction Frank Norris's railroad octopus is a clear and obvious example. Its tentacles of track spread and advance silently in every direction. They are ready to reach up suddenly to "grip with a sudden unleashing of gigantic strength." The railroad-octopus is an "ironhearted monster . . . its entrails gorged with the life-blood of an entire commonwealth" (228). Norris summons to mind what is monstrous in the natural world, implying that the machine manifests unstoppable forces of havoc. Norris is not, as has been pointed out, hostile to machine technol-

Postcard view of harvesting machine, San Joaquin County, California

ogy per se. But he evokes a fine sense of horror at machinery that manifests energy amok, which is to say the energy of instability. Such is the energy of the railroad and also the harvesting machine.

That harvester is worth a look. It shows the extent to which the naturalist writer can see the energy of machine technology as a counterpart to the horrific forces of wind and wave in the natural world. Approaching the harvester, Norris lists the component mechanical parts—header knives, beltings, cylinders, augers, fans, seeders, elevators—and names the sounds (hissing, rasping) of the machine. He mentions two goggled operators in attendance—but not really in control—for the machine seems to have a monstrous life of its own. It is the mechanical incarnation of chaotic natural energies. Thousands upon thousands of wheat stalks are sliced and slashed, "rattling like dry rushes in a hurricane" when caught up in "the prodigious monster, insatiable, with iron teeth, gnashing and threshing, devouring always, never glutted, never satiated, swallowing an entire harvest, snarling and slobbering in a welter of warm vapor, acrid smoke, and blinding, pungent clouds of chaff" (433–34).

Not satisfied with the image of the hurricane-force monster, Norris reaches for additional figures of horrific, chaotic power. He compares the harvester to a hippopotamus, then to a dinosaur whose vast jaws crush and tear with an appetite that is "incessant, ravenous, and inordinate." This last term, "inordinate," falls flat as a figure with which to summon a sense of horror. But the word precisely designates the basis for Norris's terror. It is the very excessiveness of the machine energies that strikes terror in the human heart.

Technological nightmares recur in important novels of this period, including Ignatius Donnelly's *Caesar's Column* (1889), Mark Twain's *A Connecticut Yankee at King Arthur's Court* (1888), and Upton Sinclair's *The Jungle*. All deal with technology as an agent of destructive apocalyptic power. Readers of *A Connecticut Yankee*, the story of the nineteenth-century Hartford, Connecticut, Colt arms factory foreman thrust back into Arthurian England, have been especially repelled by the horrendous concluding scene of carefully planned explosion and mass electrocution. That graphic passage on Arthurian corpses massed into "homogeneous protoplasm" signifies machine technology run amok and implicates the technological American mind as an agent of atrocity (396).

The Jungle, similarly, rejects sophisticated technology in an often-reprinted scene that shows the factory assembly line to be an American death camp. Like Twain, Sinclair shows the havoc wreaked when technology is deployed in the service of submerged passions like greed or lust for power. Both Sinclair and Twain address the limits of rationalist thought and the inordinate passions it conceals. Both were obviously alarmed by the brutal human energies masked as rational technologic efficiency. Both worked to reveal the raging, destructive force behind the mask.

Yet many writers, far from rejecting technology, put faith in its potential for the stabilization of nature and culture. There is a certain paradox here. Technology could succeed too well, like the Yankee's explosives which serve the most brutal human drives and proved effective with depressing regularity in actual wars. Yet again, technology could fail in such dramatic ways that it seemed, here too, an agent of instability. The Johnstown Flood was caused in part by a faulty dam; the "unsinkable" *Titanic* went down with shocking loss of life; fire destroyed Baltimore's metal-girdered "fireproof" tall buildings. "Instability" was a term engineers also used with great anxiety because it meant the failure of their efforts.

Be that as it may, there is a sense in which technological goals—functional regularity, efficiency, stability—were beginning to seem natural. All sorts of documents from journalism to advertising show that in a profound way the goals of technology were beginning to be projected onto the natural world. The well-regulated environment began to be felt as the natural environment, and vice versa. Severe wind and wave, tremors and geomorphic upheavals were perceived increasingly as anomalies, aberrations in nature.

From this point of view, technologists—the engineers—were not summoned to battle nature but only its aberrations. Their values were thought to be consonant with those inherent in the natural environment. In a conceptual twist, it was technology that was becoming the standard for what was considered natural. Forces counter to the technologic goals of efficiency, stability, functional regularity, etc., were seen as unnatural. They required reconstructive attention. Accordingly, popular writers appealed to the spokesmen of technology, the engineers, to be humane, knowledgeable, and powerful. They looked to these new professionals, as a class, to be wise men, men able to make machinery serve human needs, men so powerful in their ingenuity that they could design the machines, structures, and even the social organizations that would enable human beings to surmount the forces of instability. The sociologist Robert Park, for instance, sought the principles of "useful control" to stabilize city life, and thus allied himself with the social engineers.

Thus it was technology to which many Americans obviously turned in hopes of overcoming the dreadful, "unnatural" forces of instability. As we shall see, this turn required that the world be reconceived along utilitarian lines, for the polar contraries, waste and efficiency, enabled the world to be newly understood. The new utilitarian values fostered a belief that the world was a congeries of machines and structures made up of component parts subject to recombination. It encouraged everyone to become his or her own engineer.

THE NEW UTILITARIANS

The man of action can within certain limits have his way with nature. Now the men who have acted during the past century have been the men of science and the utilitarians who have been turning to account the discoveries of science. The utilitarians have . . . been able to stamp their efforts on the very face of the landscape.

Irving Babbitt, *Rousseau and Romanticism*, 1919

New utilitarian arguments emerged during this period to challenge the "truth" of cosmic instability, for certain writers and analysts repudiated the concept of an unstable cosmos and offered a utilitarian one in its place.

These writers dissented from the pessimistic, gloomy worldview. Armed with the utilitarian, industrial-age terms, *waste* and *efficiency*, they rejected the idea of "instability." In effect, they declared it invalid. More, they shifted certain terms of argument—really of perception itself—in ways that eventually altered American thought and literature in the twentieth century. Ultimately the contraries these analysts employed, waste and efficiency, opened the way for the values of machine technology to enter fully into twentieth-century imaginative forms.

This part of the story must begin in 1888 with the publication of Edward Bellamy's *Looking Backward: 2000–1887*, the tale of a late-nineteenth-century Bostonian who finds himself in a utopian America in the year 2000. Bellamy offered a glowing vision of the nation sustained by material abundance and social harmony for all. It proved so attractive that *Looking Backward* became a major best-seller in the decade following its publication. The novel argued that the United States, in fact the Western world, could become a utopia by rejecting its wasteful ways and embracing the ideals of efficiency.

As themes, waste and efficiency became the polar axis of Bellamy's novel, which we must examine here for its utilitarian notions, then encounter later on when considering popular perceptions of the engineer. For now, Bellamy's *Looking Backward* shows the entrenchment of new thematic key words in American culture. His waste and efficiency signified new modes of thought in an era of pervasive industrialization. Bellamy proclaimed the onset of the new utilitarian world when he cast waste as America's devil and efficiency as its industrial-age god. Every page of *Looking Backward* announced the new utilitarian religion just a few years in advance of the public worship that would swell into the Efficiency Movement of the 1910s, including Progressive politics and cultural baguettes like the composer Scott Joplin's "Efficiency Rag." By the 1910s the patron saint of efficiency would be the production engineer Frederick Winslow Taylor, not Edward Bellamy. Taylor would be the figure praised and pilloried in terms that rang in public debate throughout the 1920s, continuing to be a legacy in public discourse to this day. Yet it was the novelist, Bellamy, who first put America on a new utilitarian footing when he exploited the contraries, waste and efficiency, in his visionary program for the American future.

Bellamy did not dismiss contemporary convictions on instability when he proclaimed the new doctrines. In fact, his novel acknowledged the apparent cataclysmic instability that was so emphatic in the work of Stephen Crane, Theodore Dreiser, Hamlin Garland, and the others. Bellamy says outright: the "barbaric industrial and social system" is as "unstable" as a drifting iceberg, "shaking the world with convulsions that presage its collapse." As a Springfield, Massachusetts, newspaper publisher, Bellamy used headlines to telegraph the very messages on instability that were central to so much contemporary thought and writing. In *Looking Backward* the metropolitan morning paper reads like the manifest of an unstable world:

> The epidemic of fraud unchecked. . . . Orphans left penniless.—clever system of thefts by a bank teller; $50,000 gone. . . . Enormous land-grabs of Western syndicates.—Revelations of shocking corruption among Chicago officials. . . . Large failures of business houses. Fears of a business crisis. . . . A woman murdered in cold blood for her money at New Haven. . . . A man shoots himself in Worcester because he could not get work. A large family left destitute.—An aged couple in New Jersey commit suicide rather than go to the poorhouse. . . . More insane asylums wanted.—Decoration Day Addresses. Professor Brown's oration on the moral grandeur of nineteenth-century civilization. (217)

On the face of it, Bellamy's headlines ring true to the vision of those committed to an "unstable" world. (The mixture of greed and grief capped with irony also anticipates, in its technique, John Dos Passos's disjunctive use of news headlines in fiction a quarter century later.) Yet Bellamy's congruence with contemporaries like Dreiser, Norris, Crane, and so on, is limited. In plot, theme, and character, their work insisted upon an unstable cosmos. Bellamy's gave credence only to its symptoms.

To argue the difference, Bellamy effected a cunning linguistic change, a kind of verbal mutation that enabled him to make a utilitarian, functionalist argument impossible for those committed to a worldview of instability. Granted, Bellamy was something of an Emersonian mystic. He felt hopeful about the human condition as figures like Mark Twain or Edith Wharton did not. A socialist reformer, he considered his novel to be an instrument for social change. He defined the writer as an agent of social progress, not as an experimental explorer-chronicler of blind forces at work in an ever-evolving and thus unstable cosmos. Accordingly, Bellamy's Boston-2000 is a model of harmonious stability, while the naturalists' America of the foreseeable future heaves with human energy squandered blindly.

Bellamy, moreover, understood the implications of a new utilitarian argument. By opposing waste to efficiency, he made instability into a fiction, a mere snare and delusion for moderns. By employing the utilitarian terms as his premises of argument, Bellamy could show that so-called instability was really a man-made state of affairs, not an immutable condition. In this light the destitute orphans, the elderly suicides, even the syndicated land-grabbers of his newspaper headlines become the victims of culture, not of nature. They and the others in their plight can be redeemed by utilitarian efficiency. They suffer needlessly from wastefulness.

The term "waste" is crucial. As of the 1910s it would become a pejorative American byword, virtually the industrial-era devil denounced in texts of all kinds from literary criticism to advertisements. But the first exfoliation of its meaning came from *Looking Backward*, in which waste is the culprit in all human suffering. Bellamy finds it everywhere, in the wars that consume human treasure like water, in the woeful maladaptation of individuals to their work, in the middleman's redundant and costly distribution of goods, in the household toil undertaken in thousands of separate kitchens and laundries when a centralized few would suffice (67, 113, 184, 168).

But these pall before the "other prodigious wastes." Bellamy lists them in a litany of America's cardinal sins, "first, the waste by mistaken undertakings; second, the waste from the competition and mutual hostility of those engaged in industry; third, the waste by periodical gluts and crises; fourth, the waste from idle capital and labor, at all times" (168–69). The world of *Looking Backward*, by contrast, is an exemplary state of societal harmony and plenty—in short, of thoroughgoing efficiency.

Bellamy makes it so because in the world of his novel *instability* sideslips conceptually into the utilitarian realm. Here the conceptual framework of the novel—and beyond it, of human experience—undergoes a radical change away from a realm of instability. For a state of waste is not immutable. It is susceptible to correction in the achievement of its contrary, efficiency. Coupled with that contrary, "waste" invites, in fact demands, corrective action. In denotation and connotation the word is a summons to it. As such, it is humanly empowering as "instability" cannot be. The very word implies that human life in all its relationships—personal, social, environmental—is subject to planning and design. It need not be devastated or squandered by "unheralded storms out of clear skies." Bellamy even scolds contemporaries for accepting a wasteful state of affairs as if it were the cultural equivalent of droughts, hurricanes, and earthquakes. He challenges the naturalist position by turning its own terms of disaster against it. With planning and design all these disasters, both natural and man-made, are averted, really transcended in America-2000.

The nexus of waste and efficiency establishes new terms of argument for human experience, terms perhaps inevitable in a capitalistic industrial culture. As we shall see further on in this discussion, *Looking Backward* is a hymn to efficient America and to the engineers entrusted to achieve it. It is significant here as the herald of functionalist thought and values that would provoke sustained public debate through the 1910s and 1920s and eventually alter the forms of American literature. The extent of the American debate on waste and efficiency from Bellamy through the 1920s is crucial here. That debate forms the basis on which the engineer could emerge as a hero for the new American century, and the values of engineering in turn initiate major change in the imaginative life of American culture.

The baton of argument on waste passed directly from Bellamy to the Scandinavian-American economist and cultural critic, Thorstein Veblen. Veblen's first wife recalled that the couple read *Looking Backward* on her uncle's Iowa farm, and that it marked a turning point in both their lives. In Dos Passos's words, Veblen was "a grayfaced shambling man . . . subtly paying out the logical inescapable rope of matter-of-fact for a society to hang itself by" (*U.S.A.: Big Money* 101). In style and substance it was true, for Veblen soon became one of America's best critics of culture, even if his difficult, sonorous prose made him a figure more talked about than read. His one commercially successful book, *The Theory of the Leisure Class* (*TLC*) (1899), was popularly mistaken for a satire on the lives of the idle rich and the bourgeois who attempted to imitate them. In fact it was a scathing indictment of waste measured against a functionalist standard of value.

In retrospect it seems self-evident that in an age of the ostentatious display of American wealth, Veblen, like Bellamy, should find waste to be a propitious critical topic. It was the very gilding on the Gilded Age. Veblen observed that in every quarter from food to fashion, value increased according to its distance from productive, useful employment. Veblen's standard, like Bellamy's, is functional. Waste, Veblen cautions his reader, is not to be taken in an odious sense. It denotes an expenditure that fails to serve human life or human well-being on the whole. Veblen's examples of waste under this functional heading include "carpets and tapestries, silver table service, waiters' services, silk hats, starched linen, many articles of dress," including corsets and seasonal fashion and frippery (*TLC* 97–101). Readers of Dreiser's *Sister Carrie* can find Veblen's point illustrated in a restaurant dinner party at Sherry's, the mecca of "the moneyed or pleasure-loving class. . . . The air with which the [waiter] pulled out each chair, and the wave of the hand . . . were worth several dollars in themselves." Once the patrons are seated,

Veblen's cultural "waste" instanced in the sumptuous interior of the Siegel Cooper Co. store, New York, 1903 (Courtesy Library of Congress)

"there began that exhibition of showy, wasteful . . . gastronomy as practiced by wealthy Americans" (288–89).

Such waste, in Veblen's terms, is the failure to meet the functional criteria of the "economic conscience." All expenditures must be subjected to one test: do they serve "directly to enhance human life on the whole?" This criterion compels Veblen to designate "waste" in endless categories, from livery to lap dogs, from ladies' hair to gentlemen's race horses. The intelligentsia are fair game. Veblen scorns William Morris's Kelmscott Press as a ridiculous travesty of book publishing, producing volumes of "painstaking crudeness and elaborate ineptitude," which mark it as a decadent object of conspicuous waste (*TLC* 99, 163–65).

Veblen's critique of waste includes a closer scrutiny of social mores and cus-

Nonfunctional "waste" illustrated in this colonnade of the Palace Hotel, San Francisco, 1900 (Courtesy Library of Congress)

*"Wasteful" lives of New York society women in Greek pageant
(Courtesy Library of Congress)*

*Veblen's leisure class on display at the Ladies' Four-in-Hand and Coaching Society annual
parade, New York City, 1906 (Courtesy Library of Congress)*

Children imitating adults' "wasteful" displays in goat carriages in Central Park, New York City (Courtesy Library of Congress)

toms than Bellamy undertook, and in one important respect Veblen differed from his mentor. Bellamy's citizenry of America-2000 achieves its spiritual fulfillment only in retirement from the world of work after the age of forty. But Veblen prizes the instinct of workmanship, as he calls it, too dearly to sever it from the worlds of work or of play. Human beings, in Veblen's scheme of things, have "a taste for effective work, and a distaste for futile effort. They have a sense of the merit or serviceability or efficiency and of the demerit of futility, waste, or incapacity" (*TLC* 15, 16). In a barbaric business culture this instinct has been so perverted that only a pecuniary standard prevails. That standard debases the concept of "cheapness" so that goods produced at low cost become despicable, no matter how serviceable and ameliorative they are.

And no matter how aesthetically satisfying. Veblen asserts that the barbaric leisure-class culture has conditioned its victims and perpetrators to "aesthetic nausea." They have suffered the corruption of their intuitive, inborn taste. "All wastefulness is offensive to native taste," he says (*TLC* 178, 176). But to those of corrupted taste, *waste* becomes the measure of social esteem by the degree to which its symbols, objects of idleness and uselessness, surround the individual, the family, and its retinue of servants and animals. The barbarous scene in Sherry's could only occur in a wasteful culture.

Both Veblen and Bellamy will compel attention further on when we examine the figure of the engineer, who is the cultural exponent of these anti-waste, pro-efficiency values. At this point, the two writers serve to introduce waste and efficiency as cultural key words of the new utilitarians. In fact, these terms are burdened with divers meanings that call out for separate definition. Semantic distinctions become all the more necessary considering that by the 1910s and 1920s the terms, waste and efficiency, would become the common coin of management consultants and writers, of self-help evangelists, advertisers, politicians, presidents, and journalists like Veblen's acolyte, the popular economics writer, Stuart Chase. In those years the terms scattered everywhere, threatening to become buzzwords meaning everything and nothing. Yet *waste*, like *efficiency*, was a cultural key word directly pertinent to the gear-and-girder technology and its imaginative forms. It requires a closer look here.

WASTE

Waste, colossal waste! Waste, now ignorant, now careless, often criminal! There's the great scientific sociological problem. And every one can help to solve it.

Saturday Evening Post, October 14, 1905

We come to definition. What, exactly, did "waste" mean? If slashed trees, ladies' pearls, and business competition all signified it, what conceptions lay behind those examples? Because numerous writers followed Bellamy's lead and recast the world along an axis of efficiency and waste, it is important to examine the ramifications of the two terms. They took a governing place in all areas of American life from the breakfast table to novels and poems. In written texts the two terms ordinarily appear together and imply each other's conceptual presence. But the semantic strands can best be examined in a separate discussion.

As the contrary of efficiency, "waste" meant dysfunction and danger, pejoratives in many writers besides Veblen and Bellamy. All found the term equally opprobrious. As of the 1910s even advertisers could appeal to the new public antipathy to waste. Manufacturers of factory-cut houses promised to "eliminate waste," to "save 20% lumber waste." "If the 20 million housewives of America each had a [Sellers] Kitchen Cabinet," read the *Good Housekeeping* advertising copy, "a total of ten million hours, now wasted, could be saved" (67 [Nov. 1918]: 147). The Simplex electric ironer promised to "prevent waste of time and strength," while the manufacturer of gas water heaters virtually taunted readers: "You live in an age of scientific accomplishment. . . . Yet your family is using methods of a half century ago to get hot water. Many hours are wasted because water must be heated for dishes, for bathing, . . . for baby's bath" (*LD* 62 [July 12, 1919]: 92).

The intelligentsia continued to cite waste as abhorrent. Writers from Ezra Pound to Henry James, from Upton Sinclair to William Carlos Williams denounced it by name, believing waste inimical to the life of the imagination and of the society as a whole. Robert Herrick wrote a novel on it. His *Waste* (1924) was a blanket denunciation of corruption in government, business, family, and personal life in this century. It is evident that T. S. Eliot intended to evoke contemporary cultural resonances when he named his poetic indictment of modern spiritual aridity *The Waste Land*. When paired with "efficiency," waste implied all things retrograde and in the worst sense primitive. The word became a negative test of cultural and literary status. In an inverse way, as we shall see, it came to influence form and style in twentieth-century American literature.

As we proceed into definitions, it is useful to bear in mind one essential point. "Waste" is a term of opprobrium, but of a certain kind. Utilitarian, it implies a specific kind of critical thinking. It presupposes a certain form of intellectual analysis of a condition or situation. The analysis must include a breaking-down, a dis-assembly of the way something works. To pronounce a situation or condition wasteful is to have first scrutinized the whole of it by breaking it down into its component parts. To call it wasteful is to have seen or devised a better, more efficient way of doing things. That can only be accomplished by an intellectual dis-assembly and re-assembly.

The critical mind that finds a condition or apparatus wasteful has thus worked according to the defining technology of the gear-and-girder world. The whole, meaning the entire structure or system or machine, has been analyzed part by part. It has been judged wasteful because, in dismantling it into its parts, the critic has recognized a more effective or efficient means by which it can operate. To call it wasteful is to say that it needs to be redesigned, and the critic who thinks and judges in this way is working de facto as an engineer. Whether that critic is a housewife counting unnecessary steps in her kitchen or an industrialist scrutinizing the reason why factory equipment lies idle too much of the time, the individual is thinking like an engineer. The point is evident in the writer who exhorted the housewife "to examine her own day and its work and discover where the wastes occur" (E. H. Wharton 25). That home economist, like an industrialist, perceives a world in which things and social organization are complex assemblies subject to dismantling into component parts. Improvement of that world necessitates re-design part by part, eliminating the unnecessary or wasteful ones, recombining the others.

Thus critics of waste reveal the same thought process no matter which definition of the term they emphasize. As for definitions themselves, they clustered into a very few well-defined meanings, even though the *Oxford English Dictionary* lists more than a dozen definitions of "waste" ranging from "useless person" to "uninhabited or uncultivated country" (which is the sense in which seventeenth-century Puritan New Englanders used it).

American texts of the late nineteenth and early twentieth centuries revert princi-pally to three definitions of the term. One emphasized the possible exhaustion of finite resources. In this sense the historian Frederick Jackson Turner warned a 1914 university graduating class that "the national problem is no longer how to cut and burn away the vast . . . dense and daunting forest" but "how to save and wisely use the remaining timber" (294).

The historian found an echo in *The Tragedy of Waste* (1927) by the popular economics writer, Stuart Chase, who wrote, "When we review the methods by which the pioneer lays waste our unreplaceable national resources, it seems as though we touch bottom indeed—a race of weevils consuming its substance without the intelligence for the future which animates a colony of bees" (277). Theodore Roosevelt was also anxious about the diminishment or consumption of the nation's raw materials. He warned, "We have passed the time when we will tolerate the man whose only idea is to skin the country and move on" (51). And the conservationist Gifford Pinchot similarly condemned the "drain upon our non-renewable coal" (44–45). Not surprisingly, World War I sharpened sensitivi-ties to the exhaustion of material. "The world will be much poorer after the war," one writer said. "The [general] store will be less. Waste will be more quickly felt" ("Waste" 572). These kinds of statements refer, of course, to the diminishment or depletion of resources. They imply the need for new plans, new designs, for resource management.

There is, moreover, another definition of waste that took a prominent place in the lexicon: *to fail to take advantage of*. In this meaning "waste" becomes the unrecognized opportunity, the missed chance for some order of gain. In this sense the word "waste" is a summons, not a dire threat. If an improvident America could reject its squandering ways, it could also seize the previously unnoticed opportuni-ties and take advantage of them. By this logic, waste could actually become the opportunity for a new abundance.

Many writers pressed that point. Sarah Orne Jewett, the fiction writer, spoke poignantly of her "wonder at the waste of human ability in this world, as a botanist wonders at the wastefulness of nature, the thousand seeds that die, the unused provision of every sort" (95). Most others, however, who defined waste as potential, unrealized opportunity concentrated specifically on matters of business or eco-nomic life. In *Today and Tomorrow* (1926) Henry Ford's chapter on "Learning from Waste" argued to the fraction of the inch and hundredth of a cent that Ford plants maximized natural resources and manpower in order to serve the Ameri-can public. Essentially, Ford argued that his plants were the exemplary machine designs.

The conservation movement also provided ideological opportunities to exploit the semantics of "waste" as unrealized abundance. Gifford Pinchot's polemic is one good example. "There may be just as much waste in neglecting the develop-ment and use of certain natural resources as there is in their destruction," said the conservationist whose utilitarian viewpoint eventually put him at odds with the preservationist John Muir. "The development of our natural resources and the fullest use of them for the present generation is the first duty of this generation" (48, 43–44). Pinchot's forestry programs, of course, brought an engineering approach to nature, one ideologically compatible with Ford.

It is helpful to have in mind the broad cultural base of this concept of waste-as-abundance. A few further examples show the popularity of the issue. One landmark study, *Waste in Industry* (1921), was compiled by a committee of engineers headed by Herbert Hoover. It issued a spate of recommendations for four areas of industrial waste, listing its recommendations under a heading entitled "Opportunities and Responsibilities" (Committee on Elimination of Waste in Industry 24–33). A reader of the report sees at once that to undertake the diverse responsibilities is to seize the overlooked opportunities hidden under the rubric "waste." The analytical report is really a summons to action. Waste becomes the opportunity for abundance, the very plenitude cataloged in Henry J. Spooner's *Wealth from Waste* (1918). This author, an Englishman, located waste—which is to say potential abundance—in every conceivable part of Western culture, from underutilized land to the "waste of more or less trifling things" like candles, soap, and cigar ash. He celebrates the alchemy by which refuse and residues are turned into fabrics, oils, and numerous useful products (240, 197). Whether the subject is forestry, product development, or the use of personal time, "waste" is the waiting opportunity. Only ingenuity is wanting.

There was yet a third definition in frequent use—one very close to Veblen's. The idea of squandering or of useless expenditure (of money and goods, of time and effort) was prominent in diverse writings and also had activist implications. It appeared in a range of texts from scholarly journals to fiction. In *America and Alfred Stieglitz* (1934) the educator Harold Rugg reviewed industrial America from the Civil War to World War I. He listed the virgin continent, the climate, human nature, and the pressure of immigrant hordes as a cauldron in which "everything in the earth was taken in a mad, unrestricted, and unplanned race for gain." Rugg concludes, "It was an uproarious period of hectic trial and error—mostly error —and waste!" (92). His criticism of "unrestricted" and "unplanned" exploitation of natural resources aligns him with the utilitarians. Rugg implies the need for planning and regulation, in short, a need for design. Ezra Pound concurred, and broadened the indictment to include the entire American experience, which he thought corrupted by the market economy of the Protestant Reformation. Says Pound, "The American tragedy is a continuous history of waste—waste of the natural abundance first, then waste of the new abundance offered by machines" (*Selected Prose* [*SP*] 176).

From specific vantage points others defined American wastes similarly as squandering or useless consumption, always with the belief that redesign is possible. The department store merchant, Edward Filene, proclaimed that business graft wasted consumer dollars ("In a word, high prices are caused by waste") (*Successful Living* 31). Melville C. Dewey, inventor of the library system named for him, pronounced himself "an uncompromising foe to every kind of waste and lost motion." As a proponent of the simplified spelling movement (in which Theodore Roosevelt

Typewriter advertisement, 1910s (Courtesy National Museum of American History, Smithsonian Institution)

took part), Dewey remarked that "one seventh of all English writing is made up of unnecessary letters; therefore one tree of every seven made into pulp wood is wasted" ("Novel Ways of Saving Your Time" 34–35). Dewey, of course, had engineered a library cataloging system. He then dis-assembled the English language into its phonetic components in order to redesign a system of efficient spelling. In the traditional system the unnecessay letters were wasteful components; he proposed a new design that could eliminate them.

Time, too, could be broken into component parts and reformulated. To some, the squandering of this precious commodity was as loathsome as the waste of material resources. Ford called it "the easiest of all wastes, and the hardest to correct," lamenting that no salvage of time is possible. Ford took an industrial approach to the problem, which he defined in terms of inventory, meaning on-hand components. "We think of time as human energy," he wrote, explaining that the waste of it could be avoided by sustaining an adequate inventory of people, materials, and plant facilities. The design challenge was to keep the proportion of components in balance for efficient functioning of the manufacturing machine (*Today and Tomorrow* 110).

With a global sweep Walter Lippmann provided a succinct summary of the new awareness, and defiance, of waste-as-squandering. "It's a movement to end waste in the world," wrote Lippmann. "It includes almost anything, from forestry to housekeeping, from brick-laying to personal hygiene. There are more and more people in the world who hate waste," he continued, "and can't rest until they end it. The idea of doing a job in double time; the spectacle of people foozling and fuddling without plan, without standards; the whole idea of wasted labor and wasted material is a horror to them" ("More Brains—Less Sweat" 827–28).

Advertisement for factory-cut houses. Literary Digest, *1918*

Tools from a Waste-Killer's Kit

SINCE a workman is known by his tools, the partial contents of a Johns-Manville Salesman's kit will give some indication of the kind of a man that carries it.

Johns-Manville men are more than salesmen—they might be called "Waste-Killers"—because before they *sell* anything, they show how to *save* something—power, heat, energy lost through friction, or property from fire loss. So they must know industry and engineering and the relations of these to the products they handle.

Whether it be a recommendation of a particular packing for a certain pump—calculating proper thickness and kind of heat insulation to reduce heat loss in pipe lines—or again in handling a roofing problem—or specifying electrical protection—the Johns-Manville Salesman must *serve* before he sells.

More than five hundred of our salesmen are welcome visitors, so customers tell us, to the industries of America. Not surprising either when you realize that in all departments of industry, conservation is alike the key-note to progress and the slogan of these Johns-Manville Waste-Killers—a title which they have earned by consistent service over two decades.

H. W. JOHNS-MANVILLE CO., New York City
10 Factories—Branches in 63 Large Cities
For Canada, Canadian Johns-Manville Co., Ltd., Toronto

1. *Asbestos Roofing.*

2. *Blow Torch* to demonstrate fire repellency of asbestos roofing.

3. *Friction Blocks* for industrial clutches, brakes and friction drives.

4. *Sectional Insulation* to prevent heat losses in power and heating systems.

5. *Technical Data* on all power plant products sold.

6. *Fibre Conduit* for underground electrical systems.

7. *Asbestos Shingles:* fire proof, Beautiful, durable.

8. *Sea Rings:* a packing for pumps, engines and compressors that has revolutionized thought on all packings.

9. *Steam Trap:* to prevent waste in steam lines.

10. *Gasket:* to make boiler manholes and handholes steam tight.

11. *Fire Extinguisher:* motor car, industrial, and home first aid protection.

12. *Renewable Fuse:* economical electric circuit protection.

13. *Electrical Cutouts:* a complete unit system of wiring distribution.

14. *Refractory Materials:* cements for the protection of masonry against high heats.

15. *Salesman's Engineering Manual:* a complete encyclopedia of information on all Johns-Manville products and their relation to conservation.

16. ⊄. *Crude Asbestos:* in the pocket of every Johns-Manville Waste-Killer—as illustrating the basic source of the service he gives.

Through—

Asbestos

and its allied products

INSULATION
that keeps the heat where it belongs

CEMENTS
that make boiler walls leak-proof

ROOFINGS
that cut down fire risks

PACKINGS
that save power waste

LININGS
that make brakes safe

FIRE
PREVENTION
PRODUCTS

JOHNS-MANVILLE
Serves in Conservation

Johns-Manville advertisement. Collier's, *1919 (Courtesy Manville Corp.)*

American writers of imaginative literature kept clear of Lippmann's kind of jingoism and, their texts suggest, could only look askance at the journalist's zest for a war on waste "to get the business of life done." Their optimism on prospects for the riddance of waste was hedged about with a certain skepticism, with ambivalence that is evident even as they denounce waste-as-squandering in many areas of the culture. Henry Adams abhorred it in the university yet saw no institutional effort to stop it: "throughout human history the waste of mind has been appalling," and "society has conspired to promote it" (*Education* 314, 303).

Adams was as biting as Henry James was poignant when, in *The American Scene* (1906), he looked upon the new Manhattan skyline to pronounce it a "vision of eternal waste." In his discussion, "The Waste of Growth," James points out that the term means more to him than conspicuous pecuniary power. The "appealing, touching vision of waste" in the endlessly built and rebuilt onetime Knickerbocker town especially saddens James because of the loneliness he perceives in all the desperate activity. "Nowhere else does pecuniary power so beat its wings in the void," James writes, adding that "the whole costly up-town [architectural] demonstration was a record, in the last analysis, of individual loneliness; whence came . . . its insistent testimony of waste—waste of the still wider sort than the mere game of rebuilding" (113, 158–59).

In identifying squandering with loneliness, James characteristically pursues meaning to depths that elude others. Lewis Mumford offers the more conventional kind of critique, likewise occasioned by the subject of American architecture. The 1893 Chicago World's Fair's White City architects aped imperial Rome, Mumford complains in *Sticks and Stones*, because of "its skill in conspicuous waste." Mumford added that "once we assimilate the notion that soil and site have uses quite apart from sale, we shall not continue to barbarize and waste them" (204). *Once we assimilate the notion*. The phrase conveys both skepticism and yet confidence in future action.

Even those literary works that most explicitly address the issue of waste, Herrick's *Waste* (1924) and Upton Sinclair's *The Jungle* (1906), leave open the hope for redemption despite their dark vision. *The Jungle* concludes with the certainty of redemption. All along, Sinclair had recounted the futile quest for stability and for modest prosperity on the part of eastern European immigrants destroyed in the inferno of the Chicago meat-packing houses. His polemical novel concludes with a socialist lecture by a self-described philosophic anarchist. The speech, envisioning a millennial cooperative commonwealth, is a virtual reprise of Bellamy and Veblen. The speaker foresees a toil-free New Jerusalem just the other side of fifteen enumerated kinds of waste (of competition, ostentation, advertising, time, etc.). Sinclair then forecasts the elimination of these wastes as socialist political power advances in America. The mid- and southwestern voting tallies he reprints at the closing of the book prove that the end of the dreadfully wasteful period is at hand. The larger and larger socialist votes in Illinois and Indiana, in Wisconsin and Ohio are meant to prove that the jungle is soon to become efficiency's New Jerusalem (332–34, 339–41).

Of course, T. S. Eliot's *The Waste Land* (1926) is the text that comes immediately to mind in any consideration of waste in twentieth-century literature. The poem expresses the postwar sense of aridity experienced by what Gertrude Stein called the "lost generation," meaning those moderns who had lost their bearings, their direction, and their generative powers. Probing contemporary spiritual decay, Eliot proclaimed April "the cruellest month" and made modern London the locus of his baleful indictment of the loss of Christianity and its culture throughout Europe. Anarchy and futility become the hallmarks of contemporary western Europe, which has become "a heap of broken images / where the sun beats" (*Complete Poems* 37, 38).

We now know something of the biographical as well as historical impetus for *The Waste Land*, including Eliot's difficult marriage and, of course, the war ("I had not thought death had undone so many") (39). In the West, vitality has given way to assault, indifference, and the mechanization that Eliot scorns. In the poem, for instance, the sexually indifferent typist, left alone when her importuning lover departs, feels "glad it's over," then mechanically smoothes her hair, plays music on a machine, and prepares for a day of work as a human machine at a keyboard (*Complete Poems* 44). She is Eliot's automaton. The poet extends no sympathy; she is a despised type of the modern.

All readers are by now familiar with Eliot's exploitation of anthropological and classical myth and literary allusion to enrich his emphasis on the contemporary wasteland. Tiresias and Dante, the myth of Actaeon and Diana, Shakespeare—all have been found by scholars to enhance the poet's themes of desiccation. But it is Eliot's unrelenting perception of religio-cultural waste that proves significant here. As one reader remarks, the tragedy of the poem is that of "one who can perceive but cannot act, who can understand and remember but cannot communicate" (Litz 21). "Each in his prison," writes Eliot of the modern condition, "thinking of the key" (*Complete Poems* 49). A kind of narcissistic powerlessness pervades *The Waste Land*. And this is the quality that separates Eliot's poem from those of the neo-utilitarians under scrutiny here. As we shall notice in due course, Eliot's editorial cohort, Ezra Pound, cut the "waste" from *The Waste Land* in editorial excision. But the poem itself offers no alternative world and no possibility of redemption, not even implicitly. Eliot names the modern condition, based on postwar Europe. His poem, however, reverts to Europe, not America, and it takes a direction very different from that of the American neo-utilitarians.

The one serious American writer who most systematically pursued the subject of an American "waste land" is Robert Herrick. His novel, *Waste*, deserves attention because Herrick, a writer with roots in the Romantic tradition, attempted an analysis of the components of waste in one man's life in America. Herrick shows the junction between romanticism and modernism. In effect, he superimposes his contemporary consciousness of waste upon the romantic conception of a man's life. That life, conceived as an organic journey, is simultaneously dis-assembled into its components, each declared to be a waste. Herrick's version of the American "wasteland" is personal, organic, and committed to spiritual unity. Yet in the

1920s it is also a world of gear-and-girder values. Ultimately Herrick could not reconcile the two. His novel invites attention because it shows how the writer of romantic allegiances tries to represent a constructed world of component-part machines and structures. In that sense it sharpens the distinction between the two worlds and forecasts the achievement of Hemingway, Dos Passos, and Williams, who found forms wholly congruent with the defining technology of gears and girders.

Waste traces the life of its engineer-architect protagonist, Jarvis Thornton, from the early 1880s to post–World War I. It strives to capture the American geographical panorama from New England to the West, including such movements as Roosevelt-era conservationism and domestic wartime mobilization. The novel is essentially an American morality play, an indictment of waste in every component of human life, beginning with Thornton's spiritually starved boyhood in a New England family household made miserable by a shrewish mother obsessed with money, and by a despairing father, the failed provider in a culture preoccupied with material success. "The old shabby stucco house was . . . cracking . . . from something evil and disintegrating within" (13). In fact, the Thornton household is not exceptional, for every household in the novel is fatally flawed. Disinheritance, deceit, truncated pleasures, estrangement—any and all of these characterize familial waste in the novel.

But the individual can fare no better once freed from the tar pits of family life. Thornton's journey through a national-biographical wasteland proceeds as Herrick argues that people of uncomprising integrity and sensitivity will be "crushed like rotten fruit," wasted by parasites and opportunists before reaching their full powers. So with Thornton. Scrimping through Harvard as an impoverished outsider, he determines to go to architectural school "to help build up the new United States," even though his science mentor warns against that "trade school," the new technological institute that trains "mechanics and plumbers" for a "bathroom civilization." "Don't stay in their workshop too long," the scientist warns, or "there won't be much of the artist left in your soul after a few years there" (76).

The technical-artistic battle for Thornton's soul, however, is a mooted point because the honorable youngster is lured into marriage to a grasping widow with a young daughter. The disastrous marriage, which produces a son, ends in separation. But the emotional turmoil anticipates Thornton's other love affairs pursued in Rocky Mountain cabins, in Manhattan apartments, each passionate yet tenuous, consummated without fulfillment and thus, Herrick implies, a betrayal of passion, a romantic waste.

Work and livelihood afford little compensation. First, the financial obligations of marriage put an end to Thornton's architectural ambitions. At work as an engineer, he discovers business corruption in the "weedy, sandy waste" of Chicago, from which he goes west to the Rockies where, as a consulting engineer, he understands that the nation's natural resources are plundered to fatten the railroads and the mining companies, all with the congressional assent that makes a sham of conservation. "There is no comprehensive organized development," Thornton confides, "just grab and waste—waste, waste." Herrick hammers the point: "it annoyed him both as an engineer and an artist—the waste and the ugliness of exploitation in America" (160, 194–99).

If institutions are corrupt, art cannot flourish, as the allegory of Thornton would prove. Recognizing squalor behind the American facade of "pullmans and bathtubs and sanitary plumbing and concrete sidewalks," Thornton begins, "with the engineer lobe of his brain, . . . to chart his way of permanent freedom" with a monastic commitment to find beauty through disciplined detachment, poverty, and suffering (215). Here Herrick states his admiration for the engineer's aesthetic, the mating of function and form for efficiency.

Cleansed and chastened by it, Thornton revives his architectural ambition, only to find art to be incompatible with civilization. He designs a few houses which, "original and interesting," are ill-adapted "to the manifold mechanical inventions of the day." A Bohemian beer garden executed in a Chicago prairie style of architecture, an echo of Frank Lloyd Wright, stirs professional controversy before Prohibition shuts it down (224–25).

Wartime, however, brings the serendipitous opportunity for large-scale design. Thornton is commissioned as architect for shipyard workers' housing combining "efficiency and beauty" in a "suburban dream." The engineer and the artist in him speak in one idealistic voice as Thornton cries, "Modern society has learned to . . . work on a mighty scale which rivals nature in her vastest undertakings. . . . There is an unimaginable force in society that can be released for creative ends, when men's minds are ready." He prays that America will learn the wartime lesson of engineering values: "cooperation, organization, and service primarily not for profit" (314–15). His architectural suburb takes shape in "brick, cement, wood, paint and trees and shrubs" and lets him dare to hope that the engineering aesthetic will prevail in postwar America.

But all for nothing, since the war's end means the abandonment of the shipyard site before even one of Thornton's houses is lived in. The structures are "scrapped, their organizers . . . staying only to prey upon the remains" (329). The litany on waste continues as Thornton gradually recedes into the embittered isolation of a pilgrim's progress verging on despair, with no celestial city in sight. "Waste! Waste!" Thornton shouts from a desert hideaway, his voice echoed by the wind that murmurs in turn, "Waste! All waste!" (439).

The despairing tone would aptly conclude the novel. Yet Herrick could not rest, finally, with his lamentation. At the very last he wrenches his text to change its thematic course, at least provisionally. The protagonist victimized by every conceivable waste in modern America—in family relationships, business dealings, environmental management, sex, politics, war—this man nonetheless resolves at the conclusion of the novel to undertake a reform movement of sorts. He will return to teach at the Boston "Technical School" (The Massachusetts Institute of Technology), which he is determined to "humanize." He laments, "If in any way I can save some of them from waste, the waste that I went through, the waste of spirit I see everywhere about me in our life to-day, I shall be content." He continues, "I don't know that it can be done, that waste is not inherent, inevitable in the process of living, but it is worth the effort. That is my destiny" (439, 447–48). Thus, tentatively at least, the novelist holds out hope for the redemption of the nation by the eradication of its wastes.

Herrick seems to conclude with a resolve to humanize technology. Yet inadvertently he does the opposite. He really proposes to bring the painful, romantic's journey of life to the engineers in the hope that they can alleviate pain and loss by eliminating wastes. He proposes that the romantic's life journey and its American context be submitted to the engineers for redesign. A designed America will somehow, he implies, enable personal fulfillment. What's more, by making his protagonist an engineer-architect, Herrick implies that the modern consciousness belongs to the world of gears and girders. He makes the engineer the man who can dis-assemble his own life and find each component a waste. That way, of course, lies self-annihilation, a conclusion abhorrent to Herrick, and one he probably did not intend. His final chapter on Thornton's new mission teaching engineers reads like a coda.

Waste, then, stands on the cusp of historical transition. It records the cultural preoccupation with waste and attempts analysis of life and society component by component. By its example the novel shows the serious limitations of imaginative writing whose form is deeply committed to the aesthetics of an earlier, bygone era. Herrick's deepest allegiance lies with the Romantics. But faced with personal and sociocultural waste, he finds no consolation in the Transcendentalist doctrine of Emerson's "Compensation," which argues that adversity is overcome by the soul's "deep remedial force" (73). Instead, Herrick's twentieth-century protagonist seeks deliverance from waste in the polytechnic temple of the engineers.

Herrick was a essentially a romantic, poles apart from the utilitarian polemicist, Bellamy. Yet he reverts to the kind of world against which Bellamy and Veblen and others are in full revolt, a world racked by "prodigal wastes." Bellamy conceived of these wastes in political-economic terms, as did Upton Sinclair. Herrick (abetted by Veblen) personalized them within the American experience.

The point of bringing each to bear on the others is to notice, first, that all reject the notion of an unstable world. Sharing the cultural preoccupation with waste, and engaged in strategies for its diminishment or abolition, they indicate design possibilities inherent in a world subject to reconstruction part-by-part. This comes clear in the guided tour of "waste" through novels, advertisements, magazine articles, business texts, and so forth. The subject of waste thus becomes, in itself, a potential precipitant of new modes of thought and writing.

So the casebook on waste prepares us to understand the emergence of a new functional aesthetic in American literature. To recognize the broad-based cultural response to "waste" is to gain an understanding of the foundation of that functional aesthetic, one based on the values of engineering and machine technology. Bellamy, Veblen, Herrick, and the others show how the way is prepared for it.

But only prepared—for these writers saw waste to be an issue essentially confined to themes in literature. They remained unconscious of the implications for style or structure. There is no evidence that the shape of their sentences or paragraphs, their diction or syntax was in any particular way affected by their abhorrence of waste. Bellamy's plot operates like a clockwork design, but sentence by sentence he gives no indication that style can be expressive of waste or for that matter of efficiency. In fact, connecting the concept of waste with the writer's imagination and craft was a leap to be made by others, notably Ezra Pound, Dos Passos, Hemingway, and Williams. That leap ultimately involved the figure of the engineer who symbolized enactive powers. But it directly concerned the axial contrary of waste—that is, efficiency.

EFFICIENCY

Big things are happening in the development of this country. With the spreading of the movement toward greater efficiency, a new and highly improved era in national life has begun.

Harper's Weekly, November 2, 1912

As the affirmative side of the contraries, "efficiency" came into American culture from the machine shop, where the term had a specific technical meaning. It referred, then as now, to the ratio of work done or energy developed by a machine or engine according to the energy supplied to it. This was an application of the laws of thermodynamics to machinery, and it was ordinarily expressed in a percentage. By the 1910s, however, efficiency assumed a new range of meanings in American popular culture. Denotations of personal competence, effectiveness, and social harmony under professional leadership were by then included in a much broadened semantics of efficiency—though the term always reverted to the values embodied in machine technology.

In the earlier twentieth century, in fact, the machine became a perceptual model, and efficiency accordingly was the standard by which physical and intellectual activity was measured. The very term became an expression of abundant, disciplined energies. Like waste, efficiency offered an opportunity to realize new levels of abundance, for it promised to amplify space and multiply time and thus led directly to a new valuation of speed. Ultimately the aesthetic implications of efficiency brought formal changes to American fiction and poetry. These changes, however, were at first enabled by currents in the larger culture.

The Education of Henry Adams (1907) is a good example of the new, twentieth-century technological outlook. Adams casts a critical eye over American political history, seeing the political system as a mechanism judged by its efficiency. President Grant's administration, he says, marked the breakdown of the constitutional "system of 1789." Ever since, political energies have been "wasted on expedients

. . . to tinker . . . the political machine as often as it broke down. . . . As a machine, it was, or soon would be, the poorest in the world—the clumsiest—the most inefficient" (280–81).

Adams went on to explain why the government of the Founding Fathers was inadequate. "Their machine," he wrote, "was never meant to do the work of a twenty-million horse-power society in the twentieth century, where much work needed to be . . . efficiently done." "Bad work," Adams added in machine terms, "merely added to the friction" (375). Adams concludes that modern corporate capitalism "was a question of gear, of running machinery. . . . The machine must be efficient" (344).

The irony here is palpable because Adams so disliked capitalism. But he clearly participated in machine values when he declared that education is "to fit young men . . . to be men of the world," and that each young man is by definition "a certain form of energy; the object to be gained is the economy of his force" (xxx).

"Economy" is the giveaway. Of course it is a very old word, meaning the prudent disposition and planning of resources so as to avoid waste, in which sense it referred to household or estate stewardship in the Middle Ages. When Adams, however, says that "education should try to . . . diminish the friction" (314) to accomplish an economy of force, then he is clearly far from the Middle Ages or even from the nineteenth-century Romantic world of Henry David Thoreau's *Walden* "economy." In fact Adams is on the verge of the perceptual change in which machine efficiency becomes a standard for the judgment of virtually every human endeavor, thus altering imaginative forms as well.

One figure, the mechanical engineer Frederick Winslow Taylor (1856–1915), brought about that change in popular American culture. In the 1910s, thanks to a much-publicized court case, he became known as the father of the Efficiency Movement, otherwise called Scientific Management or Taylorism. His influence on industrial life was enormous, both in America and abroad (notably in France and Russia), and he was hailed by disciples as a scientific intellect comparable to Darwin.

In American literature one writer, John Dos Passos, has recognized Taylor's cultural significance. In *The Big Money* (1936), the third book of the *U.S.A.* trilogy, he capsuled Taylor's life along with those of Thomas Edison and Frank Lloyd Wright. Taylor is important here because of the implications of his work. Begun in the factory and extending into the larger culture, it shows the explicit machine-based relation of efficiency to human perception and action. Taylorism hastened the American public into a gear-and-girder world which made Everyman, and Everywoman, an engineer scouting wasteful components of life and society. The Taylorist American was the designer of an efficient world. Ultimately Taylorist thought affected a significant body of early twentieth-century American writing.

Taylor did not begin life as a technocrat, though he was a child of the industrial Delaware Valley. The son of a family with Quaker and Puritan New England roots, he grew up in Germantown (near Philadelphia) as a reportedly likeable, rigid, intense, and dutiful boy who had an upper-middle-class youth of rigorous schooling, field games, and European travel. As John Dos Passos put it, Taylor's mother dictated "selfrespect, selfreliance, selfcontrol" as the family terms of conduct (20).

Although Taylor showed early interest in medicine and engineering, his parents expected him to follow his father into the practice of law. Problems with headaches and eyesight, however, curtailed his academic work at Exeter and, following a few months of rest at the family home near Philadelphia, the young Taylor began work as an apprentice patternmaker in the factory of a family friend. He flourished, and following the apprenticeship went to work at the Midvale Steel Company as a journeyman machinist. Within six years he was chief engineer, soon thereafter devising a high-speed method for cutting steel. Taylor completed a home-study course in mathematics and physics in order to complete degree requirements in mechanical engineering. Within a few years he resigned from Midvale, became a self-employed consulting engineer for manufacturers and businessmen, and ultimately went on to become president of the American Society of Mechanical Engineers and to gain popular fame—and notoriety—as the exponent of efficiency (Copley, Kakar).

Taylor's work began with interest in the problems of mechanical efficiency. His ideas were based on the typical late nineteenth-century piecework shop and not on the mass-production factory of the early twentieth century. As a shop foreman he was troubled by managers' indifference to workmen's motivation, to their work habits, and to their various body types which he felt ought to fit them for different tasks. He was especially irked by workers' "loafing" or "soldiering," their marking time (30).

Taylor's remedy for these problems owed much to the contemporary interest in the visualization of motion in space. Essentially Taylor saw in industry the opportunities that sequential stop-motion photographs were providing the visual experimenters Thomas Eakins, Etienne Marey, and Eadweard Muybridge in the 1880s and 1890s. They captured phases of motion in sequential photographs which led to the development of motion pictures (and complemented the time-space disjunction characteristic of so much modernist painting) (Giedion 14–30).

Taylor worked with the stopwatch, not the camera. He confined his interests to industrial production on the shop floor. But like the French physiologist and the Philadelphia artist, he dissected motion visually. He broke into component parts the movement of the body through space over time. With increased productivity as his object, Taylor conducted tens of thousands of experiments in which he separated seemingly simple tasks into their smallest components, analyzed each for excess or extraneous motion, then worked to reformulate them so precisely and economically that they required no excess mechanical motion of the worker's body or of his tools. In short, he increased workers' efficiency by eliminating waste energy and therefore attributed utilitarian value to economy of motion.

In 1897–98 Taylor was invited to introduce his method into the Bethlehem Steel works. As Dos Passos writes, "It was in Bethlehem he made his famous experiments with handling pigiron; he taught a Dutchman named Schmidt to handle fortyseven tons instead of twelve and a half tons of pigiron a day and got Schmidt to admit he was as good as ever at the end of the day. He was [moreover] a crank about shovels; every job had to have a shovel of the right weight and size for that job alone; every job had to have a man of the right weight and size for that job alone" (*U.S.A.: Big Money* 23–24). In fact, Taylor conducted stopwatch studies until he found exactly which kinds of shovels and manual motions were most efficient in the shoveling of different grades of coal. After three and a half years of Taylor's work, 140 men were doing the tasks formerly done by 600, the cost of shoveling was cut by half, and the shovelers' wages had risen by 60 percent.

Taylor described this work in several papers to the Society of Mechanical Engineers and in the books *Shop Management* (1903) and *Principles of Scientific Management* (1911). His argument had a certain appeal because of his goal: material abundance for the multitudes, all achievable by higher productivity and by commensurate high wages for workers. Taylor believed high wages to be necessary to high productivity and to low manufacturing costs. His objective was to find the one best way to accomplish each work task, then to standardize that way. He insisted on maintaining the standard by controlling the work entirely. In the 1900s Taylor had a following of young engineers and others, converts like the construction contractor Frank Gilbreth, who furthered the efficiency movement with photographic motion studies that complemented Taylor's work with the stopwatch.

The most casual students of Taylor know that controversy surrounded his work from the first—and reverberates into the present. His goals and methods drew criticism and ridicule from unions, politicians, industrialists, and humanists. Dos Passos, for example, recognized that his methods led to the de-skilling of work ("the substitution . . . of the [compliant] plain handyman . . . for skilled mechanics"). Like many social critics, the novelist questioned the intrinsic value Taylor accorded abundance per se—"more steel rails more bicycles more spools of thread more armorplate for battleships more bedpans more barbedwire more needles more lightningrods more ballbearings more dollarbills" (*U.S.A.: Big Money* 24).

Others have recognized Taylor's arrogant presumption that the interests of workers were identical to those of managers. They held him responsible for an inadvertent subjugation of rank-and-file employees to a kind of industrial slavery. Taylor, moreover, never addressed the problems of the workers displaced by his system. Presumably the 460 unemployed Bethlehem shovelers found new jobs—or charity—elsewhere. Not surprisingly, the unions campaigned vigorously against Taylorism, both in Congress and on the shop floor, in some instances with notable success.

Analysts of American labor and economic history have discussed all these issues at length, and earlier twentieth-century critics found them troubling as well. For the repetitive tasks of any one human cog in the Taylorist (or for that matter Ford) shop were crushingly monotonous. Public voices from the novelist Sherwood Anderson to the onetime secretary of commerce, the engineer Herbert Hoover, worried about the consequent human damage. Anderson (*Perhaps Women*), for instance, thought industrial machinery emasculating, while Hoover warned that "the vast, repetitive processes are dulling the human mind. . . . We cannot permit the dulling of these sensibilities" (qtd. in A. Pound 51).

The qualities of Taylorist thought, however, concern us here for other reasons. At the turn of the century they signaled a change in certain American values and therefore in the imaginative forms that express them. In certain ways Taylorism presented new opportunities to writers in search of innovative form. First, Taylorist thought presented a cluster of new values based upon machine technology. It embraced productivity, economy, immediacy, and functionalism. It valued the formulation of efficient motion in space and thus espoused streamlining and minimalism. By implication it celebrated speed. By the turn of the century all these were qualities available for artists' and writers' enactment in painting as well as in fiction and poetry.

Taylorist thought also offered writers a new position of authority vis-à-vis themselves and their materials. It redefined the artists' and writers' relation to their work in an age of assembly-line manufacturing from component parts. In the waning of the crafts era, it provided a new self-identification for the artist. One could now be a designer-engineer. For the intellectual center of Taylorism was not the worker, but the mastermind. It was not the rank and file but the engineer whose formulations would prevail and endure.

The controlling consciousness in Taylorist thought has momentous implications for writers. On the part of the engineer—or, in literature, the novelist or poet—efficient designs become "a study in unity and synchronized power" (A. Pound 44). In order for writers to perceive their role as analogous to that of engineers, it remained for Taylor's ideas to permeate the larger culture.

They did so with the Eastern Rate Case, which made the engineer's name a household word in the early 1910s when the Efficiency Movement became an American fad. In brief, in 1910 the Eastern railroads sought a rate increase from the Interstate Commerce Commission in order to pay promised higher wages to workers. But the shippers filed suit to block the increase. They hired the attorney Louis D. Brandeis to represent them, and he won the case with testimony from Taylor's new apostles, who gave the name Scientific Management to their mentor's system and who argued that the railroads could be run so much more efficiently that they could save one million dollars per day.

"A million dollars a day!" became the rallying cry of the new Efficiency Movement formed in the wake of the court case and taken up by a middle-class public anxious about the stubborn persistence of an inflationary economy that was blamed on everything from the tariff and the trusts to spendthrift housewives. Efficiency societies were formed, and hundreds of books and articles began to appear in the mid-1910s with such titles as *Efficiency in High Schools*, *Efficiency in Home Making*, *Efficient Composition*, *Intellectual Efficiency*, and *Efficiency in Religious Work*. The *Ladies Home Journal* was inundated with requests for additional information when it published a series of articles applying scientific management to the household; *Good Housekeeping* offered its readers a pamphlet on *The Household Efficient*. The educators George Betts and Otis Hall argued that rural inefficiency

Institute of Efficiency advertisement. Literary Digest, *1917*

had harmed the nation, while Walter Hines Page, the editor of *World's Work*, said that "town life and modern life in general have been made efficient" through organization (qtd. in Danbom 48–90). Even Gustav Stickley, a principal figure in the anti-industrial Arts and Crafts Movement, sang the praises of Taylor and his "amazing results," finally suggesting that nature's "great powerhouse" was the best model of efficiency (qtd. in Lears 90–91). Proponents of the movement ranged from the muckraker Ida Tarbell to the feminist Charlotte Perkins Gilman. Predictably, the moral terms that clustered around "efficiency" were character, competence, energy, hard work, and success.

Taylor himself became an evangelist of the movement, for he linked morality and well-being to his scientific management. He prophesied that his methods would extend "to the management of our homes; the management of our farms; the management of the businesses of our tradesmen, large and small; of our churches, our philanthropic institutions, our universities, and our governmental departments" (qtd. in Drury 168). During the Progressive Era of the 1910s his disciples brought the methods of scientific management into American institutions ranging from education, in which Morris Cooke studied Harvard University in order to make the "machinery of education" cost-effective, to medicine, in which Frank Gilbreth undertook micromotion analyses of surgical operations in New York City hospitals.

Notable intellectuals backed the movement, as Samuel Haber has shown in his excellent *Efficiency and Uplift*. The founding editor of the *New Republic*, Herbert Croly, made it an integral part of his *The Promise of American Life*, and Walter Lippmann incorporated it into his concept of societal and governmental "mastery." William James was taken up as the philosopher of the Efficiency Movement because of his essay, "The Energies of Men" (1907), in which he wrote, "Compared with what we ought to be we are only half awake. . . . We are making use of only a small part of our mental and physical resources" (221).

In Progressive politics the introduction of these machine-based utilitarian values was greeted with optimism. To a figure like Louis Brandeis efficiency signified professionalism. It heralded a period when social policy would be formulated according to facts gathered systematically by experts. It was presumed that the public would welcome this professional expertise. For the editor-author Croly it meant the age of enlightened leaders and the end of tyrannical bosses. Political reformers like Theodore Tilden saw its nonpartisanship as the opportunity for a more equitable American democracy. The Progressives were not apprehensive about the prospect of the machine becoming the model in political life. On the contrary, they welcomed its disinterested neutrality and seemed to concur with Henry Adams's point that "the machine must be efficient."

It seems that in the 1910s "efficiency" became a catch-all word like "waste," virtually a buzzword in its own time. To some extent it was, for "efficiency" was applied everywhere from Sunday schools to baseball. The term appeared in advertisements for dishwashers and touring cars (just as "waste" was an advertising copywriter's favorite for the sales promotion of hot water heaters and ironing machines).

A Study In Efficiency
Go See If You Approve It

Mitchell cars differ—and differ vastly —from any other cars in their class.

The very styles are exclusive, because all the bodies are our designs, and all are Mitchell-built.

The present Mitchells are the final result of 700 improvements made under John W. Bate. They are distinctive in a hundred ways.

They have 31 features which most cars omit. They are extra-luxurious cars. And they are built to the standard—adopted three years ago—of 100 per cent. over-strength.

A Bate-Built Plant

The whole Mitchell plant, covering 45 acres, was built and equipped under John W. Bate. It embodies all his ideas of factory efficiency. It contains over 2,000 up-to-date machines, all designed to build this type of car economically.

Now it includes a model body plant, which saves us hundreds of thousands of dollars per year. So 98 per cent. of the Mitchell is built here, under Bate efficiency methods.

The result shows clearly in many extra values. In the extra features, the added luxury and the over-strength. Under other methods, no such cars could be built at Mitchell prices. We ask a chance to prove this before you decide on a car.

Not a Penny Kept

These efficiency methods, on this year's output, save us $4,000,000. All

this saving goes into added values. Our profit margin was never smaller than now.

For instance, this year our new body plant yields us a big new saving. So we this year have added 24 per cent. to the cost of finish, upholstery and trimming. You will be amazed at the luxurious cars which sell at these modest prices.

They embody 31 rare features, all of which you want. Things like a power

tire pump, which cost extra in most cars.

Unique Standards

You will find unique standards in Mitchells. One is 100 per cent. over-strength in every vital part. Mr. Bate has doubled our margins of safety to give you a lifetime car. Two of these cars have proved their ability to run 200,000 miles each.

Over 440 parts are built of toughened steel. Safety parts are vastly over-size. We use a wealth of Chrome-Vanadium.

Our test for gears is 50,000 pounds per tooth. Our test for springs is 100,000 4-inch vibrations. As a result, not one Bate cantilever spring has broken in two years.

The same extremes are carried into luxury and beauty. Before designing the latest Mitchells, our experts examined 257 new models, so that no attraction would be missing in the Mitchells.

A New $1195 Six

Despite all these standards, one Mitchell Six—the Mitchell Junior—sells for $1195 at factory. It has a 120-inch wheelbase, a 40-horsepower motor. You are bound to agree that no other like value is shown in a high-grade car. But the big 7-passenger Mitchell is built on the same profit basis.

Prove all these facts for your own sake, before you decide on a car. Remember how long it will last.

Mitchell

SIXES

TWO SIZES

Mitchell—a roomy 7-passenger Six, with 127-inch wheelbase and a highly-developed 48-horsepower motor.

$1460 F.o.b. Racine

Mitchell Junior—a 5-passenger Six, on similar lines, with 120-inch wheelbase and a 40-horsepower motor, ¼-inch smaller bore.

$1195 F.o.b. Racine

Also 6 styles of enclosed and convertible bodies. Also new Club Roadster.

MITCHELL MOTORS COMPANY, Inc., Racine, Wis., U. S. A.

Mitchell Motors Co. advertisement. New Country Life, *1917*

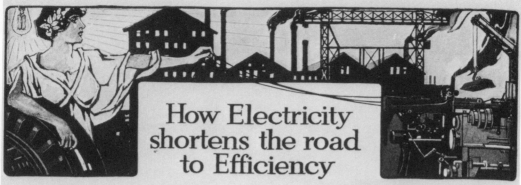

How Electricity shortens the road to Efficiency

"A ROAD made smoother is a road made shorter," said an old engineer.

This is a pretty good text for a word about the way electricity is shortening the road to that great modern goal—Efficiency. That text applies to store and office as well as to factory, machine shop or distribution room.

The steel industry offers a practical illustration. Growth means greater needs—need for bigger tonnage output, for lower production costs, for more efficient and more economical methods with an absolute continuity of process. It was these needs that linked steel and electricity. It was electricity that played a foremost part in accomplishing that high industrial efficiency that has given the steel industry its world-fame.

Allied industries have felt the same impulse, and what has happened to construction work, mining, ship, car and engine building, is happening in countless lines of industry throughout the country. Electricity has raised efficiency in the fundamental branches of production, such as lumber, mining, cement and brick laying, textiles, paper, etc., and in the vital manufacturing lines such as clothing, food products, shoes, soap, automobiles, household goods, office equipment, etc.

In other words, the application of efficiency principles led straight to electrification.

To take the textile field as another example, the leading textile mills have found it a competitive necessity and a direct economy to use electricity in subdividing power units, in answering the need for clear overhead space, unobstructed by shafting and belting, and in using power sources most economically.

In paper making, the facility with which electricity could accomplish motor drive and lighting made it a natural resource for regular power as well as for supplementary lighting and emergency power generation. With wired power the mill proper need not adjoin water supply but could be located at such distance as might be demanded by shipping facilities and labor requirements. By such separation it often became possible to select the best waterfall instead of second or third best or to combine the power of several.

Not only has electricity made it easy for cereal companies to improve their output by regularity in the speed of machines, but the cleanliness of electricity, eliminating unsightly belts and dripping oil cups, has made it possible to give plants a tidiness and attractiveness that naturally led to the show-place plan for daily visitors. The visitor to the great bake shop, the towering sugar refinery or the newspaper press room sees in all these strictly modern displays of productive efficiency the results of electrical help. The visitor may not guess the advantages of the speed control, or the wide economies of operation in electrically-run machinery, but the actual cleanliness of the modern way gives an impression of efficiency that has a selling power in itself.

The reduction in insurance rates, which often follows as a matter of course, the cleanliness which does so much for the acceleration of production, the immense increase of direct productive power through both machines and men—these are great factors that have linked electricity and efficiency in the modern industrial world.

If you have a problem to be solved, take it up today with your electric power and light company, or with any General Electric Company dealer or agent in your vicinity. You will find them more than glad to co-operate with you, and no matter how complex your problem may be, they have at their command the service of any part of our organization that may be most helpful to them or to you.

The Guarantee of Excellence on Goods Electrical

Trade Mark

GENERAL ELECTRIC COMPANY

General Electric Co. advertisement. Literary Digest, *1914 (Reprinted by permission of General Electric Company)*

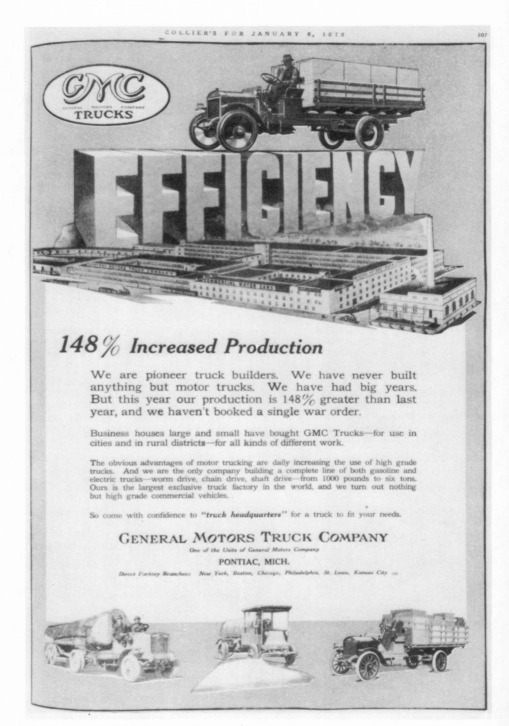

General Motors Truck Co. advertisement (Courtesy General Motors Corp.,
Truck and Bus Division)

American Tobacco Co. advertisement (Courtesy American Brands)

THE EFFICIENT MINUTE

We have speeded up our ships and railways; we have made rapid transit more and more rapid; we have developed a mile a minute in the air and much faster in an automobile.

But the Bell Telephone is quickest of all. It is *instantaneous.* No weeks or days or minutes wasted in waiting for somebody to go and come; no waiting for an answer.

It is the most effective agency for making minutes more useful, more efficient.

In almost every field of work men are accomplishing more in less time with the Bell Telephone than they could without it. They can talk with more people, near and far; they can keep the run of more details; they can buy or sell more goods, and to better advantage; they can be active in more affairs.

The Bell Telephone has placed a new and higher value upon the minute — for everybody. It has done this by means of One Policy, One System, and Universal Service.

Bell Long Distance Telephone service not only gives an added value to a man's minutes — it accomplishes business results which would be absolutely impossible without it. Every Bell Telephone is the Center of the System.

AMERICAN TELEPHONE AND TELEGRAPH COMPANY
AND ASSOCIATED COMPANIES

American Telephone and Telegraph advertisement. Literary Digest, *1910 (Reproduced by permission of AT&T Corporate Archive)*

Efficiency lent itself readily to jingles and jingoism, but we must recognize that this movement had antecedents in American literature. In part the middle-class American reading public prepared itself for Taylor's message by way of literary prophets. In the 1890s, when Taylor was known only to American industrialists, upwards of one million readers listened to Bellamy extol the virtues of an efficient America in *Looking Backward*. At the turn of the century when the Philadelphia engineer was introducing his innovative, efficient piecework system at the Bethlehem Steel plant, his contemporary, Veblen, was publishing the book that rebuked modern society for its barbaric wastefulness, a theme Upton Sinclair would echo in *The Jungle* in 1906. And as Taylor worked to eliminate excess energy from work, Henry Adams was proclaiming the purpose of education to maximize the economy of a young man's force. Taylor has been seen as the instigator (and the scapegrace) of the Efficiency Movement, but the issues he distilled were in the air. If Taylor had not been there, someone would have invented him.

The overt literary response to efficiency was, unsurprisingly, mixed. On a thematic basis several American writers expressed profound skepticism of so pat a philosophy for progress and fulfillment. In *The Jungle* Upton Sinclair, loathing waste, declared himself a partisan of socialist efficiency, though he detested the capitalists' "wonderful efficiency of . . . pork-making by applied mathematics" in the brutal Chicago packinghouses (37, 39). A. L. Byard, the author of a magazine story for women, "The Efficient Wife" (1923), disliked the images of kitchen laboratories and of cooking as "a series of chemical experiments." Her heroine, a muddled cook, is kind and generous, and her appreciative husband "wouldn't trade her for the most efficient graduate of a domestic science school" (30–32).

To one writer, at least, the movement was ripe for satire. In *Main Street* (1920) Sinclair Lewis's Carol Kennicott notices "the brisk efficient book-ignoring people," one of whom turns out to be "an advocate of culture-buying and efficiency" (13, 212). Lewis was soon at work on the male counterpart of the bustling clubwoman. The title character of *Babbitt* (1922) is "the plump, smooth, efficient, up-to-the-minute and otherwise perfected modern." Lewis's American philistine, George Babbitt, carries an "efficient" notebook filled with forgotten names, and he expounds "the spiritual and mental side of American supremacy, the . . . uh, dominating movements like Efficiency and Rotarianism, and Prohibition and Democracy [which] compose our deepest and truest wealth" (12, 29, 72).

In the two novels a contemptuous Lewis says that efficiency is only a nostrum for a vacuous culture. He further elaborated that point nearly ten years later in *Dodsworth* (1929), which in brief presents its protagonist, a manufacturer-engineer, as the mechanized man who "made his toilet like a man who never wasted motions," who "tied his tie . . . with the unwasteful and extremely unadventurous precision of a man who has introduced as much 'scientific efficiency' into daily domesticity as into his factory" (17). Here Lewis suggests that efficiency is as much the enemy of spontaneity and romance as it is the substitute for introspection and intellect.

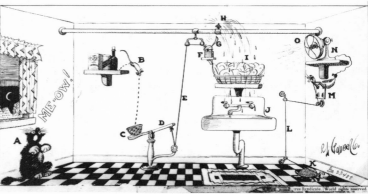

By the late 1920s-early 1930s efficiency was so thoroughly appreciated that the overdesigned, "wasteful" Rube Goldberg machine became the object of popular humor. Rube Goldberg drawings, 1929–30 (Courtesy Division of Graphic Arts, National Museum of American History, Smithsonian Institution)

By far the strongest sociopolitical antiefficiency themes appeared in the best-selling socialist novel *The Harbor* (1915) by Ernest Poole. The son of a well-to-do Chicago stockbroker, Poole (1880–1950) was a muckraking journalist who wrote on sweatshops, child labor, tuberculosis in the slums. Based in Greenwich Village as a prominent journalist and neophyte novelist, Poole wrote *The Harbor*, inspired by the leadership of the Industrial Workers of the World, the "Wobblies," in the textile strikes of 1912–14.

The Harbor is a novel of education, its protagonist a young man learning sympathy for the oppressed masses who are represented in the teeming life of the New York harbor. In boyhood young Billy sees the harbor scene as sordid, disgusting, at best commercial. He is drawn irresistibly to it, though his ideals are elsewhere, and in young manhood he discovers that these ideals—his mother's god of goodness, the Parisian god of art and beauty —have been false gods. "One by one

I had raised them up, and one by one the harbor had rushed in and dragged them down" (188).

At last he finds the god no harbor can topple. "Its name was Efficiency" (188). And it is found in the person of the renowned civil engineer and city planner, a Robert Moses type named Dillon, who works atop a Manhattan "tower of lights that seemed to be keeping a vigilant watch over all the dark waters, the ships and the docks" (138). Dillon and his cohorts are "the efficient ones [who] have the brains and the know-how to work—to use science, money, everything—to get a decent world ahead" (196). In his tower Dillon prepares the blueprints and sketches that will transform the chaotic harbor—by extension the modern world itself —from its wasteful tangle and congestion into efficient order. The idealized social order is symbolized in the figure of a departing ocean liner, its hold heavy with American products, its deck thronged with affluent passengers. Commanding officers guide the ship from the bridge just as Dillon guides the ship of state from his engineers' tower. The liner is "a mighty symbol of order and prosperity and of that Efficiency which had been a religion for so many years" (350).

By the conclusion of *The Harbor*, however, efficiency had gone the way of the other idols. Poole discredits it because the engineer-planner and his kind subvert democracy. Arrogant, they underestimate the people's ability to guide their own lives. Worse, the novel argues, they overlook the degree of misery and desperation soon to bring on global revolution beginning with massive labor strikes. The city planner-engineer is oblivious to these matters. Far removed in his tower and equally distant in his speeding harbor motor launch, he fails to see such immediate realities as the families of crippled dock workers living shattered lives in agony and near-starvation. He fails to acknowledge the "hairy ape," as Eugene O'Neill called him, who stokes the fires that power the great ship.

"If you want to help the people," says one character to the young journalist, "you've got to drop your efficiency gods. You've got to believe in the people first. . . . You've got to see that they're waking up fast—all over the world—that they're getting tired of gods above 'em slowly planning out their lives—that they don't want to wait till they're dead to be happy—that they feel poverty every day like a million tons of bricks on their chests—it's got so they can't even breathe without thinking! And you've got to see that what they're thinking is, 'Do it yourself and do it quick!" (262–63).

As the strike momentum builds, the young journalist rejects the planners' tower to embrace the "wretched refuse" struggling to stoke the fires of the huge ocean-liner nation. He accepts the teeming harbor as his own and melts into it in a kind of combined socialist baptism and epiphany. The efficiency idol teeters and soon will topple, or so the novel suggests. Confronting the master engineer, the journalist proclaims that the populace, not the planners, will prevail. They may not do the job "half so well . . . as your big men at the top," but the people will press on with a "spirit compared to which your whole clean clear efficiency world is only cold and empty!" (369).

That declaration stands as the novel ends, at which point efficiency is a call to arms. Poole sees it as a key element in the power struggle between the haves and the have-nots. The very term "efficiency" is an ideological armament by which the vested corporate interests victimize the poor and seek control over the modern world. The concept frames the political argument of the novel.

Readers of *The Harbor* thus find efficiency to be central to the novel's theme. In this, *The Harbor* is the companion volume to *Waste*. Just as Herrick decried waste, so Poole denounced efficiency because he thought it at best a cultural panacea, at worst an instrument of political tyranny. But Poole and Herrick, and the others, confined their critiques solely to thematic statement. They did not see the possibility that waste and efficiency could pertain to the style or the structure of their works of art. They had no inkling that the concept could be relevant to the shape of a sentence or a paragraph. Ironically, Poole's socialist *The Harbor* directly repudiates the efficient America of Bellamy's equally socialist *Looking Backward*. But the important point is that these writers concerned themselves with waste and efficiency as concepts useful to political ideology, not to aesthetics. None showed interest in the design possibilities of component-part efficiency in fiction. The very notion of an aesthetics of waste or efficiency would probably have struck all of them as bizarre.

Yet the terms have profound implications for style and form even if a putative modern like Lewis was as oblivious of them as Poole and the others. (Lewis's prose, in fact, is so jammed with images that it shows authorial distaste for the aesthetic implications of efficiency. The novelist who in the 1920s seemed so advanced in his portrait of the American philistine and his Main Street habitat satirized efficiency as intellectual and material gimcrackery; but Lewis's prose, a museum of Americana, is the stylistic nemesis of the efficient ideals of streamlining or verbal economy).

The Efficiency Movement nonetheless had momentous implications for literary style and form. When Taylor recognized that the input-output ratio of machine efficiency could be applied to workers and their activities, he enlarged the concept of machine technology to include human action and its organization. From there he was just a step away from the "Taylorization," which is to say the machine-based, systematic design of virtually all human activity, personal and social, private and institutional.

And literary—for Taylorist thought offered writers new opportunities for style and structure. It provided perceptual paradoxes because it promised to multiply time and space by dividing them. Its ethos of synchronized design, abundance, and functionalism, its kinetics, its utilitarian motivation and method of spatial and temporal reformulation all came to have a significant impact on American literature in the twentieth century.

If some writers rebelled thematically against the idea of human mechanization, others recognized that the waste-efficiency contraries provided new opportunities for innovative formal design. Even a writer politically hostile to the Efficiency Movement, like Dos Passos, would prove himself to be deeply indebted to its implications in his structuring of narrative. The writer, however, who best gave voice to the aesthetics of efficiency and propounded that aesthetics to Hemingway and Williams, and indirectly to Dos Passos, was Erza Pound. He deserves a close look. His theories proved crucial to artistic expression in the gear-and-girder world.

In the 1910s and 1920s the energetic, Idaho-born and London-based Pound (1885–1972) advanced efficiency as a major criterion for all arts of the written word. In the inaugural issue of the revolutionary modernist magazine, *Blast* (1914), Pound celebrated the term and unequivocally connected it with machine technology (153):

VORTEX.

POUND.

The vortex is the point of maximum energy,

It represents, in mechanics, the greatest efficiency.

We use the words " greatest efficiency " in the precise sense—as they would be used in a text book of MECHANICS.

Pound's lexicon is extremely bold, considering his contemporaries' thematic hostility toward "efficiency." His Vorticist Manifesto may appear these days to be, as one reader says, "almost charming, more a classic of . . . humor than a cry to revolution" (Kearns 11). But Pound's mechanics-text definition of efficiency was radical in aesthetics. His proclamation was more than a bellicose statement of modernist revolt. Seizing the utilitarian values swirling in American culture, Pound used the vortex or point of "'greatest efficiency'" to repudiate the naturalists' cosmos of instability. "You may think of man as . . . the TOY of circumstance," he wrote, echoing the school of Dreiser. But Pound took up utilitarian concepts to proclaim human power. His vorticist is an activist "DIRECTING a certain . . . force against circumstance" (*Blast* 153).

Pound recognized the radical change that the polar contraries, waste and efficiency, would bring to literature, once employed in style and structure. He thus made "efficiency" a revolutionist's necessity for all arts. Throughout his prolific career as poet, critic, editor, translator, "efficiency" pervaded his reviews and essays which appeared in such English and American periodicals as the *New Age*, the *Fortnightly Review*, and *Poetry*. He sustained his commitment to "efficiency" in the journey that had taken him from undergraduate study at Hamilton College, where he planned to become the epic poet of the *Cantos*, to the University of Pennsylvania (M.A., 1906), where he met and befriended William Carlos Williams. Based in London by 1908, Pound wrote reverently of the older writers, William

Butler Yeats, Henry James, and Thomas Hardy, and offered support and encouragement to such contemporaries as T. S. Eliot, James Joyce, Robert Frost, H. D. (Hilda Doolittle), Hemingway, and Williams. He allied himself closely with the English writer-artist Wyndham Lewis, a coeditor of the *Blast* issue which celebrated machine technology and its values of the "greatest efficiency."

As a critical term, "efficiency" meant several things to Pound, the first of them a verbal economy that became a fundament of his practical criticism. In *The ABC of Reading* (*ABC*) (1934) Pound said outright, "Good writers are those who keep the language efficient" (32). In a 1918 essay, "A Retrospect," he enunciated the principles undergirding the new writing, including "direct treatment of the 'thing' whether subjective or objective" and use of "absolutely no word that does not contribute to the presentation" (*Literary Essays* [*LE*] 3). He repeated this point on numerous occasions. "Use no superfluous word, no adjective that does not reveal something. . . . Good writing is writing that is perfectly controlled, the writer [speaks] with complete clarity and simplicity. He uses the smallest number of words. . . . [In poetry] I mean something like 'maximum efficiency of expression'; I mean that the writer has expressed something interesting in such a way that one cannot re-say it more effectively" (*LE* 4–5, 50, 55–56; *Selected Letters* [*SL*] 11).

Readers could judge writers' excellence by this criterion of effectiveness. Catullus was preferable to Sappho, Pound said, because of his "economy of words," and he warned that "incompetence will show in the use of too many words." "The reader's first and simplest test of an author will be to look for words that do not function; that contribute nothing to the meaning OR that distract from the MOST important factor of the meaning" (*LE* 4–5, 55–56; *Selected Prose* (*SP*) 374–77). These views governed Pound's editorial advice to aspirant writers. ("I don't see why you don't simply 'escape' instead of 'be emancipated.'") (*SL* 79). Efficiency similarly governs Pound's own form in the "In a Station of the Metro":

> The apparition of these faces in the crowd;
> Petals on a wet, black bough.
> (*Selected Poems* 35)

Pound recounted that this twenty-word poem began as a poem of thirty lines, which he destroyed, six months later writing a shorter poem, which he also discarded until, years later, he arrived at the now-familiar form we know (Kenner 184).

Pound's poetic practice of efficiency became clear with the 1971 publication of the facsimile of the original drafts of *The Waste Land*, including Pound's annotations. As one reader remarks, "Ezra Pound's service to Eliot in cutting the manuscript . . . will remain a symbiotic triumph of his editing conjoined to Eliot's composing" (Vendler 82). Throughout the manuscript, readers see Pound's excision of unnecessary words, conventional connectives, lines and stanzas of personal bathos and excess. One good example of poetic efficiency occurs in Pound's edited lines on the typist, that modern mechanical woman we noticed in earlier remarks on *The*

Waste Land. Eliot's manuscript version struck Pound as prolix and burdened by inversions. He wrote in Eliot's margin, "Verse not interesting enough as verse to warrant so much of it" and "inversions not warranted by any real exigence of metre." He changed the phrase "typist . . . who begins / To clear" to "typist . . . who / clears," and similarly cut other nonfunctioning terms (45). Eliot's final version reads:

> The typist home at teatime, clears her breakfast, lights
> Her stove, and lays out food in tins.
> Out of the window periously spread
> Her drying combinations touched by the sun's last rays.
> (*Collected Poems* 44)

The Waste Land thus became a poem of what Pound called "swift moving apprehension" (*Gaudier-Brzeska* 20). The spirit of that work is clear in his 1912 commendation of H.D.'s poems, which Pound called "objective—no slither; direct—no excessive use of adjectives, no metaphors that won't permit examination. It's straight talk" (*SL* 11). In 1940 he reflected that "the poetical reform between 1910 and 1920 coincided with the scrutiny of the word, the cleaning-up of syntax" (*SP* 32).

In one sense Pound was obviously reaffirming writers' and critics' centuries-long commitment to concision, to "what e're was thought but ne're so well expressed" or to poetry's ethos of the "best words in the best order." To some degree "efficiency" was Pound's endorsement of the compression, pointedness, and clarity of the epigram, which he knew from ancient Greek poetry, from the Roman poet, Martial, and from Renaissance and eighteenth-century English poetry. In Emersonian terms Pound restated the power of the poet whose "delicate ear" enabled him to write the primal cadences especially amid the vacuous, attenuated Romantic and Victorian poesy that Pound scorned as blurred, indistinct, conventional, and soft (Emerson, *Selected Writings* 224).

In important ways, however, Pound's injunctions on verbal economy were new. In an industrial era Pound could make his vorticist argument on maximal energy from the model of machine technology, not of organic forms. His remarks on efficiency surpass schoolmasterly strictures on diction and syntax. Pound used machine-based terms as the foundation for a new activist theory of poetry, in fact of all the arts. He argued the necessity of stylistic efficiency from an urgent belief that literature could—and must—enact maximal energy. Efficiency thus became a measure of the artist's activism. It meant escape from the human passivity inevitable in an unstable world. And the source of Pound's liberating vortex lay in the example of machine technology, in which engineers can deliberately exploit the point of maximum energy or "greatest efficiency" in their designs.

Pound's affinity with machine technology and the engineer can be traced to a specific source. In fact his insistence upon machine-based verbal efficiency owes much to a theory of language espoused from an unlikely quarter. In 1910 an

American munitions manufacturer and gadfly literary critic, Hudson Maxim, published a treatise on language which came to Pound's attention. Maxim had ample time in which to speculate on linguistics because he had sold his profitable chemical explosive, immodestly called maximite, to the Du Pont Corporation, which retained him as a consulting engineer, whereupon he wrote occasional magazine pieces like "Man's Machine-Made Millennium," which appeared in *Cosmopolitan* (1908). In 1910 he published a book-length study, *The Science of Poetry and the Philosophy of Language*, which Pound reviewed in an essay entitled "The Wisdom of Poetry" (1913).

Maxim's goal for the arts of the written word was identical to his engineering goal: efficiency of operation. The rationale of Maxim's treatise owed much to contemporary industrialists' and engineers' goals of standardization and evaluation in manufacturing. "The main object of this book," wrote Maxim, "is to provide a practical method for literary criticism and analysis, and a standard for uniform judgement for determining the relative merits of literary productions, and, further, to supply a more practical and efficient means than we have had heretofore for the standardization of poetry, whereby any poem may be assayed and the amount of its poetic gold determined and separated from the slag and dross" (*Science of Poetry* ix).

Maxim made literary criticism sound like mining extraction and like machine-tool guaging. But his theory of poetic efficiency, formulated with the help of Herbert Spencer's essay, "The Philosophy of Style" (1852), clearly enabled the young Pound to codify his own theory of the poetic imagination in ways that allied it with machine technology. "Poetry obeys the law of conservation of energy," wrote Maxim. "By poetry a thought is presented with the utmost economy of word symbols." He compared the poem to the sweep of a beckoning hand, a nonverbal gesture whose meaning is grasped immediately. "Poetry . . . thereby economizes in the use of the word symbols by selecting only those most pregnant with meaning. . . . Any surplussage of word symbols in a line weakens it." Maxim argued that poetry conserved energy but also "energized perception" by converting energy into "pleasurable emotions." Maxim's argument was exactly suited to the poetic and critical aspirations of the young Pound, even if Maxim lapsed from his theory by resorting to traditions of nineteenth-century oratory in order to explain the emotional power of poems.

The engineer-critic went even further. In a chapter entitled "Potentry" Maxim tried to merge power and poetry in a concept presenting language as a productive machine. He paraphrased Spencer, calling language "an apparatus for conveying thought. . . . Like any other apparatus, [it] is most nearly perfect when it is of the simplest construction and does its work with the least expenditure of energy." Accordingly, the goal of composition is to minimize friction and inertia. Maxim augments Spencer by extending the definition of the language-machine: "besides being . . . an apparatus for conveying ideas, language is also an instrument for the conversion of energy into pleasurable emotions, which serve to energize perception. . . . Hence, . . . that language apparatus is best which, while consuming energy with economy for a given purpose, converts the most energy into useful work —effective expression" (78–79).

Pound never adequately acknowledged his debt to the eccentric theorist, but his ideas on efficiency in language were evidently nourished by Maxim's statement (via Spencer) that language itself was an elegant, efficient machine. Hudson Maxim gave Pound the basis for his theory of language efficiency. More, he provided the linkage between language and literature and the "machinery, factories, new and vaster buildings, bridges and works" of which Pound and Lewis boasted in *Blast* (4).

Pound thus ranged freely in his appreciation of machine-based design efficiency. In "The City" he proposed that the "stream line or speed line" replace the "inefficient" grid and concluded (erroneously, from a professional engineer's standpoint) that in "solving this perfectly clear engineering problem the beauty comes of itself" (*SP* 224–25). In *Gaudier-Brzeska*, his memoir of the deceased Polish sculptor, he praised the aesthetics of automotive design. "The forms of automobiles and engines . . . are very beautiful in themselves and in their combinations" when "they follow the lines of force" and "are truly expressive of the various modes of efficiency" (26). Pound knew that "the school of sentimental aesthetics," in which he put the "well-meaning goose," Ruskin, found "the fact of this beauty . . . offensive." He himself, however, had made common cause with it in literature and in culture (*SP* 224–25).

In this light it was virtually inevitable that Pound should respond warmly to the British Major Clifford Hugh Douglas's social credit theory set forth in *Economic Democracy* (1920), and probable that he should employ the major's theories in the *Cantos*. For the utilitarian axis of efficiency and waste pervades Douglas's text, which argues that capitalists and financiers impede machine-based abundance. Douglas charged that these miscreants perpetuate inequity by draining off profits to pay bloated sums for interest and thus burden workers with low wages and consumers with unnecessarily high prices. Reading Douglas, Pound heard the Veblenesque denunciation of waste in industrial sabotage, make-work, bureaucracy, byzantine accounting, and tawdriness of goods, in addition to the major's acknowledgment of "the awful tragedy of waste and misery" of the war years (70–73, 130).

But Pound also saw Douglas's explicit recognition of tremendous factory productivity made possible by the work of the efficiency engineer, Frederick Taylor (31). He saw Douglas reject the views of William Morris and John Ruskin as retrograde ("It cannot be seriously contended . . . that men should abjure the use of anything more complicated than a hammer and chisel or a spinning wheel"). And he heard Douglas's repeated invocations to "Ultra Modern" efficiency in an economic system designed to achieve "higher economic efficiency" and "higher psychological efficiency" (91, 78, 8, 36). Pound could not help but find Douglas's argument compelling, given the values he imbibed and espoused in literary theory. His commitment to a literary-cultural linkage undergirded his decision to make an efficient economics as much a part of his poetry as was efficient language. It goes

without saying that Pound is not open to the charge of machine-based deper-
sonalization. Democratic equity and "effective expression" were the goal, and
they encompassed the full range of human feeling and experience. So there could
be no question of machine-based efficiency being dehumanized. It was, on the
contrary, intensely human, suprahuman.

Not that Pound blindly worshiped machine efficiency. Like all his contemporaries, he loathed mechanism turned against human life. He deplored the hapless
students hammered "into a piece of mechanism for the accretion of details" and
scorned the unimaginative magazine editor whom he compared to "the factory
owner [who] wants . . . each man in his employe to do some one mechanical
thing that he can do almost without the expenditure of thought" (*SP* 128, 111).

But Pound's Vorticism allied him necessarily with the one profession committed
to the "'greatest efficiency' in the precise sense—as . . . used in a text book of
MECHANICS." When Pound accepted the idea of language as an apparatus, as a
machine converting energy into useful work or effective expression, he implicated
himself as an engineer, just as his friend William Carlos Williams would do when
he called the poem "a machine made of words . . . with no redundant part."
Pound understood and accepted the analogy. He compared an engineer in a
machine-filled laboratory with a figure like himself, the art critic in a gallery of
masterwork paintings. The paintings, like the diverse machines driven by steam,
gas, and electricity, "all 'produce power'—that is, they gather the latent energy of
nature and focus it on a certain resistance. The latent energy is made dynamic or
'revealed' to the engineer in control, and placed at his disposal" (*SP* 24–25).

Pound admired that controlling engineer. His critical prose gave the rationale for
that admiration, and it authorized the entry of the engineer's values into imaginative literature. Pound's statements on efficiency flew in the face of the skepticism
of writers like Sinclair Lewis and Ernest Poole. Pound, unlike them, presumed the
salutary impact of technological values in literature. He did so because he prized
two attributes of engineers' machine design, the patterned energy and the beauty
which the pattern manifested. The writer, like the engineer, could see the latent
energy made dynamic in the designed arrangement of words. Pound recognized
that the writer, an artificer in the age of great machine and structural technology,
had a powerful counterpart—even analogue—in the engineer. As Pound understood, the time was propitious for his values of functional efficiency to be embodied in literature. In fact, Pound's images acknowledged the prestige and power of
the modern engineer, a figure we must now examine in some detail.

CHAPTER THREE

THE ENGINEER

*It is a great profession. There is the fascination of
watching a figment of the imagination emerge through
the aid of science to a plan on paper. Then it moves to
realization in stone or metal or energy. Then it brings
jobs and homes to men. Then it elevates the standards
of living and adds to the comforts of life. That is the
engineer's high privilege.*

Herbert Hoover, *Memoirs*, 1951

LOOKING BACKWARD, LOOKING FORWARD

n Sinclair Lewis's novel *Dodsworth* (1929) young Sam
Dodsworth, a graduate of Yale and "Massachusetts Tech,"
peers over Long Island Sound to reflect on his post-
college plans to be "a civil engineer . . . riding a mountain trail, two thousand sheer feet above a steaming
valley." Instead, Dodsworth works on his mechanical
drawing, convinced in 1903 that the new-fangled auto-
mobile ought to be streamlined instead of boxy and that he is the man to make
the design change "in the urgent new motor industry." A quarter century later in
Paris this same Dodsworth, a successful engineer and manufacturer of automobiles ("the first man to advocate four-wheel brakes"), stands contemplating
the Cathedral of Notre Dame and feels a kinship with the artisans who built it
centuries ago. Reflecting on his achievement, he goes even further to claim identity as an artist of the twentieth century. Like painters and writers and composers,
"he had created something," for "every one of the twenty million motors on the
roads of America had been influenced by his vision . . . of long, clean stream-
lines" (12–17, 133, 228–29).

Lewis's Dodsworth was attuned to the times. From the turn of the century
through the 1920s countless American youngsters yearned to master the secrets of
technology and to become engineers, whom one writer called "true poets, makers
whose creations touch the imagination and move the world" (Maclaurin xxv). By
the late nineteenth century the engineer's signature was everywhere on the American landscape, in railroads, bridges, and tall buildings, in tunnels and in systems
for water, gas, and electricity. As the historian Samuel Eliot Morison recalled in his

memoir, *One Boy's Boston*, his boyhood "opened [in 1887] with the horsecar and . . . closed [in 1910] with the Cadillac and the airplane" (81).

As engineers made their presence felt in the American scene, they began to figure prominently in imaginative literature. Yet critics and analysts have been oddly blind to their presence. Students of American texts, avid seekers of national types, have failed to recognize the engineer's presence or to notice the embodiment of engineering values either in popular or enduring literature. Other American occupational types—doctors, lawyers, ministers, businessmen—have become our familiars from the novels of Ernest Hemingway, Herman Melville, William Dean Howells, and Theodore Dreiser. The characteristics of those figures, pro and con, are taken into account in college classroom lectures and in scholarly journal articles. In this sense the missing engineer is simply an empty frame in the national gallery of occupational portraits.

But the issue is more complex than that. It surpasses mere occupation to concern itself with national myth and ideology in an era of industrialization and pervasive technology. It calls to mind the precedent set by the study of another national type, the cowboy, a symbol of rugged individualism, egalitarianism, and heroism in the western dime novels of the nineteenth century. By the turn of the century, as Alan Trachtenberg points out, the cowboy reflected the post–Civil War incorporation of America, becoming the guardian of the private property of the conservative ruling class (*Incorporation of America* 21–25). Reflecting social change, the cowboy has compelled attention as a symbolic figure who can be shown to embody distinct values in the American experience. He reflects cultural change even as he participates in the myth and ideology of the nation.

So does the engineer, this invisible man of American studies who appeared as the hero in over one hundred silent movies and in best-selling novels approaching five million copies in sales between 1897 and 1920. From Edward Bellamy's *Looking Backward* (1888) through *The Education of Henry Adams* (1906) and the writings of Thorstein Veblen, the engineer appears as a crucial figure in modern American civilization. He is in Emerson's sense the representative man for the era, a symbol of efficiency, stability, functionalism, and power. In the imaginative literature of industrialized America he figures as a new hero who enacts the values of civilization. He is at once visionary and pragmatic.

Even writers who cast him in minor roles exploit these qualities. Dreiser does so, for instance, in the figure of the electrical engineer, Robert Ames. In *Sister Carrie* Ames is the one man *not* dazzled by luxury ablaze in incandescent restaurant lights. Carrie thinks the young engineer a "scholar" who is both "innocent and clean," and "wiser, saner, and brighter" than her lovers, the traveling salesman and the failed restauranteur (291–94, 361, 389). For once she is right, since Dreiser endows Ames with unusual analytical powers. The young engineer criticizes wasteful consumption, critiques current literature, and, sexually unmoved by Carrie, foresees her potential as an actress because he recognizes in her facial features the objectification of popular longing. Ames is the ethical man of clarifying vision, and he is the only figure in the novel who transcends the materialistic romanticism that holds all others in a tight, even fatal, grip.

Dreiser's engineer, once identified, beckons us toward similar engineer character-types in imaginative writings. He alerts us to the possibility that a knowledge of literature and culture is incomplete without the recognition of the figure in popular and enduring texts. To scrutinize industrialized, technological America without due regard for the engineer is like studying the idea of the American West without attention to the cowboy, or agrarianism without noticing the farmer. Each is indispensable to an adequate understanding of ideology and of the values that underlie social change and define an era.

Engineering, moreover, has important aesthetic implications, as Sinclair Lewis suggests in Sam Dodsworth's drive to supplant the horseless carriage with the sculptured automotive streamline, the very line we heard Ezra Pound praise for its vibrant efficiency. In fact, Dodsworth's claim to be a modern artist is authentic and authoritative. It suggests the basis on which the engineer could become a role model for twentieth-century artists, including poets and novelists. In an age in which machine manufacture took precedence over handicrafts and artisanry, the engineer was the new kind of author. He created efficient, functional, component-part designs. He set a new example for the twentieth-century artist, no longer a craftsman fashioning unique objects from raw materials, but a designer committed to the functional, efficient arrangement of prefabricated components into a total design. Ezra Pound emphasized that language is "made out of concrete things . . . arranged" in precise relations to each other (*SL* 49; *SP* 41). It is fair to say that engineering values entered the national literature virtually as a matter of course, once the national landscape burgeoned with engineers' achievements.

It is essential to recognize the ways in which engineers and their work were presented to the American public. A masculine figure in a male profession, the spokesman for a gear-and-girder world, the engineer became a vital American symbol between the 1890s and 1920s. In popular fiction, as we shall see, he signified stability in a changing world. He was technology's human face, providing reassurance that the world of gears and girders combined rationality with humanity. And he represented the power of civilization in the contemporary moment. Popular texts present the engineer as the descendant of once-powerful ministers and statesmen; his is ethical *and* utilitarian power. In an industrial era, in a gear-and-girder world, the engineer wears the mantle of civilizing power and ethical judgment.

As we shall see, the engineer is also a critical figure in the enduring imaginative literature of the era. To understand why, we must revisit Edward Bellamy and Thorstein Veblen. They insist that the engineer poses a compelling and powerful alternative to the profit-minded businessman or industrialist. We must also examine the writings of Henry Adams. His respect for the achievement and potential of engineers has so far not been recognized, though it is compatible with the popular images of engineers and helps to anticipate the election of America's only engineer president, Herbert Hoover. All these strands so interconnect that the engineer needs full and separate treatment.

In sheer numbers and geographical range the growth of the engineering profession signaled its cultural importance in the United States of the late nineteenth and early twentieth centuries. In 1917 New York's City College planned its School of Technology for five hundred engineering students, only to find it enroll over five thousand students by the late 1920s. The phenomenon was not only urban. A handful of engineers' biographies suggests that engineering attracted youth from logging towns of the Pacific Northwest to the Finger Lakes region of upstate New York to rural Idaho and to the very shadow of the Brooklyn Bridge teeming with the hyphenated, immigrant Americans. Engineering lured its (overwhelmingly male) students from diverse households — that of the Methodist minister whose watchwords were "peace and order," of the lower East Side laborer's family, of Idaho farmers whose children interrupted their university training in engineering to help their families with urgent farmwork (Ratigan, Kimball, Vauclain, Hammond).

The allure of engineering surfaces in American fiction of the time, reflecting the breadth of its popularity. In Abraham Cahan's *The Rise of David Levinsky* (1917) a young New York City clothing manufacturer saves money in order to "take up medicine, engineering, or law" (168). In an early Edna Ferber novel, *Roast Beef, Medium* (1913), the college-age son of the heroine exclaims, "Mother, you know how wild I am about machines, and motors, and engineering" (74). And in Robert Herrick's *Together* (1908) the young engineer gets the opportunity to work on the Panama Canal, saying, "They have interesting problems down there. It is really big work, you know. A man might do something worth while." Ferber's young man cries, "Professions! Why, you talk about the romance of a civil engineer's life!" (296–97).

That romance was served up in a towering book stack of children's literature of the 1910s and 1920s. Readers of H. Irving Hancock's series on *Grammar School Boys* and *High School Boys* could follow the youngsters into their grown-up heroic exploits in a four-volume *Young Engineers* series (in Colorado, in Arizona, in Nevada, in Mexico). Those same readers could venture into the war zone in James R. Driscoll's *The Brighton Boys with the Engineers at Castigny*, all the while keeping abreast of Victor Appleton's *Tom Swift* books whose titles suggest the excitement of the fantastic yet plausible new technologies: *Tom Swift and His Motor Cycle*, *Tom Swift and His Motor Boat* (*and* his airship, submarine, wireless message, sky racer, electric rifle, wizard camera, photo telephone, etc., each a separate full-length novel).

Tom Swift's followers received lessons in mechanics along with vicarious adventures. Their appetites for invention and engineering were surely whetted by this fictional mix of technology and adventure. When Tom's plane engine fails in mid-air in *Tom Swift and His Air Glider* (1912), for instance, the boy inventor is forced to land in a rural field where he pokes "among the numerous cogs, wheels, and levers," then diagnoses the problem: the magneto is broken because the

Book cover design for The Young Engineers in Mexico, *1913*

bearings and contact surfaces are fused and crystallized. Here the action stops for a narrator's lesson in mechanics. "The magneto of an aeroplane performs a service similar to one in an automobile; it provides the spark that explodes the charge of gas in the cylinders" (12). The narrator restarts the extraordinary engine of a plot, which features a Siberian quest for the platinum necessary for Tom's magneto and other machinery.

It is not known how many American boys were first lured into engineering through adventure books like the *Tom Swift* series. But it is probable that many of these readers realized their fantasies of technology in play with A. C. Gilbert's Erector Sets, which, as we saw, featured the small electric motors and square girders that could be bolted together to form machines and structures. Boys who attained a certain level of ingenuity in their models were awarded diplomas certifying them as Engineers or Master Engineers of the Gilbert Institute of Engineering. The Erector instruction manual of 1915 boasted that "Erector is the only builder with girders that resemble the real structural material used in the great sky-scrapers, offices, factories, and public buildings." It promised, "You can build derricks —machine shops—battleships—aeroplanes—duplicates of celebrated bridges, arches, etc. that can be operated with the electric motor." In his autobiography A. C. Gilbert recounted that over the years hundreds of engineers had written to tell him that their professional commitment began in boyhood with an Erector Set.

In part such boyhood interest accounts for the findings of William F. Book, who surveyed six thousand high school seniors for vocational preference and published the results in 1922. The occupation favored by 31 percent of the boys was engineering. It eclipsed agriculture by seven percentage points and showed the prestige of technology (*Intelligence* 139–42). Back in 1870 Ralph Waldo Emerson had described the American farmer minding a "machine of colossal proportions." "The earth," wrote Emerson, "is a machine which yields almost gratuitous service to every application of intellect" ("The Farmer" 404–5). Struggling to dignify the farmer, Emerson came close to the credo of the engineer, set forth in 1828 by the British bridge and rail designer, Thomas Telford, in the charter of the British Institute of Civil Engineering: "engineering is the science of controlling the forces and utilizing the materials of nature for the benefit of man" (qtd. in Beyer 419). In 1872 in a post–Civil War sermon Henry Ward Beecher looked into the American future and proclaimed that "the higher instincts, when civilized, become engineers' forces." By the turn of the century many agreed (qtd. in H. N. Smith x-xi).

The imagination of Americans warmed to engineers and engineering values for complex reasons. To some extent the "romance" that thrilled Ferber's young man came from popular contemporary images of such massive projects as the Panama Canal (1902–14), the Wilson Dam on the Tennessee River (1922–26), and the Alaska Railroad (1914–23). Engineers made so many indelible marks on the American scene that even in 1869 the *New York Times* reported the "revolution in every mode and attribute of [American] life." The *Times* defined this "revolution" through technological achievements: "the dissolving and recomposing of materials, the utilization of natural forces, the wonders of chemistry, the feats of engineering,

A. C. Gilbert Co. advertisement. Good Housekeeping, *1916*

the triumphs of machinery . . . the steamship, the locomotive, the telegraph, the iron bridge, the Bessemer process, the machinery of agriculture, of water supply, of illumination, or weaving, or printing . . . or turning power into infinite channels, and the machinery that makes machinery" (qtd. in Merritt 32).

Very slowly, in the 1860s and 1870s, the American public came to recognize that individual engineers and their growing profession were responsible for this "revolution" whose breadth can be measured, in brief, in statistics. The *United States Census Reports* from 1850 to 1880 indicates that engineering was the fastest-growing profession, increasing sixteen times over thirty years. (The numbers of physicians and clergymen, by contrast, just more than doubled.) In 1850 there were 512 civil engineers, in 1880, 8,261, with the heaviest concentration of them in urban, industrial centers (Merritt 9–11; D. F. Noble 38–39).

Many engineers were schooled, in those years, in informal apprenticeships on the shop floor, but formal engineering education increased at the land-grant colleges as a direct result of the first Morrill Act of 1862. That law mandated land to be set aside in each state for the support of a "College of Agriculture and Mechanic Arts." Institutions like Cornell University, the Pennsylvania State College, and the University of Idaho joined the older polytechnic institutions (Rensselaer, the Polytechnic College of the State of Pennsylvania, the Massachusetts Institute of Technology) and such additional centers as the University of Michigan, the Columbia School of Mines, and the Lawrence Scientific School at Harvard to provide education for the more than 3,800 engineering graduates of the 1880s. One historian reports, "In the third quarter of the nineteenth century the most rapid and extensive development of American higher institutions of learning took place within the so-called polytechnic education." By 1900 there were approximately 45,000 engineers, by 1930, 230,000, a fivefold increase (Merritt 11).

The public, nevertheless, largely overlooked the engineer himself in those latter decades of the nineteenth century, even if engineering achievements were ubiquitous. Perhaps, as one historian of the period argues, engineers' work so well accorded with the goals and objectives of established groups that the people who spoke for them—farmers, clergymen, educators—appropriated technological achievements and reformulated them in schemes congruent with their own beliefs. Thus the railroad promised farmers higher land-and-crop values, while its passenger service promised to sinew the nation in Christian brotherhood. In poetry Walt Whitman (whose brother was chief engineer of the St. Louis waterworks) argued that "chef-d'oeuvres of engineering" endured only as the objectification of the nation's "personal qualities," of its "muscle and pluck" (Merritt 23–25; Whitman 188).

Engineering "muscle" was amply evident in the final decade of the nineteenth century, when steel-framed bridges arose to span the rivers and bays of the eastern seaboard, the rivers of the Ohio Valley, and the Mississippi itself (following the stunning example of the Eads Bridge at St. Louis, 1867–74). Every major city boasted the tall, steel-framed buildings made possible by fabricated steel and by the elevator powered by electric motors. Newspapers and magazines kept readers abreast of these phenomenal engineering feats, which much of the population experienced at firsthand in such major cities as Chicago, Pittsburgh, and New York, and in smaller locales like Sioux City, Iowa; Marietta, Ohio; Tyrone, Kentucky; and Nebraska City, Nebraska. Sinclair Lewis marked the trend in his fictional mid-size American city, Zenith, whose office buildings are "austere towers of steel and cement and limestone, sturdy as cliffs and delicate as silver rods" (*Babbitt* 5).

As these structures reshaped the American scene, the engineer became the exemplar of technological power and began to appear, at last, as a new kind of American hero in popular fiction. Yet he was more than a dashing figure of industrial-age romance and adventure, the director of "the terrific chorus of steel and stone and glass" (Huneker 39–40). In the American imagination he was also much more than a boys' role model for the strenuous life urged by Theodore Roosevelt, the Young Men's Christian Association, and the scouting movement.

The figure of the engineer apparently satisfied other, deep psychological needs that were specific to the new age. The enginee played a critical role in an America that was trying to surmount its anxieties about instability. He became vital to a nation striving to achieve efficiency while ridding itself of the dreaded waste. In 1883 the soon-to-be mayor of New York City, Abram Hewitt, spoke directly to this point in his address at the opening ceremonies of the Brooklyn Bridge. The structure "looks like a motionless mass of masonry and metal," Hewitt observed. "But as a matter of fact it is instinct with motion. . . . It is an aggregation of unstable elements, changing with every change in the temperature and every movement of the heavenly bodies." Hewitt then posed the challenge central to engineering and, by extension, to American society itself. "The problem was, out of these unstable elements, to produce absolute stability" (308–9).

Absolute stability: that, in the politician Hewitt's view, was the enviable societal goal, which he saw successfully realized, materially, in the engineering of John A. and Colonel Washington Roebling. For Hewitt, their bridge satisfied the yearnings documented in so many contemporary American writings, even if few believed that stability could be "absolute." As Oliver Wendell Holmes wrote, "Our stability is but balance, and wisdom lies in masterful administration of the unforeseen" (qtd. in Fitch, *Engineering and Civilization* 329). A broad spectrum of the public looked to the engineers to provide this mastery, to bring a fast-changing culture into balance or stability just as the Roeblings' calculations brought stone and steel into the dynamic equipoise of the Brooklyn Bridge.

The engineer was the exponent of efficiency and the slayer of that dragon, waste. In the age of pervasive machine technology he was a messianic figure, at least a priestly one. His values—efficiency, organization, production, functional and elegant design—enabled Americans once again to expect national salvation. The engineer renewed the spiritual mission embedded for over two and a half centuries in the national experience. He promised, so it seemed, to lead industrialized America directly into the millennium.

Bellamy's best-selling *Looking Backward 2000–1887* (1888), once again com-

Photographs showing survey, construction, and operation of Florida East Coast Overseas Railroad (Courtesy National Museum of American History, Smithsonian Institution)

pels attention, this time because the novel heralded a new millennial vision and signaled a popular endorsement of the engineering mentality in America. Like Washington Irving's story of Rip Van Winkle, *Looking Backward* uses the ploy of time-change to develop its themes. The central figure, a Bostonian named Julian West, awakens from a trance-induced sleep of more than a century to be reborn in the American future of the year 2000. Sheltered in the futuristic household of Dr. and Mrs. Leete and nurtured by their lovely daughter, Edith, Julian West also finds himself in a new America of full employment, material abundance, efficiency, social stability and harmony, and technological sophistication. Vanished is West's familiar, late-nineteenth-century Boston (and America) of instability, class tension, waste, strikes, misery, and extremes of wealth and poverty.

The novel tells the story of West's gradual conversion of faith to a utopian America-2000. Under Dr. Leete's tutelage he comes to reject his lifelong beliefs in the nineteenth-century status quo, to become angry at its inequities even as he participates in the daily life of Boston-2000, shopping, dining, strolling—and falling in love with Edith Leete.

In fact, Bellamy sets up his plot with Edith Leete's allure and with West's insatiable, amnesiac craving to have the American metamorphosis explained to him as he copes with his sudden double identity. His readers, citizens themselves of an imperfect world, share the Bostonian's skepticism about the cultural transformation. Bellamy exploits both the attraction and the resistance of his audience, its optimism and its defense against gullibility.

Steel-frame building, San Francisco, 1889 (Courtesy National Museum of American History, Smithsonian Institution)

Bridges of Pittsburgh, 1890s (Courtesy Carnegie Library of Pittsburgh)

William Steele & Sons Co. advertisement.
Literary Digest, *1918*

Generically, *Looking Backward* is both a stock-in-trade romance and a reformist tract. The sage father-doctor, Leete, becomes the interlocutor for a story whose philosophical base is Christian socialism and whose religious presumption of brotherhood is a version of Emerson's Transcendentalism. The doctor must first prove to his visitor that this new city is in fact Boston. From a roofed gallery of the Leete house they behold Boston-2000:

> Miles of broad streets, shaded by trees and lined with fine buildings, for the most part not in continuous blocks but set in larger or smaller enclosures, stretched in every direction. Every quarter contained large open squares filled with trees, along which statues glistened and fountains flashed in the late-afternoon sun. Public buildings of a colossal size and architectural grandeur unparalleled in my day raised their stately piles on every side. (55)

Julian West exclaims that he surely has never seen this or a comparable city before (though Bellamy's post-1893 readers might know that nearly five million Americans saw exactly that city in Chicago's Jackson Park, where the World's Columbian Exposition featured its unified White City in the "wedding cake" Beaux Arts architectural style) (Badger 109). But West recognizes Boston's topography, and from that moment knows he must confront the truth of his time travel.

Looking Backward is largely the story of Julian West's conversion to the socialist principles of nationalism. He is Bellamy's specimen of the nineteenth-century gentleman whose sensitivity to injustice is channeled at last into belief in the feasibility of social change. Gradually during strolls, shopping trips, sojourns to restaurants, and in hours-long talks with Dr. Leete the young man recognizes the barbarism of his era and comes to understand that individuals like himself can redeem an inhuman social order.

Meanwhile the new, enlightened West succumbs inevitably to the charms of Edith Leete, who is sensitive to his suffering and, coincidentally, bears the same name as West's Boston-1887 fiancée. An element of mystery is cleared with the revelation that Edith Leete is that very fiancée's own granddaughter. The bloodlines are intact, and West can pledge his troth to the new Edith. He is not, after all, a stranger in a strange land—though his fitness for Boston-2000 is sorely tested in a dream scene late in the novel when the new Julian West revisits the old Boston, finds it unendurably grotesque and cruel, yet cannot persuade his friends and acquaintances that together they can reform this "Golgotha."

The nightmare from which West awakens is really the certification of his citizenship in Boston-2000 and the reader's own injunction to take reformist action. The vital center of *Looking Backward*, however, is the American millennium made possible by a research-and-development office of American engineers. At heart a socialist reformer, Bellamy paid the dues of a mystery writer and romancer. But the author clearly got his deepest satisfaction from the engineering of the American future.

Bellamy was not, it must be said, an engineer. But his Christian mysticism was overlaid with logical habits of mind and a pragmatic approach to problems of all kinds. Bellamy even considered fiction in this light, saying that "nothing outside of the exact sciences has to be so logical as the thread of a story, if it is to be acceptable" (qtd. in Kasson 259). In boyhood he yearned to become a cadet at that citadel of American engineering, West Point. Failing the physical examination in 1867, he enrolled at Union College in Schenectady, New York, for one year of independent study in philosophy and political economy.

The year at Union was perhaps crucial. The college had enjoyed unusual, long-standing faculty and administrative leadership in the field of engineering. The outspoken William Mitchell Gillespie took charge of the civil engineering course in 1845, published two treatises on surveying and road construction at mid-century, and went on to translate and publish a portion of Auguste Comte's *Cours de philosophie positive*, a work Bellamy reportedly studied at Union. If this very young collegian was, at that time, far from reinventing the United States of America within the framework of a novel, it is possible that the tone set by figures like Gillespie and his successor, Cady Staley, enabled Bellamy to embrace the idea of systematic, utilitarian, practical application of thought to all problems of American life.

Newspaper journalism eventually became Bellamy's route to the functional intellectualism of *Looking Backward*. By his mid–1830s he had studied German socialism and law, and was also a cub reporter for William Cullen Bryant's *New York Evening Post*, a newspaper involved in reform issues like sanitary regulation and tenement problems. In 1872, at his father's suggestion, Edward returned to his Chickopee Falls, Massachusetts, hometown to become an editorial writer and book reviewer for the *Springfield Union*, and five years later to form a partnership with his brother to publish their own paper, the *Springfield Daily News*. Married, the father of two children, his health always precarious, Bellamy nevertheless drove himself with reformist ardor. His editorials of the mid–1870s are revealing: "Overworked Children in Our Mills," "Riches and Rottenness," "Wastes and Burdens of Society." Meanwhile, he wrote novels and short stories, some two dozen of which appeared in periodicals like the *Century*, the *Atlantic Monthly*, *Harper's*, and *Scribner's*. William Dean Howells, who was then the nation's foremost literary critic and editor, admired Bellamy's fictional romances (though he remained silent on the young writer's tendency to solve characters' psychological problems with the kind of plot gimmicks soon to be featured in O. Henry's stories). Bellamy, nevertheless, so well mastered the techniques of fiction that in *Looking Backward* he held readers rapt while expounding the very social theories which a mass audience had found tedious in other writers (introduction to *Looking Backward* 7–27).

Looking Backward piques readers' interest in part because its advanced technologies (electric lights, electronic broadcasting, indoor climate control, credit cards, enclosed shopping malls) make Bellamy seem a canny futurist. The novel has

compelled attention for its political vision of a socialist America, one that trans-
forms an American "Black Hole of Calcutta" into a "paradise of order, equity, and
felicity." This bloodless revolution occurs when competing, ruthless capitalist
corporations, trusts, syndicates, and pools merge into one Great Trust operating
for the mutual benefit of all citizens who are organized into an Industrial Army.

The novel's appealing argument is that every class, "rich and poor, cultured and
ignorant, old and young, weak and strong, men and women" can recognize the
mutual advantage to be had in sharing equally in the production and distribution
of wealth. In economic theory, as readers have noticed, Bellamy was indebted to
Henry George's *Progress and Poverty* (1879) with its "single-tax" system based on
agrarian socialism. George closed his book with a futuristic glimpse of "the
Golden Age . . . the city of God on earth" (522). *Looking Backward* presents that
American millennium in full function.

Bellamy's images reveal his engineering bias. He looked backward (and askance
at) the nineteenth century, scorning its society as a badly designed, precarious
structure. It is "a pyramid poised on its apex . . . maintained upright . . . by an
elaborate system of constantly renewed props and buttresses and guy-ropes in the
form of laws." Twenty thousand new annual state and federal legislative acts fail to
buttress it. The props break down or become "ineffectual through some shifting of
the strain." The structure threatens to topple while America-2000, in fortunate
contrast, "rests on its base" (156).

That base is an engineered structure, even if Bellamy reverts to images from
nature to invoke the pyramidal stability of the "everlasting hills" and to laud
America's communal union as a "mighty heaven-touching tree whose leaves are
its people." Overlooking the distinction made by engineers themselves between
structures and machines, he praises America-2000 for its elegant simplicity of
design. He assures us that "the machine which [the modern Washington function-
aries] direct is indeed vast, but so logical in its principles and direct and simple in
its workings, that it all but runs itself." In contrast, Bellamy criticizes the nineteenth century for its cumbersome, intricate design of the sort soon to be identified
with Rube Goldberg. ("There is not with us, as with you," says Dr. Leete, "any
complex machinery to get out of order and magnify a thousand times the original
mistake.") As for the engineers of America-2000, they are eligible, along with great
authors, artists, physicians, and inventors, for the highest of all national honors.
Their bridges and transportation systems are categorically as valuable and aesthetic as performances and exhibitions in theaters, art galleries, and music halls
(183, 140, 174, 130, 177).

Bellamy's engineering ethos, however, surpasses figures of speech and his validation of engineering as a prestigious contribution to America-2000. His alliance
with the "functional intellectuals" is best revealed in his zest for the efficient
systemization of every aspect of American life. The officers in his Industrial Army
have indeed learned to "control the forces and utilize the materials of nature for
the benefit of man." Urban design, including water and sewerage systems and
climate control, for instance, are presupposed. Citizens need not even get wet in a

storm, thanks to a retractable canopy—a device of public-health significance at a time when physicians prescribed travel to congenial climes and when a sophisticate like William Dean Howells thought that harsh climes could be ameliorated if, for the cost of a medium-sized war, the jet-stream currents were redirected by razing the Alaskan mountains (*Through the Eye of the Needle* 163).

Readers of *Looking Backward* hear Dr. Leete expound at length on the Boston-2000 systemization of education, domestic labor, economics, book and newspaper publishing. But Bellamy waxes warmest in his engineering of the social order. The population of the entire nation is reconstituted in the Industrial Army, which is led by the "highest-class men" but enrolls everyone, male and female, for three entry-level years of manual labor in service to the nation. Thereafter the competition for advancement is intense. In place of monetary incentives there are elaborate prizes, privileges, and honorable mentions at all levels, together with manipulations of rank in an elaborate guild system culminating in an elite officer corps. The army as well as the presidency is emphatically apolitical, insulated from partisan politics by an electorate of retirees who, after age forty-five, are mustered out of the army and are free to cultivate new interests for the remaining decades of their lives. Repeatedly Bellamy emphasizes the humane motivation of the army, unified by "the solidarity of the race and the brotherhood of man," even if dissenters find themselves on bread and water in solitary confinement (111).

Readers who disagree on the political and psychological ramifications of the Industrial Army must concur on one point. Bellamy's is an America by design. To read Dr. Leete's lengthy monologues on the structure of the army is to recognize both Bellamy's commitment to the amelioration of social conditions and his engineering ethos. His scheme for a new social order anticipates the broadening of professional engineers' concerns in the United States in the early twentieth century. As one essayist, an engineer, wrote in 1922, "It is of fundamental significance that the American engineering profession has of late considerably widened the scope" of its effort. Now, says the writer, engineering is not only "the science of controlling the forces and utilizing the materials of nature for the benefit of man"—but also "*the art of organizing and of directing human activities in connection therewith*" (Beyer 419).

Bellamy's America-2000, in fact, heralded the work of Frederick Winslow Taylor. Like Bellamy, Taylor argued that maximal national prosperity depended upon the utmost efficiency of the individual engaged in the work best suited to his natural abilities. Taylor, too, envisioned the abundance of low-cost consumer goods and presupposed that the interests of workers and managers—in fact, of the entire society—meshed like gears. As one reader remarks, Taylor could have been a general in Bellamy's army (Kasson 197).

Looking Backward inspired a welter of utopian and dystopian novels in an era notorious for political corruption, corporate power, and social upheaval. Significant in literary and political study, the novel is also a landmark in the history of technology and culture in the United States. As a serious book for a mass audience it proclaimed the power of technology to solve the most vexing and debilitating national problems, those both moral and material. Its sale of over 500,000 copies in the several years following publication, together with the formation of some five hundred politically activist Bellamy Clubs, signifies the public readiness to welcome engineering and its values into every area of national life. To bring humane order from chaotic instability, to banish waste and achieve efficiency, to serve others in benevolent disinterest—these were the promises of Bellamy's engineered America. They represented the future, even if Bellamy conservatively chose a minister, not an engineer, to deliver the eloquent peroration on America-2000 toward the closing of his book.

Bellamy and his readers may seem naive one century later. In hindsight both author and audience appear unaware of the totalitarian implications of America-2000. Both, it seems, mistook the attainment of comfort for the achievement of happiness. Both overestimated the ability of engineering to bring about the industrial-age millennium, as the presidency of the engineer Herbert Hoover was to make painfully clear by the early 1930s.

But the extraordinary popularity of Bellamy's novel through the 1890s is significant in another way. *Looking Backward* announced that engineering had come of age in the imaginations of Americans. Henceforth it would be a discrete yet integral part of the national consciousness. Thus in 1905 William James's Harvard University colleague, Hugo Munsterberg, wrote that "the utilitarians," embracing science and technology, comprised fully one half of the American character (354–59). By 1914 Van Wyck Brooks wrote that men merely dilated over vague catchwords like democracy and patriotism, reserving "careful thought and intellectual contact" for "engineering, finance, advertising, and trade" (166). In 1918 George Santayana praised the vigor of young philosophers by comparing their minds to those of doctors, engineers, or social reformers (102). When the cultural analyst, Harold Stearns, enlisted writers to undertake "a critical examination of our [American] civilization" in the early 1920s, he invited the engineer Otto S. Beyer, Jr., to join such figures as Lewis Mumford, H. L. Mencken, Van Wyck Brooks, Conrad Aiken, and Ring Lardner. Their anthology, *Civilization in the United States*, featured Beyer's essay, "Engineering," along with those on topics like "The City," "The Literary Life," "The Law," and on racial minorities, sex, sports, and medicine—all issues that American intellectuals thought crucial for the invigoration of the national culture.

In fact, the popular usage of the very term "engineer" through the 1920s shows a continuing regard for a profession valued for expertise, authority, and power. In *The American Language* H. L. Mencken satirizes the many borrowings of the word with his characteristic scorn for pretension. He begins, "I once knew an ancient bill-sticker, attached to a Baltimore theatre, who boasted the sonorous title of *chief lithographer*. Today, in all probability, he would be called a *lithographic-engineer*" (289–91).

Mencken shows just how probable as he surveys Americans' efforts to dignify their mundane jobs with the imprimatur of engineering. There is the bedding manufacturer "who first became a *mattress-engineer* and then promoted himself to the lofty dignity of *sleep-engineer*." There is the "beautician who burst out as an *appearance engineer*, and the *demolition-engineers* who were once content to be house-wreckers." Mencken relishes the "*sanitary-engineers* who had an earlier incarnation as garbage-men," and the "*wedding-engineer*, a technician employed by florists to dress churches for hymeneal orgies." He spoofs the "*packing engineer*, a scientist who crates clocks, radios, and chinaware for shipment," and the "*income-engineer*, an insurance solicitor in a new false-face." Doubtless he would have scorned Edward Bernays's definition of public relations, the field Bernays virtually founded in the 1920s, as "the engineering of consent" (*Boston Globe* [June 27, 1984]: 72).

In any case, as much as Mencken relished his own satire, the egregious examples multiplied and outran his willingness to sustain what Sinclair Lewis dubbed his "gay anarchy" (*Dodsworth* 133). He resorted at last to the researcher's format, listing as data some sixty-five engineering euphemisms that include "a *printing-e.*, a *furniture-e.*, a *photographic-e.*, a *financial-e.* (stock-market tipster), a *paint-e.*, a *clothing-e.*, *wrapping-e.* (a dealer in wrapping paper), a *matrimonial-e.*

The source of Mencken's humor was, understandably, an irritant to the professional engineers, at least one of whom kept a scrupulous tally of the pseudo-professionals. In a revealing footnote Mencken says that Theodore J. Hoover, dean of the School of Engineering at Stanford University, combed *Who's Who in Engineering* to report in 1935 that entrants listed themselves under 2,518 different engineering titles, most well suited to the satirist's barbs at the American "Booboisie."

Mencken's jibe at America's linguistic sins underscores a serious point. The self-styled engineers not only sought higher status but revealed, inadvertently, what engineers represented to the public. The beautician and the mattress manufacturer who paraded themselves as engineers did so with every expectation of gaining customers' respect and approval as specialists and professionals. In proclaiming themselves to be engineers, these and similar individuals reveal the positive connotations surrounding the very term "engineer" in earlier twentieth-century America. To find out just what those connotations were, it is helpful to have a look at some of the popular novels of the time.

CIVILIZER OF OUR CENTURY

From the turn of the century through the 1910s a new American hero—the engineer—entered popular American fiction. In titles like *Soldiers of Fortune* (1897), *Fighting Engineers* (1918), *The Quickening* (1906), *The Trail of the Lonesome Pine* (1908), *The Iron Trail* (1913), and *The Winning of Barbara Worth* (1911) popular novelists fashioned a new American hero whose actions and qualities of mind reveal the hopes and anxieties of the cultural moment. The story settings varied from the Alaskan frontier to the Cumberland Mountains, and the plots ranged from mountaineers' feuds to entrepreneurs' rivalry. Yet whether the author was the journalist-adventurer Richard Harding Davis, or John Fox, Jr., Francis Lynde, Rex Beach, Harold Bell Wright, or Zane Grey, the hero-engineers in these novels are so much alike that they seem to have been cut from the same pattern. This typing is useful, since it enables access to a cluster of cultural values focused within one figure to which the American reading public responded with extraordinary enthusiasm.

The heroes of these novels are typically civil engineers living roughneck lives in the American (or Latin American) outback. They design and construct railroads, mines, bridges, dams, and ironworks in such places as West Virginia, Kentucky, Alaska, Cuba, and California's Imperial Valley.

Neither crude nor parochial, these men straddle the eastern clubroom and the western camp. In fact, they must. They are ruling-class figures. If eastern by birth, like Willard Holmes in *The Winning of Barbara Worth*, they must imbibe the western spirit to become certifiably American. If western born, they must venture east to be civilized. In *The Quickening* the Appalachian Thomas Jefferson Gordon seeks education in Boston, while the hero of *Soldiers of Fortune*, a boy born in the shadow of Pike's Peak, his hero Kit Carson (and his youth spent as sailor and cowboy), intuitively seeks acculturation in the capitals of Europe and is professionally renowned in Edinburgh, Berlin, and Paris, as well as the eastern United States.

A visit to the East, in fact, becomes a device by which the novelist authenticates the civil engineer's civility in stories enacted in primitive conditions. In *The Iron Trail: An Alaskan Romance* Murray O'Neil, desperate to raise new capital, goes east from Alaska to New York City, where readers watch him in suites and clubrooms over cigars with financiers. His crude, temporary camp life in the Alaskan interior is thus permissible, as is Warren Neale's boisterous toil with a work gang laying track toward the end of *The U. P. Trail*. For readers have already seen Neale travel to Washington, D.C., invited by the president of the Union Pacific Railroad who introduces him to the "frock-coated, soft-voiced, cigar-smoking" congressmen, senators, and other officials who "talked of gold" with "an air of luxury, of power, of importance" (295). Neale, like O'Neil, may choose the West. Holmes, in *The Winning of Barbara Worth*, even intends marriage to it by proposing to Barbara, the onetime foundling whose lineage is the desert itself. But the breeding of all these engineer-heroes is certified to readers by their family origins and gentlemanly eastern manners.

Even in rough territory the engineer may become disheveled, but never barbarous. Robert Clay (*Soldiers of Fortune*) cites Shakespeare in the tropical jungle. Jack Hale (*The Trail of the Lonesome Pine*) is "adept in Latin and Greek." Though his life is always "rough," Hale keeps a volume of Keats's poetry with him to read even in his most primitive Appalachian encampments. Bearers of civilization, these engineers are at all times self-possessed and rational in judgment. Hale is "fearless," "thoughtful," and "calm" (40–45). So are the others. They never yield to impulse or to intense feelings of the moment. Passionate, they nonetheless subordinate emotion to controlled rationality in numerous crises that demonstrate the power of their leadership. Mobile, adaptive, tough yet gentlemanly, these engineers are literally all-American men, integrating the nation's regions as birthplace and workplace conjointly manifest the national character in them. They are American stability incarnate.

To a man, they are visionaries and idealists. "You're one of these dreamers," a cynic remarks to young Warren Neale, the future chief engineer of "maintenance of way" of the Union Pacific Railroad in *The U. P. Trail* (285). Indeed he is, as is Thomas Jefferson Gordon, the Cumberland Valley boy who in *The Quickening* graduates with honors in engineering from "Boston Tech" but sees his native valleys as the Promised Land that Moses glimpsed (15). So too in *The Trail of the Lonesome Pine* is the engineer Jack Hale a man "with the vision of a seer, as innocent as [Daniel] Boone." Surveying, Hale sees the Cumberland "Gap" and thinks it to be "the heaven-born site for the unborn city of his dreams" (40–45).

The visionary engineer is especially prominent in *The Winning of Barbara Worth*. There the elderly patriarchial engineer who first envisions the reclamation of the arid King's Basin (the Imperial Valley of California) is called, simply, the Seer. In an early scene in the desert the foundling baby, Barbara, who comes to symbolize the West, intuitively puts out her infant arms to embrace him, implicitly to embrace all that he stands for. "So it was the Seer who became . . . [a] dominant influence in forming the character of the motherless girl," says Wright. "His dreams of Reclamation, his plans and efforts to lead the world to recognize the value of that great work, . . . she shared at an early age." This fictional engineer is a biblical prophet who must watch others undertake the work mandated by his vision. Kept offstage during the course of the action, the "brave, great-hearted, generous Seer" is brought back late in the novel to offer a benediction when the dream of reclamation has been realized (44, 71, 366).

In these popular novels the engineer's vision is both prophetic, in that it foresees the future, and poetic, since it originates within the realm of imagination. The engineer is explicitly put forward as an artist. In *The Iron Trail* the novelist Rex Beach emphasizes this point with his hero, Murray O'Neil, an entrepreneur with an engineer's capabilities. In the inhospitable Alaskan landscape O'Neil discovers a potential railroad route thus far unnoticed by the engineers for five competing rail companies. "The idea took possession of his mind," writes Beach. "He had begun to dream" (74).

The novelist opens this dream of the engineer, who is an artist of the functional. "The world owes all great achievements to dreamers," Beach writes. "No matter how practical the thing accomplished, it requires this faculty, no less than a poem or picture. Every bridge, every skyscraper, every mechanical invention, every great work which man has wrought in steel and stone and concrete, was once a dream." Beach's character is endowed with "the imaginative power that makes great leaders, great inventors, great builders" (74). By temperament he dares what others fear to undertake and insures progressive change. As Zane Grey writes in *The U. P. Trail*, the "engineers had been seized by the spirit of some great thing to be . . . and that strange call of life which foreordained a heritage for the future" (16). In *The Winning of Barbara Worth* Harold Bell Wright strove for eloquence to match the grandeur he thought inherent in the subject:

The Desert waited, silent and hot and fierce in its desolation, . . . holding its treasures . . . against the coming of the strong ones; . . . waited for this age —for your age and mine—for the age of the Seer and his companions . . . all strong, clean-cut, vigorous specimens of intelligent, healthy manhood, for in all the professions, . . . there can be found no finer body of men than our civil engineers. (86–87)

These novelists make a grand claim vis-à-vis the engineer and the artist. They say the engineer-hero is an entitled artist implicitly superior to those who merely paint, sculpt, or write in the studio or atelier. In controlling and utilizing the forces of nature, the engineer makes the continent itself his studio as well as the medium in which he works. He is, moreover, an instrument of (and at the same time the embodiment of) national destiny.

These engineers realize their dreams. They bring the bold, visionary schemes from the imagination into tangible reality. They are poets for the quotidian. That, in essence, is Santayana's 1918 definition of the American at his best. "An idealist working on matter," says the Spanish philosopher of the composite American. "His imagination is practical and the future it forecasts is immediate; it works with the clearest and least ambiguous terms known to his experience," namely, "number, measure, contrivance, economy, and speed." To an audience of Englishmen, American intellectuals, and Bryn Mawr College women Santayana glossed the American character in terms which all of the popular novelists would approve:

[The American] dreams of helping to carry on and to accelerate the movement of the vast, seething, progressive society, and he actually does so. Ideals clinging so close to nature are almost sure of fulfillment. The American beams with a certain self-confidence and sense of mastery; he feels that God and nature are working with him. (124–25)

The novels testify in support of Santayana's view, for "the [transcontinental] railroad can and will be built" (*U. P. Trail* 85). The Appalachian hills, "storehouses for iron and coal," become factory boomtowns. The Alaskan wilderness becomes "fruitful." The engineers survive "five long years of toil and snow and sun, and the bloody Sioux, and the roaring camps" (*Iron Trail* 316, 131–32, 191). They surmount unceasing rains, paralyzing cold, dispirited workmen, a snarling river, and (in glacial Alaska) charging icebergs. In the squalor of the Appalachian Mountains they contain clan hatreds that threaten social havoc.

They are "indomitable." "I wish I could tell you," says Warren Neale to his lover, "how tremendously all this has worked upon me—upon all the engineers. . . . If you can, imagine some spirit seizing hold of you and making you see difficulties as joys—impossible tasks as only things to strike fire from genius" (86, 386). Neale's lover is not the only auditor asked to understand "the wonder of such progress" which "only an engineer can know." In the Alaskan wilds Murray O'Neil's listener is the reader who overhears this expostulation on the prophesy and the poem come true:

> "I've won. I hold the keys to a kingdom. . . . I saw it in a dream, only it was more than a dream. . . . I saw a deserted fishing village become a thriving city. I saw the glaciers part to let pass a great traffic in men and merchandise. I saw the unpeopled north grow into a land of homes, of farms, of mining-camps, where people lived and bred children. I heard the mountain passes echo to steam whistles and the whir of flying wheels. It was a wonderful vision that I saw, but my eyes were true." (*Iron Trail* 243)

There is millennial fervor in all this, for historically, Beach and the other novelists hearken deep into the American past. They tap nearly three centuries of anticipation that the utopian New Earth prophesied in the New Testament Book of Revelation would soon be realized on American soil. They follow an ideological tradition embedded in American culture from the Colonial era, and recorded by writers like the New England Puritans Cotton Mather and Edward Johnson and such Revolutionary figures as Joel Barlow and Timothy Dwight, and through nineteenth-century Romantic writers like the historian George Bancroft and the poet Walt Whitman.

These and many others had exploited the American belief in joint spiritual and material progress which was expected to culminate, imminently, in the millennium. This thousand-year period of social, spiritual, and environmental harmony is based conceptually upon Judeo-Christian prophesy. In American thought the issue has a complex, well-documented theological history concerned with religious typology and eschatology. Suffice it to say here that for upwards of three centuries virtually every writer or orator, whatever his or her level of education, found the apt millennial phrasing in the Old Testament prophesy of Isaiah, who foretold the desert blossoming like the rose. That is exactly the reference Rex Beach expected his readers to recognize when, in *The Iron Trail*, the ladylove thinks of her engineer's achievement, "He made the wilderness fruitful" (316). It is the very prophesy which Harold Bell Wright echoed in *The Winning of Barbara Worth*, when someone says of the Seer, "I've heard him say that hundreds [of] thousands [of] acres [of] these big deserts will be turned into farms, and all that by what he calls 'Reclamation'" (24).

The once popular, now-forgotten writers like Wright and Beach exploited millennial visions even as enduring writers of twentieth-century America largely abandoned them in disaffection. (Edward Bellamy was perhaps the last to engage intellectuals in the feasibility of the American New Earth.) One new element, however, enters the American imagination in these popular books, as Bellamy's *Looking Backward* hints in its anticipation of the thoroughly industrialized future. In these twentieth-century novels the impetus for the New Earth changes, for the key figure to bring about the American millennium is no longer, as in the past, the minister, the statesman, or the poet. It is instead the engineer. Power has passed from theology through politics, statecraft, and literature to settle upon technology. As the president of M.I.T. wrote in 1911, "Our grandfathers, looking down upon us, would feel that they observed a new heaven and a new earth" (*Mechanic Arts* xxv).

Technological expertise is only part of the story, though of course readers are invited to admire the engineering skills of these heroes. Is the proposed Union Pacific rail grade too steep?—"set a compound curve by intersections and we'll get much less than a ninety-foot grade to the mile" (*U. P. Trail* 214). Does financial recession threaten ruin?—develop a low-cost, automated "pit machine process for molding and casting [the] water- and gas-pipe" which municipalities must buy even in hard times (*Quickening* 207–8). Is the construction of an Alaskan bridge impossible?—show the reader how it can be done against the clock with caissons, abutments, falsework, piers, cantilevers, a "traveller" crane "somewhat like a tremendous cradle" (*Iron Trail* 333, 355–91). Then show readers the engineer-hero alone in the center of the span while the bridge withstands the smash of glacial ice in the Alaskan spring (a reassuring scene to readers well aware in 1913 that in the previous year icebergs sank that triumph of marine engineering, the *Titanic*).

Engineering feats in these novels refer directly, in fact, to successful projects, to the Union Pacific Railroad, the foundries of the Ohio River Valley, the Susitna Bridge of the Alaska Railroad—all of them readers' references intended to authenticate the values in the fiction. In a page of acknowledgments prefacing *The Winning of Barbara Worth*, Harold Bell Wright issues a disclaimer. He says that the novel is "not in any way a history of the Colorado Desert now known as the Imperial Valley, nor a biography of anyone connected with this splendid achievement." But Wright cites by name nine engineers, among them William Mulholland, chief engineer of the Los Angeles Aquaduct. Their work "in the past ten years has transformed a vast, desolate waste into a beautiful land of homes, cities, and farms" and has been, says Wright, "my inspiration."

The engineer's technological triumphs, however, are only in part the basis for heroism in these earlier twentieth-century popular novels. The other—and it is crucial—is the engineer's imperviousness to corruption. Inherently ethical, he resists every effort at political or financial influence liable to compromise his work or liable to endanger those whose safety depends upon it.

As the uncorruptible American surrounded by corporate and political greed, the engineer embodies the nation's purity of vision. The very spirit of the Republic endures in him. John Fox, Jr., emphasizes this point when he traces the genealogy of his modern engineer, a man whose "forefather had been with Washington on the Father's first historic expedition into the wilds of Virginia" and whose "great-grandfather had accompanied Boone . . . and come again with a surveyor's chain and compass" that the modern engineer inherits, in turn, from his father and uses to site "the unborn city of his dreams" (126, 40–45).

The hero-engineers in these novels not only resist corruption. They transcend it. Willard Holmes resigns from his uncle's corporation rather than proceed with a water-intake design whose specifications would leave settlers in jeopardy of ruinous floods. Later, as flood waters rise, Holmes saves both populace and property by building the dam whose necessity he had foreseen. His fictional counterpart, Warren Neale, is equally high-minded. He spurns bribes, fires the grafters, completes the work. Beyond that, he belongs to the engineering cognoscenti. "Neale," says the patriarchal chief engineer of the Union Pacific (a character modeled on the actual chief, Grenville Dodge), "Neale, there are two kinds of men building the U. P. R.—men who see the meaning of the great work, and men who see only the gold in it." Neale knows. He understands that the railroad directors and their partners think only "of money, of profits" while those like himself work for "an ideal," "a nobler motive" (295–96).

As national virtue inheres in the engineer, the soulless "company" of corporation executives, financiers, and politicians preoccupied with profits, stocks, and gold hatch their "labyrinthine plots." The "company" represents "the smoke and steam and bustle and greed of the Twentieth Century." Its demonic Moses is "the frenzied, ruthless spirit of commercialism." Its financial manipulations intermittently blight the work of engineers with boomtown crassness and desolate depressions. Consistently business, finance, and politics are the villains (*Trail of Lonesome Pine* 39; *Quickening* 315).

Yet the hero-engineer, which is to say America itself, prevails. In popular fiction the cowboy came to represent either a corporation overseer or a vanishing America embodied in the figure of an isolate on horseback. But the engineer suggests a different national future. It is emphatically social, civil, and stable. The engineer is its trustee and agent. "It [is] his business to win the wilderness over to order" (*Iron Trail* 45). His ambition is "to know how, and to do things; to compel iron and steel and the stubborn forces of nature . . . but better still, [to] be a leader of men" (*Quickening* 143). "The civil engineer . . . is the chief civilizer of our century" (*Soldiers of Fortune* 82). In the engineer the national vision remains pure and America's destiny intact.

Like much popular writing, the engineer-novels are mired in contradiction and internal conflict that probably escaped the notice of their authors and contemporary audiences as well. Opposing values are apt to collide in such books, which typically function to allay the anxieties of their cultural moment. Popular fiction may sharpen contemporary conflicts, but authors (and their readers) tend to want pacification and assurance, not ambiguity and ambivalence. These engineer novels, in particular, exhibit tortuous environmental values. Readers of *The Quickening* are told, for instance, that Thomas Jefferson Gordon has "the appreciative eye and heart of one born with a deep and abiding love of nature," while Jack Hale of *The Trail of the Lonesome Pine* has a "long submerged sense of the beauty of . . . [the] hills." Pristine nature is itself a character trait of these heroes (252).

Engineering work, however, hastens the transformation of the pristine environment. As a result of the heroes' labors the desert, at least large tracts of it, will disappear. So will the forest dwellings of Daniel Boone's heirs. A part of the engineer's own self would seem to be in jeopardy. But do the authors enact a struggle within a divided consciousness? Not at all. Do they force their engineers to confront the environmental conflict the authors themselves have focused on? Only briefly, when the heroes face the ecological costs attendant on their work. "Floating sawdust whirled in the eddies [of a stream] and the water was black as soot. . . . The black wash from the coal-mines had driven the perch from the pools and spoiled the swimming holes in the creek; [and] in the farther forests of the rampart hills the chopper's ax had been busy" (*Trail of the Lonesome Pine* 252, 201). A buzz saw savages a tree trunk, demon miners dig a shaft, and "the cruel, deadly work of civilization" proceeds (*Quickening* 161).

The engineers recoil in horror, but only for the moment. Anyway, they are exonerated. The authors imply that business and politics, not engineering, are the real culprits. Above all, these novels evade conflict with the panacea of romance. Is pristine nature disappearing?—no matter. It can be displaced and distilled into the very women the heroes fall in love with and marry. These women, the quintessence of front-parlor civilization in these books, ironically become totemic figures representing the vanishing America unmarked by industry or civil order. That America lives on in them, symbolically, into perpetuity. In *The Trail of the Lonesome Pine* the heroine, an Appalachian Pygmalion, is methodically schooled and civilized, yet always represents "the coolness of the shadows, the scent of the damp earth, and the faint fragrance of the wild flowers." The inventory goes on, for the heroine is "the incarnate spirit of it all." She and her engineer plan to efface all traces of industry from their secluded mountain cove ("I'll stock the river with bass again. I'll bury every bottle and tin can in the cove"). This park cleanup is an anodyne for readers encouraged to believe that the engineer's marriage to "the incarnate spirit" of nature will forever join pristine and industrialized America in conflict-free holy matrimony (257, 252, 415–16).

Accepting the engineer's proposal, the woman-as-nature also confers her blessing on his vision of transformation. Together Barbara Worth and her engineer, Holmes, survey the Imperial Valley now filled with the farms and towns made possible by an ample, engineered water supply:

> "You like my desert?" asked the young woman softly, coming closer to his side—so close that he felt her presence as clearly as he felt the presence of the spirit that lives in the desert itself.
>
> "Like it!" he repeated, turning toward her. "It is my desert now; mine as well as yours." (508–9)

The American earth, in the person of Barbara, symbolically blesses and legitimates the engineer's transformation (and possession) of it. It yields to his possession. Ambiguity and ambivalence are banished as the author refashions contradiction into conciliation.

The reading audiences loved it all, at least according to sales figures. Two of these engineer novels, *The Trail of the Lonesome Pine* and *The U. P. Trail*, were the number one best-sellers in 1908 and 1918 respectively, with combined sales conservatively set at 1,750,000. *Soldiers of Fortune* sold at least a half million copies in

Shooting the film, Soldiers of Fortune, *Santiago de Cuba, 1919*
(Courtesy Charles Scribner's Sons)

1897, while *The Winning of Barbara Worth* remained at the top of the best-seller list for two years, 1911–12, with sales of 1,635,000 copies. Though *The Iron Trail* never rose to such heights of popularity, its author, Rex Beach, was a best-selling author in the years 1906, 1908, 1909, and 1911, which suggests his intuitive grasp of the potential of engineering as a subject ripe for American fiction likely to perform well in the marketplace (Mott 225–33, 237, 312–13; Hackett 109, 113, 115, 124, 106, 210).

On the basis of these novels it is easy to see why, much to H. L. Mencken's bemusement, Americans of every occupational stripe would appropriate the title, engineer. His popular image as a figure of action and expertise, of personal restraint, and especially of unassailable ethics made the engineer the perfect occupational namesake, especially for those involved in trade and commerce, since, as "engineers," they could use semantics to allay customers' suspicions about the quality of materials and the margin of profit. They could, in addition, partake of the American destiny. Sinclair Lewis understood this mentality on the part of "sales-engineers." His middle American, the realtor George Babbitt, thinks of himself as "a prophetic engineer clearing the pathway for inevitable changes" (*Babbitt* 255).

The popular image of the engineer diverges from historians' findings on the actual experience of professional engineers from the late nineteenth century through the 1920s (and beyond). Engineers were not necessarily free of personal animus toward their peers, as the bitter professional rivalry between the bridge designers,

Vilma Banky as Barbara Worth and Ronald Colman as the hero-engineer in the Samuel Goldwin production, The Winning of Barbara Worth, *1926. The* New York Times *reviewer, mindful of the current spate of engineer movies, remarked that "the conflict between rival engineers in this picture struggles along in a rather tedious fashion, which may be due to the familiar aspect of this idea," though* Variety *hailed "this epic of the reclamation of the desert lands." (Courtesy Collector's Book Store, Hollywood, California)*

The
ENGINEER
looks into the FUTURE

WHEN the clock hands meet at midnight he is still at work... dreaming over streets and structures he will never live to see. He toils behind the scenes of great civic enterprises, the unsung prophet of comforts and economies which will bless the lives of generations as yet unborn.

Yet the engineer must contend with the fantasies of idealists, the rhetoric of demagogues, the lobbying of propagandists. He must check every contingency of the future against the facts and figures of today. He must bring the cool wisdom of science to every choice of methods or materials. He must properly appraise the "tremendous trifle"—the all-determining detail. Such a detail, for instance, as the kind of pipe to be used for underground gas and water mains.

The engineer who looks into the future specifies pipe which will long outlast the streets under which it is laid. He must guard against the heavy expense of tearing up thoroughfares for the replacement of short-lived pipe. And for *proved* long life he chooses cast iron pipe—for he knows there is cast iron pipe in use today which has served for more than two hundred and fifty years. Every engineer knows that cast iron pipe has served a century or more in leading American cities. That it is the *longest* wearing pipe being used for gas or water mains today. That cast iron pipe can be laid *and forgotten*. And that these facts hold great importance for the future—the decades which will bring staggering traffic difficulties, more costly street structures, greater tax burdens.

Civic minded taxpayers, conscientious public officials, shrewd city planners are listening attentively to the engineer who looks into the future, who is insistent upon the importance of the proper choice of pipe for gas and water mains. The Cast Iron Pipe Research Association is assisting with information on the use of cast iron pipe for water, gas, sewers, road culverts, and industrial needs.

This information is supplied for the asking. Address: The Cast Iron Pipe Research Association, Thomas F. Wolfe, Research Engineer, 122 South Michigan Avenue, Chicago. Copyright 1929, by C. I. P. R. Ass'n

CAST
IRON
PIPE

Cast Iron Pipe Research Association advertisement. Collier's, *1929*

This Body of Engineers
Build a *New* "33"—Self-Starting

Hudson Motor Car advertisement. Collier's, *1912*

David Steinman and Othmar Ammann, reveals. In the popular literature the hero-engineers are not only powerful and autonomous but free of antagonistic corporate interests as well. Robert Clay (*Soldiers of Fortune*) recognizes that he is only a salaried employee working to please and enrich the owner of a mine. "[But] I don't say, 'I am a salaried servant'; I put it differently. I say, 'There are five mountains of iron. You are to take them up and transport them to North America, where they will be turned into railroads and ironclads.' That's my way of looking at it" (98, 149–50).

One can only speculate on the degree to which actual engineers similarly rationalized their professional status. As the historians Edwin Layton and David Noble have shown, engineers were typically the employees of large corporations. When their judgment conflicted with the interests of their employers, they had no recourse to the professional autonomy enjoyed by physicians and attorneys, despite their efforts to gain strength in numbers through the formation of professional engineering societies. The career path of ambitious and successful engineers, moreover, often led directly into corporate management. Edwin Layton writes, "These [managerial] men did not repudiate the ideology of engineering, but instead they sought to use it to reaffirm the engineer's loyalty to his employer" (*Revolt of Engineers* viii).

*" Came Prometheus, the Fire-Bringer, he who snatched
from the sun's glowing chariot thrice-precious fire
and brought it, hidden in a fennel-stalk, to earth,
that men might live like gods in its pleasant warmh."*
(Transl. Greek Myth)

THIS is today's Prometheus . . . . . Bringer
of comforts . . . . The Chemical Engineer!

One of civilization's pioneers, it is he who has
brought to mankind comforts and conveniences
that a century ago were only wishes.

It is he who, searching in the hidden depths of
Nature, has bared her secrets and laid at the feet
of the world's industries new substances, new uses
for them, new ways of using the present materials of commerce in the satisfying of man's wants.

It is he who, watching on the frontiers of science,
has seen in his test-tubes visions of industries yet
unborn that are to drive commerce to the far corners of the earth in the service of man's needs.

The world's debt to The Chemical Engineer is
one that can never be paid.

*This is one of a series of advertisements published
that the public may have a clearer understanding
of E. I. du Pont de Nemours & Co. and its products.*

E. I. DU PONT DE NEMOURS & COMPANY, Inc., *Wilmington, Del.*

TRADE **DU PONT** MARK

Collier's The National Weekly, July 15, 1922. Volume 70, Number 3. Entered as second-class matter, July 22, 1915, at the Post Office, at New York, N. Y., under the Act of March 3, 1879, and at the Post Office Department, Ottawa, Canada, by P. F. Collier & Son Company, 416 West 13th St., New York, N. Y. Price: 5 cents a copy, $2.50 a year; 10 cents a copy, $3.00 a year in Canada and Foreign Countries. Manufactured in U. S. A.

Du Pont de Nemours & Co. advertisement. Collier's, *1922 (Courtesy Du Pont Corp.)*

Gathering Raw Materials   *for OSBORN BRUSHES*

Not merely built but "engineered"

THERE are two ways of making brushes. The *Osborn* way is to study the *use* for which the brush is intended and then design the best brush for that use, regardless of whether or not the result follows past brush-making habits. Guess-work steps out—science steps in.

That method of procedure assures every purchaser of an *Osborn* Brush the best combination of design (shape), materials (fibre, wire, bristles or hair) and construction (method of fastening bristles in place) which can be achieved at the price offered.

Brush Divison of

THE OSBORN MFG. CO.
INCORPORATED

New York CLEVELAND Detroit
Chicago   San Francisco

A sanitary brush for cleaning closet bowls should be in every home—but should have no metal to rust. Osborn No. 33 is scientifically constructed for this specific and vitally necessary use.

The Osborn "KITCHEN-AID"—a brush that lightens the labor of cleaning milk bottles, washing dishes, scrubbing vegetables or cleaning the sink. Some housewives keep three handy in a kitchen.

A "delightful household convenience"—that's the way one owner describes Osborn Floor Brush No. 14. Ideal for hardwood floors; sweeps the kitchen without raising dust; is equally convenient for porches, sidewalks and basements.

Don't let washing your auto break your back. Let an Osborn No. 417 dig the dirt from the chassis and beneath the fenders. The stiff genuine palmetto does not soften in water. The long handle saves your back and keeps your arms and hands out of water.

Osborn No. 364—a scrub brush with a handle. In the navy it's called a "deck scrub". The stiff Palmetto fibre digs the dirt out of wood and concrete floors. Note the rubber squeegee along the back.

Cleaning the furnace! ! ! ! At last it has been made a reasonable task. Osborn No. 5733, newly invented, bends its way into any part of a furnace. The wire of the brush portion is specially tempered for this particular use.

OSBORN
BRUSHES OF MERIT

Osborn Mfg. Co. advertisement (Courtesy Osborn Manufacturing, Unit of Jason, Inc.)

❧ Balboa crushed savage human foes; the engineer conquered disease, a far more deadly enemy.

❧ Balboa brought bloodshed and ruin to the natives of the Isthmus; the engineer brought prosperity and peace.

❧ Balboa aimed to monopolize the Pacific and the lands it bathes; the engineer united two oceans by a world-free waterway.

❧ Balboa left no trail; the trail of the engineer will endure for ages.

❧ The Conquistador hungered for loot and selfish gain; the engineer builded that men might live and profit by a greater freedom of the seas.

❧ Conquerors both, which was the greater?

The Panama Canal project prompted one anonymous writer to contrast modern engineers to the Spanish conquistadors. (Courtesy National Museum of American History, Smithsonian Institution)

It is noteworthy that the hero-engineers in these novels are not modeled on inventors familiar to the public. There is no Cyrus McCormick or Eli Whitney among them, no "Wizard of Menlo Park" or Henry Ford. They are not figures of idiosyncratic genius, but types of a new professional class. "In all the professions," says Harold Bell Wright in his preface to *The Winning of Barbara Worth*, "there can be found no finer body of men than our civil engineers." These men are, as a class, the industrial-age conservators of America. Together they form an elect who advance democracy over and against the corruptive perils of corporate capitalism and its politics.

Popular America was no onlooker to the engineers' internecine wars or struggles with their professional identity, certainly not in best-selling fiction with its reliance on adventure, action, and romance. In fiction the engineers are heroes, not technocrats. The novelists' historical inaccuracies are finally less significant than their affirmation of national destiny in the representative figure of industrialized America. From their checkered backgrounds in mining, fire-brick manufacture, journalism, railroading, banking, and the ministry these novelists, together with their millions of readers, saw the engineer as the American ideal in modern guise.

"By Their Works, Ye Shall Know Them"

AVID H. MOFFAT, one of the outstanding men in the history of the State of Colorado, dreamed a dream of empire-building—a vision that dared to release the resources of a vast territory inconveniently locked away by the unconquered Colorado Rockies.

This is a story of a fulfillment of that dream, a narrative of seasoned construction skill towering bigger and bigger, translating rosy romance into practical accomplishment. In the doing, there was a continuous struggle between man and nature, a conflict between resourcefulness and the raw, unfettered, primitive forces within a gigantic mountain.

Against the cutting of steel drills and the bite of the shovel, the mountain released rock pressures so great that time and time again, massive Douglas fir plumb posts, set less than a foot apart, were bowed to the breaking point. Great floods of water from vast subterranean reservoirs were flung headlong to crush human ingenuity. Hardened granite gave way to a shear zone of rock that was heated and twisted, ground and kneaded by some prehistoric disturbance that had changed the face of the world. Indeed, a new work on the geology of the Rocky Mountains needs to be written.

Construction ability and the loyal support of courageous workmen met every crisis successfully. In the winning of the struggle against the obstacles of nature, brilliant discoveries were made that are a definite contribution to tunnelling science.

Our triumph was shared by the world when on February 18, 1927, President Calvin Coolidge touched the golden key in Washington, D. C., to blast away the last barrier in the Water Tunnel.

We leave you here to take up the story of the great achievement, feeling that by their works the Contractors may be judged.

Engineers sometimes portrayed themselves and their work in the same heroic terms as in film and fiction. Reprinted here is the dedicatory page from The Contractors' Story of the Moffat Tunnel, *1927. (Courtesy National Museum of American History, Smithsonian Institution)*

THE SOVIET OF TECHNICIANS

The late-twentieth-century reader may smile at the naiveté of the popular novels. The notion of the engineer as the embodiment of American democracy may strain credulity. Encountered in novels or movies, it is the stuff of melodrama. But it cannot be dismissed only as grist for the mill of popular culture. The aggrandizement of the engineers broke the confines of popular novels consumed by "golden multitudes" of readers—because the American intelligentsia also approved of the hero-engineers. To a remarkable degree, the argument made in *The Winning of Barbara Worth* and similar novels is the very argument made for an intellectual and academic audience by the socialist economist, Thorstein Veblen.

Veblen, as we saw earlier, aroused readers to an awareness of waste in his first and only popular book, *The Theory of the Leisure Class*. Sinclair Lewis no doubt had that very title in mind when in *Main Street* he described his character Carol Kennicott drowsily listening to her husband stoke the furnace for the night, then trying "to read a page of Thorstein Veblen" (255). Had she succeeded, Carol could have followed Veblen's technologically redemptive argument through *The Theory of Business Enterprise (BE)* (1904), *The Instinct of Workmanship and the State of the Industrial Arts (IW)* (1914), *The Higher Learning in America* (1918), *The Vested Interests and the State of the Industrial Arts* (1919), and *The Engineers and the Price System (EPS)* (1921).

Readers have found these titles to constitute an oeuvre. Consistently it argues that the culture of business and finance is an archaic, corrupt impediment to the material abundance which technologists could bring about in America if freed to exercise their instincts or proclivities of workmanship. These instincts surpass the manual dexterity and aesthetic taste which customarily define the artisan or craftsman. Veblen's scheme makes room for machine technicians. In the machine culture the instinct of workmanship comes into play "whenever a challenging objective is established and materials are competently manipulated to reach it." Veblen thus opens the way to an appreciation of machine technology in and of itself. In the modern world it is the disciplinarian of clear-headed thinking and of effective work methods (West 75; D. W. Noble 72–105).

Veblen's is a world in class conflict, but the antagonists are not those familiar to readers of Karl Marx. Veblen's division is not between those who control the means of production and a proletariat empowered only by its capacity to work. Instead, Veblen's classes divide by their habits of thinking. On the one side are the archaic, preindustrial-minded businessmen and their minions, the attorneys, clerks, clerics, sportsmen, and military. On the other are the engineers, scientists, technicians, and industrial workers, a confederation whose way of thinking accords with evolutionary change and has been shaped by the machine process itself. They represent the potential for "revolutionary overturn" of old ways. As one reader remarks, Veblen had been "preaching the coming millennium for almost thirty years" by the time he wrote his self-styled memorandum on a "soviet of technicians" in 1919 (*Theory of Leisure Class* x; D. W. Noble 101).

It is possible that Veblen's embrace of the engineers began with his discovery of Bellamy's *Looking Backward*, which he read with his first wife, Ellen Rolfe, on her uncle's farm in Stacyville, Iowa, in the years before Veblen launched his multivolume dissection of capitalist culture. Ellen wrote of the couple's response to the Bellamy novel, "This was the turning-point in our lives" (Dorfman 68).

If so, Veblen was biographically prepared for it. As Henry Steele Commager has remarked, Veblen's theories and insights were common coin of Middle Border farmers who learned firsthand the distinction between business and engineering. Any Kansas Populist or western farmer, Commager observed, could compare "the constructive work of building the transcontinentals with the destructive work of exploiting them" (238). As farmers they could recognize that such legislation as the Homestead Act of 1862, the Desert Land Act of 1877, and the Timber and Stone Act of 1878—all intended to benefit settlers and farmers—instead enriched speculators and the railroad, mining, and timber interests. Farmers' politics may have given Veblen grounds ultimately to flay American business for its spirit of compromise, collusion, and corruption.

But farm life also gave him good reason to prize the power of technology. During boyhood he saw his father, a Norwegian immigrant farmer, succeed in large part because of his technological innovations. Thomas Anderson Veblen ordered the first two-horse power thresher in Manitowoc, Minnesota, and was first in the area to install drains and buy a "platform binder" or "harvester," which the young Veblen liked to operate. By nature the boy had a personal proclivity for the efficiency of well-designed machinery. Veblen's biographer notes his "mechanical ingenuity" and "highly developed sense of economy of effort." A farmhand observed that he had never seen "such a lazy-looking person who performed his job with so few motions." As an unemployed intellectual in the early 1880s, Veblen occupied himself by inventing farm implements (Dorfman 6, 10, 12, 57, 272). In a rural, agricultural setting he learned to appreciate the ameliorative value of machine technology in lives burdened by unremitting toil.

Veblen identified "the machine culture" with the twentieth century, urban and rural. Like Bellamy, he characterized it in machine terms as "a delicately balanced moving equilibrium of working parts, no one of which can do its work by itself" (*TBE* 55, 119). It is "self-balanced," "a system of interlocking mechanical processes" (52–53). This is not the Newtonian clockworks world of the eighteenth-century Deists, but an evolutionary, post-Darwinian world of constant change. Finely calibrated, its tolerance for error diminishes with its increasing complexity.

Worse, it is constantly subject to sabotage and obstruction by businessmen, financiers, and the "one-eyed captains of industry." In machine terms they represent "lag, leak, and friction." Their beneficiaries are "the kept classes," in Veblen's ironic phrasing the very concubines of capitalism. From the socialist perspective they are superstitious, barbaric, financially self-interested, retrograde (*EPS* 64, 74).

Veblen had particular historical reasons for his beliefs. While teaching at Stanford University in the mid-1900s he grew friendly with Guido Marx, a professor of mechanical engineering who later, in the 1910s, made him aware of the reform movement within the American Society of Mechanical Engineers (A.S.M.E.). Through Marx, Veblen learned something of two reform-minded activists, Morris L. Cooke and Henry L. Gantt, who were rallying younger engineers concerned about industrial waste and mismanagement because they were dismayed by engineers' captivity to big business and the utilities.

Between 1917 and 1920, as Veblen learned, Cooke had succeeded in reforming the A.S.M.E., which Gantt considered a prelude to the engineers' control of the economy through public service corporations for which precedent was set during World War I by the federal government. Gantt had read and admired Veblen's earlier work and, thanks to Guido Marx, Veblen now read Gantt's writings and used them as a source for *The Engineers and the Price System*. In 1916 Gantt had formed New Machine, a group of mechanical engineers whose ultimate objective was to gain political and economic power. It seemed to Veblen the beginning of the "soviet of technicians" and, when the New School for Social Research opened in New York City in the fall of 1919, Veblen, who was teaching there, was instrumental in an attempt to organize the engineers (Dorfman 453–55; Layton, *Revolt of the Engineers* 227 and "Veblen and the Engineers"). Ironically the effort failed, as a historian of engineering recounts, because from the outset Veblen had misperceived the essentially middle-class and status-seeking nature of the reform movement. Like the novelists, Veblen was ignorant of the nature of the professionals he characterized in heroic terms.

Veblen apparently needed his fiction of a class of functional intellectuals "whose end is very simply to serve human needs" (*EPS* 132). His engineers, progeny of the machine process, are free of the business culture's animism and its make-believe of "anthropomorphic subtleties" (*IW* 310–11). Impersonal, the machine process which schools them "gives no insight into questions of good and evil, merit and demerit; it knows neither manners nor breeding." It disciplines them to handle impersonal facts for mechanical effect. The engineers deal solely, in Veblen's favorite phrase, with "matter-of-fact," for their thought contains "no mysterious element of providential ambiguity." They work only on the basis of "ascertained quantitative fact." Their proficiency is itself a measure of their mastery of "the matter-of-fact logic involved in mechanical processes of pressure, velocity, displacement, and the like" (*IW* 306–7; *BE* 310–11). As the training ground of the engineers, the machine process is, in Veblen's view, the liberator. It provides the opportunity for freedom from the historical baggage of the business culture. It can liberate America from its historical misdirection. It is, in sum, transformational.

Veblen was circumspect about the outlook for a transformed state of things. He never ventured to describe a technological utopia and was not mesmerized by machine technology per se. (He saw the telephone, typewriter, and automobile, for instance, as serviceable inventions appropriated by the business class as armaments in competitive warfare.) (*IW* 311–15). But he saw a social ideology devolving from the engineer, that professional exponent of efficiency and stability. The engineer would function as guarantor of the material welfare of "civilized peoples" and of "the underlying population" (*EPS* 58, 69, 75, 142, 163–66). Reacting against the Gilded Age, he envisioned a class of ruler-managers free of historical superstition and pecuniary interests, one uniquely qualified and positioned to allocate resources, to plan the employment of people and machines, to supply goods and services equitably and sufficiently.

All this may sound at once soulless and techno-mystical, but it must be remembered that Veblen saw the engineers as redeemers of a culture debased by predatory businessmen. In his view, religion, education, work life, even war and patriotism had become hostile to human interests as each succumbed to the predations of business enterprise in the modern world. Now, in the midst of the Red scare with its anti-Bolshevist riots (and in frank admiration of the goals of the Russian Revolution), Veblen espoused the revolutionary cause of an American soviet of engineers. Starting in April 1919, readers of the *Dial*, a magazine of artists and intellectuals, would find Veblen's hymns to engineers as the "General Staff of the industrial system," and as the leaders of the workmen and "officers of the line and rank and file" (*EPS* 69, 80). Behind them stand "the massed and rough-handed legions of the industrial rank and file, ill at ease and looking for new things" (80–81). A "revolutionary overturn" is imminent, even if a self-conscious Veblen hedges his millennial bet (e.g., "no move of this nature has been made hitherto," not "just yet") (138). His title, nonetheless, betrays his motive: "A Memorandum on a Practicable Soviet of Technicians." *Practicable*: the word is a call to action as economist Veblen tries to become the catalyst of the imminent revolution.

It is helpful to juxtapose Veblen against the contemporary popular writers, though his readers seem uneasy, even embarrassed, that such a rigorously skeptical, searching mind—as John Dos Passos put it, a mind "dissecting out the century with a scalpel so clean . . . that the professors and students . . . and the magnates and respected windbags . . . never knew it was there"—could succumb to a quasi religion of technocracy. In sympathy, Dos Passos summarized Veblen's alternatives: "a warlike society strangled by the bureaucracies of the monopolies . . . or a new matter-of-fact commonsense society dominated by the needs of the men and women who did the work and the incredibly vast possibilities for peace and plenty offered by the progress of technology" (*U.S.A.: Big Money* 102, 109).

The novelist identifies the political basis of Veblen's thought. But we can see that Veblen's "soviet of technicians" is by no means an eccentric ideal, given the popular fiction and language usage of the time. On the contrary, Veblen is in full accord with the popular writers and with those who became the butt of Mencken's satire. All of them believed that power and action in the twentieth century centered in the engineer. In this sense Veblen's "soviet of technicians" belongs with the popular fiction of the American mainstream.

It does, that is, with one crucial qualification. Veblen stands apart from the popular novelists by virtue of his indeterminacy. The novelists' hero-engineers sustain a foreordained American destiny. They are agents of its unfolding, and America patiently awaits them. They transcend and prevail because they are destined to do so.

The case of Veblen's engineers is different, problematic. They are part of a changeful historical process whose outcome is uncertain, for their industrial-age millennium is not nationally predestined, much as it is to be desired and sponsored. Veblen's rhetoric is urgent but stops short of declaring that the barbarians of business will be defeated or circumvented.

DYNAMO, VIRGIN, ENGINEER

Henry Adams was another who shared the historicist's anxiety about social change. Like Veblen, Adams was skeptical of the notion of moral and material progress, yet he resorted to the engineer to convey his hope for the future of civilization. Adams, like Veblen, enjoyed dissecting systems of politics, society, and religion, revealing their contradictions and illogic in tones of irony. Yet Adams too looked to the example of the engineer for the potential redemption of the wayward culture. He expressed his intellectual (and temperamental) doubt in arguments based in the physical sciences as Veblen located his in anthropology. Like the second-generation Norwegian-American, moreover, this grandson and great-grandson of presidents thought the engineer represented an intelligentsia empowered to stabilize, and even to advance, twentieth-century civilization.

A member of the fourth generation of one of America's most prominent families, Henry Brooks Adams (1838–1918) was variously a world traveler, diplomatic private secretary, reformer in the vein of the muckraking journalists, college professor, editor, and historian. In American literature his novels (*Democracy* 1879; *Esther* 1884, published under a pen name) are regarded as a minor achievement, but his mastery of form and style in his quasi-autobiography *The Education of Henry Adams* (*E*) (1907) has prompted comparison with the work of his contemporary, Henry James (Harbert 190). Critical of machinery, the *Education* has been read as a trenchant critique of technology and its values, even as a doomsday prophesy of the inhuman technocracy. The discursive part, however, is not the whole, and a close look at Adams shows that the achievement and potential of the engineer informs all his major texts, buoying his esteem for democracy and undergirding his tenuous hope of the attainment of a future "some day" when he and his closest friends might return to "find a world that sensitive and timid natures could regard without a shudder" (*E* 505).

If *Looking Backward* is a hymn to an engineered America, *The Education of Henry Adams* has warned many readers that the engineer's devices are Faustian objects. To many, Adams's juxtaposed symbols, the modern dynamo and the medieval Virgin Mary, speak volumes on the soulless machine which has supplanted the world of mediation and compassion, of unified purpose and communal energies. Adams's chapter, "The Dynamo and the Virgin (1900)," has been repeatedly excerpted from the *Education* and reprinted, its central figures seeming less like symbols than cultural artifacts telling the ghastly truth about historical change.

As one reader remarks, "On the one side [of the Virgin, Adams] lines up heaven, beauty, religion, and reproduction; on the other [of the dynamo,] hell, utility, science, and production" (Marx 347).

Yet the ethos of the engineer is much in evidence in Adams's writing, including the *Education*, *Mont Saint-Michel and Chartres* (1904), and the *History of the United States during the Administration of Thomas Jefferson . . . [and] James Madison* (1884–89). If Henry Adams deplores a machine-age wasteland, he argues covertly for a technological-philosophical redemption of America. The *Education* is directed to "active-minded . . . young men of the world" whom Adams's biographer identifies as "philosopher technicians of a new society" (Samuels 362). They are virtually a Young America able to retrieve the industrial, governmental machine from the barbarians and to redirect its purpose.

That Young America populates Adams's *History* (*H*) in a roll call of early 1800s inventors who went far to realize American ideals. The nine-volume *History* is framed in tributes to engineering inventiveness and its implementation of the national vision. Adams's historical search for the corps of "active-minded" philosopher-technicians of America was a quest for those "who count as force even in the mental inertia of sixty or eighty million people" (*E* 315). They include inventors as well as political leaders.

The *History* sets forceful engineers against inert agrarians, including Thomas Jefferson. In opening chapters Adams praises Jefferson's "liberality of ideas." If the Virginian political heritage were missing, "no small part" of American history would be lost (1:138). But in reproof Adams notes that Jefferson was typically Virginian in discouraging manufacture and urbanization. Without them, "no new life could grow." The height of Virginian ambition, writes Adams, "was to fix upon the national government the stamp of idyllic conservation [of] . . . a future Arcadian America."

The term "arcadian" is fraught with connotation. Literally it means simple manners and tastes. But Adams's usage implies a pastoral ideal suited to Elizabethan poems, not to the sociopolitical and economic realities of a rugged continent. Adams depicts America of 1800: "After two centuries of struggle the land was still untamed; forests covered every portion, except here and there a strip of cultivated soil; the minerals lay undisturbed in their beds, and more than two thirds of the people clung to the seaboard" (1:1–5). The problem, in Adams's view, was both simple and monumental: "nature was rather man's master than his servant." Five million struggling Americans were hardly better at bridge- and road-building than the beavers and buffalo. The question was, How could human beings equipped with axes and wagon wheels become better civil engineers than the dumb beasts?

Adams had his two-word answer, steam power. In 1800, he writes, "every American knew that if steam could be successfully applied to navigation, it must produce an immediate increase of wealth" and settle "the most serious material and political difficulties of the Union." Adams regrets that for too long the government and the people thought steam power a novelty or chimera and failed to sponsor its research and development. He presents a sad roster of prophets without honor, starting with John Fitch, ("a mechanic without education or wealth, but with the energy of genius"), who in 1789 plied the Delaware River in a ferryboat with an engine and paddles of his own design. Spurned by the public, Fitch ended his life a suicide. "But he did not stand alone." One Oliver Evans, "the American Watt," also engineered a "locomotive steam-engine which he longed [in vain] to bring into common use." A rueful Adams writes that even the best-known engineer of his day, Benjamin Latrobe, was dubious of the new power.

"But within four years a steamboat was running," and "Latrobe was its warmest friend." Why?—because "a few visionaries" like Chancellor Livingston, Joel Barlow, John Stevens, Samuel L. Mitchill, and Robert Fulton "dragged society forward." Adams casts the situation as a problem in physics. Innovative force overcame conservative inertia embodied even in "radicals as extreme as Thomas Jefferson and Albert Gallatin." Unimaginative, they aspired only to the American replication of a simple, vice-free "European Republican society." Adams teaches his lesson. With "half a continent to civilize," Americans "must devise new scientific processes" (1:66–74).

And they did, according to his discussion of "American Ideals." There Adams took the opportunity to praise "the average American," using his favorite kinetic phrase, "active-minded." His examples begin with Benjamin Franklin, who antici-pated the hapless Fitch but also the successful Eli Whitney, the clockmaker Eli Terry, the inventor of a machine for carding wool, the inventor of a nail-making machine, the inventor who "revolutionized cotton printing," and the designer of an improved flour mill. These were men who raised America's standard of living and its creative power. "All these men," says Adams, "were the outcome of typical American society, and all their inventions transmuted the democratic instinct into a practical and tangible shape" (1:181–83).

Adams's honor roll of American visionaries mixes names that might startle those accustomed to sort technology and the humanities into separate categories. Lincoln, Ralph Waldo Emerson, the Unitarian William Ellery Channing, and the Quakers keep company with the inventors John Fitch, Oliver Evans, Robert Fulton, John Stevens, and Eli Whitney—"all classed among visionaries" (1:171). (Even Jefferson comes in for tribute as "the inventor of the first scientific plough, the importer of the first threshing machine known in Virginia, the experimenter with a new drilling machine" [1:32].)

Engineering achievement subsides to a minor place in Adams's account of the administrations of Jefferson and Madison. But in the closing chapters of his final volume of the *History* the author revives the subject. He defines the "national character" by the "quickness of intelligence" demonstrable in successful inven-tions. Many are military, including naval gunnery, Fulton's torpedo, the screw propeller, the pivot gun, and improved ship design, itself the result of expedience. Battles themselves are testing laboratories which prove American efficiency of "scientific engineering . . . achieved at West Point." Adams sings hymns of praise to the military engineers, who "introduced a new and scientific character into American life" (9: 218–42).

To read Adams's passages on "American Ideals" achieved by home-grown engineers is perhaps to feel caught in a time warp. The notion of democracy objectified in engineers' designs had once been a futuristic vision of certain Enlightenment and Jacksonian figures. But Adams, a habitual skeptic, wrote his *History* in the Gilded Age and knew the lessons of hindsight. He was an adult during the Civil War (that "waste of immense energy") (*E* 240). He knew that the primeval bridges and roads of the beaver and buffalo became the trestles and track monopolized by corporate moguls swilling at the federal trough during the "stone age" of the Grant administration. He knew of the violent railroad strike of 1876 which exemplified the social unrest that was ancillary to the mechanization of transport. Adams, always a caustic social critic, knew as well that some contemporary voices were dubious of life shaped by machine technology. As of the late 1870s certain writers suggested that mechanization was "beyond control" and a contributor to "American nervousness" (G. Beard, *American Nervousness*).

Adams, then, was in a perfect position to write a jeremiad, at least to suggest that Fitch, Whitney, and others were illusionists and not visionaries, as Henry David Thoreau had suspected. Disabusing others of their illusions was always Adams's forte. Instead he argued, without qualification, that American engineers had transmuted their democratic instincts into a practical and tangible shape. He reserved criticism for the laggards who impeded them.

Henry Adams's attitude remained consistent as he went on to the writings of his "major phase," his study of the medieval cathedrals and religious life, *Mont Saint-Michel and Chartres* (*Mont*), and his autobiography, the *Education*. Not all readers have recognized this constancy. Some find *Mont Saint-Michel and Chartres* to be an "antimodern" text of a writer recoiling in protest from the frenzy of contemporary civilization (Lears 285–87). Adams, after all, did spoof himself as a "twelfth century monk in a nineteenth-century attic" and surrounded himself with men like the artist of stained glass, John La Farge, and the poet of fin-de-siècle weariness, Bay Lodge, both of whom were deeply involved in the pre-Raphaelite movement fathered by John Ruskin. There is a good basis on which to say of Adams that "beneath the swirling chaos [of contemporary life] he stood poised on his granite foothold of the past" (Samuels 217).

It is, however, more accurate to say that Adams looked at medieval France with a modern eye. He studied the Middle Ages as a man of contemporary outlook and not as a poignant, turn-of-the-century misfit. For Adams gazed at medieval France with the consciousness of one accustomed to mechanization and, in particular, to the functional aesthetic of the tall iron- and steel-framed structures engineered and built in the contemporary moment.

Adams's imagination, as his *History* reveals, warmed to the potential of steam-powered machinery, the kind with visibly moving parts, like the Philadelphia pump powered "at the rate of twelve strokes of six feet, per minute . . . or one stroke every five seconds" (*H* 70). But in the 1880s one of the most impressive achievements of the engineers was not strictly speaking a machine, but a structure. Tall iron- and steel-framed bridges and buildings were rising in every major American city and testified to the newest success of the engineer. Accordingly, the structural side of engineering—or structural art, as it has recently been defined—interested Adams as he turned to his study of French cathedrals of the Middle Ages.

In large part Adams qualified by virtue of his experience as a Harvard College professor of medieval history (1870–77). But there was another side to his preparation. For decades the cosmopolitan Adams had undergone a different, equally important schooling in the informal, random education of rail travel and passage through the great terminals and cities. He would have seen London's Paddington Station (1852–54), whose engineers "created a huge vault of wrought iron ribs carrying a shell of glass and iron," and New York's Grand Central Terminal (1869–70), the first comparable structure in the United States. As a railway passenger he traveled through industrial zones and saw the webbing of bridges, the structural forms of an "organic architecture appropriate to the mechanized industrial culture." These were the designs of such figures as James B. Eads, the Roeblings, and Gustave Eiffel, structural artist-engineers who were, in Carl Condit's words, "imbued with a sense of the harmony and proportion of trained architects" (Condit 4, 5; Stilgoe 17–46, 73–104; Billington 99–128).

As a traveler, moreover, Adams saw the new urban buildings such as Louis Sullivan's Bayard Building (1897–98) and Daniel Burnham's Fuller (or "Flatiron") Building (1901–3), both in New York. Adams's onetime college classmate, Henry Hobson Richardson, the architect of Adams's own house in Washington, D.C., designed the "first architectural masterpiece" of the new Chicago. Richardson's Marshall Field Wholesale Store (1885–87) has been described as a "magnificently rugged masonry box" whose articulation depends "almost solely on the pattern of window openings," which were themselves a principal feature of the new Chicago commercial style (Condit 70). Since the 1870s combinations of cast and wrought iron had allowed minimal walls and maximal openings for glass and, therefore, light for the interiors.

The steel framing of the 1880s continued the new style whose architects were, as William Jordy notes, remarkable for their youth and for their backgrounds in engineering, a point David Billington develops at length. A Scottish journalist of 1900 surveyed the new skyscrapers of Chicago and New York and called them "simply astonishing manifestations of human energy and heaven-storming audacity" (qtd. in Jordy 44–45).

By 1890 the new Chicago commercial style of structural art was on full view. Visiting the city in 1893, Henry Adams could have seen Richardson's Romanesque Marshall Field Wholesale Store, in addition to such structures as Daniel Burnham and John Wellborn Root's steel-framed Ashland Block, the Monadnock Building (1884–92), and the Masonic Building (1891–92), which at the time of its construction was the tallest building in the world. It is inconceivable that in Chicago Adams ignored this architectural world's fair.

In fact, we can best route Henry Adams to twelfth-century France by way of his travels to the World's Columbian Exposition in Chicago in 1893. In May he made a two-day "whistle stop" visit to the fair with friends bound for Europe and already planned his return in late September for a "fortnight" stay that actually stretched to twenty days. Perhaps Adams traveled to Chicago via the New York Central's luxurious *Exposition Flyer*, which carried thousands of passengers from New York City to the fair. In any case, architecture was on his mind at the exposition's White City, that "Beaux Arts artistically induced to pass the summer on the shore of Lake Michigan" (*E* 340). Adams had some personal interest in this fair, for his friend, Augustus St. Gaudens, was its official adviser on sculpture. St. Gaudens had once declared that the fair's principal architects constituted "the greatest meeting of artists since the fifteenth century" (Badger 68). Such ecstasies virtually predetermined Adams's report in the *Education* that the White City's architects felt they cast their pearls, if not before swine, then before the bovine infidels who saw their designs as so many diamond shirt studs (*E* 341).

Adams sympathized. He mused that if the middle westerners "knew what was good when they saw it," they would talk about the architects and artists "when their politicians and their millionaires were otherwise forgotten" (*E* 341). He himself had in mind a book of travels "with a volume or two . . . [on] the Fair." He would "talk about architecture, and discuss the relation of a galaxy of architects to the world" (Samuels 122). Meanwhile in Chicago, according to the *Education*, he sat on the steps of Richard Hunt's Administration Building like Gibbon at the Ara Coeli trying to divine the cultural symbolism of its dome (*E* 340).

And yet Adams often left the campus of the White City, drawn by the "seductive vanity" of the "other" fair, the adjacent Midway intended by the Beaux Arts architect-planners to be separate and decidedly unequal. "We haunt the lowest Fakes of the Midway, day and night," wrote Adams. "We have turned somersets in the Ferris wheel" (*Letters*, ed. Ford 2:33n).

It was no ordinary wheel. The Pittsburgh bridge engineer, George Washington Gale Ferris, had reportedly designed the structure in direct response to Burnham's criticism that the engineers had fallen short in their proposals for the fair and had submitted nothing as novel or original as Gustave Eiffel's tower erected for the Paris Exposition of 1889–90. When the Chicago Fair Planning Committee (including engineers) rejected Ferris's plan and excluded his wheel from the White City, the enterprising engineer formed a joint stock company and won a concession in the entertainment zone, the Midway. Behind its facade of anthropological education lay a bazaar of donkey and camel rides, jugglers, dancing girls, and ethnic foods. A Californian operated an ostrich farm, and the Fleishmann's Yeast Company "engaged Jim Corbett to give [pugilistic] demonstrations of how he had defeated the great John L. Sullivan" (Badger 107–9).

In 1893 Henry Adams thus made his way through the Gypsy band, the "instant-replays" of the boxing championship, the French pavilion in which peasants pressed cider served by Normandy maids. Towering over all of them, tremendous in size and popularity, was the Ferris Wheel on which Adams turned his "somersets" at fifty cents a ride. Actually, it was two wheels, each 264 feet in diameter, between which thirty-six cars were suspended, each one larger than a Pullman coach. On a full car Adams would have been one of sixty passengers on a swivel seat or standing up. At capacity he would have been one of 2,100 passengers on the wheel and, at the top, would have been as high as the Statue of Liberty. The axle of Ferris's wheel was the largest piece of steel ever forged, and its towers were designed to withstand winds of one hundred miles per hour. An engine of two thousand horse power turned it. One chronicler marveled, "What next? Shall we not in time be able to invade the lunar territory?" (Badger 108). And one civil engineer wrote that the wheel encircled the domes of the White City like a halo (qtd. in Kouwenhoven, *Half a Truth* 113).

How we might wish that Adams had commented further on the wheel and, during his visit to the Paris Exposition four years earlier, had remarked on Gustave Eiffel's tower. For if the relative merits of those two structures are debatable, the visitor's experience of them is quite similar. Roland Barthes's comment on the Eiffel Tower is helpful. On approach, he says, pure line gives way to the perception of "countless segments, interlinked, crossed, divergent." The appearance of "the straight line [or additionally, in the case of the wheel, of the circle or ellipse] becomes its contrary reality, a lacework of broken substances." Barthes understands this close-up perceptual change to be a demystification as "the visitor becomes an engineer by proxy" (15).

An engineer by proxy. The phrase is so apt for Adams, a man who tells us he wasted a pencil and several sheets of paper at Chicago "trying to calculate exactly when, according to the given increase of power, tonnage, and speed, the growth of the ocean steamer would reach its limits" (*E* 341). It is Adams who asks engineering questions about the new dynamo: "Did it pull or did it push? Was it a screw or thrust? Did it flow or vibrate? Was it a wire or a mathematical line?" (341–42). This man, whose statistics on coal and steam power recur insistently in his major book, looked past the Beaux Arts architectural ideal to take considerable interest in the practical structural problems of an engineer in fact and by proxy.

Adams's interest held fast in his study of the French Middle Ages. He had a French mentor to help him and a sort of midwife in the American translator, Henry Van Brunt. One of the architects of the White City, Van Brunt had translated Eugene Emmanuel Viollet-le-Duc's *Discourses on Architecture* for American readers back in 1875. Van Brunt recognized that the United States lived in "an atmosphere of haste," was "impatient of delay," and was above all practical in its concerns. It needed an architecture compatible with "conditions as they are" ("out of prosaic exactions our architecture must be developed") (xiv-xvii). The translator Van Brunt obviously felt that Viollet-le-Duc, who became Adams's own mentor, could help the American public and its builders. In the pages of his translation readers would find the advice of a practical man who had mastered construction techniques, had "measured and analyzed" Greek and Roman monuments, rebuilt and restored chateaus, town halls, and churches, repaired fortifications, and prepared the exhaustive *Dictionnaire raisonné de l'architecture français, du Xe au XVIe siècles.*

But Viollet-le-Duc (1814–79) was more than this. An iconoclastic French theorist of architecture, he had enraged students and faculty at the prestigious Ecole

Ferris Wheel, Chicago, 1893 (Courtesy National Museum of American History, Smithsonian Institution)

Ferris Wheel close-up (Courtesy Chicago Historical Society)

The "engineer by proxy" at the Eiffel Tower (Photograph by William Tichi)

des Beaux Arts. They openly revolted when, in lectures (1863–64), he pointed out their ignorance of construction methods, of materials, of styles of the past, their academic rigidity, their "mania for producing monuments." Viollet-le-Duc remains a father of modern architecture (though his reputation was sullied by participation in dubious restoration projects). His were the credentials of a "shop-floor" man trained at the construction site rather than in the academy. According to his great-granddaughter, a thirty-years' student of his career, he was "clever with his hands" and "could handle all the instruments used by builders and stone cutters." Self-taught, he worked with contractors "in a practical fashion." He pioneered the use of iron and concrete. "For him, structure was paramount," and in Gothic architecture he found the functional aesthetic he championed until his death (Hermann 14–18).

Adams discovered Viollet-le-Duc in 1871, enthusiastically commended his book on medieval military architecture to a friend ("It will give you a new interest in architecture") and took Van Brunt's translation of the *Discourses on Architecture* as his guidebook when he set out to write *Mont Saint-Michel and Chartres*. The *Discourses*, as Adams knew, urged architects (as Frank Lloyd Wright would do in 1902) to use "the immense resources furnished by modern industry . . . to produce a new style" (405; *Letters*, ed. Levenson et al. 2:103).

Adams's mentor encouraged the convergence of architecture and engineering. He urged those in both groups to stop their territorial battles, reminding each of the strengths and resources of the other. The modern architect, he says, "complains that the engineers intrench upon the domain of art" yet resists meeting the new and practical requirements of the day. On the engineers' side, the French theorist urged those professionally accustomed to "nice calculation" to take satisfaction in simplicity, economy, and "unaffected manifestation of construction." If they do, the engineers can achieve "remarkable results, from a purely artistic point of view" (*Discourses* 291, 509). His repeated theme is that "the theoretical and practical" must be joined, and the *Discourses* make it abundantly clear that for Viollet-le-Duc the structures that bond the two in exemplary fashion are those of the French Middle Ages.

In *Mont Saint-Michel and Chartres* Henry Adams cited Viollet-le-Duc as a scholar cites a master, which is to say that the Frenchman is the authority with whom Adams must, at points, respectfully disagree even as the name, Viollet-le-Duc, remains a constant thread in the fabric of Adams's book. It is important to notice that neither Adams nor his mentor are antiquarians. Viollet-le-Duc searched the past for structural forms and principles that could enlarge the contemporary "capacity for design," that could enable the moderns "to produce an original style of architecture based truly and firmly upon modern civilization" (*Discourses* 478).

By the turn of the century Adams, of course, had seen Viollet-le-Duc's theories made tangible, in part in Richardson's designs but principally in the metal-framed tall buildings that burgeoned in New York and Chicago. There the architect-engineers, notably William Le Baron Jenney and John Wellborn Root, explicitly put into practice the design theories of Viollet-le-Duc (Billington 105–6). Adams,

Eiffel Tower, 1889–90 (Courtesy H. Roger-Viollet, Paris)

From the elevator in the Eiffel Tower, 1889–90 (Courtesy H. Roger-Viollet, Paris)

preparing to study medieval structures, was tutored by these contemporary buildings and was fully conscious of their commercial impetus. His imagination was
well equipped to move back and forth fluidly between the medieval and the
modern. Far from retreating into the past, he searched it as the counterpart of his
own era in which commerce and industry were fostering new structural forms.
Adams, the habitué of world's fairs, knew that "the great cathedrals of the Middle
Ages always reflected the [commercial and technical] industries and interests of a
world's fair" and that "no world's fair is likely to do better today" (*Mont* 104–5).

Viollet-le-Duc could help Adams in part because the French theorist addressed
the very issues of form and use that Adams saw interplayed in the new buildings
around him. With the help of the *Discourses* Adams studied the architecture and
engineering of the French Middle Ages in order to find its resolution of problems
confronting designers of his own day. Adams, for instance, was interested in the
medieval architects' "necessity for light." ("They needed light and always more
light. . . . They converted their walls into windows . . . until their churches could
no longer stand" [*Mont* 97].) A man who for twenty years had seen the advance of
metal-framed building with its opportunity for vastly increased window space
might well ask how medieval architects had "converted their walls into windows."
As Van Brunt had said of the American city in his translator's introduction, "We
must have narrow facades on our streets, and these must be built to the skies and
crowded with windows" (xv). As an American Adams would recognize that the
ugly-sounding word, fenestration, "became the most important part of the architect's
work" (*Mont* 97).

Adams was also sensitive to the conflict between practicality and beauty in
building design. He had seen that struggle inscribed in the buildings of urban
America. He recognized that designers in the Middle Ages had also grappled with
the problem of beauty versus practicality in their division of tall structures into
storeys. "This particularly American problem of the twentieth century" found a
practical solution in Norman architecture and one of grace and beauty in the
French. "And when tourists return to New York," Adams writes, "they may look at
the twenty-storey towers which decorate the city, to see whether the Norman or the
French plan has won" (*Mont* 54–55).

At times Adams explicitly considers the interests of the engineer. The great hall
and refectory of the order of Saint Michael, studied together with the cathedral and
abbey, "are an exceedingly liberal education for anybody, tourist or engineer or
architect" (*Mont* 40). He ponders the multifunctional abbeys with their design
problems of dormitory space, provisioning, and traffic flow. "To administer such a
society required the most efficient management," he observes, noting that when
the abbot decided upon a monumental plastering project, the architect had a
rather simple task before him, but that "the engineering difficulties alone were
very serious" (*Mont* 38).

Mont Saint-Michel and Chartres, as Adams's biographer says, is a work in which
"technical knowledge will challenge us on nearly every page" (Samuels 260).
Weight, stress, buttressing, mathematical calculation—all recur as an integral

Travelers like Henry Adams could reach Mont St. Michel, ca. 1900, by motorcar or railroad. (Courtesy H. Roger-Viollet, Paris)

part of this discussion of technics in the service of faith. Architecture, says Adams, is "an expression of energy" (*Mont* 8). Of course *Mont Saint-Michel and Chartres* is a literary work, as many readers have proven, speaking as R. P. Blackmur has of its poetry and music, of its central symbol of the Virgin Mary. But the book was first published under the auspices of the American Institute of Architects, which serves as a reminder that Adams's interests are structural in technics as well as in literary design. Those interests found their fullest expression in Adams's *Education*, for there he presents the technological dynamo as the symbol of the modern age and the engineer as the exemplar of contemporary action and power.

We must first recognize that Adams's dynamo and Virgin are not found objects, but deliberately crafted literary symbols of a writer who, to be credible and authoritative, presents himself as a man of the contemporary moment. He may criticize Theodore Roosevelt as a creature of "pure act" (*E* 417), but the narrator of fifty-odd self-professed educations is also a restless man in a kinetic culture. "What he valued most was Motion, and what attracted his mind was Change" (*E* 231). He pointedly rejected the life of an English dilettante or of an American antiquarian. "He had no choice but to march with his world. . . . The current of his time was to be his current, lead where it might" (*E* 427, 458, 460, 232).

In the latter, kinetic chapters of the *Education* he keeps current on the newfangled bicycle and the Daimler motorcar, traveling among the medieval cathedrals at the rate of "a century a minute" (469, 470). True, Adams's recollected boyhood summers in preindustrial Quincy, Massachusetts, seem of a piece with the world of the French Middle Ages in *Mont Saint-Michel and Chartres*. Both are worlds of artisanry, agriculture, solar rhythms, and of higher authority to which the individual can readily assent. But at the turn of the twentieth century Adams is not nostalgic for that past. Struck by the power of the new dynamo, he feels that the "old-fashioned, deliberate, annual and daily revolution of the planet [is] less impressive" than before (380). He is the global traveler remarking on the telephones and electric lights strung close to the polar ice cap of Norway, where he receives telegrams of doings half a world away. There is no trace of elegy in his proclamation, "The electro-dynamic-social universe worked better than the sun" (413).

It is important for Adams to present his credentials as a participant in the new era. As a symbolist of its forms of power, he needs credibility. It is one thing to pose as a failure in a culture ridiculously ravenous for success, but quite another to brandish an autobiographical buggy whip in the age of the Daimler. In fact, there is just such an anachronistic figure in the *Education*. Adams's sculptor friend, St. Gaudens, is "a lost soul that had strayed by chance into the twentieth century." Instinctively he "preferred the horse" as a symbol of power (387–88). St. Gaudens exhibits a certain Victorian dualism, in Adams's view. Like other artists he "felt the railway train as power . . . yet complained that power embodied in a railway train [or any such machine] could never be embodied in art." So all summer long St. Gaudens put his "interminable last touches" on a sculpture of General William Sherman and his horse even as the term "horse power" gained new vitality in its application to machines. Like St. Gaudens, Henry Adams says he too is a sculptor. His pen "acts like a hand, modelling the plastic material over and over again to the form that suits it best" (387–89). But in the era of machine technology Adams knew exactly from what source his sculptural effort must come. In the new age, power was in the realm of the engineer and not the equestrian.

As a machine-age modern Adams admits readers to his fairgrounds where we watch his sculpting of symbols based upon one principle, power or the "sequence of force" (*E* 382). The historian in Adams had already discarded several useless kinds of sequences (social, chronological, intellectual), none of them valid in the light of current scientific thought. Now force preoccupies him, especially since the eminent physical scientist (and aspirant designer of flying machines), Samuel Langley, took him in hand at the Paris Exposition of 1900. Langley taught Adams to ignore the entire industrial exhibit, touched in brief upon motors for airships and automobiles, and then showed Adams the great hall of dynamos. "As he grew accustomed to the great gallery of machines, he began to feel the forty-foot dynamos as a moral force" (*E* 380). Immediately Adams's mind worked symbolically

Augustus St. Gaudens, The Sherman Monument, *at Central Park South, New York City (Photograph by Marjorie Wekselman)*

and sequentially, for in the age of electricity he searches the Middle Ages for the icon of equivalent power. Like a metaphysical poet who yokes images that are shockingly different, Adams matches the Virgin to the dynamo. Together they form two halves of an equation that spans centuries. They are equivalents, not opposites or contraries. "A miracle or a dynamo . . . a cathedral or a world's fair . . . all that the centuries can do is express the idea [of infinity and force] differently" (*Mont* 104).

Adams knew how outrageous was his yoking of the two forms, each posing great difficulty for the symbolist. First, the figure of the Virgin Mary was problematic for an American writer working in a culture that valued women only as figures of sentiment but never of sexual power. Even in the modern age of rapid transit and communication, the Virgin remained a French national whose residual influence stopped at the coastline of France (though Adams must have known that the Virgin had slipped into America by steerage class to take up residence belowstairs in households like his own). As for the dynamo, the "huge wheel, revolving . . . at some vertiginous speed" may be Adams's chosen "symbol of infinity" and "moral force," but the object itself had yet to partake of those declared meanings.

To confer them, to equate mechanics with charismatics, Adams crisscrosses religious and technological-scientific terms in plain view of his readers. His Virgin is (at Lourdes at least) "as potent as X-rays." She is herself an "animated dynamo" when allied with the sexually powerful Venus. Over time her output of energy can be measured, favorably, against the standard of the engineers, for hers was "the highest energy ever known to man . . . exercising vastly more attraction over the human mind than all the steam dynamos ever dreamed of" (383, 384, 351). In *Mont Saint-Michel and Chartres* Adams had similarly said that the power of the Virgin "had built up these World's Fairs of thirteenth-century force that turned Chicago and St. Louis pale" (469). This, then, is not the Virgin of beauty, taste, reflected emotion, and purity, which is to say the old-fashioned Virgin of St. Gaudens (*E* 388). She is not even the Virgin of maternity, which is different from reproductive power. Adams's Virgin is, in a word, the queen of force.

As for the dynamo, Adams works to invest it with a counterweight of religious meaning. It is a "moral force" like the Cross of primitive Christianity; it is "occult" and compels Adams to pray to it. Like the Virgin it is supersensual, and its electricity, like religious faith, seems to exist only by "absolute fiat" (*E* 380–81). Its vocal hum promises to become a voice, for if the dynamo "was not so human as some [symbols], it was the most expressive" (*E* 380). Little babies may safely nap alongside it (as the Virgin's baby slept in her arms?). Adams even hints that he will look into the sex of the dynamo at such time as he can measure its energy.

For all Adams's effort to show the dynamo and the Virgin as "convertible, reversible, interchangeable attractions on thought" (*E* 383), many readers persist in seeing these "two kingdoms of force" as Manichaean figures of heaven and hell. Why?—because as literary symbols, they fail. Despite his effort, Adams could neither transform nor pair them. He could not successfully wrest the Virgin from traditional associations any more than he could animate the dynamo.

The Virgin, Chartres Cathedral (Photograph by William Tichi)

Virgin in Majesty, Chartres Cathedral (Photograph by William Tichi)

Adams's own ambivalence impaired him. His respect for technology had its well-known negative side, which undermined his efforts at symbolism. He wrote that the "throb of fifty or a hundred million steam horse-power, doubling every ten years," was "more despotic than all the horses that ever lived." The new pulse, he said, thwarted intellectual life and disoriented the poet.

And defaced the landscape. En route to the St. Louis World's Fair, Adams saw a baleful scene from his Pullman window. "From Pittsburgh through Ohio and Indiana . . . tall chimneys reeked smoke on every horizon, and dirty suburbs filled with scrap-iron, scrap-paper and cinders formed the setting of every town." The Anglo-Saxon Adams hints his revulsion at the "mixed humanities," the "millions of Germans and Slavs, or whatever their race-names" who "overflowed these regions" to become "the new American," the "child of steam and brother of the dynamo." The industrial scene is clearly, intentionally repellent, and Adams makes it even more so by calling the industrial workers a "squeezed and welded . . . product of mechanical power" (*E* 408, 466). Adams's revulsion is not qualified in these passages. His loathing of the industrial scene, stated outright, forms no part of a symbol in which antagonistic qualities coexist as paradox.

But Adams's dynamo symbol fails for reasons that have little to do with ethnic bigotry or even with the intrinsic qualities of machine technology. In the industrial era of "trees, animals, engines" there is good reason to believe that the successful symbol need not even be organic. In a chapter on "The Dynamo and the Virgin

Revisited" the theologian Harvey Cox urges us to take a broader view of symbolic possibilities. "We need you, Henry Adams," he begins, arguing that technological artifacts could well become symbols of the sacred. These are characterized, Cox says, "by a high degree of power and ambiguity" and "arouse dread and gratitude, terror and rapture." He emphasizes that a symbol is defined "not by its content but by its relative degree of cultural power" (280–83).

In fact he is not the first to make this point. In the late 1920s Michael Pupin, a Columbia University professor of science, argued a parallel relation between pious Christians worshiping the spirit of Christ beyond the paint and wood of the crucifix, and scientists and engineers worshiping "the spirit behind . . . the material machine." "The machine," Pupin concludes, "is the visible evidence of the close union between man and the spirit of the eternal truth which guides the subtle hand of nature" (28–29). Pupin did not use the term "dynamo" in this religious context, but in 1914 Van Wyck Brooks had done so, referring to the dynamo's ability to convert electrical energy to mechanical energy when he said that Harvard College theologians had "founded themselves each on a remote system of dogma, and all their wheels turned in relation to the central theological dynamo" (19). Thus in diction as well as in metaphysics Harvey Cox had predecessors when he concluded that "clearly there is nothing to prevent technologies of any kind from becoming sacred symbols" (282). From a theological viewpoint he, together with the others, would seem to be Henry Adams's empathetic apologists, understanding what Adams was trying to do, praising the precocity of his vision, and urging contemporary readers toward spiritual lives consonant with their own technological twentieth century.

But the sacred symbol is not necessarily the literary symbol, which has requirements of its own, ones that Adams committed himself to fulfill. It is tempting to say that Adams did not bring the mechanistic dynamo sufficiently into the realm of the organic, as did his symbolist predecessors in the classic American literature. The history of American literature, we might think, could have been instructive to Adams, from the Puritans' spiders to the Romantics' pond, the white whale, the multimedia "A," and even the dilapidated manor house that stands for the psyche in a tale of Edgar Allan Poe. An admirer of Walt Whitman, Adams evidently overlooked the example of "Song of the Broad-Axe," in which the technological artifact quickens to life to become a symbol of American energy. Adams, so eager to span centuries, evidently ignored both Whitman's ferry ("Crossing Brooklyn Ferry") and the possibilities Hart Crane would soon see in the Brooklyn Bridge. (In the 1900s–1910s even the children's writer, L. Frank Baum, understood that mechanism can be successful in literature only if it speaks to human feeling; in the Oz books his Tin Woodman and the copper automaton, Tik-Tok, function as rheumy-jointed pals of Dorothy and her friends.) Even the railroad of the novelist Frank Norris achieved the status of an industrial-age symbol only when expressed in the monstrous yet organic figure of the octopus.

But the organic quality of the symbol is only a part, perhaps a minor part, of Adams's problem, which principally concerns the freedom to develop symbolic

The new cathedral, the Palace of Machines, where Henry Adams saw the dynamos at the Paris Exposition, 1889–90 (Courtesy H. Roger-Viollet, Paris)

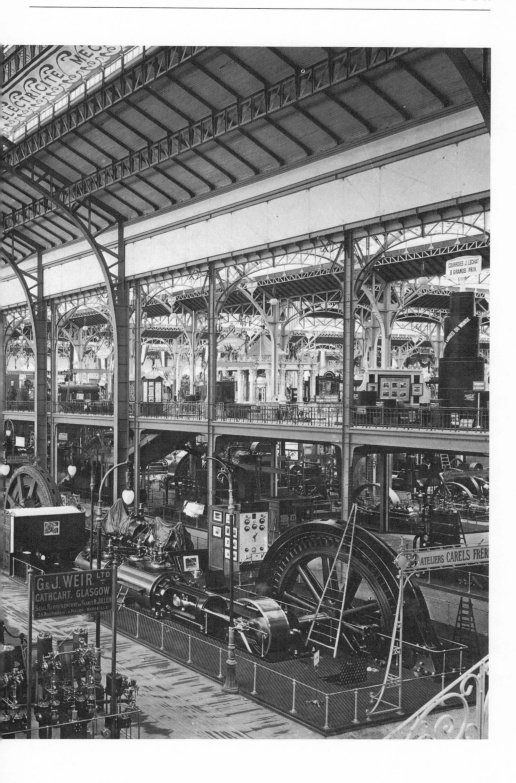

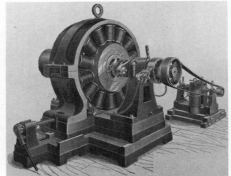

Dynamos at the Paris Exposition, 1889–1900

meaning. It is a freedom fully exercised by the American Romantic writers but foreclosed to Adams. Strange to say, the author of the *Education* could have taken a lesson in such freedom from his English contemporary, H. G. Wells, whose journalistic account of the dynamos of the Niagara Falls Power Company is filled with possibilities for symbolic development. Wells, traveling in the United States to record the American scene in 1905, saw the dynamos as human "will made visible, thought translated into easy and commanding things." They are "starkly powerful . . . noble masses of machinery, huge black slumbering monsters, great sleeping tops that engender irresistible forces in their sleep." "They sprang," says Wells, "armed like Minerva, from serene and speculative, foreseeing and endeavouring brains. First was the word and then these powers." Wells's dynamos rest in "cloistered quiet" and form "an empire," yet are "the heart of a living body" (54–55).

Wells's images—imperial, mythic, organic, religious—tumble one after another, then peter out in a trail of elliptical dots. Stymied on what the dynamos finally mean in the United States, he constructs a "day-dream of the coming power of men . . . the greatness of life still to come," then abruptly changes the subject. His passage on dynamos remains only as a set of notes for a symbol whose meaning eludes him.

The initial process of symbol-making, however, is left on record, and it is instructive precisely because of the great freedom Wells exhibits in his evocation of associations. Repeatedly he works outward from the dynamos of the Niagara Falls Power Plant to endow the machines with a wide range of complementary meanings. In his prose we feel the free expansiveness of the symbolist impulse.

It is this quality of evocative freedom that Adams lacks and that points us toward the reason why his symbols fail. For Adams' major difficulty lies in his positioning of the dynamo and the Virgin in such a way that he severely limits the possibilities for symbolic meaning. Adams doomed his symbols to failure precisely by joining them in an equation. In doing so, he burdened himself with a problem perhaps unique in Western literature: he wrote an equation of two symbols which could only cross-reference each other and therefore ultimately restrict each one's meanings.

To understand the reason for Adams's insurmountable difficulties, we must be reminded that in imaginative literature a symbol has a concrete referent in the objective world and a permanent objective value. The symbol goes beyond its referent to evoke or suggest meaning beyond itself. It embodies an idea or quality, partakes of the thing symbolized. The writer may choose a symbol deliberately or subconsciously. The task is elementary if the symbol is as universally suggestive as the sea or the seasons. But the symbol whose meanings are secured only by literary treatment is much more difficult. In *Moby-Dick* Melville's chapters on the tail, the head, the spout of the white whale are exhibitions of symbol-making, just as are Whitman's transformation of the axe (*Song of the Broad Axe*) and Crane's of the Brooklyn Bridge.

Adams, however, does not have just one major symbol; he has two of them. The dynamo and the Virgin do, of course, have meanings beyond themselves. But these meanings are strictly confined, restricted each to the other. Adams's symbols do not speak of one thing *in terms of* another, but *as* another. Their meanings are severely restricted. Neither can mean anything more or anything else than the other means. The meaning of each, therefore, becomes less evocative than designated. Joined together, the dynamo and the Virgin become more like an algebraic equation than a pair of literary symbols.

A poem by Emily Dickinson can clarify the point. When Dickinson wrote of the train embodying the characteristics of the horse, she spoke of one thing (train) in terms of another (horse) to evoke the qualities of power ("I Like to See It Lap the

Industrial Pittsburgh, ca. 1900 (Courtesy National Museum of American History, Smithsonian Institution)

Miles"). But we would never equate the train with the horse in her poem. In Adams's symbolic treatment of power, however, the two objects are presented in an equation, so that in effect the dynamo equals the Virgin equals the dynamo equals the Virgin, and so on. Instead of liberating his symbols, Adams restricts them despite prodigious efforts to the contrary. In bondage to each other, the dynamo and the Virgin become the Siamese twins of literary symbols, attached, mutually restrictive, and ultimately grotesque.

Perhaps subconsciously Adams knew he had failed to transmute either St. Gaudens's Virgin of good taste or the object which he, like most everyone else, considered only "an ingenious device for conveying somewhere the heat latent in a few tons of poor coal hidden in a dirty engine house carefully kept out of sight" (*E* 380). "As dumb as dynamos," he says at one point, unwittingly contradicting his statement that the electrical device is the "most expressive" symbol of the age (*E* 421). As an aspirant symbolist Adams crawled unsuccessfully along his acknowledged "knife-edge." His posture of worship of the dynamo strikes readers as so repellent that most recoil and take sanctuary in the humane and genteel realm of St. Gaudens's Virgin.

Foundry workers, Pittsburgh, 1890 (Courtesy Carnegie Library of Pittsburgh)

Adams, it is fair to say, was not the last American writer to try, without success, to make the dynamo a symbol of modern power. In the late 1920s Eugene O'Neill attempted to install it as a contemporary female deity in his play *Dynamo* (1928). O'Neill's dynamo is the "Divine Image on Earth . . . of the Great Mother of Eternal Life, Electricity." "Her power houses," he writes, "are the new churches." The stage directions called for "a massive female idol . . . the main structure like a head with blank, oblong eyes above a rounded torso." Evidently O'Neill, like Adams, tried to bring the dynamo into a quasi-human realm, though his context is classical Greece, not the Christian Middle Ages (91–105).

O'Neill's dynamo is a kind of Sophoclean Jocasta in an Oedipal scheme mixing sex, technology, engineer-priests, and love-hate relations with mothers. The protagonist, one of O'Neill's many sexually tortured young men, finally meets his fate in simultaneous orgasm and electrocution. Theater audiences were not pleased, and *Dynamo* closed after fifty-four performances, making it O'Neill's only conspicuous failure. We can only guess what O'Neill and Henry Adams would feel could they have known that in the mid-1920s in Muncie, Indiana, some citizens felt quite cheerful invoking the dynamo in the kind of civic ritual Sinclair Lewis loved to satirize as "boosterism." Yet Muncie's muscular Christianity effortlessly absorbed the very symbol with which Adams, then O'Neill, struggled. Each Monday at noon, according to the sociologists Robert and Helen Lynd, Muncie's "Middletown" Protestant men gathered to sing these lyrics to the tune of the World War I infantry song, "Over There":

> Dy-na-mo, Dy-na-mo,
> We're the bunch, we're the bunch,
> Dy-na-mo!
> We're alive and coming,
> And we'll keep things humming:
> We're surely always on the go. (374)

The dynamo was not Henry Adams's last word on technological America. The engineer has a prominent place in his thought as well. Adams, like Veblen and the popular novelists, saw the potential of engineers as a force in the redirection of American society. In the *Education* Adams exemplified that potential in the figure of his close friend, the geologist and mining engineer, Clarence King, who in the *Education* has a significant symbolic role in modern America.

Adams met him in the Rockies, but King (1842–1901) was actually a New Englander, Yale-trained in the physical sciences with concentration in geology. In several ways his biography reads like the plot of one of the popular engineer-novels. After graduation he went west to what he later called "that industrial gulf stream," the Placerville Road across the Sierras. He attached himself to the California Geological Survey, later assisting Frederick Law Olmsted in gold mining and participating in other surveys in the Sierras. (Mount Clarence King, in the Sierra Nevada, is named for him.) In the post–Civil War years King headed two major projects, the geological exploration of the Fortieth Parallel and the United States Geological Survey, of which he was appointed the founding director. These surveys not only expedited westward settlement but, more important to Congress and industry, formed the basis for the exploitation of natural resources. King wrote that "a Geological Survey . . . may be directed to the vigorous study of the . . . soils, metals, coals, mineral fertilizers, building stones, clay, etc., which are the foundations of human industry and the basis of national wealth" (Wilkins 245). His biographer remarks that King conceived of the U.S. Geological Survey "as an ally, first and foremost, of the mining industry" (264). In an era unregulated by conflict-of-interest laws, King regularly served as consulting engineer for mining companies.

Like the engineer-heroes of the popular novels, Clarence King was at his ease in clubrooms, galleries, and at dining tables. In the East in 1870 he was a sought-after speaker and friend of the recent western literary sensation, Bret Harte. James T. Fields of the *Atlantic Monthly* invited him to contribute essays, and the publisher James Osgood urged him to write a book about his western adventures. King's *Mountaineering in the Sierra Nevada* (1870) was well received, admired particularly by Howells. He became a member of New York's Century, Metropolitan, and Knickerbocker clubs. Admirers had never "heard a conversationalist so versatile, so brilliantly clever." "The trouble with King," said one, "is that his description of the sunset spoils the original" (qtd. in Wilkins 197–98). By the 1880s King traveled in London and Paris, a dashing figure in a green velvet traveling suit with knee breeches and a tam-o'-shanter. Endlessly charming and convivial, he was an art connoisseur who held tête-à-têtes with the prince of Wales and so captivated John Ruskin that he sold King two Turners from his collection of paintings (Wilkins 245, 264, 197–98).

In the *Education* Adams called King "a bird of paradise rising in the sagebrush." He met the geologist "coming from the west, saturated with the sunshine of the Sierras," while the vacationing Adams "drift[ed] from the east, drenched in the fogs of London" (311–12). Their intimate friendship lasted until King's death. In the *Education* Adams cast him as an exemplary figure of energy and capacity, as "the ideal American" all men wished to be. But Adams's Clarence King was more than a personal memoir or a memorial brass rubbing. The mining engineer served both a cultural and literary purpose. He was exactly the figure Adams needed to complete the structure of his *Education*. As it turned out, Adams needed Clarence King for the American future..

Adams's portrait is eulogistic. His King "knew more than Adams did of art and poetry; he knew America, especially west of the hundredth meridian, better than anyone; he knew the professor [of which Adams was one] by heart, and he knew the Congressman better than he did the professor. He knew even women; even the American woman; even the New York woman, which is saying much. . . . [He] saw ahead at least one generation further than the textbooks." Adams continues in these glowing terms in a Latinate sentence that builds excruciating suspense. King's "wit and humor; his bubbling energy which swept everyone into the current of his interest; his personal charm of youth and manners; his faculty of giving and taking, profusely, lavishly, whether in thought or money as though he were Nature herself, marked him almost alone among Americans" (*E* 311).

Adams goes on to portray King in terms reminiscent of a Richard Harding Davis novel. King "directed his life logically, scientifically, as Adams thought American life should be directed. He had given himself education all of a piece, yet broad. . . . King's abnormal energy [which Adams confessed sickened him in comparison to his own] had already won him great success. None of his contemporaries had done so much, single-handed, or were likely to leave so deep a trail." Adams surveys King's achievements. "He had managed to induce Congress to adopt its first modern act of legislation [authorizing the Fortieth Parallel survey.] He had organized as a civil—not military—measure, a Government Survey. He had paralleled the Continental Railway in Geology. . . . He was creating one of the classic scientific works of the century. The chances were great that he could, whenever he chose to quit Government service, take the pick of the gold and silver, copper or coal, and build up his fortune as he pleased. Whatever prize he wanted lay ready for him—scientific, social, literary, political—and he knew how to take them in turn. With ordinary luck he would die at eighty the richest and most many-sided genius of his day" (*E* 312–13).

Instead Clarence King died tubercular and virtually bankrupt from failed mining enterprises at the age of fifty-nine. Adams saw his death in tragic terms. The "best and brightest man of his generation, with talents immeasurably beyond any of his contemporaries," succumbed, Adams suggests, to America's gold fever. The nation which gauged success by the dollar figure seduced King. He attempted to amass a great fortune, even at the cost of his health, his sanity, his life. "He knew more practical geology than was good for him," and fell victim to the siren song of the American El Dorado. Adams did not flinch from the dissoluteness he sensed in King. "He had in him something of the Greek," he said, "—a touch of Alcibiades" (*E* 311–13, 328, 346–48).

"Or Alexander." For it was this latter image of strength, leadership, and conquest that Adams needed in the closing chapters of his *Education*. The book that began recollectively with place-name chapters (on "Quincy," "Boston," "Washington") concluded in kinetics, in chapters whose titles emphasize movement ("*Vis Nova*" [The New Force of Energy], "A Dynamic Theory of History," "A Law of Acceleration," "*Nunc Age*" [Now Go]). Movement preoccupies Adams in these closing passages, especially in the authorial send-off which is focused on contemporary cultural conditions. A hysterical citizenry cries that "the new forces must at any cost be brought under control" even as "the cylinder had exploded, and thrown great masses of stone and steam against the sky" (*E* 499). Culture threatens to disintegrate in a spin cycle of social anarchy and renegade technological power.

But Henry Adams had not lost faith in the "active-minded" or "visionaries," not even in frantic modern times. To rescue civilization—and Adams's account of it—from dissolution, he calls for a "new type of man—a man with ten times the endurance, energy, will, and mind of the old type." Adams feels he may be at hand, this "new man" or "new American" who can successfully battle the powerful trusts and corporations. "The new American must be either the child of the new forces or a chance sport of nature" (*E* 500–501).

Such a figure may seem the wishful figment of Adams's imagination, until we recall Adams's portrait of Clarence King, the scientist-engineer bred among the westering surveyors who enjoyed complexity and for whom "catastrophe was the law of change." King, unlike the native Californians, also understood New York and the Mississippi Valley and thus understood the nation as a whole, in fact the modern world (*E* 313). If he fell victim to the gold bug's bite, he remains nonetheless Adams's type of the new American Constantine, the emperor-engineer for the age of the dynamo. Adams, like the popular novelists, felt the yearning that Emerson had expressed for a figure of "energy and practical ability," of "enterprise and command" to bring about "engineering for all America" (*Selections* 393).

CODA: HERBERT HOOVER

Henry Adams's new American was waiting in the wings, even if history has not been kind to him. The name Herbert Hoover (1874–1964) may call to mind the infamous Hoovervilles, the ramshackle huts of the homeless who migrated to the fringes of America's cities during the Great Depression of his presidency (1928–32). But Hoover Dam on the Colorado River honors the engineering ideology of the man who succeeded Calvin Coolidge in the White House.

Hoover was as reticent as Clarence King was voluble, but he showed the prodigious energy that Adams found awesome in King and mandatory for leadership in the new century. Hoover was reportedly a "high pressure . . . pushful American," and his career struck certain parallels with King's. As a Stanford University student and recent graduate, Hoover served on the United States Geological Survey originated by Clarence King. And he worked as a mining engineer in China during the Boxer Rebellion of which Adams speaks in the *Education*. By 1928, the year of his election, Hoover was an internationally renowned mining engineer, a self-made multimillionaire who organized and directed the relief of Belgium during World War I, then became the United States food administrator in the postwar reconstruction of Europe before becoming the secretary of commerce ("Business Manager of the Nation," as one biographer put it) in the Coolidge administration. By the time he became a presidential candidate Hoover had spent an adult lifetime "controlling the forces and utilizing the materials of nature for the benefit of man, and organizing and directing human activities in connection therewith" (Nash 570 ff.; Wilson 149).

Behind Hoover lay a monumental fictional image, for the engineer portrayed repeatedly in the popular engineer novels and movies went far to prepare the American public for Hoover's presidential candidacy. Campaign-era magazine articles recall the adventures in the novels ("How Hoover's Forces Fought the Flood"; "Hoover: Specialist in Public Calamities"), and Will Irwin's campaign biography followed the fictional formula to the letter. The Hoover hero is controlled yet passionate, cultured yet rugged, visionary, powerful, and destined to advance civilization. During his western boyhood Hoover grows to love the hills and forests, fishing with Indian children with a bent pin even as he cultivates a taste for classical English writers, including Shakespeare. Diligent in his farm chores with the livestock, young 'Bert becomes absorbed in mechanics, constructing a mowing machine from metal parts junked on his uncle's farm, and continuing his interest in machinery until a mining engineer asks him, "Son, why don't you go in for engineering?" The question, virtually a divine calling, works in Hoover "a change as sudden and revolutionary as a religious conversion. . . . [H]e wanted to go to Stanford, to become a mining engineer" (Irwin 11, 24–25, 30, 32, 99, 245, 249, 314).

The campaign biographer, like the novelists, worked to show the depths of feeling behind the implacable facade of the engineer. Thus Hoover's emotion "translates itself not into tears but into action. 'What can I do?' he asks himself; and the mind once more takes control. While others sleep, he works!" Lest readers suspect the candidate to be a man of mechanism, the biographer insists that "Hoover organizations more resemble a living thing than a machine" and that Hoover "always takes into account the human factor." The popular campaign biography, which went through six printings by July 1928, fully prepares voters to say yes to the contemporary hero as it concludes, "Without goose-stepping the human spirit, blue-printing the human soul," Hoover "is engineering our material civilization as a whole."

The engineer Hoover was apt to use language biased in favor of his profession. The capitalist-engineer sounded like Bellamy when he spoke of "the delicate machinery of social organization, of production and commerce upon which our civilization is founded." In 1920 he urged Americans to adopt "the attitude that marks the successes of America, the attitude of the business man, of the engineer, and of the scientist" (Hoff-Wilson 151–52). This language was, as we know, virtually commonplace by that time.

Hoover's record in American political history is currently undergoing revaluation. His aura of personal force and his views of engineering are pertinent here because Hoover is, in effect, Clarence King's second chance. He is the figure Henry Adams invokes for the American future. "Most people do not know it," Hoover wrote of "The Profession of Engineering," but the engineer "is an economic and social force. Every time he discovers a new application of science, thereby creating a new industry, providing new jobs, adding to the standards of living, he also disturbs everything that is. New laws and regulations have to be made and new wickedness curbed." Apparently the engineer is just the figure to curb it, since Hoover concludes, as had Adams, that the engineer "is also the person who really corrects monopolies and redistributes national wealth" (*Memoirs* 1:134; Nash 498, 501, 588).

Ironically, Hoover dismissed *The Education of Henry Adams*, which was the number-one best-selling nonfiction book of 1918, as "the puerilities of a parasite," obviously overlooking any connection between himself and Clarence King (Nash 498). Although he entertained Richard Harding Davis at his California home, Red House, Hoover failed to recognize that the public was largely prepared to elect him president because writers like Davis had successfully embodied America itself in the figure of the heroic engineer.

CHAPTER FOUR

DANGER AND OPPORTUNITY

So the poet in the engineer and the engineer in the poet.

Frank Lloyd Wright, *A Testament*, 1957

WRIGHT'S BLOCKS, ALEXANDER'S BRIDGE

The gear-and-girder world of the engineer affected artists, including poets and novelists,
in one of two ways during the period of 1890s–
1920s. Either they saw it as danger or as opportunity. Either they felt jeopardized by it or welcomed
its potential to solve contemporary problems of
form.

Frank Lloyd Wright typifies those who felt optimistic about a dynamic world of
component-part construction. From kindergarten, we recall, Wright played with
prefabricated design components, the Froebal blocks his mother precociously
chose for a son growing up in the industrial United States. He called them "smooth
shapely maple blocks with which to build," using the term "block" as a catchword.
For the "Froebal Gifts" included diverse geometrical solids. Their container, Wright
recalled, could become the base for a mast "on which to hang the maple cubes
and spheres and triangles, revolving them to discover subordinate forms." He
recalled that the sense of those forms "never afterward leaves the fingers: *Form
becoming feeling*" (*Autobiography* 13).

Wright was perfectly positioned in adult life to welcome the machine and the
structural aesthetics of component parts. True, much of his work was done in the
plastic material, cast concrete. But, in childhood, he had learned the tactile and
visual pleasure of component forms, which he systematically arranged and rear-
ranged to achieve different designs. He was fully prepared to herald the potential
of its aesthetics of simplicity in harmony "with man's spiritual and material needs."
In 1901 Wright called upon contemporary artists to abandon the decadent crafts
tradition and exploit the possibilities inherent in the machine. In an address to the
Chicago Arts and Crafts Society at Hull House he told his listeners that the engineer's
machine had dealt a "death-blow" to "art in the grand old sense," meaning
handicrafts in which work was accomplished "through man's joy in the labor of
his hands." Artists who continued to cling to that craft tradition in the twentieth
century could only echo a bygone era. "Echoes," Wright warned, "are by nature
decadent" (*Writings and Buildings* 55–73).

Children at play with Froebal blocks in Bennington, Vermont, 1896 (Courtesy the Weichert-Isselhardt Collection)

In the year of Wright's Hull House talk, William Carlos Williams was a high schooler of eighteen, Dos Passos a kindergartner of five, and Hemingway a toddler of three. By the mid-1920s all were writing the poems, novels, and stories that showed how the machine afforded new formal opportunities to contemporary artists. All took advantage of component parts as building blocks of imaginative literature, for these writers came to understand what Wright had learned in boyhood and never forgot, namely, that the machine could produce component parts that the artist would arrange to make the design. In the age of machine production, Wright saw, artistic achievement no longer lay in the fashioning of a single, unique object. Artists, instead, could select and arrange the prefabricated components at their disposal. The artistry lay in the arrangement and selection of those components, and the artists who continued in the former crafts tradition could only be "decadent."

Wright's summons—and his warning—were as applicable to writers as to painters and architects. Writers, like the workers in wood and metal and clay, often identified themselves as craftspeople in an age of encroaching machine technology. Percy Lubbock's emphatic title, *The Craft of Fiction* (1921), can stand alongside novels in which craftsmen like Robert Herrick's blacksmith (*Together*, 1908) and Sherwood Anderson's harness maker (*Poor White*, 1920) are cherished figures. The literary critic who in 1929 identified "natural human faculties" with "the tradition of craftsmanship" was typical of many writers who were devotees of John Ruskin and William Morris. They were accustomed to view themselves as the staunch defenders of that civilization threatened by an onslaught of machine technology. But when Wright warned that the machine had dealt the death blow to the traditional worker in crafts, he implicated writers too. He implied that their continuance in the traditional ways meant that written forms of imaginative expression would fall into decay (O'Brien 76–77).

Yet, Wright argued, they need not. He welcomed the newest technological revolution and found reason to hope that the engineer's machine would engender a creative "poetic fire" as deep and intense as that burning in Shelley's poet yet compatible with the new age. Artists need only "unlock the secrets of the beauty of this time" and discover the machine-age ethos of "SIMPLICITY," of materials wrought "without waste" but in harmony with "man's spiritual and material needs." "The machine," said Wright, "is a marvelous simplifier: the emancipator of the creative mind, and in time the regenerator of the creative conscience." In rhetoric filled with organic figures Wright waxed eloquent on the "poetical . . . rational freedom made possible by the machine." He predicted that its art would be orchestral and democratic and, like the city, embody the vital human spirit, the soul itself. Art, Wright said, could regain contemporary power by exploiting the potential of the machine (*Writings and Buildings* 64).

The key lay in the redefinition of the term "artist." Artists were no longer craftspeople but designers. They no longer shaped raw materials into a unique finished object. Instead they masterminded the assembly of prefabricated parts produced by the machine. The artist's form was intrinsic to the arrangement of materials. The key to this aesthetics was the components, whether they were steel beams, gear wheels, words, or paragraphs. Writers like Dos Passos, Hemingway, and Williams apparently grasped this point in maturity, surrounded on all sides as they were by the component-part construction of bridges and skyscrapers and automobiles, and guided as they were (Hemingway and Williams in particular) by Ezra Pound's lessons on machine-based efficiency.

As we shall see, these writers brought radical change to narrative design, style, and aesthetic form as a result of the embodiment of engineering values in fiction and poetry. All accepted the challenge to use the machine to invigorate the art of the written word. All understood the opportunities of the gear-and-girder world.

Wright's blocks, however, stood opposed to a different conception of the world of the engineer. This alternate conception implied that the engineer's world was dangerous to all art forms. This was the world of *Alexander's Bridge* (1912), the title of Willa Cather's first major novel, which concerns a master bridge engineer of worldwide renown. Cather's form is at least as important as her subject. *Alexander's Bridge* is committed to the values of the waning Romantic era. If Wright speaks for artists exploiting the machine age, Cather typifies those others who felt threatened by the engineering power from which they felt excluded. In the novel, Alexander's bridge is not a structure but an organic symbol. It is not an artifact of component parts but an evocation of the spiritual-psychological state of the man whose life it represents. Its significance does not lie in its statement on design, but only in what the symbol reveals about the spiritual state of the person it represents. Its importance lies in what it means, and its meaning lies beyond itself. As a structure with its own design integrity, it is negligible, unimportant.

Cather only flirts once with the idea of a component-part aesthetics of engineering. The bridges of her engineer-character do have, she concedes, artistic value. "Have you ever seen his first suspension bridge in Canada?" asks her engineer's wife, showing a photograph of the bridge to Alexander's former professor. The impeccably tasteful Mrs. Alexander describes the "bridal" bridge as spanning the "wildest river, with mists and clouds always battling about it . . . as delicate as a cobweb hanging in the sky" (17–18).

The figure of the cobweb has great potential for perception of the gear-and-girder world. It could have given Cather easy access to an appreciation of component-part design in nature and culture. As one journalist wrote, "A suspension bridge represents the highest mechanical, mathematical, and engineering skill, and yet is only the adaptation of a spider's web to man's requirements" ("Natural Form and Mechanical Design" 463). Cather could have looked into the aesthetic values of the structure, exploited them, and welcomed the engineer as a fellow in the arts. In turn, she could have gained an invaluable sense of the potential that the novelist could have as a designer in the contemporary world.

Yet Cather felt threat, not fellowship. In fiction she held fast to the traditional romantic worldview. In that world fiction was synonymous with story, its form presumed to be organically whole. It was formally natural, not constructed. It hearkened always to a preindustrial world of spiritual values thought to be inherent in nature. Cather's identity and fictional realm belonged to the world Thoreau described when he called poetry a "natural fruit" and said that "man bears a poem . . . as naturally as the oak bears an acorn and the vine a gourd." That fidelity to a unified, spiritually whole, organic world set Cather in opposition to the world of gear-and-girder technology in which trees, animals, and engines were all perceived as constructions. The romantic Cather could only see the encroachment of engineers and their worldview as a threat. She used fiction to try to expose the danger of the engineers and to plead for the restoration of a waning world.

Cather typifies those writers and artists who were frightened and angry, and motivated principally by their sense of immediate danger. They, too, lived in urban areas replete with machines and steel-framed structures. But they saw no imaginative opportunities in the component parts of structural or mechanical engineering. Feeling threatened by technology, they reacted with attacks on the engineer, his bridges, his buildings, his machines. They disparaged the technological mind as narrow, dangerous, and unimaginative, and invited readers to rededicate themselves to the traditional source of spiritual vitality, the written word kept pure and uncontaminated by technological influences. Willa Cather, Sherwood Anderson, and the young Lewis Mumford belong in this group.

Early in the twentieth century, then, Alexander's bridge was directly opposed to Frank Lloyd Wright's blocks. They represented two separate and distinct worlds. In 1912, in fact, Cather declared war on modern technology in two works of fiction, a short story and a novel.

Cather's story, "Behind the Singer Tower," is set in the aftermath of a catastrophic hotel fire in which over three hundred people have died, among them many corporation presidents and dignitaries. The luxury hotel "was the complete expression of the New York idea in architecture." In price and proportion it "outscaled everything in the known world." Yet its interior burned with "incredible speed." Its fire escapes melted as some guests plunged hundreds of feet toward "cobwebby life nets." As the aura of invincibility vanishes, the charnel house exposes the myth of so-called fireproof tall buildings and discredits the skyscraper per se. "The New York idea [will] be called to account by every state in the Union, by all the capitals of the world."

From a motor launch offshore in the Hudson River the narrator, a newspaperman, recounts the events of the fire and observes the city skyline. The "incredible towers of stone and steel" seem a lonely, confused grouping, and he imagines the city to be protesting, asserting its helplessness and its outrage at those responsible for this new vertical profile. He ponders American values gone awry. "Our whole scheme of life and progress and profit [is] perpendicular. There [is] nothing for us but height. . . . [W]e depend upon the ever-growing possibilities of girders and rivets as Holland depends upon her dikes" (44, 46).

The conversation in the launch turns toward other buildings and the engineers who plan them. Here Cather's tone turns vitriolic in its anti-Semitism. One of the passengers remarks on "what a Jewy thing the Singer Tower is when it's lit up" (46). The group blames the ideals of open immigration for the enormity of the commercial skyscraper. Then the story recounts the life of the engineer who built the burned hotel. He is half Jewish and thereby genetically corrupt. All his motives are commercial. Readers are left to surmise that the catastrophe has been caused by criminal negligence fostered by his Semitic greed.

In its own structure "Behind the Singer Tower" is uncertain. Its narrative parts seem cobbled together. But the story makes a clear, strong statement against the power Cather discerns in the engineer. A greedy heathen, he builds the structures to which human life is sacrificed, from the foundation workers to the window washers who plunge to their deaths at the rate of one a day, to the guests and employees seduced and destroyed by the engineers' hubris masquerading as expertise. But the story also suggests the extent to which Cather felt threatened by the engineers' new world. Even as a charred ruin it is "massive and brutally unconcerned," the very material embodiment of its designers. The author's bigotry is a measure of her anxiety.

The source of that anxiety was amply revealed in *Alexander's Bridge* (1912), the novel focused on another engineering failure. We meet Bartley Alexander, the great engineer, in mid-life and discover that Cather's protagonist conforms biographically to the engineers of the popular novels. By birth a poor westerner, Alexander worked his way to Paris to study, thereafter becoming the protégé of an eminent bridge engineer who, facing death, designates Alexander his heir apparent. The young engineer succeeds and has since married a wealthy and elegant Bostonian who represents fine taste and eastern tradition. We see their Beacon Hill life together as one of formal ritual, of elegant dinners, of tea in the drawing room. Cather makes it clear that the couple deeply love and admire each other. As for

Alexander's career, at forty-three he is a man rich in honors, moving with professional ease between Britain and America, and lecturing in Japan at the emperor's request. He has several bridges under construction throughout the United States but is primarily involved in "the most important piece of bridge-building going on in the world," a Canadian bridge over the St. Lawrence River "designed to be the longest cantilever in existence" (36–37).

Alexander, however, is a man in crisis. "His existence was becoming a network of great and little details" (38). The success he thought would bring freedom and power has proven to be confining. Vowing in youth to preserve his personal liberty, he finds himself instead "a public man . . . a cautious board member, a Nestor *de pontibus*." He yearns to recapture the vitality of his youth, the "wild light-heartedness" and vibrant consciousness he calls "Life itself." Instead, facing the "dead calm" of middle age (and in a foreshadowing of his death by drowning) Alexander begins to feel "buried alive." The novel recounts the story of his life-and-death struggle between his youthful and mature selves.

Cather exploits the engineer's youth-and-mid-life crisis through the traditional literary opposition between fair and dark women. She sets the brunette Bostonian, Winifred Alexander, against the blond Irish actress, Hilda Burgoyne, the engineer's former lover now celebrated for her work on the London stage. Their reacquaintance during his stay in London turns into a resumption of the old love affair of his youth, which in turn intensifies his personal battle. Alexander's wife appeals to that civilized part of him which has learned to value "the harmony of beautiful things that have lived together without obtrusion of ugliness or change . . . those warm consonances of color . . . blending and mellowing before he was born" (9–10). The free-spirited Hilda, on the other hand, speaks to his pagan energies, which Cather accents by imbuing her life—from her dress to the food she serves —with the tones of golden yellow that signify sexuality. The engineer's divided self is enacted in his attraction to both women and dramatized in his transatlantic crossings on a "bridge" of steamships as he tries in vain to stabilize the conflict within.

That conflict, meanwhile, takes another symbolic form in Alexander's professional life. The niggardly commission for the Canadian bridge forces him to specify construction materials about which he feels uncertain and to design the structure close to its maximal stress limit. "They've crowded me too much on the cost," he says to the house guest who is Alexander's former college professor. "It's all very well if everything goes well, but these estimates have never been used for anything of such length before" (63–64).

Here Cather makes the Canadian bridge the symbol of the engineer's tortured psyche. The professor's intuition of Alexander's "weak spot where some day strain would tell . . . a big crack zigzagging from top to bottom" proves to be accurate, as Alexander himself acknowledges (12, 114). No sooner does he envision the terrifying personal cataclysm of "the crack in the wall, the crash, the cloud of dust" than he is brought face to face with the moment of his death at the collapse of his great bridge, the symbol of himself. Responding to an emergency call to its construction site, Alexander has found the bridge members ready to buckle from stress. Moments too late he orders work stopped and the workmen off, then dies as the uncompleted bridge on which he stands tears "itself to pieces with roaring and grinding and noises that were like the shrieks of a steam whistle" (125). He drowns in the clutches of panicked workmen, but we are meant to understand that the collapse of the bridge symbolizes the destruction of a man unable to reconcile two antagonistic parts of his psyche.

In Alexander's torment Cather's readers can recognize at once her recurrent preoccupation with themes of the divided self, which can also be found in such novels as *My Ántonia* (1918) and *A Lost Lady* (1923). *Alexander's Bridge*, however, engages us here because it makes a trenchant statement about the antagonism Cather felt between the literary artist and the engineer. For one thing, she saw the master engineer as a figure whose distinction she thought dubious. In London her protagonist need be introduced only as "Bartley Alexander, the American engineer," and he is recognized on sight while traveling upcountry in New England on a railroad day coach (27, 112). As a journalist Cather had interviewed many artists and literary lions, and she appreciated celebrity status as an index of power. To cast Alexander accordingly in her novel was to acknowledge the contemporary prominence of the engineer.

By basing her novel on an actual engineering disaster, however, Cather implies that such prominence is unwarranted. In 1912 she would have expected her readers to grasp a dreadful historical connection between her story and recent events. In August 1907, the Quebec bridge on which Alexander's own is based had collapsed when a main compression member buckled, turning 19,000 tons of structural steel into twisted wreckage and killing eighty-two workmen. In the government inquiry that followed the disaster, the board charged that the bridge was designed for economy and not strength and that the dead load estimate was too low—both problems Cather attributes to the failure of Alexander's bridge. Just as in the story, "Behind the Singer Tower," Cather exploits a major engineering failure in fiction. This time she relies on public memory to support her suggestion that the engineer is fallible and that his personal flaws can kill and maim those who rely on his expertise.

Cather goes further, in fact, to characterize the master engineer as a machine-age barbarian. Bartley Alexander's very physique is the grotesque embodiment of technological power. His head is a catapult, his shoulders a bridge pier (9). "The machinery was always pounding away in this man . . . [who] was only a powerful machine" (13, 39). (Cather, like most writers, fails to make a distinction between machines and structures, and so intermixes images from both.)

She also shows the engineer's barbarity of mind. The antithesis of the artist, her engineer is neither reflective nor introspective. "Away with perspective! No past, no future for Bartley; just the fiery moment" (7, 8, 13). His former professor remembers him as "the most tremendous response to stimuli [he has] ever known" (8). It is significant that an elderly aunt of Alexander's wife greatly admired the young engineer, for the aunt "liked men of action . . . and had a great contempt for music and philosophy" (18–19). The contempt extends to literature. In the course

Quebec Bridge collapsed, 1907 (Courtesy Public Archives of Canada C57836)

of the novel Alexander writes two lengthy and important letters, one to his wife and the other to his lover; yet Cather, overlooking this, has him claim that mere "marks on paper" mean nothing to him (108).

Cather's portrait of Bartley Alexander could be dismissive were she not fearful that the future belonged to him and his kind. He is the modern American successor to the great Victorian activists, Benjamin Disraeli, "Pasha" Gordon, and the explorer David Livingstone (11). He is a "natural force . . . always on the edge of danger and change." He is a "bridge into the future" because he is one of the people "who make the play," while most others "are only onlookers at the best" (15, 17, 101, 138).

As one of the "onlookers," the novelist can only seek consolation in the qualities thought to be lacking in the engineer, reflection and perspective. These too, Cather argues, are powers. They enable her to see and to understand the fault line in Alexander's nature. They endow the writer with the power of insight lacking in those whose minds can only formulate "definite" things. For those of technological minds are baffled by the collapse of the bridge and shocked at the accidental death of its designer. "According to all human calculations, it simply couldn't happen," says a young engineer, incredulous amid the twisted steel and the bodies of the drowned workmen (129). Of course the novelist knows better. The artist

Quebec Bridge completed, 1917 (Courtesy National Museum of American History, Smithsonian Institution)

working routinely in the world which surpasses that of mere mathematical calculation understands the naiveté of the young engineer, even if he represents modern America.

If the public continues to believe that the American mind at its truest is the mind of an engineer or mechanic, as one character suggests, then America, says Cather, is a nation in jeopardy. Her eulogy for the drowned engineer contains a warning of the kind only the writer can provide. The novelist's voice, introspective and reflective, teaches that "the mind that society had come to regard as a powerful and reliable machine, dedicated to its service, may for a long time have been sick within itself and bent upon its own destruction" (131). By showing the disastrous personal and social consequences of that sickness, Cather suggests that the literary voices are those best heeded by a people otherwise condemned to be the victims of their own misplaced faith in technology and its proponents. Her Alexander is an emperor of havoc, and one feels she takes a certain resentful satisfaction in the failure of his bridge.

The novel also shows a degree of authorial anxiety not allayed by the catastrophic fictional climax. For now, Cather must acknowledge the power of the engineer. Her best hope is that in the long run the the writer will prevail, not the engineer. Surrounded by the industrial technology of Pittsburgh, Cather spoke of herself and of all artists when she said that the music of her Pittsburgh friend, the composer Ethelbert Nevin, "will live when the armour plate made at Homestead [steel works] is eaten away with rust," since "it is possible for a lyric to outlive a battle-ship and a nation's songs to outlive its navy" (Byrne and Snyder 34). This, in essence, is the argument she tries to write large in *Alexander's Bridge*, even though readers suspect the sentiment must come from massive denial of the industrial-age realities confronting her daily in Pittsburgh and New York, the cities where she lived in maturity.

VICTORIANA

Not that everyone involved in art in a technological society felt the pull of opposing allegiances. Some in the arts were untouched by the opposition between Wright's blocks and Alexander's bridge. For them, the tension between the two was unnecessary and even unseemly. Their position on these matters was clear and free of ambiguity. They simply felt that art inhabited a province properly exclusive of machine and structural technology. In their view the arts belonged by definition to a higher spiritual realm untainted by machines or structures. These aesthetes really represented the old Victorian dualism separating art from technology. The engineer, in that scheme, was fit to mine, to dredge, to build bridges, or to put up railway sheds. But he had no legitimate place in the arts, whose devotees were committed to keep the muses' shrines free of him.

Harriet Monroe (1860–1936), the founder of *Poetry* magazine, is an instructive case in point. Chicago-born and bred, she moved in the city's literary circles. As a Chicagoan in the 1880s, she saw the great engineering-architectural triumph of the commercial skyscrapers, as had Henry Adams. As a friend of the Chicago novelist, Henry Blake Fuller, she no doubt had listened to his outspoken critique of these very buildings. Fuller's *The Cliff-Dwellers* (1893) complains that "all a building is nowadays [is] one mass of pipes, pulleys, wires, tubes, shafts, chutes, and what not, running through an iron cage of from fourteen to twenty stages." The engineer, the novel complains, has hamstrung the architect-artist, who becomes a mere decorator "asked to apply the architecture by festooning on a lot of tile, brick, and terra cotta" (95–97).

Fuller's critique cut close to home for Harriet Monroe, because her brother-in-law, the architect-engineer John Wellborn Root, was a principal designer of the tall buildings Fuller found distasteful. At his untimely death in 1891 Monroe decided to write a biography of his career. *John Wellborn Root: A Study of His Life and Work* (1896) is a work of familial devotion and of admiration for the artistic achievement of its subject. Monroe's book is striking in one respect especially relevant to this discussion. She shows a remarkable determination to preserve the aesthetic purity of her subject precisely by *not* taking full cognizance of his interest and achievement in engineering.

Root was "an architect who did engineering" (Billington 107). He took a degree in civil engineering from New York University and soon was espousing the principles of Henry Adams's mentor, Viollet-le-Duc. In Chicago he formed a highly successful partnership with Daniel H. Burnham. Their firm, Burnham and Root, designed twenty-seven major Chicago buildings in the 1880s and over two hundred buildings in all. A recent scholar remarks that "because of his technical training, Root approached the two Chicago engineering problems —marshland subsoil and metal superstructure—without hesitation. He invented the concrete foundation reinforced with a grillage of steel rails, and he was the first designer to use the metal skeleton as the complete wall structure" (Billington 107).

Harriet Monroe could not be expected to know these facts when she began to sort through Root's papers in preparation for her biography. Her completed book, however, shows a remarkable obliviousness—or perhaps imperviousness—to Root's technical expertise and its relation to his architectural achievement. Both were manifest, for instance, in the acclaimed Monadnock Building (1892), a continuously vertical structure whose walls, freed of structural weight that was borne by the metal skeleton within, became "weather protection and a source of light" (Billington 111). Monroe does concede briefly that "ability as a designer [combined] with ability as a constructive engineer has always been rare among architects," and she reprints long passages from Root's 1890 essay on the construction of modern office buildings (120). But Monroe failed to appreciate the integrity of technics and artistry in Root's work, even though she quotes, with approval, Root's statement that anyone who thinks science crushes "the rising fancies of the poet or painter" is "grossly misled" (206–7).

Monroe's method, finally, was to commemorate Root's artistic purity by minimizing the importance of his engineering work. "John Root's equipment for the practice of his profession was rather in the quality of his mind than in his training," and "the degree of bachelor of science and civil engineering . . . availed him little in architecture" (18). Monroe makes these remarks even as she sets forth Root's brother's own discussion of Root's engineering innovations.

Monroe exalted her subject in the only way she knew, in romanticized hymns doubtless intended to rescue Root from anti-engineering sneers like those we noted in *The Cliff-Dwellers*. "Beauty was the chief thing in the world for him" in boyhood. "His heart thrilled to the appeal of the arts." His best buildings "have a way of singing to the blue sky" and are "dedicated to the Muses by every line and ornament" (11, 151). Her biography, intended as an act of tribute, is a schizoid work not only because Root's engineering aesthetics are interleaved with Monroe's effusions, but because the book works misguidedly to remove its subject from his own proper aesthetic achievement. In the late 1890s Harriet Monroe typified the genteel literary mind that saw no possible bonding of technology and the fine arts, even when the connection was evident in works of structural art that rose up from the very street. The functional, "Utilitarian Theory of Beauty" inscribed in Root's buildings would reach Monroe's consciousness only in the 1910s, when Ezra

Burnham and Root, Monadnock Building, 1889–91 (Courtesy Chicago Historical Society)

Pound, the first European-based correspondent of her newly launched *Poetry* magazine, began in his letters to tutor her in the poetics of efficiency (Pound, *Selected Letters* 11, 49).

DANGER

It was a time . . . when learning and thought paused. Without music, without poetry, without beauty in their lives or impulses, a whole people, full of native energy and strength of lives lived in a new land, rushed pell-mell into a new age.

Sherwood Anderson, *Poor White*, 1920

The struggle between Wright's blocks and Alexander's bridge was one version of the larger struggle, which Cather recognized, between literature and technology. It was a struggle between the writers and the engineers. Wright, once again, is helpful here. Though optimistic about contemporary artists' opportunities to exploit the machine, he grasped the dimensions of the contemporary crisis in literary-technological terms. In his 1901 Hull House address, "The Art and Craft of the Machine," he indicated that social and aesthetic power were in fact shifting away from the written word toward structural and machine technology, from the authors to the engineers and their cohorts. As he said in a revised version of that talk, "Today we have a scientist or an inventor in place of a Shakespeare or a Dante" (qtd. in Roth 365). He meant that the written word was no longer intellectually dominant in Western culture. He indicated that the writer had been displaced by those enacting human thought in new technological forms. He meant that the bridge, the steel-framed building, and the machine had dethroned the book.

The optimistic Wright, however, understood that although this power shift involved the artists in ways potentially damaging to them, it also held out great promise for their immediate future. It could be exhilarating and inspiring to artists of all kinds. The rapid ascendance of the machine and its values was affecting every area of civilization and precipitating a crisis in the arts. But Wright's grasp of the situation is best stated in the definition of the Chinese characters for crisis (weū gū), which, in English, translate conceptually into the terms "danger" and "opportunity." The architect recognized that the power shift away from the written word toward the machine endangered all artists but was convinced that technology provided the basis for a splendid revitalization of the arts.

Frank Lloyd Wright was no lone eccentric. The young architect was a plausible spokesman for the position of poets and novelists in the new century. He made the argument to which others assented, often in the figures of speech which acknowledge that aesthetic and social power had gravitated to the new structural and machine technology. As we saw, the popular novelists Rex Beach and Harold Bell

Wright identified the engineer as a poetic visionary. Other voices joined in, one of them a writer for the *Atlantic Monthly* (1913), who extolled "the engineers whose poetry is too deep to look poetic" and whose gifts "have swung their souls free . . . like gods." The *Atlantic* essayist suggested that the machine age ought to discourage "minor" poets whose decayed romantic figures of "nightingales, poppies, and dells" were now trite and irrelevant. "Machinery is our new art-form," the essayist said, calling for a machine-age generation of poets (Lee 201, 199).

Writers like this, calling the engineer the "true poet," underscore the art-technology crisis. The crux of the matter is the relation between imagination and civilization—and thus is one of aesthetic and social power. That power in America had a long written tradition in religious, political, and belletristic documents. The powerful texts of America were in large part verbal, extending from the seventeenth century to the contemporary moment. Yet now, at the turn of the twentieth century, and in the face of stunning engineering feats, analysts began to state, and writers to feel, the threat of diminishment, even of the displacement that Wright perceived with stark clarity. We need now to examine one text, a novel, which works to define this crisis in terms of the danger it presents to a writer allied wholeheartedly with the world of Alexander's bridge.

Sherwood Anderson (1876–1942), like Cather, thought technology dangerous to literature. His were "crude times," he said, "when thoughts leaped forth, / Conquering, destroying, serving steel and iron" (*Mid-American Chants* 78). Alluding both to machine technology and to its wartime uses, Anderson vowed to combat technological thought with "prayers and dreams," by which he meant the imagination of the writer. Anderson, like Cather, felt that writers and inventor-engineers were locked in a struggle for imaginative dominance, in fact for proprietary rights to the imagination itself. Anderson acknowledged that the arts of the written word had not been adequate to the new machine age. "Thought and poetry," he said, "died or passed as a heritage to feeble fawning men who also became servants of the new order" (*Poor White* 62).

Now robust writers must wrest the rights to "dreams" from the invasive utilitarians of that new order—so Anderson argued. In fiction Cather had set a critical precedent. In romantic terms she tried to champion the writer by showing the superiority of the contemplative, humanistic mind to the frenzied and disordered mind of the engineer. In this same vein an anxious Anderson tried to affirm the primacy of the writer's imagination. Like Cather, he attempted an exposé of the technological mind. In *Poor White*, he tried to demystify the man-made heroes, the inventor-engineers he feared had become "a new set of semi-mythical heroes" for the machine age (246–47). *Poor White* is Anderson's indictment of the pathology, sexual repression, and perversion of nature he thought represented by the technological imagination.

Poor White belongs to the world of Alexander's bridge. It pledges allegiance to an organic, unitary view of the natural world and the human place in it. This world is a romantic landscape from which the arts of the written word emerge naturally as emanations of spiritual wholeness. This is not a world of assembly or of construction but of seamless organic harmony. At its pristine best this once was a world in which older men walked the "moonlit roads" talking of God. The young men, listening, "caught the drift of the talk and made poetry of it" (62). In America this "poetry" was made possible by the traditions of village life, which Anderson idealizes as perfectly communal and enriched by generations of "old humanness." The men farmed or followed the crafts of carpentry, wagon making, smithing, etc. "On the farms and in the houses in the towns the men and women worked together toward the same ends in life" (129). Above all "it was a time for art and beauty to awake in the land" (131).

But not now. This unitary world has been invaded, suddenly, by history, for the era of gear-and-girder industrialism has come to blight the land, its people, and its art. It is an intrusive—and it is to be hoped, temporary—aberration from the spiritually unified, romantic cosmos. For now, the age of the factory has destroyed the village idyll and jeopardized the life of the imagination. Now the same young men who used to listen to their fathers' voices and make "poetry" from what they heard are "swept away from thinking and dreaming." "Definite things" are the order of the day, and the young men, confused by the clamor, now go off to technical school (62). "I want [my son] to be a mechanical engineer," a father is heard to say. "It's a mechanical age and a business age. I want him to keep in the spirit of the times" (358). Anderson represents the new spirit in the figure of Hugh McVey, an inventor of complicated agricultural and industrial machinery. Just as Willa Cather chose to etch an iconoclastic portrait of the bridge-building civil engineer, so Anderson turned his critical energies upon the designer of complex machinery.

In one important way Anderson differs from Cather, who presented her engineer as a phenomenon of nature. Anderson, on the contrary, argues that the technological mind is developmental, not phenomenal. To him, the engineer is a figure shaped by warped cultural values and perverse social trends. *Poor White* is an effort to trace the genesis and development of a technological intellect. Anderson, who had written for the company trade journal *Agricultural Advertising*, undertook the anatomy of the kind of mind represented in the harvesters and threshers familiar to him in the midwestern fields and in magazine layouts. In *Poor White* he attempted an anatomy of the imagination embodied in mechanistic forms.

Hugh McVey, "the man of iron and steel," begins life as an industrial-age Huck Finn. A native of Mudcat Landing, Missouri, he is born into a world of "filth, flies, poverty, fishy smells" and of the birthright of indolence befitting the semiorphaned son of the town drunk and wastral (352). A slouching, gangly boy, Hugh is predisposed to sleep and, when awake, to daydream. By this Anderson suggests an incipient poetic imagination in the boy. "Half formed thoughts passed like visions through his mind" (27).

His most powerful poetic vision prophesies the dire technological age. The daydream begins on the banks of the Mississippi when a supine, relaxing Hugh imagines one cloud detaching itself from others, voyaging off, then returning, "a half-human thing" that agitated the others until the entire sky became a scene of disturbance. Hugh, still on the riverbank, next imagines himself airborne, looking down to see the countryside destroyed in an industrial apocalypse. Agrarian America is literally uprooted and washed away by the raging river. Forests are destroyed, hills torn open. "The white faces of drowned men and children, borne along by the flood, looked up into [Hugh's] mind's eye" (27–29). Though a struggling Hugh manages to awaken, this dream of disaster recurs almost nightly. To escape his own prophetic dreams Hugh turns to his "definite things," ironically to the very technologic objects that help to convert the dream into a nightmarish industrial-age reality.

Anderson employs "definite things" as a code term for the industrial-era thought he deplores. Real poets, real dreamers engage the ineffable and intangible, which is to say the spiritual world. They concern themselves with the immaterial, with ambiguity and ambivalence in human thought and feeling. The definite-minded people, on the contrary, are quantifiers and materialists. They deal in numbers and in objects, usually at the expense of humane values. They are the utilitarians, the workers at girders and gears. *Poor White* is virtually a laboratory in which Anderson shows the conditions under which a natural dreamer can be warped into a person of "definite" things.

How does it happen?—first, from an uprooted life, implicitly the life of thousands of young Americans streaming to the cities and thus deserting their hometown farmsteads and villages in the late nineteenth and early twentieth centuries. Hugh is a specimen of the displaced villager. Shy and withdrawn, he remains a lonely alien living in the Ohio village community which is not his own.

Hugh's work is thus presented as the defensive act of an alienated man. For the lonely, isolated Hugh has absorbed the protoindustrial values of a railroad station-master and his puritanical wife, who were virtual foster parents to the boy back in Mudcat Landing. Because their insistence upon constant industriousness constitutes the young man's only appreciable schooling, Hugh forces himself to concentrate on the objects and numbers that are foreign to his poetic nature. On residential streets he counts the fence pickets and the trees, then calculates the per-tree yield of pickets, gradually increasing his rule-of-thumb accuracy. In utilitarian fantasy he builds imaginary houses with lumber cut from trees lining the streets and ponders how the smallest treetop limbs might be utilized. He is becoming, of course, the man who mentally dis-assembles, who thinks about component parts and creates a gear-and-girder world.

Anderson insists that mental exercise in quantification is, in and of itself, pathologic. It signifies sexual repression and the avoidance of intractable human problems that engage the poet. Hugh deliberately keeps himself awake at night with thoughts of "definite things" because, once asleep, he is plagued by the recurrent nightmare about the fate of humanity in the industrial age. It is a dream he cannot begin to contend with.

Hugh McVey lacks the psychological insight of the writer. Knowledge comes only to his subconscious mind when he sleeps. Interpretive power eludes him. He is a mass of voiceless intuition and longing, of powerful feeling thwarted by its very inarticulateness. He yearns for sexual intimacy, friendship, and acceptance, but all in a mental maze of undifferentiated longing. A reticent man who speaks in monosyllables, Hugh has no words, no language in which to express himself. In the novel the narrator must explain him because he cannot explain himself —which becomes one way for Anderson to affirm the powers of the writer at the expense of the engineer. The man of definite things is dumb, tongue-tied even with his new bride. She knows why and says so in terms Anderson could only approve: "thinking of machinery and the making of machines had been at the bottom of her husband's inability to talk with her" (326). Unless or until he can learn to speak, he must have a spokesman, a narrator-poet, or a wife. In the meantime the inventor-engineer is hostage to his own inarticulateness and vulnerable to the predations of the glib entrepreneur.

Yet Anderson cannot easily dismiss Hugh McVey as a "definite-minded" utilitarian or as a mere victim of cunning businessmen. Repelled by the industrial age, the novelist nonetheless acknowledged its potent energies and even attempted to imagine the ways in which a Hugh McVey could be defined as a modern poet. We recall that Willa Cather, facing the opportunity to explore the component-part aesthetics of a suspension bridge, turned away without nodding in the direction of sculpture or architecture or engineering. But when journalists and others were proclaiming the engineers to be the modern American poets, Anderson evidently tried to be empathetic.

The novelist did sense a certain kinship between the writer and the engineer-inventor. Anderson must have imagined that a man like Hugh McVey would work under conditions similar to a writer's. Both would labor in solitude, withdrawn from the world which often misunderstood them. "All men lead their lives behind a wall of misunderstanding," writes Anderson, who led a covert literary life himself, drafting his first four novels while outwardly leading a businessman's life in Ohio. "Now and then a man, cut off from his fellows by the peculiarities of his nature, becomes absorbed in doing something that is impersonal, useful, and beautiful" (221).

The arduous route to that "something" offered another point of fellowship, since Hugh McVey's mind is not, as Anderson's was not, facile or precocious. The novelist saw this parallel: the novice writer must master the rudiments of grammar and the mechanics of punctuation (which Anderson himself learned only in adult life) and school himself with literary models; so the aspirant inventor pores over mail-order books on mathematics and mechanics, dismantles a clockworks, and "carefully" studies the newest agricultural machines that arrive at the local freight house. We are meant to see genius earned even as Anderson gains a certain empathy with the inventor-engineer by identifying Hugh's struggles with his own.

Anderson even tries a crucial crossover in which Hugh's fixation on "definite things" flowers into an imaginative vision. "His inclination to dreams . . . began to reassert itself in a new form." His brain "played no more with pictures of clouds and men in agitated movement but took hold of steel, wood, and iron. Dumb masses of materials taken out of the earth and the forests were molded by his mind

into fantastic shapes. . . . He saw in fancy a thousand new machines, formed by
his hands and brain, doing the work that had been done by the hands of men"
(68).

The key to Anderson's approval lies in the humanitarian motive prompting
Hugh's vision. The novelist can appreciate Hugh's aspiration to lessen the human
burden of incessant toil. Concealed at dusk by a cabbage field, Hugh watches a
farm family toiling to plant the spring cabbage crop. "They came down the long
row toward him . . . like grotesquely misshapen animals driven by some god of the
night to the performance of a terrible task" (77). He overhears them complain
about their "slavery." "What's the good of being alive," says one of the farm boys,
"if you have to work like this?" Observing the repetitious, machine-like motions of
the young bodies, Hugh begins to imagine a mechanism that could alleviate brutal
drudgery. He now has a definite task with a humanitarian purpose. Though his first
machine, a plant setter, fails, he succeeds brilliantly with a lifter that dumps entire
carloads of coal for ship or factory boilers, and with the successful agricultural
machinery which includes the McVey Corn Cutter.

Fortified with this morality of technology, Anderson manages to confer the
accolade, *poetry*, on Hugh's machinery. The corn-cutting that is now semimech-
anized by Hugh's invention is "poetry . . . set to another rhythm" (224). The coal-
car lifter which sends forth "a long reverberating roar" along loading docks has
"made a new kind of poetry in railroad yards and along rivers" (225). For a time
the young woman Hugh eventually marries sees him as a poet: "He was a creative
force. In his hands dead inanimate things became creative forces" (247).

But fundamentally Anderson remains committed to the organic, romantic world
of *Alexander's Bridge*. And that world is directly opposed to the gear-and-girder
world Hugh McVey represents. *Poor White* shows the case of the writer with
primary allegiance to preindustrial America trying hard to endorse the engineer as
a poet for his age, when he deeply believes that the engineer is a destroyer of an
older, better world. Underneath he feels animosity, not kinship. As a result, he
subverts even his own deliberate efforts to praise the inventor-engineer as a cousin
of the artist.

For one thing, the novel is consistently negative about the engineer-inventor's
work. Hugh moves from the picket calculations to systematic machine design
because he is "desperate," not because he feels engaged or challenged. And
Anderson takes every opportunity to say that work with machine parts is only the
tortuous act of a twisted mind. Here, for instance, is Hugh at work in his shop:

> How many days, weeks, and months he had already worked there, thinking in
> iron—twisted, turned, tortured to follow the twistings and turnings of his
> mind—standing all day by a bench beside other workmen—before him
> always the little piles of wheels, strips of unworked iron and steel, blocks of
> wood, the paraphernalia of the inventor's trade. (309)

Elsewhere Anderson has said that Hugh's work consists of "twisting" parts of iron

Coal-car dumper, an invention Sherwood Anderson attributes to his fictional character, Hugh McVey, in Poor White. Collier's, *1916*

International Harvester exhibition, St. Louis World's Fair, 1904. A similar photograph appeared in the July 1904 Agricultural Advertising, *for which Sherwood Anderson worked as editor.* The Greatest of Expositions, Completely Illustrated, *1904*

and steel and that his dreams have been "twisted into new channels so that they expressed themselves in definite things" (352, 246). Repeated, these terms of contortion urge readers to see technological invention itself as the contorted, unnatural act of a tormented psyche. It goes without saying that Anderson deprives his protagonist of every artist's deepest pleasure in the solution to a problem of aesthetic form.

Perhaps Hugh McVey was coming too close to Anderson. It is just a step from "little piles of wheels" to little piles of words, from the "paraphernalia" of the engineer to that of the writer. In retrospect, it seems so easy for the novelist to have recognized an equivalent relation between words and machine parts, both demanding an artful, functional integration. That relation was one that William Carlos Williams understood and welcomed.

But Anderson could not. His romantic, organic world would have shattered had he recognized that point of identity between himself and his character. This point is crucial. To see himself and Hugh McVey as brothers, both designers manipulating component parts, would have violated the novelist's worldview. To see the poet in the engineer would also have meant seeing the engineer in the poet. Anderson would then have to acknowledge his role as a constructor of fiction. He could no longer define himself as a singer of poetic story-songs, but as a designer of fictional forms. His own identity would be forced to change radically. He could no longer bear the torch of the organically unitary world. Alexander's bridge would fall to pieces—rather, to component parts. The world that Alexander's bridge represents, moreover, would be destroyed. Keeping it intact meant denying the writer's identity with Hugh McVey, and vice versa. Thus Anderson kept his distance by denying engineer aesthetic legitimacy as a designer.

Hugh's fate, however, is not sealed. He began as a protopoet and was side-tracked by circumstance. His engineering is really a mistake because Hugh, by temperament, is a dreamer. Thus he can be redeemed, brought back to his true self. He need only undergo a conversion experience that frees him from technological absorptions and brings him back into the realm of the poets and dreamers. The conversion originates in Hugh's sexual awakening following his marriage. A postnuptial week of agonized inhibition concludes with Hugh's sexual fulfillment, which Anderson describes in the image of a bird taking flight, traditionally a figure of spiritual freedom. Not surprisingly, Anderson makes sexual expression, man-hood itself, tantamount to the awakening of the imagination, which is not possible for the man obsessed with invention, itself an escape from suppressed sexual desires and from society. Aroused by his wife, Hugh feels that "within himself something new had been born or another something that had always lived with him had stirred to life" (318).

Before Hugh can qualify as a bona fide poet, however, he must also repent. That is, he must gain an awareness that industrial technology is the Pandora's box releasing every kind of evil into the world. First, he must realize his culpability as an inventor-engineer responsible for ruining the craftsman, in the novel the martyred, sainted figure. Anderson's harness maker "feels the touch of the heavy finger of industrialism," which dwarfs him (133). Anderson plays the harness maker's story in counterpoint to Hugh's. A superb master craftsman, the harness maker has taken lifelong pride in his trade, which is soon to disappear with the proliferation of a factory-produced harness (and with "a new machine that [goes] along roads at a startlingly increased rate of speed" [324]). The harness maker suffers unendurable humiliation when his commercially minded assistant stocks his shop with low-cost factory-made harnesses. At last the distraught, brooding man turns upon the assistant and kills him. Once captured and brought into town, he whirls upon Hugh, crying, "It wasn't me. You did it," then sinks "his fingers and teeth into Hugh's neck" (349).

Hugh McVey's spiritual task is to grasp the full import of the craftsman's accusation. Bitten and infected, in Anderson's term, with his "disease of thinking," Hugh comes home to himself (that is, his poetic self), by recognizing that his work with machinery has wrought incalculable evil. Hugh's redemption is virtually programmatic as he changes, so to speak, from a technological Pinocchio into a real boy. He gains the power of empathy, which is the monopoly of poets in *Poor White*. For Hugh can only appreciate the full horror of the machine age if he first imagines lives other than his own. Resolving not to infringe on another man's patent, Hugh thinks about that man, then recalls his own dissolute, alcoholic father and for the first time asks himself why the man so craved liquor. The question, Anderson argues, is generically the writer's own, since it requires conjecture about human nature and character. There, says Anderson, was "a problem that could not be solved in wood and steel." At the moment Hugh is virtually helpless to deal with it because "he had lived but little in the life of the imagination, had been afraid to live that life" (352, 361–63).

Beginning his quest to understand others, Hugh sees the evils of machine technology. The berry fields have given way to grim warehouses and factories, and the farm family once slaving in their cabbage fields now toil as factory hands, industrial slaves under a brutal piecework system that results in a violent strike in which three are killed and poisonous feelings linger on. Groups become factions, and friends rivals. Swarms of strange men, many of them foreigners, press into town for work, forcing the sectioning of agricultural lands into streets and houses "all alike, universally ugly." The community has been destroyed. In its place stands a filthy industrial city. Facing up to all this in late-night ruminations, Hugh complains in utilitarian terms, "The evening has been wasted. I have done nothing" (354). We know better. For the first time he has looked inside his mechanized Pandora's box.

A chastened Hugh is now ready to join the ranks of the poets. Traveling on business through the industrial Midwest, he begins a meditation on a handful of colored stones, which he sees symbolically and metaphorically, which is to say poetically. Anderson writes, "The same light that had played over the stones in his hand began to play over his mind, and for a moment he became not an inventor but a poet. The revolution within had really begun" (358). For Anderson, Hugh is reborn and thus redeemed. He will deal with life's hard questions, the ones technological minds avoid. "The time of comparatively simple struggle with definite things, with iron and steel, had passed." Thus Anderson elevates Hugh as a prophetic figure, precocious in the machine age and now, reborn as a poet, "still in advance of his fellows" (356). Hugh becomes Anderson's symbol for the poetic future in which machine technology will be repudiated, in fact transcended. Everything about it points toward the 1820s America of, say, John Greenleaf Whittier's *Snow-Bound*.

Poor White presents the dilemma of the twentieth-century writer intrenched in the world of Alexander's bridge in the age of Frank Lloyd Wright's blocks. Anderson is the nostalgic romantic in the gear-and-girder era. He is trapped between sentimentality and rage. His novel is weakened by its worldview.

Hugh's early, prophetic dream of industrial apocalypse sends up a warning signal early in the novel. The dream of a troubled sky and a flooding Mississippi are meant to provide a glimpse of the boy's native imagination which is so regrettably suppressed by a utilitarian culture. The dream ought to give us some basis to regret the young poet we have lost. But because the symbols of the clouds and the river are disappointingly banal, we are left without any conviction that the poetic mind has suffered in its conflict with "definite things."

Hugh's play with a handful of colored stones in a closing scene refocuses Anderson's problem. From his Pullman coach window Hugh sees the grimy Ohio industrial cities. He wants "light and color to play over them as they played over the stones." At this point readers are also prepared to see the light and color of Hugh's poetic mind. At last Anderson will show us Hugh's liberated imagination at work. He makes up "words over which lights played," words, says Anderson, which form "a good phrase and lights . . . play over it as they played over the colored stones" (369).

Hugh's actual statement, however, is embarrassing. The poetic expression for which we have waited throughout the novel falls flat in banality. It is, to quote, "'The gods have scattered towns over the flat lands.'" One rereads the line in mounting dismay. If this is poetry, the reader may think, then give us instead more brilliant mechanical inventions. Trying to have Hugh sound poetically robust, Anderson only manages to make him sound insipid.

Unintentionally, Anderson makes a procrustean bed for the poet. Dreams are judged principally on the basis of their content. The important thing, it seems, is not to dream, but to dream correctly. The content, the message, is what counts. The dreamer qualifies only if his vision is politically antitechnological. Language, form, imagery, symbol—all the elements of imaginative literature—are subordinate to the extractable message. Hugh's dream slides from poetics to propaganda, but the novelist seems not to have noticed. This whole problem is greater than Anderson's use of a flaccid poetic line and his failure to sculpt his literary symbols. These only indicate the fundamental problem, which is the novelist's inability to put forward the poetics able to challenge what is, by his own definition, the technological hegemony of his time. *Poor White* really demonstrates that the world of Alexander's bridge is not a viable alternative to that of Frank Lloyd Wright's blocks. In 1920 an attenuated romanticism was not an adequate response to the gear-and-girder world.

The outcome of Hugh's poetic life shows why. In Anderson's scheme the dreamer, the figure representing the poetic view of life, is presumed to have a vision opposed to the machine age. By Anderson's definition, to have an imagination is to possess that vision. Yet Hugh's poetry fails even to hint at it, except insofar as the skies, fields, and towns endorse an agrarian, preindustrial America and make the dreamer an anachronistic, even atavistic figure.

Worse, a paralytic one. For Hugh's redemption requires that he give up serious efforts at machine design. To be spiritually saved is to be made "useless for the work of his age," meaning machine work. So the redeemed Hugh dabbles at his bench, presumably enjoying family life with his wife and children, all of whom live a quasi-agrarian life on her father's farm. To scratch the surface of that life, however, is to see that Hugh McVey is immobilized. He has no real place in the world. He has nothing to do. Hugh can only be the reformed engineer-inventor. His value lies ultimately in what he is *not*.

Hugh's immobilization says a great deal about the relation of the world of Alexander's bridge to that of Wright's blocks. To withdraw from the world of design is to retire. It is to retreat into some idea of the past. It is to become an effigy, for the world of Alexander's bridge offers no alternative terms of individual engagement. That romantic world, the novel says despite itself, is unreal. In fact, the world of Alexander's bridge is the fiction of *Poor White*. Just as the former inventor is identified by what he is not, so *Poor White* defines itself according to the machine technology it rejects. Convinced that the times call for a powerfully imaginative alternative to an industrial culture, Anderson cannot provide one.

OPPORTUNITY: IMAGINATION EX MACHINA I

It is the novelist's business to set down exactly manners and appearances: he must render the show, he must, if the metaphor be permitted, describe precisely the nature of the engine, the position and relation of its wheels.

Ezra Pound, "Patria Mia," 1913

Sherwood Anderson and Willa Cather represent those writers who feared that the technological mind had become preeminent and threatened to disempower them. As Ezra Pound's statement indicates, however, some writers felt differently. If Anderson and Cather fought the engineer, Ezra Pound and others embraced his values. Pound, along with the novelists John Dos Passos and Ernest Hemingway and the poet William Carlos Williams, found that engineers' machines and structures provided opportunities for innovation in form and style. Their writings show that Ezra Pound's linkage of fiction with machinery was more than a rhetorical flourish, more than an effort to update a traditional form with a current machine-age figure of speech. Of course Pound knew that his metaphor of fiction's enginery and gear wheels presented the novel in a contemporary way. In a world of "trees, animals, engines," it gave currency to a traditional, preindustrial imaginative form.

But Pound spoke theoretically when he described the modern novel as an engineer's drawing. His machine metaphor suggested that society could be delineated as a machine and the novel formally reflect its interworkings. We can imagine the protests this concept would have provoked from an outraged Anderson or Cather, to name only two contemporary writers on record for their resistance to an aesthetic of the machine. But Pound, the modernist, asserted the machine metaphor with just a touch of self-consciousness. He spoke as one who welcomed the aesthetic possibilities of machines in the arts. He joined figures like the British critic T. E. Hulme, who noticed the painters "expressing admiration for engineer's drawings" and the sculptors "expressing admiration for the hard clean surface of a piston rod" (97).

Pound's homage to the precisionist ethic of clear-cut, mechanical lines allies him with Frank Lloyd Wright. It indicates an allegiance to the values of machine technology at the expense of the handicrafts. But it also goes far to point up the basis for innovation in the novel, a form so different from painting and sculpture that it might seem to defy any serious analogy with machine design. Whether he fully understood it or not, Pound pointed toward the solution of a major problem facing any novelist who, like John Dos Passos, aspired to write fiction from an omniscient point of view in an age that no longer believed in an omniscient, God-like presence.

The machine and the engineered structure became liberating models for fiction in a secular and subjective age. Their dynamic and integrated system of component parts, whether presented in a bridge, a skyscraper, or an automobile engine, became the model on which the novel could be constructed. It is fair to say that in the twentieth-century United States machines and structures opened the way for radical innovation in the premises for fiction (and as we shall see, for poetry). In an age that no longer felt the presence of an omniscient and omnipotent deity, the engineer replaced God as the designer with whom the writer could identify. Even the critic hostile to machine technology recognized this point. "It is only the architect or the engineer who can really practice a craft today. . . . In modern industry the artist . . . is a designer" (Randall 293). A writer like Dos Passos, who called himself an architect, evidently grasped this point, as the very structure of his fiction reveals (Introduction, *Three Soldiers* n.p.). The engineer's machines and structures became the designs which, fashioned from component parts, enabled the novelist-architect to present a story in ways congruent with the times.

Dos Passos's machine-based design for novels was perhaps the result of biographical origins. Unlike Cather or Anderson, he had no roots in agrarian America. As the son of a prominent attorney and his mistress, he grew up in a demimonde of hotel suites in the United States and Europe. Apart from intermittent years spent at his father's Tidewater Virginia farm, Dos Passos traveled extensively with his mother, experiencing a cosmopolitan boyhood of frequent journey by rail and steamship. Scenes of crowds, of hotel lobbies and dining rooms, piers and concourses, of anonymous aggregations of people massed and gathered, fugitive encounters, overheard conversations, impersonal and fleeting relationships—such were the scenes of Dos Passos's boyhood. Enacted in Chicago, New York, Washington D.C., and in Mexico, Belgium, and England, such scenes must have convinced Dos Passos that the world was vast, impersonal, populous, shifting, interregional and multiethnic. If any twentieth-century writer should attempt to encompass it from an omniscient point of view, a writer of Dos Passos's background would be the likely candidate. As Edmund Wilson observed in an essay on Dos Passos, "Most of the first-rate men of Dos Passos's age—Hemingway, [Thornton] Wilder, Fitzgerald—cultivate their own little corners and do not confront the situation as a whole. Only Dos Passos has tried to take hold of it" (35).

He did not immediately try, in his writings, to "take hold of it." For Dos Passos's first three books marked out the same subjective territory of the young-man protagonists of Fitzgerald's and Hemingway's fiction. By the mid-1920s, however, Dos Passos grew dissatisfied with the subjective narration presented from the young man's viewpoint. He sought a way to cast the novel from the point of view of the omniscient, God-like narrator—yet knew he worked in a secular and subjective era which doubted the existence of an omniscient God. Not all novelists would find this situation problematic. A writer oblivious to this secular avant-garde climate of opinion, or a writer faithful to traditional sectarian belief in an all-knowing, all-powerful deity would simply proceed unabashed to write novels from the omniscient viewpoint. Yet Dos Passos knew he would be at cross-purposes with his age if he did so, since he identified himself as a modernist. An avant-garde writer, he was well aware that his artistic imperatives were on a collision course with his contemporary beliefs.

We can appreciate the crisis of a writer in Dos Passos's position if we recognize the depth of twentieth-century secularism. The critic J. Hillis Miller argues that from the Victorian era writers coped with "the disappearance of God" in their world and thus in their writings. Miller observes that for modern writers like Franz Kafka God "no longer inheres in the world as the force binding together all men and all things" (2). Prior to the modern period the Judeo-Christian culture presumed that God had authored the book of nature and that verbal symbols and metaphors incarnated the things they named. The poet was instrumental in setting forth divine analogies of God's world. But, as Miller says, modern literature records the history of the breakup of this union between man, God, nature, and language. Industrialization, the rise of science and technology, urbanization, and the rise of the middle class all led to the sense of isolation and destitution experienced by the Victorian writers and those who followed them.

Writers like John Dos Passos (1896–1970) were born into this post-Victorian world, which Miller and other critics have defined by its salient subjectivism. "Modern thought has been increasingly dominated by the presupposition that each man is locked in the prison of his consciousness. . . . [T]he assumption has been that man must start with the inner experience of the isolated self" (8). Miller reminds us that Henry James's novels exemplify this subjectivism by showing not the facts but characters' interpretations of them.

So in the fiction of F. Scott Fitzgerald, Ernest Hemingway, and others, there is the built-in subjectivity of the quasi-autobiographical novel. *The Great Gatsby* (1925), *The Sun Also Rises* (1926), and the collection *In Our Time* (1925), landmark texts of the 1920s, are presented through the narrator-protagonists Nick Carraway, Nick Adams, and Jake Barnes. These young men, in the course of the novels and stories, inevitably show their personal biases, prejudices, and perceptual limits. The format of the fiction in which they appear virtually announces the presumption of subjectivity. The authors can exploit this very quality to suggest a wider realm of knowledge inaccesible to the individual protagonists. But novels like these deny even the possibility of an encompassing omniscience on the part of their authors. It could hardly be otherwise, since their texts were conceived in a world from which an omniscient God was thought to have disappeared. In their art, accordingly, these writers were not free to take a God-like stance. If one lacks belief in an omniscient presence, one cannot authentically create a fictional world from that point of view.

Dos Passos, nevertheless, did seek to create a form of authorial omniscience true to the modern ethos of secularism but also faithful to the scope of a world presumed to be knowable beyond the self. In fact, Dos Passos's early, subjective fiction shows his impulse to present the components of a wider world beyond the consciousness of the young men protagonists, the adventuring Telemachus and Lycaeus of *Rosinante*, and even Martin Howe and John Andrews of *One Man's Initiation* and *Three Soldiers*. Their consciousness in all three works is expanded with song lyrics, poems, snatches of overheard conversation, statements of social criticism, brief encounters with figures representing a wide range of socioeconomic groups. Dos Passos was trying to widen the scope of each novel with enriching artifacts of culture and history. These early novels, accordingly, indicate an author in search of a narrative form that could expand the world of the novel beyond the mind of any individual, no matter how capacious his consciousness or catholic his interests.

Dos Passos found his form by the mid-1920s. *Manhattan Transfer* (1925) was his first novel of authorial omniscience, a point of view continued and strengthened in the *U.S.A.* trilogy which included *The 42nd Parallel* (1930), *1919* (1932), and *The Big Money* (1936). These novels show Dos Passos's commitment, in narration, to a national consciousness, a sociocultural totality of America. That commitment found expression in a particularly modern form of narrative omniscience. As of *Manhattan Transfer* Dos Passos had succeeded in moving the world of the novel out of the protagonist's mind and into the material universe. The question is, On what basis was he able to do so? In fiction this thoroughly secular writer found a way, in modern terms, to assume an omniscient stance vis-à-vis himself and the novel. But the grounds on which he did so remain to be recognized. We must seek the rationale by which he achieved a new omniscient design for fiction. Dos Passos's enablement is rooted in contemporary technology. The narrative innovation that began with *Manhattan Transfer* and continued through the *U.S.A.* trilogy originated in structural and machine technology. It implicates the self-styled "architect" as an engineer.

Dos Passos understood the nature of his narrative task. "In a great city," he wrote, "there is more going on than you can cram into one man's career. I wanted to find some way of making the narrative carry a large load" (qtd. in Wagner, *Dos Passos* 63). Whether or not Dos Passos intentionally used the load-bearing figure from engineering, it is certain that he conceived of the novel as a structure that must embody all of metropolitan America, which he conceived in component parts. In *Manhattan Transfer* these included such mass-media forms as advertising ("FOUR OUT OF EVERY FIVE GET . . . EX-LAX, NUJOL, O'SULLIVAN'S") (293), popular music ("an the big baboon by the light of the moon / Was combing his auburn hair. . . . a querulous Sunday grinding of phonographs playing *It's a Bear*") (34, 197), newspapers (ADMITS KILLING CRIPPLED MOTHER . . . Nathan Sibbetts, fourteen years old, broke down today . . . and confessed to police that he was responsible for the death of his aged and crippled mother") (17), and movies ("Nickelodeon," as one section of *Manhattan Transfer* is entitled).

Dos Passos needed, moreover, to create a narrative form reflective of fast-paced metropolitan rhythms. The title, *Manhattan Transfer*, suggests the rapid-transit life portrayed within a novel named for a northern New Jersey rail station at which trains switched to electric power to begin their underground voyage into New York City. The novel is filled with rapid transit via the subway, the railroad, the elevator, and the automobile (*"Glowworm trains shuttle in the gloaming through the foggy looms of spiderweb bridges, elevators soar and drop in their shafts.* . . . [T]he endless stream of automobiles whirred in either direction past the yellowbrick row of stores") (305, 197). Dos Passos let the technology of rapid transit mandate his own fictional technique of fast movement from one character's story to another. He also underscores the rapid-transit age with the technique of jamming words together to suggest rapid-fire speech and instantaneous perception. We read, for example, of "topstory light," a "walnutpaneled diningroom," a "chocolatebrown haze," "whitegold light," "plumcolored clouds," "orangerinds," "sunsinged grass," "talcumpowder," and of "machineshops, buttonfactories, tenementhouses." In spoken language and on the printed page these breathlessly jammed words collapse time and space. They emphasize perceptual speed as a trait of the modern. To participate in twentieth-century life is to see, hear, speak, read, and write fast (118, 251, 136–37, 353).

When we discuss another "rapid-transit" writer, the poet William Carlos Williams, we will look closely at modernist America's preoccupation with "the God of speed" (*Dodsworth* 154–55). It affected virtually all writers of the 1910s–20s when the automobile and the "rush hour" signified a new rapid-transit culture. But Dos Passos's fast-paced fiction, we must recognize, grew out of a larger realm indicated by the Taylorist Efficiency Movement. Perceptually, we recall, the Taylorites' time-motion studies paradoxically multiplied space and time by dividing them. They raised the status of the mastermind able to dis-assemble and redesign matter-in-motion. The result was a streamlined kinetics. In fiction, this reformulation of matter in space and time gave Dos Passos's *Manhattan Transfer* and *U.S.A.* an emphatic rapid-transit structure which exploits, yet transcends, the fast pace of the urban settings.

Apart from popular culture and the mass media, Dos Passos's modern omniscient novel also included a representative sampling of the metropolitan population. The novelist loaded his narrative with a very large number of characters. The leading figures are Ellen Thatcher, a woman just born as the novel opens, and Jimmy Herf, a newspaperman who wants to become a writer. Ellen, who grows up to have a successful career in theater and fashion, loves "not wisely but too well," devoting herself first to a bisexual man of the theater, then falling deeply in love with an irresistible, irresponsible young drunkard, Stan Emery, who instead marries a casual date during a weekend binge at Niagara Falls, then dies in a fire. Dos Passos continues Ellen's story as an important thread in the novel. Pregnant with Stan's child, she will marry the devoted and steady Jimmy Herf, who offers to become the baby's father. The marriage fails, but, more important to Dos Passos's theme of wasted lives, Ellen has begun to turn brittle and metallic. She has lost her faith in

Jumping horse, matter-in-motion, in Eadweard Muybridge, Animal Locomotion, *1887 (Courtesy Special Collections, Van Pelt Library, University of Pennsylvania)*

love itself and feels "an invisible silk band of bitterness tightening around her throat. . . . [E]verything about her seemed to be growing hard and enameled," her mind "like a busted mechanical toy [going] brr all the time" (375, 400). As she moves cynically toward another marriage, one of material comfort, we are to understand that Ellen is a woman destroyed.

Jimmy Herf, whom some readers have identified as Dos Passos's alter-ego, reaches an equally pathetic terminus. Having refused an uncle's offer to take him into his business, Herf tries to make his way as a *New York Times* reporter. "It's a hellish rotten job and I'm sick of it," he confides to a cousin he happens to meet (247). Herf's stated ambition is to become a writer, and ostensibly to that end he finally does quit his job—only to find himself mired in a depressing domestic life "of diapers and coffeepots and typewriter oil and Dutch Cleanser" (303). By the end of the novel Herf desultorily continues to seek life, liberty, and the pursuit of happiness, the very phrasing now an ironic declaration of disillusionment, not independence. Flat broke and trailing a failed marriage, Herf hitchhikes out of New York, though Dos Passos gives us no reason to believe that a better world awaits him. As another character has said earlier in the novel, "The terrible thing about having New York go stale on you is that there's nowhere else. It's the top of the world. All we can do is go round and round in a squirrel cage" (220).

Although Herf and Ellen are Dos Passos's main characters, many others fill the novel, each with a life story. There is Bud Korpenning, a country bumpkin in Manhattan who commits suicide when he fails "to get to the center of things" or even to find a place on the margin of society (4). There is George Baldwin, an ambulance-chasing lawyer who wheels and deals his way into financial success and has contacts but no friends. Congo Jake, a French seaman without particular ambition, makes a fortune in bootleg liquor and assumes a new identity as Armand Duvall. These and other characters exist in a constant flux of arrival, departure, momentary pause, divorce, desertion, death.

Minor characters' fugitive encounters also fill the novel. Some are prosaic, others cries from the heart, but all seem to mix indiscriminately. "I used to think all I wanted was to get a good job an marry an settle down, and now I dont give a damn," says an unnamed sailor (387). A troubled seamstress, Anna, confesses to her lover, "I never did nothin to hurt anybody in my life. All I want is for em to leave me alone an let me get my pay and have a good time now and then" (389). Others merely gripe or make small talk that sounds like background "white noise." Their overheard voices, too, form a component of modern life.

Once the reader understands Dos Passos's format, it is easy to move along, alternately attuned to the momentary exchanges and engaged in the intertwined lives that tend to have the fleeting yet immediate interest of figures in oral histories. To begin to understand Dos Passos's debt to machine and structural technology, however, one must step back from this multiplex of lives. One must ask first, What is Dos Passos's basis for this mix of characters who form an aggregation but not a society? To read *Manhattan Transfer* or *U.S.A.* is to realize how radically Dos Passos rejected the established fictional tradition in which characters' relationships are based on lineage, ancestry, kinship patterns, or the common culture of a region.

At least one of his contemporaries noticed Dos Passos's nontraditional configuration of characters. The critic Matthew Josephson pointedly declined to compare *U.S.A.* with Zola's fictional epic of the Rougan-Macquarts or to Thomas Mann's *Buddenbrooks*, both family sagas (Sanders 1). Dos Passos's characters, as Josephson understood, coexist without kinship or home territory. Unlike George Eliot or Dickens, or for that matter James Fenimore Cooper or Mark Twain, Dos Passos's figures are neither rooted in a kinship pattern nor tied to locale. There is no familial or spatial rationale for their lives, which, by Victorian standards, makes theirs an arbitrary coexistence, one disturbing to some readers who complain, as Lionel Trilling did, of this "epic of disintegration" (Sanders 21).

In theme Dos Passos emphasizes a certain spiritual enervation. In the course of his novels hopes and dreams are blighted, ambition misplaced, love thwarted. Politically Leftist, Dos Passos persuades us that monopoly capitalism—in fact, any large and powerful organization—brings out the most barbarous human traits and that it crushes lives of individuals helpless to oppose it. In this sense *Manhattan*

Transfer is a fictional analogue to *The Waste Land*, and *U.S.A.* an echo of "The Hollow Men" (Hook 53–60; Krause 97–107).

The configuration, however, of Dos Passos's characters is highly structured. This in itself is a point of immediate interest, and one that bears upon Dos Passos's role as a novelist-engineer. Alfred Kazin has written that Dos Passos was "the first of the 'technological' novelists, the first to bring the novel squarely into the machine age and to use its rhythms, its stock piles of tools and people, in his books" (353–59). If only Kazin had spoken at greater length, for his intuition was accurate: Dos Passos *did* bring machine design into fiction. The basis of his innovation, however, has not been understood. It really begins in the crisis facing a twentieth-century novelist trying to move into the omniscient point of view and yet facing a secular world no longer held together in traditional bonds of culture and society.

In fiction Dos Passos was clearly unwilling to perpetuate those human relationships which he regarded as anachronistic. Like Henry James, he understood twentieth-century metropolitan life to be impersonal. To reflect an industrial, urban, immigrant, restless, disjunctive American scene with accuracy, the characters could *not* be drawn along the lines of those in the Victorian novel. Dos Passos sensed the pitfall awaiting a writer who populated the contemporary scene with characters constellated in outworn relationships. He needed a basis on which his novel could govern a large cast of characters unconnected by class, caste, family or community origins, or even friendship or temperament or ideological commitment to a political, religious, or artistic movement. To fall into traditional, that is, outdated, patterns would be to misrepresent the world and to falsify the novel. It would be to repeat the errors of such American predecessors as Robert Herrick, Frank Norris, even Dreiser. All of them, as we saw, deplored an unstable world which they represented, nonetheless, in conventionally stable narrations. Their themes spoke one language, their forms another.

Dos Passos sought a way to avoid their contradictions, knowing, however, that the novel demanded its own unity. No matter how experimental, it must exhibit its own aesthetic form. Dos Passos thus needed fictional coherence for a world that did not cohere through blood ties or allegiance to place. The novel had to cohere when the world it represented did not, at least not in traditional ways. Dos Passos needed, in other words, a way to encompass an arbitrary aggregation of people and symbols even as he faithfully evoked a metropolitan style of life characterized by its fast pace and its disjunctions. He was challenged to find some basis on which he could meet the demands of his art form while remaining true to his sense of metropolitan modernity. The scope of his fiction had to be large and his structure stabilizing of a world that seemed on its face fluctuant and unstable.

Here, at this crisis point, is where the machine and structure come in. Here we can recognize a crucial way in which structural and machine technology provided the model for the composition of the modern novel, for the machine and the structure offered Dos Passos a new conception of characters and their relationships to one another. Machines and structures presented the model of a functionally integrated design. They exhibited wholeness from impersonal parts dynamically integrated in a system. They therefore offered the novelist a new design possibility, one that enabled formal coherence without compromising the novelist's belief in an impersonal world including the major characters Ellen Thatcher and Jimmy Herf down to the lunch-counter waitress and the "longnosed Roumanian waiter" (374). Dos Passos's numerous characters are presented as human components integrated in a large-scale, dynamic system conceived on the model of machine and structural technology. In this sense the characters function virtually as parts interchangeable throughout the American scene, a point Kazin hinted at when he said that Dos Passos used "stock piles . . . of people" and which F. R. Leavis recognized when he called them "a representative assortment of average men and women" (71). Dos Passos severely criticizes a world in which people are so vulnerable to sociocultural forces that drive them apart; his novels, however, are marvels of integrated structure. He is America's engineer-novelist.

Dos Passos's novels really invite a new view of the fictional stock character, emphasized because he is replicable, not because he is historically familiar or because he is uniquely an individual. In the world of *Manhattan Transfer* there is no individuation of character, no crafting of the unique figure. Each character is an "everyman" from a stock inventory. Familiar characters, therefore, are not meant to resonate from the literary past. Readers are to see the character, for instance the country bumpkin, in a different light from those in literary tradition. When Hawthorne created the bumpkin, Robin, in "My Kinsman, Major Molineaux" in the mid-nineteenth century, he called forth a host of literary associations, including Shakespeare's Bottom (*A Midsummer Night's Dream*) and, in American literature, the rustics of Charles Brockden Brown and even the Benjamin Franklin who recollected his younger self gawking on the Philadelphia city streets with armfuls of bread.

Dos Passos's rustic, however, is not meant to recollect tradition. The recognizable bumpkin, Bud, is not notable for his familiarity through time as a figure often encountered in stage and story. Instead, Dos Passos emphasizes that in the era of the machine production of component parts, the stock character is but one standard figure interchangeable with countless others. Bud, like so many of Dos Passos's characters, comes from a demographic inventory. He is part of the "stock pile . . . of people," one of countless others just like himself. Nor should we deplore any robotlike quality. To recoil from Dos Passos's "automata," as one reader does, is to miss the point. Bud suffers, fails, kills himself. Ellen turns brittle. Their anguish, Dos Passos suggests, is literally typical, representative of life experience multiplied throughout America. The uniformity is the uniformity of experience in a culture of types rather than one of kinfolks.

Like many of his generation, Dos Passos had a love-hate relation to the machine age. He expressed the negative side as a Harvard senior when he wrote an essay critical of the human condition in an era of "science and its attendant spirits, Industrialism and Mechanical Civilization" (qtd. in Ludington 84). Like many

POWER users have become so accustomed to buying from local dealer's stocks that "specialty-built" equipment, however praised, holds no compensating advantages for the *immediate delivery* of pulleys, hangers, bearings, clutches, couplings, etc., built by one organization to operate as a complete unit in any plant.

And while Dodge equipment continues to serve all industrial plants as faithfully and as economically as it has since 1882, the mere offer of "something new" because it is *new* will mean little to those who have bought Dodge products because they know them to be reliable.

Dodge Sales and Engineering Company

Mishawaka, Indiana, and Oneida, New York

Canadian Manufacturers, Dodge Mfg. Co. of Canada, Ltd., Toronto and Montreal

Advertisement for standardized component parts. Literary Digest, *1920*

others, he used figures of machines in pejorative ways. "Machine-like promptness," "the machine that has been crushing us all," the "new religion of steel and stamped paper," the human "sausagemachine" are all typical phrases in which the novelist uses figures of machine technology to describe its hostility to human interests (Ludington 108, 158, 180, 238). In 1919 Dos Passos expressed his anxiety that modern man might be "swallowed and ground under the heel of forces that would make us cogs in the machine" (Ludington 183). Two of the biographies in *U.S.A.*, those of Henry Ford and Frederick W. Taylor, indict the technological mind for worshiping production and efficiency at the expense of human beings, who after a day on the assembly line were reduced, in Dos Passos's term, to "gray shaking husks" (*U.S.A.: Big Money* 57). And in 1932 Dos Passos separated serious writers like himself from the popular "daydream artist merely feeding the machine, like a girl in a sausage factory shoving hunks of meat into the hopper" (*Three Soldiers* viii).

But Dos Passos was also inclined to welcome machine technology and its values. They suited his self-conscious determination to be an avant-garde writer exploring new literary forms. We can, in fact, anticipate his exploitation of technology from his admiration for William Thackeray's *Vanity Fair*, the Victorian novel whose author defined himself as a puppet master, his characters as "puppets" (Ludington 64). Thackeray's figure of centralized control of a complex mechanism ultimately proved attractive to the author of *Manhattan Transfer*. He found its model for fictional structure irresistible, even though he disliked its political implications. Corporate capitalism, with its centralized control and its ethos of mass production, repelled Dos Passos. In order, however, to achieve the omniscience necessary for the novel, he found it necessary to participate in the power center of that very structure.

Dos Passos's biography shows other evidence of his engagement in contemporary technology. The novelist's urbane father may have helped to make the boy conscious of engineering feats, since John Randolph Dos Passos was interested in diesel engines and in plans to build tunnels under the Hudson River. The novelist himself was a child of the railroad, recalling "the speed and madness of the train," "the lurid glare" of industrial scenes glimpsed in passing from railway compartments (Ludington 18–19).

During travels in Italy in 1917–18, moreover, the young writer eagerly absorbed the writings of the Italian Futurists, including the 1909 manifesto of F. T. Marinetti, which celebrated machine technology as power and liberation from the constraints of the past. "A racing car whose hood is adorned by great pipes, like serpents of explosive breath," declared the manifesto, "is more beautiful than the *Victory of Samothrace*" (qtd. in Hughes 43). After the war years, as a correspondant for *New Masses* in the early 1920s, Dos Passos came under the influence of Veblen, who would become one of the heros in *The Big Money*. In later life Dos Passos recalled that "he had been extremely interested in the 'technocrats' during the 1920s and 'was certainly much influenced by [his] enthusiastic reading of Veblen'" (qtd. in Ludington 244). It is significant that three figures identified solely with technological inventiveness, Thomas Edison and the Wright Brothers, and the technologist-botanist Luther Burbank, emerge in *U.S.A.* as American heroes, as does Frank Lloyd Wright, whose innovative use of machine-made materials Dos Passos openly admired in *The Big Money*:

> Delightedly he reached out for new materials, steel in tension, glass, concrete, the million new metals and alloys.
> The son and grandson of preachers, he became a preacher in blueprints,
> projecting constructions in the American future instead of its European past.
> Inventor of plans,
> plotter of tomorrow's girderwork phrases. (*Big Money* 585–86)

Dos Passos, moreover, shared with his readers the generalized technological education of an early twentieth-century public exposed to engineers' structures and machines in metropolitan life. We must ask, therefore, What specific qualities of the engineers' structures or machines proved useful to the young novelist? First, the engineer attained a masterful overview of a complex system, whether it was a gearbox or an aquaduct. Of course Dos Passos had no technical expertise in any area of engineering. But as a twentieth-century metropolitan man, he observed railway systems and construction projects and glanced through the abundant illustrations of mechanical and structural systems featured in American periodicals, advertisements, and even postcards. Like other laypeople, Dos Passos became what Roland Barthes calls "an engineer by proxy." Barthes, as we noticed earlier, referred specifically to the visitor approaching the Eiffel Tower, whose structural members come clearly into view at close range.

Early twentieth-century metropolitan Americans were oftentimes engineers by proxy as a result of their overview of technological systems. They became so as onlookers at the steel-frame construction of bridges and buildings. In *Manhattan Transfer* the character who stares into the "girder forest" of a construction site is momentarily an engineer by proxy (24). In their armchairs Americans were engineers by proxy when they paused to look at the plentiful magazine machinescapes, illustrations of machines and structures in such magazines as *Cosmopolitan*, *Scientific American*, and *Collier's*. They even became engineers by proxy when peering at the urban complex of transit and traffic on view from the upper storeys of the skyscraper or, as the century progressed, from the airplane. In an urban environment the onlooker could become a proxy engineer when viewing the patterned energy of the city, its flow of population and transport.

This patterned energy is exactly what Frank Lloyd Wright attempted to invoke in the prose-poem that concludes his "Art and Craft of the Machine" and is the kind of overview Dos Passos brilliantly exploited in fiction. Wright invites his listener to join him at nightfall atop an office skyscraper. Before him lies "this greatest of machines, a great city [that] rises to proclaim the marvel of the units of its structure." Wright insists that his companion recognize each structural unit, from the drainage

Postcard view of Hudson Terminal and Tubes, New York City

THE TALLEST BUILDING IN THE WORLD

Illustration showing elevator system of Woolworth Building, New York City.
The Book of Wonders, *1916*

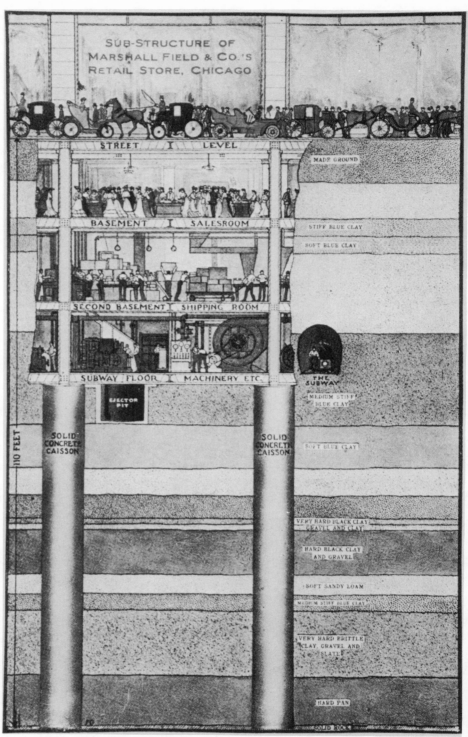

Postcard view of substructure of Marshall Field & Co., Chicago, ca. 1910s

THE LAND END OF A GREAT TUNNEL UNDER THE HUDSON

Illustration showing New York rail and subway systems. The Book of Wonders, *1916*

canal to the Bessemer converter. He invites his listener, the vicarious fellow onlooker, to feel knowledgeably rapturous about the scene before him. "Ten thousand acres of cellular tissue . . . the city's flesh" lie in view, "enmeshed by intricate network of veins and arteries." Like a tutor, Wright points out the integral systems that comprise the city, the sewerage system comparable to the "sanitation of the human body," the nervous system likened to the electrical circuits. He names the machine components—the fly wheels, tube boilers, governor gear, induction coils—to say that his rhapsodic tone is grounded in full knowledge of the mechanisms involved. He describes a delicacy in factory production and celebrates the newspaper, "millions of neatly folded, perfected news sheets, teeming with vivid appeals to passions, good and evil; weaving a web of intercommunications so far reaching that distance becomes as nothing."

Wright's purpose is to assert the urban machine as organic and democratic, the embodiment of "A SOUL!" (*Writings and Buildings* 72–73). His method, however, is what concerns us here. Wright asserts the vitality of the city by presenting its engineering components in a panoramic survey. Interweaving figures from nature and machine technology, Wright shows the perception of the gear-and-girder world. From the master's vantage point he asserts the integrity of its interlocking systems. He is the engineer by proxy, which is the perceptual mode Dos Passos exploited in fictional narrative.

Dos Passos, of course, extended his fictional world beyond a given city. The *U.S.A.* trilogy takes place in Mexico and throughout the United States. The panoramic overview, in that case, becomes an extension of the outlook of the engineer by proxy, a kind of aerial view. Thus Dos Passos's Introduction to *U.S.A.* originates from a systems overview:

> U.S.A. is the slice of the continent. U.S.A. is a group of holding companies, some aggregations of trade unions, a set of laws bound in calf, a radio network, a chain of moving picture theatres, a column of stock-quotations rubbed out and written in by a Western Union boy on a blackboard, a public library full of old newspapers and dogeared historybooks with protests scrawled on the margins in pencil. U.S.A. is the world's greatest rivervalley fringed with mountains and hills. U.S.A. is a set of bigmouthed officials with too many bank accounts. U.S.A. is a lot of men buried in their uniforms in Arlington Cemetery. U.S.A. is the letters at the end of an address when you are away from home. But mostly U.S.A. is the speech of the people. (*U.S.A.: 42nd Parallel* xii)

Reading this list, a reader is apt to think of Walt Whitman. The congeries of human activities and cultural institutions seem to echo Whitman, whose own poetic lists were characteristic of transcendentalist writing. In *Song of Myself* Whitman's sequence of "politics, wars, markets, newspapers, schools," and the like, his list of "mayor and councils, banks, tariffs, steamships, factories, stocks, stores," etc., were meant to define democratic America and to indicate its energies. His "land of the pastoral plains, the grass-fields of the world!," his "cities . . . with paved streets, with iron and stone edifices, ceaseless vehicles, and commerce," however, differ radically from Dos Passos's prose packed with Americana (*Leaves of Grass* 77, 24, 27).

The difference between Whitman and the twentieth-century writer is not apparent in the items themselves, which are quite similar. But the perceptual rationale by which they are seen and presented is vastly different from Whitman to the others. Whitman's lists, which originate in biblical rhetoric, form a catalog meant to show the manifestation of a divine plenitude. They exalt "the greatness of Love and Democracy" and above all "the greatness of Religion" (*Leaves of Grass* 21). As catalog rhetoric, they reveal the bounty and divinity of nature. They are pantheistic in their basis, revealing the self through symbols presumed to manifest nature, and vice versa. Whitman's premise for enumeration is thoroughly subjectivist. Each of his items melds into all others to form a romantic whole. Their presumed unity manifests an organic infinitude. The objects themselves are symbols of a divine spirit.

Dos Passos, on the contrary, presents an itemized America from the gear-and-girder world. His premises are true to "the culture of the machine." His list originates from the premise that the world is a complex structure of component parts, each existing in a precise, discrete relation to the others. When Dos Passos presents his airplane panorama, he presumes a continental system of integrated parts. He offers a list of Americana in order to show the component parts of an integrated system. Its reality is that of a constructed world, not of divine immanence. In short, Dos Passos's America exists purely as structure and mechanism. The resonance is intended to be from Whitman, but the cognitive basis is the gear-and-girder world.

To some extent Dos Passos's readers have grasped this cognitive basis of his fictional structure. Critics and reviewers have resorted to a cluster of related, indicative terms. They have described *Manhattan Transfer* and *U.S.A.* as kaleidoscopic, architectural, and contrapuntal and as "the hull of a huge literary cargo vessel, in the process of building." Two critics, in addition, call Dos Passos's characters "integers" in a larger system. Different as they are, these terms complement each other and point toward the novelist's fictional model. From the ship to the contrapuntal music, these images all denote integrated and interactive systems comprised of discrete component parts. All denote man-made pattern and design. None is applicable to the divine plenitude of a pantheistic spirit. Every one is a term applicable to structural or machine design (qtd. in Rohrkemper viii; Sanders 1, 11, 52, 67; Ludington 180).

A second, related attribute of engineering design proved indispensable to Dos Passos as he wrote *U.S.A.* In *Manhattan Transfer* the novelist had learned that an impersonal, twentieth-century metropolitan culture could be encompassed from an omniscient point of view if the novelist took the engineer's stance vis-à-vis himself and his materials. That is, the contemporary novel of omniscient viewpoint was possible, Dos Passos had learned, if the writer took a comprehensive overview of an integrated, dynamic system. In *U.S.A.*, however, Dos Passos sought to encompass personal history and the history of his time in fiction, all the while remaining true to the conviction of a disjunctive, impersonal world. His problem was to sustain but enlarge his fictional form along the lines of the enabling technological model.

Beginning with *The 42nd Parallel* and continuing through *The Big Money* Dos Passos found another way in which the engineered design could further his narrative innovation. In *U.S.A.* he found that the design components of the machine or structure could function in fiction just as they did in a bridge or building or automobile. The piers, trestles, trusses that contributed to the bridge structure; the drive train and electrical system that were integrated into the automobile; the wiring, plumbing, and girdering that helped to form the whole of the skyscraper —these could have their counterparts in fiction. The novel, too, could be designed and constructed of separate but integrated systems contributing to the total unity of the design. *Manhattan Transfer* anticipates how this could be done, but *U.S.A.* fulfills and exhibits the idea.

Dos Passos's structural components are familiar to readers of the trilogy. There are four of them throughout *U.S.A.*, including Newsreels, the Camera Eye, Biographies of prominent Americans, and fictional studies of representative lives much like those that appear in *Manhattan Transfer*. These four components intersect and, of course, complement each other. As in a machine or structure, all are necessary for the integrity of the fictional design.

U.S.A.'s Newsreels consist of popular songs and slogans, and of machine-produced, mass-media newspaper headlines and articles (BRITISH BEATEN AT MAFEKING, LABOR GREETS NEW CENTURY, GAIETY GIRLS MOBBED IN NEW JERSEY) (*U.S.A.: 42nd Parallel* 2, 3). These evoke a cultural climate of popular opinion and mark the passage of time by epochal events. They are headlines and articles Dos Passos found in actual newspapers, many cut and pasted into his text. The point is itself significant in that each headline or song lyric is used as a component part fabricated elsewhere but fitted into the novel to contribute to its structure. (T. S. Eliot, it must be noted, did much the same thing by fitting fragments of overheard speech into *The Waste Land*, and William Carlos Williams exploited the technique in his quasi-epic poem, *Paterson*, which is structured with similar components from history and popular culture.)

The subjectivity Dos Passos so suppressed in *Manhattan Transfer* emerges as a structural element in *U.S.A.* The Camera Eye, a series of autobiographical segments (with "Eye" evidently a pun on "I"), presents personal impressions of a Dos Passos-figure just becoming sentient at the turn of the century, which coincides with the opening of *The 42nd Parallel*, the first volume of the trilogy. His is the monologue of a person coming of age along with the century. In boyhood he recalls the rapid-transit moments with his mother. "We hurry . . . in the musty stably-smelling herdic cab . . . and we had to run up the platform of the Seventh Street Depot . . . and the conductor Allaboard lady quick lady" (12–13). Just approaching manhood at the period of World War I, the Camera Eye, now incisively ironic, observes the militarist Roosevelt boys parading about in uniforms, saying, "We must come in we must come in / as if the war were a swimming pool" (409). He himself reaches the front and notes the irony that "up north they were dying in the mud and the trenches but business was good in Bordeaux and the winegrowers . . . ate ortolans and truffles and mushrooms" (410). At age nineteen, in wartime, the narrator feels "the winey thought of death" like a sting throughout his body, and by the closing of *The Big Money* is politically allied with striking miners against the representatives of established power, the "prosecutingattorney," the judge, the political boss, the "miningsuperintendent" (*U.S.A.: 1919* 77; *U.S.A.: Big Money* 584–85). Throughout *U.S.A.* the Camera Eye is an overtly subjective part of the fiction. In the progression of the three novels it becomes the poetic voice and the political conscience of *U.S.A.* It is emotion as an integrated system within the machine-structure of the whole.

The Biographies, the third component, profile contemporary political figures (Woodrow Wilson, Eugene Debs), inventors (Edison, the Wright Brothers), business entrepreneurs (Andrew Carnegie, Minor Keith of United Fruit), popular entertainers (Isadora Duncan, Rudolph Valentino). In toto they form the American character. They become the national psyche. And of course they serve Dos Passos's political themes, though the figures are not immediately identifiable by the rubrics under which they appear. The "LOVER OF MANKIND," for instance, is the author's idolized labor leader, Eugene Debs, while the despised Frederick Taylor appears under the heading, "THE AMERICAN PLAN." It is tempting to sort the figures into categories of heroes and villains. Some readers have done so in order to see that Dos Passos's political allegiances lie always on the side of individuals in quest of liberty but never on the side of those affiliated with large-scale, powerful organizations. Thus the laudatory Edison versus the contemptible Ford.

The Biographies, however, are relevant here more for their structural significance than for their thematic emphasis. Like the Newsreels, the Biographies are telegraphic, sometimes reprinting their subjects' statements verbatim (examples, once again, of the prefabricated component). Always they encapsulate their subject's life with the compression of journalism and poetry, faithful to the machine standards of maximal efficiency achieved with minimum working parts:

In eighteen-seventysix [Edison] moved to Menlo Park where he invented
the carbon transmitter that made the telephone a commercial proposition,
that made the microphone possible
 he worked all day and all night and produced
  the phonograph
   the incandescent electric lamp
 and systems of generation, distribution, regulation, and
 measurement of electric current, sockets, switches, insulators, manholes.
(*U.S.A.: 42nd Parallel* 340)

As parts of the national psyche the Biographies externalize the national character. Dos Passos's early notes for *U.S.A.* indicate that he thought of the Biographies as an "Idea of the great / interesting people / people who do things" (Wagner, *Dos Passos* 88). These doers, in Dos Passos's design, manifest America in the material world. In *U.S.A.* the nation largely *is* what it *does*, whether to the benefit or detriment of the culture. As a structural entity the Biographies argue that the omniscient novel is an interdisciplinary enterprise on the part of the writer. The Biographies are the historiographical system in the novel. Each biography is a structural unit, and all together form an intrastructural system in the trilogy.

The fourth fictional system is made up of the intertwined characters who are much like those in *Manhattan Transfer*. Instead of Jimmy Herf and Ellen Thatcher, we have Mac ("Fainy") McCreary, a poor but ambitious labor agitator who travels from Connecticut to Chicago, the West Coast, and Mexico. His story is juxtaposed with that of J. Ward Moorehouse, the Wilmington boy who grows up to find success as a public relations man for the steel industry in Pittsburgh. Dos Passos, predictably, scorns Moorehouse's allegiance to capitalists' interests and his eager manipulation of words for their benefit. The narrative presents women's lives, too, as alliances either with the people or with huge, inhuman organizations. Janey Williams becomes an "organization woman" as a corporate stenographer whose life crosses with Moorehouse's. Mary French works devotedly for the oppressed and is one of Dos Passos's most sympathetic characters. In all, these and numerous other lives are played out against each other in serial fashion. Together they constitute the narrative system of *U.S.A.*

The notion of the novel as a design of integrated systems may sound coldly impersonal, far from life and from the art which springs from it. It is helpful, therefore, to notice that several early twentieth-century voices—those of Dos Passos's contemporaries—also praised art and society as dynamic, integrated systems. They did so in imagery rich in favorable connotations. Here again Frank Lloyd Wright's "Art and Craft of the Machine" provides a key to the aesthetic premises of Dos Passos's machine design. Says Wright, "The artist today is the leader of an orchestra, where he once was a star performer" (*Writings and Buildings* 69).

The key term here is "orchestral," for the orchestra is a synchrony of different component parts poised in a dynamic relation to one another purely for aesthetic purposes. It is revealing that several writers of different viewpoints all favored that term. In *John Sherwood, Ironmaster* S. Weir Mitchell says that his protagonist, an engineer, "loved . . . to stand still [when inspecting the machine shops] and hear the thunderous orchestra" (36). The architect Walter Gropius envisioned his Bauhaus colleagues as "a band of active collaborators whose orchestral cooperation symbolizes the cooperative organism we call society (*The New Architecture* n.p.). Waldo Frank, who detested machine technology, nonetheless hoped that the chaos of American life could be resolved by "*symphonis[ing]*" it. "This," says Frank, "would mean to control the elements of our variety" (205, 237–61). All these writers use orchestral or symphonic figures in affirmative tones.

These writers, thinking of art and culture, doubtless had in mind the late nineteenth-century orchestra whose characteristics, they felt, represented an idealized form of contemporary conditions. They were thinking of the orchestra that had tripled in size to more than one hundred pieces in a century noteworthy for important technical improvements in instruments. They referred to the trained musicians who, by the end of the century, could produce stable, replicable tones, thus enabling composers to orchestrate greater numbers of parts, each of which called for technical precision in ensemble playing. Whether they had in mind the New York, Vienna, or Berlin Philharmonic or the Boston or Chicago symphonies, the term "orchestral" implied a standardized performance practice.

Thus the figure of the orchestra applied to art and to society referred to multiple design components existing in a synchronized, dynamic relation to one another —all for aesthetics. Art and society, like machines and structures, could be conceived as an orchestra having components corresponding to the sections of stringed, wind, brass, and percussion instruments. Gropius and Waldo Frank hoped to banish the egoistic leader (be it the great man or the despot) by calling for an ensemble free of the conductor.

Frank Lloyd Wright, however, saw the conductor as the symbol of *the* modern artist, and he did so in a way directly relevant to Dos Passos. When Wright predicted that the twentieth-century artist would be a symphony conductor instead of a virtuoso, he meant that art would center in the designer's power to integrate diverse component sections or parts in order to form the aesthetic whole. He presumed the prefabrication of parts, which the artist-conductor would coordinate to achieve the desired design. "The art of the old," said Wright, "will be as the sweet, plaintive wail of the pipe to the outpouring of full orchestra." He added, "I feel modern conception and composition to be simply the essence of refinement in organization" (*Writings and Buildings* 62, 71).

In a sophisticated sense, refined organization was exactly Dos Passos's achievement when he orchestrated *U.S.A.* as a synchrony of Newsreels, Camera Eye, Biographies, and story narrative. He became the engineer-novelist, the designer exploiting the machine in ways Frank Lloyd Wright had urged contemporary artists to do. As a reviewer for *Time* magazine accurately observed in 1938, Dos Passos "never talks about creation in connection with his work. His job, he feels, is simply to arrange the materials" (Sanders 11). Back in 1929 Lewis Mumford had identified such arrangement as the hallmark of contemporary art. Mumford could have spoken of *U.S.A.* when he wrote that "individuality, in terms of machine esthetics, does not consist . . . in the uniqueness of a single object: it consists in the selection and arrangement of standard units in terms of the exact purpose for which they are to be used" ("Economics of Contemporary Decoration" xxi). Dos Passos, it must be noted, worked more in the mode of the modern atonal ensemble. The reader experiences the stories, Newsreels, Camera Eye, and Biographies of *U.S.A.* as a sequence of dissonance and of hard-edged, interruptive tempos. Dos Passos's orchestration is more like that of Charles Ives, or perhaps of Igor Stravinsky, whom he much admired.

Dos Passos felt ambivalent about his relation to machine and structural technology. "The writer," he said, "has got to put his mind on the world around him. He has got to understand . . . the industrial set-up that is so ruthlessly changing the basis of society. . . . His business is to justify the ways of machinery to man" (qtd. in Wagner xvi). This paraphrase from Milton's *Paradise Lost* reveals the epic socioliterary task to which Dos Passos felt committed as a self-styled "architect of history." But it also indicates the split he felt between the theme and the form of the novel. On the one hand, Dos Passos feared that modern man might become mere cogs in an industrial-capitalist machine, and in theme both *Manhattan Transfer* and *U.S.A.* consistently emphasize that point.

On the other hand, as a novelist in search of appropriate contemporary form, Dos Passos exploited the machine and structure, their synchrony of cogs, gears, shafts, bearings, etc. They became the basis on which Dos Passos brought a fluctuant, unstable world into aesthetic order. The machine gave him the example of simultaneous, continuous motion within a comprehensive, ordered system. He preferred to say that his method was the photographic and cinematic montage which enabled him to achieve "simultaneity" in the predominantly linear form of the novel (qtd. in Wagner xix–xx). His explicit use of the Camera Eye and the Newsreel in *U.S.A.* support his point.

But the filmic montage is a figure that does not go far enough to capture the full sense of Dos Passos's innovation. It fails to evoke Dos Passos's conception of character as type, and it fails to designate the synchrony of the component elements of his fiction. Though Dos Passos identified his fiction with film and cinema and called his own writing an intrinsically satisfying craft, his omniscient fictional form comes from the contemporary model of machine and structural technology.

OPPORTUNITY: IMAGINATION EX MACHINA II

[*The artist's task is*] *a task in the same sense as the making of an efficient engine.*

T. S. Eliot, *Literary Essays*, 1924

John Dos Passos invigorated the novel with engineering design, but his contemporary, Ernest Hemingway (1898–1961), brought engineering values into prose style. Dos Passos used structures and machines as the organizational model for the modern novel, but Hemingway enacted the values of engineering in his tight, functional prose. His was the efficient modern style for which Ezra Pound had argued. In the era of the antiwaste Efficiency Movement Hemingway's terse, economical lines brought engineering values into the very sentence itself. He reduced the sentence to its essential, functional components. The famous Hemingway style was essentially the achievement, in novels and stories, of the engineers' aesthetic of functionalism and formal efficiency.

Hemingway's engineering aesthetic, it must be noted, did not come unheralded to American readers. A 1911 best-selling novel explicitly encoded engineering values in a prose style warmly welcomed by the American reading public. We have no evidence that Hemingway read Edith Wharton's *Ethan Frome* (1911) (*EF*), but the style of Wharton's novel of thwarted passion in up-country New Hampshire announced the engineering aesthetic Hemingway would display in his own fiction of the 1920s. The reception of *Ethan Frome* anticipated the broad-based popularity of Hemingway's style from the 1920s onward. It is therefore useful to take notice of Wharton's one effort to master the prose style she felt characteristic of the engineering mind.

For Wharton, *Ethan Frome* was an anomalous work, a single, deliberate experiment in technique intended to capture what Wharton termed the "granite outcroppings" of rural New England. The book has an odd history. Begun as a copybook exercise in French composition, it was abandoned until Wharton caught sight of a mountain that reminded her of "Ethan" one summer at her home in Lenox, Massachusetts. She recounts writing the novel the following winter in Paris. It dealt, in her terms, "with the lives led in those half-deserted villages before the coming of motor and telephone" (*Backward Glance* 296).

In a retrospective preface like those of Henry James, Wharton described the problems of the "construction" (her own term) of the novel. Its hard-edged regionalism demanded, she felt, a stark and summary treatment, much like that which the modernist American painter, Charles Sheeler, would give the angular barns of rural America in the 1920s. Wharton needed to avoid what she called "added ornament, or a trick of drapery or scenery" (vii). Her style and structure must match her subject, both being hard-edged. If the modernist writers preferred to evoke that hard-edged quality with images of metals, especially steel, Wharton was just as insistent upon it with her figure of granite. She felt it would not be appropriate to treat "rudimentary" characters in the voice evocative of cosmopolitan elegance. She must reject the kind of narrator who would utter the characteristically ornate Wharton sentences, those that had brought her into stylistic comparison with Henry James. The "granite outcroppings" in *Ethan Frome* demanded a narrator who would not, in fact, speak the typical Edith Wharton sentence of the sort exemplified in Wharton's *Madame de Treymes* (1907). That novella had opened with an American businessman, John Durham, standing in a Paris hotel doorway overlooking the Tuileries gardens: "His European visits were infrequent enough to have kept unimpaired the freshness of his eye, and he was always struck anew by the vast and consummately ordered spectacle of Paris: by its look of having been boldly and deliberately planned as a background for the enjoyment of life, instead of being forced into grudging concessions to the festive instincts, or barricading itself against them in unenlightened ugliness, like his own lamentable New York" (165). At once a reader sees the Latinate phrasing, the liberal use of adjectival and adverbial structures, the string of qualifying phrases that contrast Paris with New York, the very fact of a mind characterized by the long, ornate, intricate sentence.

Wharton needed a very different narrative voice for *Ethan Frome*. She felt the novel demanded an educated narrator who spoke directly in plain, declarative statements. The subject matter, those "granite outcroppings," required a plain-spoken sophisticate who could communicate subtlety and nuance without the syntactical labyrinths of compound-complex sentences.

Wharton found a solution. For her narrator she chose an engineer. In the course of the novel he must piece together the story of Ethan Frome's tragedy and report his findings to those of "complicated minds," meaning the readers. Wharton virtually takes a page from the engineers' own guidelines for composition. As a onetime dean of a college of engineering wrote in 1939, looking back upon his half-century in engineering, "Those who attempt high-flown descriptions and impressions in writing reports make a mistake. The man who is thoroughly acquainted with his subject has no trouble in finding just the words to express his meaning, and when his meaning is expressed, he quits. There should be no padding, just sufficient detail to tell a story and no more. . . . [T]hat's all there is to a report. The simpler, the better" (Hitchcock 112).

As if designing her narrator's voice to these specifications, Wharton has her engineer-narrator in *Ethan Frome* identify himself in this statement at the opening of the novel: "I had been sent up by my employers on a job connected with the big power-house at Corbury Junction, and a long-drawn carpenters' strike had so delayed the work that I found myself anchored at Starkfield—the nearest habitable spot—for the better part of the winter. I chafed at first, and then, under the hypnotising effect of routine, gradually began to find satisfaction in the life" (8). The engineer's statement is directly declarative. It avoids participial phrases and is sparing of adjectives and adverbs. His style, that of a sensitive, educated, and expressive person, is nonetheless as spare as the businessman's in *Madame de Treymes* is ornate.

By this style Wharton gained concision, an economy of phrasing that never compromises—in fact, intensifies—the emotional impact of the discourse. Her narrator's occupation suggested, in its values, the traits she thought necessary for the narrator of her novel. To achieve her stylistic objectives, however, Wharton needed more than an occupational label; she had to imagine herself in the mind of an engineer. In this Wharton evidently had help from her close friend, the lawyer-diplomat Walter Berry, who scrutinized each day's work on the manuscript of *Ethan Frome* in her Paris apartment in successive evenings. Wharton's memoir, *A Backward Glance* (1934), recalls Berry encouraging her always to follow her instincts but adds that this friend prized, above all, "clarity and austerity." Upon the completion of a manuscript draft, Wharton recalled, Berry joined her in "'adjective hunts' from which [they] often brought back such heavy bags." With each book her friend "exacted a higher standard in economy of expression, in purity of language." We must surmise that Wharton's design for *Ethan Frome* gave Berry an unparalleled opportunity to press for the "economy of expression" characteristic of the novel. On that text his tastes converged with her technical-aesthetic objectives (116, 209, 296).

This editorial and imaginative rigor gave Wharton a double advantage of the vernacular and the sophisticated. For example, in the story Ethan's whining, hypochondriac wife, Zeena, complains of the young cousin who has come to help out in the household: "She don't look much on housework" (33). The narrator designates the same quality in the modern term "the girl's inefficiency," the very phrase one of efficiency itself (35). Wharton's engineering style also proved the power of understatement, as readers learned from the unfolding story of Ethan Frome, himself a frustrated engineer. Caught in a wretched marriage on a marginal farm, Ethan falls in love with the cousin-housekeeper with whom he tries to commit suicide when faced with the impossibility of running away with her or continuing as they are. Ironically, the failed suicide attempt ends with Ethan lamed, his lover paralyzed and demented, and the shrewish wife permanently in charge. The power of the novel comes from its stylistic restraint, its ability to convey extremes of emotion and action in an understated style. Wharton said that with the writing of *Ethan Frome* she "suddenly felt the artisan's full control of his implements" (*Backward Glance* 209). A full decade before Ernest Hemingway published the first of his major works, Edith Wharton had discovered the power of the machine-age plain style.

When *Ethan Frome* appeared, Hemingway was just entering his teens, writing for the newspaper and literary magazine of his suburban Oak Park, Illinois, high school that emphasized the classics, not contemporary writings like those of Mrs. Wharton. The son of a doctor and a musician and the oldest of six children, Hemingway was raised as an upper-middle-class white Anglo-Saxon Protestant. (His first pair of long pants were worn to a reception his parents gave in their Oak Park home for the Sons and Daughters of the American Revolution [C. Baker 18].)

Hemingway's route to the postwar avant-garde Parisian literary scene began with work on the *Kansas City Star* in 1917 as a cub reporter. His service as a World War I Red Cross ambulance driver took him to Europe, where he was wounded and to which he returned after additional journalistic experience in Chicago and on the *Toronto Star*. Encouraged by Sherwood Anderson, he spent the early 1920s in Paris, where he was befriended and helped by Gertrude Stein and Ezra Pound.

Although he grew up in the era which celebrated engineering feats, Hemingway's efficient style, unlike Wharton's, was not developed in self-conscious empathy with the mentality of the engineer. He did occasionally reveal the machine-age sensibility common to the time. In 1922 he submitted a poem to Harriet Monroe's *Poetry*, comparing his typewriter to a machine gun which "chatters in mechanical staccato, / Ugly short infantry of the mind" (C. Baker 90). At least once he spoke of himself in machine imagery, remarking that the mind and body need exercise "as a motor needs oil and grease" (*Ernest Hemingway on Writing* [*EHW*] 120–21). Overtly mechanistic figures, however, are rare in his writing; organic terms predominate, for instance in his comparison of F. Scott Fitzgerald's talent to "the pattern made by the dust on a butterfly's wings." Readers alert to Hemingway's technological outlook may only see hints of it in his reference to the "construction" of those wings (*EHW* 106).

Major evidence of Hemingway's engineering values lies elsewhere. He did not enter imaginative literature by pretending to write engineering reports, but Hemingway's preparation in journalism was analogous in one important way to the rigor of technical writing. The former dean who advised young engineers to seek simplicity, to include salient but minimal detail, and to avoid padding sought to reassure them that they need not be reporters or "literary" writers (Hitchcock 112–13). Yet the style sheet Hemingway was given as a young reporter on the *Kansas City Star* at the height of the Efficiency Movement similarly directed news reporters to "use short sentences," "short first paragraphs," smooth and vigorous English. "Avoid the use of adjectives," said one stylebook rule, "especially such extravagant ones as *splendid, gorgeous, grand, magnificent*" (C. Baker 34; Fenton 33).

Hemingway benefited from these strictures at a timely moment, for during the years of the Efficiency Movement the *Star*, a leading American paper, was in the vanguard of change in issuing such guidelines. Its editors and reporters helped American newspaper journalism emerge from a period of "heavy, turgid prose," which the novelist Robert Herrick complained about in 1904 when he described a news account of a fire: "the newspaper account wandered on, column after column, repeating itself again and again, confused, endlessly prolix, [a] waste of irrelevancy" (Fenton 33; Herrick, *Common Lot* 325). *Star* reporters of the 1910s, Hemingway included, were forced to free themselves of those offenses. "On the *Star*," Hemingway wrote, "you were forced to learn to write a simple declaratve sentence" (*EHW* 38).

In the early 1920s, when he wrote entertaining feature articles for the less rigorous *Toronto Star* and *Star Weekly*, Hemingway sustained the concise, direct style of his Kansas City apprenticeship. The economics of telegraphy helped him do so when he became a foreign correspondent. In an era of telegraphic dispatches the journalist, like the engineer, underwent the discipline of severely economical expression. Here by cable, for instance, Hemingway describes the opening of the Conferenza Internazionale Economica di Genova in a report dispatched to the *Toronto Daily Star* from Genoa on April 24, 1922:

> Delegates began to come into the hall in groups. They cannot find their seats at the table, and stand talking. The rows of camp chairs that are to hold the invited guests begin to be filled with the top-hatted, white-mustached senators and women in Paris hats and wonderful, wealth-reeking fur coats. The fur coats are the most beautiful things in the hall. (*By-line, Ernest Hemingway* [*By-line*] 30–31)

The rudiments of Hemingway's efficient style are in place here. Words are pared to a minimum. The declarative sentence dominates, free of subordination and of surrounding complex or compound-complex sentences. The adjectives are common ones, made powerful in the context by juxtaposing camp chairs to the top hats and fur coats. The critical tone surfaces in the figure of the "wealth-reeking" furs, but the passage, in fact the entire dispatch, avoids explicit editorializing. Like the other newspaper pieces collected in the volume *By-line: Ernest Hemingway*, it is tight, compact, concise. If the passage lacks the experiential intensity of Hemingway's fiction, it is important to recognize that the young writer retained the stylistic traits of such telegraph-wire journalism after he left newspaper work to write fiction full time.

A 1940 Hemingway letter to Charles Scribner contains a revealing statement on the relation between his efficient style and journalism. "Don't worry about the words," he told Scribner, "I've been doing that since 1921. I always count them when I knock off. . . . Guess I got in the habit writing dispatches. Used to send them from some places where they cost a dollar and a quarter a word and you had to make them awful interesting at that price or get fired" (*EHW* 57).

Hemingway joked, in this Mark Twain fashion, about achieving an economical yet engaging style from the rationed words of a telegraphed dispatch. It is, however, an achievement whose power he valued and one that ought not be taken for granted, as if the newspaper journalist would inevitably adapt his concise style to fiction. Nothing was further from the truth, and we can gain a renewed appreciation for Hemingway's innovation in stylistic efficiency by glimpsing a now-forgotten novel of 1921 that concerns the relation between art, journalism, and telegraphic dispatches.

Samuel Adams's *Success* (1921) recounts the rise of a young journalist, Banneker, who eventually writes successful "mood pieces" for New York City newspapers. The opening scenes of the novel especially pertain to traditional literary attitudes against which Hemingway rebelled. In a remote western railroad hamlet we meet the aspirant writer, the rustic young Banneker, a telegraph operator whose principal connection with civilization is the mail-order catalog. The nearby wreck of a passenger train becomes "his first inner view of tragedy," and immediately he begins to telegraph reports on the accident. His telegram, says the novel, "was a little masterpiece of concise information. Not a word in it that was not dry, exact, meaningful" (*Success* 18).

Meaningful, yes, but not imaginative. According to the author of *Success*, the "dry, exact, meaningful" dispatch could not in any way be imaginatively expressive. Young Banneker's state of mind, to be sure, is imaginatively excited. "His brain was seething with impressions, luminous with pictures, aflash with odds and ends of significant things heard and seen and felt" (18). As described, this state is much like that on which Hemingway based his own advice to an aspirant writer. "Remember," Hemingway advised, "what the noises were and what was said. Find out what gave you the emotion; what the action was that gave you the excitement" (*EHW* 30). These intensely felt recollections are the authentic origins of imaginative expression, says Hemingway, apparently in full accord with the traditional views of the author of *Success*.

The two part company, however, on the question of legitimate channels for the aesthetic expression of experience. *Success*, voicing the traditional viewpoint, assumes that the young telegrapher must fulfill his imaginative drives in a form permitting unlimited verbal expansiveness, which is to say a form antithetical to the telegraph. His official dispatches sent, Banneker sets to work on "some sheets of a special paper." "He wrote and wrote and wrote," says the novel, "absorbedly, painstakingly, happily. . . . [T]he soul of the man was concerned with committing its impressions . . . to the secrecy of white paper" (18–21).

This portrait of the young writer at work indicates an aesthetics of writing opposite to Hemingway's. Of course Hemgingway, too, repeatedly said that writing made him happy and, like any writer, he worked in painstaking absorption. *Success*, however, works to validate the writer's imagination in his profusion of words, his voluminous outpouring of the soul. Banneker's journal, not the telegraph, provides his real "outlet of expression." The concision of his telegraphy is irrelevant to his imagination as a writer. Worse, it constrains him, distracts him from his genuinely imaginative state of mind.

Success really presents the traditional view of literary action. Its post-train wreck scenario says that the imagination of the true writer finds expression in verbal profusion. The more intense the experience (for example, a deadly train wreck), the more the words necessary to its expression. The writer may earn his living telegraphing dispatches (whether for the railroad or, by extension, for a news organization). His telegraphic concision may be exact and meaningful, but it is not really imaginative and has no place in genuine literature.

In hindsight it is easy to see how wrong the author of *Success* was in thinking that telegraphic concision precludes the expression of powerful emotion. *Success* argues that the verbal economy imposed by telegraphy is a kind of discipline that is hostile to imaginative expression. The novel follows its author's dictates; it is long (553 pages), thick with description and dialogue. By current standards it is prolix, melodramatic, and sentimental—qualities that are apparent now precisely because Hemingway helped to pose a successful challenge to them.

Telegraphic technology and its economics gave Hemingway the basis on which to invent a style of writing in which emotional power would be conveyed virtually in an inverse relation to the number of words used. Here is one of the concentrated true sentences Hemingway wrote in Paris in 1922: "I have watched two Senegalese soldiers in the dim light of the snake house of the Jardin des Plantes teasing the King Cobra who swayed and tightened in tense erect rage as one of the little brown men crouched and feinted at him with his red fez." It is not by chance that he copied the group of six such "carefully pruned statements"—"declarative, straightforward, and forceful as a right to the jaw"—in long hand on telegraph blanks "as if they had been despatches to the *Star*" (C. Baker 90–91). The power of this concentrated style was immediately apparent to some of Hemingway's contemporaries. Upon publication of *Three Stories and Ten Poems* (1923) and *In Our Time* (1924), Ford Madox Ford's secretary, Marjorie Reid, described Hemingway's rendering of "moments when life is condensed and clean-cut and significant" and doing so in "minute narratives that eliminate every useless word" (C. Baker 125). Virtually all the critical commentary on Hemingway has elaborated upon these insights. The journalist's verbal economy, Hemingway learned, could comprehend and evoke a full range of human experience.

Hemingway's fidelity to the concision he learned in journalism goes far to explain why he was so receptive to Ezra Pound's teachings on efficient writing in Paris in the early 1920s. Pound, as we saw, compared the position of the literary person with that of the powerful engineer, praising efficiency in machine design, in social credit economics, in writing itself. All this put Hemingway in the perfect ideological position vis-à-vis himself and Pound. The writer-editor was in the ideal position to ratify Hemingway's journalistic ethos and to help him perfect it by urging an appreciative Hemingway to distrust adjectives (*EHW* 34; Wagner, *Hemingway and Faulkner* 31). Pound, by way of Imagism and Vorticism, taught that severe concision was the basis for contemporary writers' formulations of power, energy, action, and intensity. Hemingway's barter, with Pound, of boxing lessons for lessons in writing was a swap in methods of power. Hemingway's reference to prose "so tight and so hard" resonates male sexual intensity and thus reinforces his knowledge that the efficient style is that of power (*EHW* 79).

What precisely was the aesthetics of the efficient style? What was the underlying theory of its power? And what was its connection with engineering values? First, Hemingway's efficient style is axiomatic with his obsession with how things work, especially at their most efficient—or as he termed it, properly (C. Baker 17). Hemingway, like the American painter Thomas Eakins, shows a covert preoccupation with technics. In the late nineteenth century Eakins revealed his technological interest in paintings of surgical procedures, of musical instruments, of oarsmen. He showed an attraction to mechanical precision both in his subjects, for instance the Schuylkill River oarsmen of *The Pair-Oared Shell* and the engineering-type drawings he prepared as preliminary studies for the work. In the 1920s Hemingway expressed his similar interest in mechanism in his portrayals of bullfights and outdoor sports.

Like Eakins, Hemingway gravitated to subjects susceptible to analysis of their interworkings, and like the Philadelphia artist, he treated those subjects with precision of line, which he achieved with severe verbal economy. Hemingway's treatment, in short, was congruent with his appreciation of efficient structural or mechanistic entities, including those he discerned in the out-of-doors. In "The End of Something" in *In Our Time*, for instance, we see Nick Adams and his girlfriend, Marjorie, setting their fishing lines in a Michigan lake:

> She came in with the boat and ran the second line out the same way. Each time Nick set a heavy slab of driftwood across the butt of the rod to hold it solid and propped it up at an angle with a small slab. He reeled in the slack line so the line ran taut to where the bait rested on the sandy floor of the channel and set the click on the reel. When a trout, feeding on the bottom, took the bait it would run with it, taking line out of the reel in a rush and making the reel sing with the click on. (33)

The visual composition here is minimalist, formed of two angled lines, those of the rod and taut filament, coupled with the essential (as Ezra Pound would say,

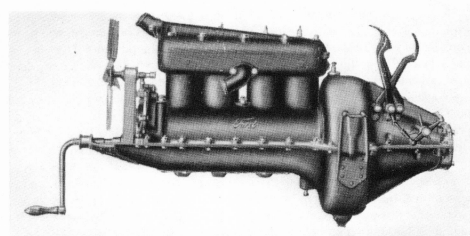

Left Side of Model T Motor; notice the simplicity of
the Ford en-bloc motor; the freedom
from unnecessary parts

Illustration and legend in Ford Model T owner's manual, 1916 (Courtesy Ford Motor Co.)

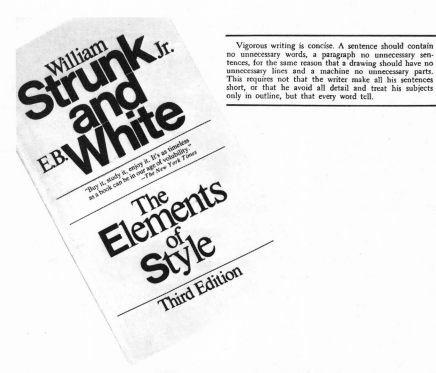

Vigorous writing is concise. A sentence should contain no unnecessary words, a paragraph no unnecessary sentences, for the same reason that a drawing should have no unnecessary lines and a machine no unnecessary parts. This requires not that the writer make all his sentences short, or that he avoid all detail and treat his subjects only in outline, but that every word tell.

Cover of Elements of Style *together with introductory statement attributed to William Strunk in 1919 (Courtesy Macmillan Publishing Co.)*

luminous) details of the driftwood and sandy channel floor. Thematically, Marjorie's fishing know-how allies her temperamentally with Nick and makes his imminent breakup with her all the more poignant. But the passage shows us something else. Characteristic of Hemingway's economical prose, it also exemplifies his need to show the reader exactly how the action, in this case fishing, is to be undertaken, what sequence of procedures is necessary. Slabs of wood stabilize the rods, whose reels, mechanisms themselves, are adjusted for optimal use. The entire apparatus is deployed for maximal efficiency and described accordingly, as if in a summary report.

Hemingway continues this method in "Big Two-Hearted River," the concluding story of *In Our Time* in which Nick Adams, now a writer and war veteran, returns to the Michigan forest to regain his psychological equilibrium by camping and fishing in solitude. Making camp, cooking, and fishing have a personal ritual value for Nick, as all readers have recognized, but these sequences can also be read virtually as a handbook on the efficient techniques of outdoor life. Here, for instance, are the step-by-step components of tenting. They show Nick's intense consciousness in the moment but provide as well an aesthetics of the technical interworkings of procedures and materials. Each component part of the action is revealed. First we see Nick find a level spot between two trees, chop out protruding roots with an ax, smooth the soil, then spread three blankets in certain precise ways, after which he pitches the tent:

> With the ax he slit off a bright slab of pine from one of the stumps and split it into pegs for the tent. He wanted them long and solid to hold in the ground. . . . Nick tied the rope that served the tent for a ridge-pole to the trunk of one of the pine trees and pulled the tent up off the ground with the other end of the rope and tied it to the other pine. The tent hung on the rope like a canvas blanket on a clothesline. Nick poked a hole he had cut up under the back peak of the canvass and then made it a tent by pegging out the sides. He pegged the sides taut and drove the pegs deep, hitting them down into the ground with the flat of the ax until the rope loops were buried and the canvas was drum tight. (138–39)

The passage concludes with a perfect tent and works aesthetically on several levels. Visually, readers once again see the achievement of an angular composition comprised solely of straight lines. The "drum tight" canvas shows Nick's own satisfaction in the lines and flat planes, and Hemingway's declarative sentences become themselves the discursive equivalents of those visual lines. But the description is grounded in the step-by-step mechanics of tent-making. These and similar passages make "Big Two-Hearted River" a camper's guidebook. Hemingway finds and conveys an aesthetics in the mechanics themselves. How the thing itself —tent, fire, fishing—works when done efficiently is of intrinsic interest and value to him. Each component part is discrete and valued.

Other familiar scenes from Hemingway's fiction work similarly to present the technics of operations. The packing of trout in ferns in *The Sun Also Rises* is a good example. In the novel the protagonist, Jake Barnes, and his close friend, Bill Gorton, go off for a day of trout fishing in the Spanish countryside near Burguette. Jake quickly catches six trout, lays them out to admire them, cleans and washes them, and then packs them in a deliberate, step-by-step process that many readers have identified as a secular ritual of personal restoration. Jake recounts that he "picked some ferns and packed them all in the bag, three trout on a layer of ferns, then another layer of ferns, then three more trout, and then covered them with ferns. They looked nice in the ferns, and now the bag was bulky" (119–20). Once again Hemingway emphasizes the intrinsic importance of the precise operational steps. In fact he divides his characters according to their ability to understand or to fail to understand the spiritual importance of these technical procedures, properly executed.

Hemingway's fascination with the bullfights is an extension of this aesthetic of function. All readers have recognized the ritual importance Hemingway attached to bullfighting, its elegant *mano-à-mano* test of courage pitting man against deadly natural force. Yet the very mechanism of the bullfights has great appeal for the novelist. The worthy onlookers qualify as aficionados because they understand the aesthetics of form and function united in the bullring. The superb torero "becomes one with the bull" in a properly efficient execution of functional procedures.

From the bullfight to camping, this aesthetics of mechanism is a part of Hemingway's deliberately efficient style. In fact, his engineering values show a stylistic alliance with Frank Lloyd Wright. Hemingway's ideas on machine-inspired art appear in his well-known statement on writing in the retrospective (and posthumous) *A Moveable Feast* (1964). There we see Hemingway in full accord with the goal of simplicity which Wright thought inherent to the machine process and exemplary for contemporary artists hemmed in on all sides by affectation. Hemingway's statement begins with this often-cited directive for the writer: "'All you have to do is write one true sentence. Write the truest sentence that you know . . . and then go on from there.'" Critics have found that the phrase on the "one true sentence" succeeding itself lies at the heart of Hemingway's method (*EHW* 28). In fact, the "one true sentence" is Hemingway's structural component of fiction.

Yet the follow-up passage is more important here, because it underscores Hemingway's allegiance to the values of engineering in efficient prose style. In particular, it allies Hemingway with the principles of Wright's "The Art and Craft of the Machine." "If I started to write elaborately," Hemingway said, "or like someone introducing or presenting something, I found that I could cut that scrollwork or ornament out and throw it away and start with the first true simple declarative sentence I had written" (*EHW* 28).

Hemingway's scorn for ornament and scrollwork is significant. It points up his engineering values of functionalism and efficiency. Back in 1922, as a correspondent for *Toronto Evening Star*, he had expressed his repugnance for nonfunctional ornamentation in a feature article on "The Hotels in Switzerland." The young journalist scorned the "monstrous" Alpine hotels built "on the cuckoo clock style of architecture." They looked, he wrote, "as though they had been cut out . . . with the same scroll saw" by which he meant the thin, ribbonlike saw used for cutting wood into spirals or other ornamental shapes (*By-line* 18). Much of the so-called gingerbread of Victorian architecture and furnishings was the product of the scroll saw. To reject the Alpine "cuckoo-clock" hotels was to reject bourgeois European tradition and, by extension, to repudiate its ornate counterpart in American middle-class architecture and home furnishings.

Hemingway's persistent distaste for such nonfunctional ornament, whether in architecture or literature, marks him as a modernist. And his remark on ridding his own work of "scrollwork or ornament" explicitly allies him with Wright's point of view. From the 1920s onward the writer of fiction was really restating the architect's position. As Wright emphasized, all artists must repudiate the inessential and thus discard inauthentic ornament or scrollwork ("jig sawed beams and braces, butted and strutted, to outdo the sentimentality of the already overwrought antique product") (*Writings and Buildings* 65). Wright, designing houses in Oak Park, the very Chicago suburb in which Hemingway grew up, anticipated Hemingway's theory of writing when he praised the machine for its capacity to accomplish the "wonderful cutting, shaping, smoothing" which produced "clean, strong forms" (65). Hemingway's "true simple declarative sentence" is exactly the verbal "clean, strong form" rid of the "waste," as Wright put it, of nonfunctional scrollwork. Wright's tortured wood is Hemingway's verbiage, but both amount to the same thing—fakery. Hemingway was everywhere sensitive to it, even in the bullring, where inept toreros would enact the wasteful scroll saw motion when they "twisted themselves like corkscrews . . . to give a faked look of danger." The authentic bullfighters, on the contrary, "never made any contortions, always it was the straight and pure and natural in line" (*Sun Also Rises* 167–68).

"Prose is architecture, not interior decoration," Hemingway wrote in a virtual echo of Wright, adding "the Baroque is over," equating its restless curves with the detestable work of the scroll saw (*EHW* 72). The nonfunctional decoration and ornamentation must be thrown out, Hemingway meant, because they are by definition inauthentic. In writing they are padding, mere rhetoric, a charge Hemingway even leveled against Melville, saying his "knowledge is wrapped in the rhetoric like plums in a pudding." Occasionally, he conceded, Melville's knowledge "is there, alone, unwrapped . . . and it is good" (*EHW* 94). But clearly he was too much on guard against nonfunctional ornamentation to undertake the close stylistic analysis that might have vindicated *Moby-Dick*. Stylistic intricacy meant just one thing, lies and evasions. Only essential, demonstrably functional structures were trustworthy.

Hemingway's repugnance for the circular and spiral forms, his appreciation for what he called the "straight" natural line has implications for the shape of the sentence itself. His ethic of efficiency finds expression in the declarative sentence. That sentence becomes geometry's straight line, quite simply the shortest distance between two points. It is the sentence comprised solely of its functional com-

Charles Sheeler, Bucks County Barn, *1923. Crayon and tempera. 19¹/₄×25¹/₂ inches (Courtesy Collection of Whitney Museum of American Art)*

ponents. It represents discourse as speed in a fast-paced culture. It is thus a different conception of efficacy from that which had governed American writing in the Romantic nineteenth century.

For the American Romantic writer found discourse to be represented adequately in the forms of the circle and spiral. Emerson's essay, "Circles," makes the point. It argues that the expansion of human consciousness takes the form of "a self-evolving circle, which, from a ring imperceptibly small, rushes on all sides outwards to new and larger circles, and that without end" (*Selections* 180). The Romantic conception of history accordingly embraced the figure of the spiral, which described the steady enlargement and progression of human society through time (Levin 1–40). In an age of machine production and speed, however, Hemingway rejected these forms in favor of the declarative straight line.

He revealed the meaning of that line in his responses to the aesthetics of bullfighting. *The Sun Also Rises* disclosed the depth of Hemingway's commitment to the efficient straight line. The passage on bullfighting is a comment on his own literary style. In his capework the marvelous young bullfighter Romero moves "smoothly and suavely, never wasting the bull." He makes no "contortions," always achieving a line that is "straight and pure and natural," a line of "absolute purity" that he holds even when most exposed to danger. That line, Hemingway believes, is the only form adequate to evoke authentic emotion. It never wastes its materials. The inauthentic writer, like the inept torero, can hide emptiness behind fantastic scrollery. But only the artist who dares to expose himself in the efficient line can achieve the form of truth. Aesthetically, the declarative line surpasses journalism because it transcends the events of the moment. It is unparalleled in power. Stated purely, it endures.

Hemingway shows how it is that writings on a range of subjects can embody the values of machine technology. Stories and novels about hunting or fishing, bullfighting or boxing can exhibit a machine aesthetics, even when machines or structures play no part in the fiction. The pictorial representation of a machine or structure is not necessary and may be irrelevant. The form is what counts, and formally Hemingway's style marks the achievement of machine values in imaginative literature. He proves that the dominant technology does define or redefine the human role in relation to nature. He is full of nostalgia for a preindustrial "natural" environment, but his sentences are irrevocably of another, a gear-and-girder, world.

CHAPTER FIVE

MACHINES MADE OF WORDS

KINETIC POETICS

"In the past human life was lived in the bullock cart; in the future it will be lived in an aeroplane; and the change of speed amounts to a difference in quality."

Alfred North Whitehead, *Science in the Modern World*, 1925

he machine-age imaginations of Hemingway, Dos Passos, and others responded directly to the new value of speed which permeated American culture. Hemingway's syntax of the straight line, for example, represented the shortest distance between two points. Compressing space, it also collapsed time and so enacted industrial-age speed. Dos Passos, as we noticed, also worked to represent speed and the immediacy of the moment in prose that jammed words together and deluged the reader with simultaneous stimuli. It is time now to look more deeply into the American world of speed and kinetics, and to turn specifically to the poet's response to them. The writer's imagination ex machina was as much one of poetry as of prose fiction. This part of our discussion, therefore, concerns the writer principally of poems. It focuses on the achievement of William Carlos Williams in defining a modernist, machine-age poetics.

The poet and physician Williams called the American artist "a universal man of action." He swore poetic allegiance to the "exact moment," vowed to embody the day's "advantageous jumps, swiftnesses, colors, movements," and described literary first drafts as "headlong composition" (*Selected Essays* [*SE*] 109, 219, 217). His readers have long noticed this kinetic quality, both in phrases like these and in Williams's essays and poems. They have spoken of his "rapid-fire prose" and "rapid transit poems" and of the "speed" of his experimental fiction (Whitaker 62, 161–62; Breslin 35, 40, 132).

Williams's kinetics was a correlative of his poetics of efficiency. Both were a deliberate reponse to the new fast pace of an industrial United States whose tempos were set by machine technology. Dos Passos and Hemingway, as we saw, participated fully in the rapid-transit age. As poet, Williams too determined to participate in the new national preoccupation with speed. He believed that the writer's imaginative life must keep pace with the constantly accelerating cultural changes and rhythms in the nation. T. S. Eliot, recognizing these American tempos, scorned this "world which will at any price avoid leisure," a world in which that exemplar of the strenuous life, Theodore Roosevelt, is hailed as patron of the arts (qtd. in Moers xiv–xv).

Scorn notwithstanding, Eliot joined a chorus of Americans from Henry Adams to the Muncie, Indiana, "Middletowners," who described their era as an industrialized age dominated by speed and motion, an age of instantaneity in which the momentary present would vanish in a societal rush toward the future. Williams, who believed deeply in literary-cultural bonding, well understood these currents (and moved with them in his montage of lives as physician, father, writer, husband). More than that, Williams sought ways in which American values and assumptions about speed and motion could "shine in the structural body" of his writing, and so "embody America and [him]self in it" (*SE* 17; *Embodiment of Knowledge* [*EK*] 47).

Like Dos Passos and Hemingway, Williams looked to contemporary culture for sources for literature. "The world force today is here," he said, "here in our own country. We must take advantage of it, work with it, use it. . . . I believe that the characteristics of the age help your writing when you go along with them. . . . I believe that the age should govern what you write" (qtd. in Mazzaro iii; *Interviews* [*Int*] 34, 79). Eliot, from a different literary viewpoint, called up the preindustrial, Romantic America of Emerson and Hawthorne in order to cite leisure or repose as the sine qua non of American (in fact, of all) literary effort. But Williams had spent more than a decade laboring misguidedly in the anachronistic cul-de-sac of ersatz Keats. He insisted ever afterward upon the utmost contemporaneity. "The poet," says Williams, is the man who "invent[s] . . . today" (*SE* 197). Guided by the "characteristics of his age," he worked to exploit both velocity per se and the imaginative grasp of the pressing moment. It is time now to recognize, in the work of Williams, an axiom of the modernist poetics of efficiency, namely, the embodiment of America and himself in the very tempo of American life.

It is useful to recall how fiercely Williams asserted his literary and cultural contemporaneity once he had abandoned his Romantic poems of the world of Alexander's bridge. "Camphorated" and "embalmed" became his new epithets for outworn forms. The values of the old words were "static" and thus a betrayal of the kinetic present. Williams, accordingly, inveighs against the sonnet as a static, rigid form. It is an "archaic oxcart" because "we do not live that way any more," because "nothing in our lives, at bottom, is ordered to that measure." The industrial-era "Zeitgeist" requires the poet to find "a new construction to conform with our age" (*SE* 109, 110, 165, 90, 281, 291, 337–38; *EK* 145).

What, then, defined the age? And what was the cadence of American life? In large part it was one of speed and hurry, qualities assumed to pervade American society. The journalist Mark Sullivan and the eminent physician William Osler, together with such social critics as Charles Merz, Stuart Chase, and others, all used similar phrases on America's "hurried way of life," on "the age of hurry," on "a nation that lives at top speed most of the day," on "this most rapid age in history," and on "life [that] moves faster than it ever did." One analyst remarked that "a European in the United States is inevitably struck by the speed, the hurry, the restlessness of it all." In a mid-1920s social critique, cast in the form of a Socratic dialogue, Phaelon asks what, besides sheer size, constitutes a test of American superiority. Socrates answers in a word: "Speed" (Sullivan 1:431; Osler 206; Merz 50; Chase, *Men and Machines* 329; Martin 6; Mowrer 168–69; Woodruff 32).

The twentieth-century American preoccupation with rapid movement was anticipated, in the preindustrial era, by the pony express and the clipper ships. But in the new century machine technology was the most obvious basis for the American ideas about speed and hurry. "There can be little doubt," as one critic wrote, "that American speed is influenced by and is harmonious with an age of high power machinery" (Mowrer 168–69). The journalist Sullivan suggested that the new American hero, the "go-getter," was a type "stimulated to conform to the machine" in an age of "the speeding up of industry" (3:296–97). The public regarded certain technologies—from the "lightning lines" of Morse's telegraph to the crack trains of the major railroads and the record-setting internal combustion engine automobiles—as marvels in their enactment of speed. In 1901, for example, the New York Central's "fastest train in America" traveled the nine hundred miles between New York and Chicago at an average speed of forty-nine miles per hour, the double dactyls of its name—The Twentieth-Century Limited—seeming to mimic the very clip of the wheels on the track. Just four years later a crowd of twenty-five thousand persons gathered in Chicago to watch the departure of the rival Pennsylvania Railroad's "fastest long-distance train in the world," which, crossing Indiana, traveled a measured mile in forty seconds (Sullivan 2:640). Before the decade ended automobile races intensified the public focus upon speed. Henry Ford first gained national attention by winning an automobile race in one of his own motorcars at over seventy miles per hour on a racecourse of ice. A shaken Ford thereafter hired the fearless Barney Oldfield to drive Ford cars in races that prepared the public to welcome the Model T.

It was inevitable that speed, wondrous in the telegraph, the train, and the automobile, would enter American life not only as a presumed trait, but as a modern value. The "go-getter" hero implies as much. In 1930 the literary critic and scholar Fred Lewis Pattee reflected that, as of 1893, there were "amazing new applications of electricity, the phonograph, the germ of the cinema, the perfected telephone," and the "gas engine [ready] to turn civilization upside down in two decades." Pattee concludes that "the old static world was vanishing like a dream of the night" to make way for "the vital twentieth century" (3–4, 6–7). To some, that vitality was beyond question. A chauvinistic Ford agreed that "certainly we are moving faster than before." He praised the young man who "hops across the continent in a day" and hails both the manager and laborer "willing to scrap today in favor of tomorrow" because both are "marching the way progress is going" (*Today and Tomorrow* 4–5). In the 1910s the novelist Edna Ferber echoed Ford in approving "the twin condiments known to the twentieth century as pep and ginger." And in 1928 Ezra Pound envisioned the vital city of tomorrow in which the streets "will sweep like the curves in a railroad siding" and thus follow the "speed line" (*Selected Prose* 224).

The very breadth of America's cultural valuation of speed may be instanced from two quarters usually poles apart, those of the academician and the advertiser. From the university lectern George Santayana cited speed or rapidity as a positive American value. Santayana repudiated the vapid genteel tradition in praises for the vigorous half of the American mind "leaping down a sort of Niagara rapids," its "sharp masculine eye see[ing] the world as a modern picture—rapid, dramatic, vulgar" (134). Meanwhile, in the same years (ca. 1914) the Eastman Kodak Company promised the sensations of speed to buyers of its snapshot cameras. Its "advt." copy reads like a commercial gloss on Santayana: "Every motorist feels the fascination of speed whether he indulges in it with his own car or not. The mile-a-minute automobile, race horses, exposures—these are all as one to this remarkable Kodak" (*Motoring with a Kodak* n.p.).

Santayana, the Kodak copywriter, Pattee, and the others all imply that speed is a valuable trait because, in and of itself, it demonstrates vitality in the modern age. It becomes a defining property of twentieth-century America. Sinclair Lewis exploited this point in theme and plot in a 1917 *Redbook* story. Lewis's "Speed" is a modern fairy tale whose princess is doubly confined. In imagination she is bound by secret yearnings to go to the New England seacoast of her family's origins, though circumstances confine her to Apogee, Iowa, which thinks her only a prim schoolmarm. Predictably, the prince of "Speed" takes one look at her and knows better. He is an automobile racing driver "smashing the cross-continent road record" in a car "where nothing in the world existed save the compulsion to keep her at top speed," where "the earth was shut off from him by a wall of roar and speed." They meet in her town during his refueling stop, and he urges her to remember him ("wireless me some good thoughts") and thrills to her reply that "there aren't so many seventy-an-hour men in Apogee!"

Of course the prince soon returns to rescue her, this time by train, and breathless to make connections westward en route to the Orient. In a twenty-six minute courtship in Iowa he frees her, largely by reporting his discovery, while back east, that her cherished New England ancestry is genealogically bogus. In the nick of time he carries her into the sunset via transcontinental express.

Lewis's story, apart from firing the fantasies of *Redbook* readers, defined modern values clearly as those of speed and motion. To affirm them, it was important to debunk the legend of his heroine's nineteenth-century New England ancestry, which is to say the values of the bygone preindustrial era. The heroine, cut free of that past, can now embrace the values of the man who typifies modern life. To get married while in motion ("somewhere between here and San Francisco") to the man who holds the world's records for automotive speed is to become a woman purely of the twentieth century (*Selected Short Stories* 301–18).

Speed records, meant endlessly to be broken, imply a corollary value in this new high-velocity America, namely, one of constant acceleration in its rhythms and in the pace of social change. Santayana remarked that public life "has been transformed and accelerated in a way that conscience can't keep up with, yet is dazzled by" (134). A British observer said bluntly, "The real end Americans set for themselves is Acceleration" (Dickinson 104–5). In *Today and Tomorrow*, Henry Ford put it in concrete images: "Soon we shall be making in an hour by air what were days' journeys by motor" (4–5), while an emigré in Robert Herrick's *Together* returns after several years to feel "bewildered" by "the increased pace of living on this side of the ocean" (356). Perhaps Charles and Mary Beard put the case most graphically in their assessment of the initial decades of the new century. "The accumulations of the machine age," they wrote, "made those of the gilded age seem slow and pitiful by contrast, outrunning in rapidity and force all calculations . . . while the pace of . . . the older plutocracy seemed like the movement of a snail" (747).

If the tone of many of these remarks on speed and acceleration sounds like chauvinistic cant, other writers were quick to criticize these characteristics of modern life, even as they presumed them to be true. By 1929 Sinclair Lewis spoke harshly of "the new divinity, the God of Speed." Lewis's Dodsworth, returning from Europe, sees the "rush-hour" at Grand Central Station and feels that the self-important traveling salesmen, exhausted brokers, fretful women, and "sleek" young men "seemed driven to madness by the mad God of Speed" (155). Frank Lloyd Wright warned that "urban accelerations . . . always preceded such decay [of the cities], and we are seeing just such acceleration in our own cities today." He warned that in New York City "accelerations due to the skyscraper—itself one of the accelerations—may be singularly dangerous" (*Autobiography* [*A*] 317). Years earlier, in the 1910s, the young Walter Lippmann wrote similarly of the destructive effects he perceived in the rapid cultural changes. "We are unsettled to the very roots of our being," wrote Lippmann. "There are no precedents to guide us. . . . We have changed our environment more quickly than we know how to change ourselves" (*Drift and Mastery* 92–94). Lippmann's contemporary, Stuart Chase, feared that Americans were emotionally debilitated by the fast pace: "There is far more to experience and rather less emotional stability with which to experience it" (*Men and Machines* 329). A British writer was more ascerbic. "To be always moving, always moving faster," he wrote, "is what Americans consider the beatific life," while leisure is for them "a kind of standing still, the unpardonable sin" (Dickinson 104–5).

It is not surprising in the 1910s to find criticism of American pace from the medical profession. Osler, as a physician and medical educator, regretted that his colleagues lacked the leisure time for beneficial reading "because of the ever-increasing mental strain in this age of hurry." He wrote of the difficulties in training "first-class students . . . in the hurry and bustle of a business world, which is the life of this continent." Osler also remarked that "one of the saddest of life's tragedies is the wreckage of the young collegian by hurry, hustle, bustle, and tension—the human machine driven day and night, as no sensible fellow would use his motor" (206, 246, 174).

There seemed no end of voices critical of the accelerating speed in American life. One Leon Samson, a critic whom readers may suspect of misanthropy disguised as Marxism, is nonetheless most articulate on what he calls "the American marathon." "Action with speed is the religion of the practical American," he writes. "And when flights of imagination prove too taxing, the aeroplane and the automobile are ready at hand to send him speeding through space, and so to translate a cultural incapacity into mechanical movement." Samson sees America as "a nation where the people are ever on the run . . . running over friends and away from ideas." Samson even indicts the front porch, the nation's ostensible "holiday from the skyscraper," which is "always running" even as it stands at rest, its occupants incessantly in motion in their rocking chairs (288–89, 300).

If Samson sounds cranky, the respected Waldo Frank was every bit as critical of the "nervous, restless" American life, "a constant agitation, a violent moving hither and beyond, in which the country strives to emulate the city." "Speed is the disease of power which," says Frank, "having no present feverishly strives to hurry to the future." He observed that the young, in need of recreation, were forced instead "to movie and gin and speed" (266). Frank's focus on the movie may seem as risible as Samson's indictment of the porch rocker. But both, in the mid-1920s and early 1930s, sought only to objectify their complaints against American speed and acceleration. The compatible argument in rhetoric that remains fresh can be found in Henry Adams, who was clear about the price to be paid for the American life of speed and cultural acceleration:

The typical American man had his hand on a lever and his eye on a curve in his road; his living depended on keeping up an average speed of forty miles an hour, tending always to become sixty, eighty, or a hundred, and he could not admit emotions or anxieties or subconscious distractions, more than he could admit whiskey or drugs, without breaking his neck. He could not run his machine and a woman too; he must leave her, even though his wife, to find her own way, and all the world saw her trying to find her way by imitating him. (*E* 445)

From Henry Adams to Henry Ford, these voices addressed to issues of speed and acceleration in American life tend to be intellectuals or public figures. To gain some sense of broad-based public involvement, it is useful to consider contemporary customs and mores. The neurologist George Beard, for example, had warned Americans back in 1881 about "rapid eating," but by 1907 the "quick lunch," which began in railroad station cafés, was spreading into American towns and cities, ultimately to become the diner whose streamlined design mimicked the speeding railway car (Beard, *American Nervousness* 159; Sullivan 3: 474).

In daily life middle-class readers—or scanners—of magazines saw a range of products presented in images of speed. Entrepreneurs planning a new building read that "a steel building can be erected, extended, remodeled, or removed with

MODEL 11-F—SPECIAL 7-PASSENGER
TOURING CAR, FORE-DOORS, $2900

Standard Chassis has 121-inch wheel base and 50-H. P.
Motor. Equipment does not include top and wind shield.

Seek Speedwell Luxury Above $4000, But Not Below It

Speedwell Motor Car Co. advertisement. Harper's Weekly Advertiser, *1911*

astounding speed." The Ansco Company marketed a photographic film called "Speedex." Numerous producers of prepackaged food boasted fast preparation: "Hot breads for breakfast in 10 minutes. . . . hot, steaming [spaghetti] in less than ten minutes. . . . [peanut butter] so quick and simple. . . . Quick Quaker [oats that] cook in 3 to 5 minutes." In all such ads, consumers were urged to see themselves as moderns, full participants in the new era even when occupied in the most prosaic daily activities (*Literary Digest* 94 [Aug. 27, 1927]: 63; *Colliers* 57 [Mar. 25, 1916]: 39; *Woman's Home Companion* 53 [Jan. 1926]: 36; [Feb. 1926]: 46).

One splendid source for the everyday concerns about velocity in middle America from 1890 through the 1920s is the Lynds' *Middletown* (1929), the sociological study of Muncie, Indiana, chosen especially because its citizenry evinced a "standardized, patterned avoidance of unusual living." The usual in Muncie meant the manufacturing of glassware and auto parts, industries of high-volume, machine-technology production characterized by "speed and specialization." "The speed of the iron man" and "the demands of the iron man for swiftness" have, said the Lynds, "brought new health hazards" to Muncie.

Machine production raised other issues as well, several of which concern val-

—'tis the speedy brush

—you wouldn't travel by ox-cart when an express train was available.

—then why not shave the quick way—the pleasant way—the Warner way?

—here is a fine Badger-hair brush—Rubber-set—that would cost you almost as much without the remarkable improvements.

—it is absolutely sanitary.

—a keen blade and this fine tool make the kit *complete*.

—the price is five dollars.

—your dealer has it—or we'll mail it for Christmas as you direct—write Warner-Patterson-Perry Company, 1024 South Wabash Avenue, Chicago.

WARNER
SHAVING BRUSH

Warner-Patterson-Perry Co. advertisement. Collier's, *1919*

WORLD'S LARGEST GROWERS AND CANNERS OF HAWAIIAN PINEAPPLE

Most people who visit our cannery speak of the white rubber gloves our workers wear. Perhaps it is unusual—but it is just one more example of what James D. Dole has done to make his cannery the model of the industry.

Speed . . . speed . . . split-second speed . . .

Hawaiian Pineapple Co. advertisement. Good Housekeeping, *1927 (Courtesy Castle and Cooke, Inc.)*

ues of speed. When in 1924 Muncie citizens first used the new voting machines, they were told to "vote quickly . . . four to a minute! Only fifteen seconds to a person on the voting machines!" One newly enfranchised woman complained that she voted straight Republican because "they hurried me so much that I just gave up trying to select my candidates." Speed was also a characteristic that set generations apart. An old-fashioned boy-girl date at home was, in youthful slang, "slow." One mother lamented that her son only "wants a Studebaker so he can go seventy-five miles an hour." "Ours is a speedy world," boasted one boy, who said of his parents, "They're old."

The parents, of course, felt otherwise. They too were caught up in the new faster pace. "Folks today want to eat in a hurry and get out in the car," complained a Muncie butcher who exhausted his supply of fast-cooking steaks and chops, only to be left with a large inventory of cuts requiring long preparation time. One

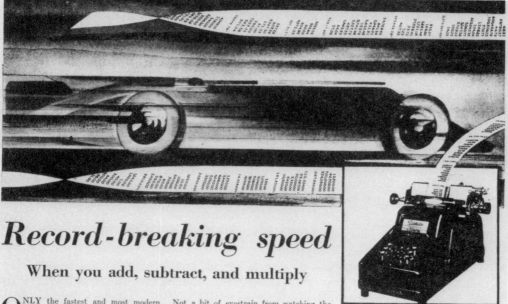

Record-breaking speed

When you add, subtract, and multiply

ONLY the fastest and most modern machines will do for the fingers that attend to your typing . . . why not the same advantages for the fingers that do your business figuring?

The lightning-fast Sundstrand will place record-breaking speed at the disposal of any operator. For the Sundstrand is not only manually faster, but it saves an incredible amount of time through features which insure greater accuracy.

Give the Sundstrand keyboard your attention for a moment. Did you ever see anything more logical — more simple or compact? Only ten numeral keys and all of them grouped in an area which the fingers of one hand can cover. In a few minutes anyone can memorize their location. Unusual speed quickly results from this natural method of touch operation. Not an inch of lost motion.

Not a bit of eyestrain from watching the keyboard.

Automatic column selection is a Sundstrand feature that saves wasted time in the selection of columns. With this feature the dollars and cents of every item align themselves in the proper vertical columns automatically. You simply touch the keys in the order that you would write down the figures with a pencil. The machine does the rest.

Another time-saving advantage of the

> **IMPORTANT**—*Only on the Sundstrand will you find all of these time-saving features*
>
> *Automatic direct subtraction . . . Automatic shift multiplication . . . One hand control . . . Automatic column selection . . . Speed beyond the fastest human fingers . . . Convenient space-saving size . . . Durability . . . Credit balance feature . . . Only ten numeral keys . . . Touch method of operation naturally and quickly acquired . . . Automatic sub-totals . . . Portability . . . Dependable accuracy . . . Visibility.*

Sundstrand is the automatic credit balance feature. This enables you to figure debits and credits in the same operation and at the end get a total of the difference between the two. If credits exceed debits, or if you subtract a larger number from a smaller, the credit balance feature gives a true answer with clear printed proof.

Wherever there is figuring to do, the Sundstrand quickly pays for itself . . . in time saved and accuracy. It is priced as low as $100. Let us send you more complete information. Use the coupon below.

ONLY TEN NUMERAL KEYS

One hand covers the entire keyboard. Close your eyes and operate it. The quickest method possible for all your business figuring.

Sundstrand

10 Key Adding-Figuring Machines

GENERAL OFFICE EQUIPMENT CORPORATION

Division of Underwood Elliott Fisher Company

342 Madison Avenue, New York City

"UNDERWOOD, ELLIOTT-FISHER, SUNDSTRAND, SPEED THE WORLD'S BUSINESS"

GENERAL OFFICE EQUIPMENT CORPORATION
542 Madison Avenue, New York City
Gentlemen: Please send me your illustrated booklet, "Under Your Finger Tips."

Name_____

Address_____

City_____ State_____

Sundstrand General Office Equipment Corporation advertisement. Collier's, *1929*
(Courtesy Olivetti USA)

foreman's wife might have been his customer. "It keeps me hustling just to keep up with my husband and the boys," she said. "I can't take the time to make fancy things [like pumpkin pie] and still keep up with my family." This woman, like many Muncie housewives, probably welcomed women's magazine advertisements for fast-food products like ten-minute hot breads, five-minute oatmeal, and instant fruits and vegetables in cans.

Middletown reports that in a Sunday school class one teacher asked, "Can you think of any temptation we have today that Jesus didn't have?" to hear a boy answer, "Speed!" Adult Middletowners enjoyed "ever-speedier auto trips," and the figure of the "go-getter" or "hustler" was reportedly much admired. The civic fathers even named a special week Pep Week. And though the Lynds quote one dissenting Middletowner as saying "we're too busy being busy," their language reveals, in places, their own presumption of cultural speed and acceleration, as when they refer to "the swiftly moving environment" in which life "goes on at a brisk pace, speeded up at every point" (*Middletown* 494, 69–70, 73, 154, 258, 151, 134, 406, 418, 491, 495, 132, 181).

The Muncie Middletowners may seem far afield of the literary concerns of William Carlos Williams, John Dos Passos, or Ernest Hemingway. But some of those very writers concerned with speed and acceleration also comment upon their effects on imaginative literature. The Beards suggested that the "brusque and breezy style" of contemporary American writers might represent a transition "to a modern vernacular appropriate to the higher velocity of living" (804). And Pattee implies that the compression of the novel, from the multivolume chronological narrative to the one thin book concentrating on "brief intervals of life," is the result of the new tenor of the times (467–68). Further, John Dewey observed, in an essay Williams frankly admired, that a whole class of periodical literature, typified by the *Saturday Evening Post*, had emerged specifically for those in transit. Such periodicals "subsist for those who are going from one place to another and haven't as yet arrived. They cannot have depth or thickness—nothing but movement" (*Characters and Events* 2:540). Another critic felt that this state of affairs was damaging short story art, which now must be "snappy" because "the magazine's craving for speed puts movement and patter at a premium" (O'Brien 168). These critics could have pointed out that periodicals, in the 1920s, helpfully provided their time-pressed readers with average reading time for each article or story. In the fast-paced machine age every minute counted.

This excursion from the quick lunch to the Kodak camera is meant to outline an important American sensibility from the turn of the century through the 1920s. In that era speed and the belief in cultural acceleration were proclaimed from every quarter to be, for better or worse, *the* defining characteristic of the United States in the twentieth-century. Both urban and outlying areas were included, even if the major cities seemed best to exemplify these traits. The Beards wrote, "The modes of New York, Boston, and Chicago . . . swept into remote mountain fastnesses . . . [and] became the modes of Winesburg, Gopher Prairie, and Centerville" (759). As Ezra Pound similarly observed a year later, "An idea or notion dropped into New

York Harbour emerges in Santa Fe or Galveston, watered, diluted, but still the same idea or notion . . . and the time of transit is considerably lower than any 'record' hitherto known" (*Literary Essays* 389–90).

For that matter, urban modes penetrated into Riverdale, the fictionalized version of Williams's hometown of Rutherford, New Jersey, from which he shuttled as a teenager to New York's Horace Mann High School and later on to the Manhattan bailiwick of his artist friends. Williams was exposed to the "idea or notion" of speed both before it was dropped into New York harbor, as Pound put it, and after it emerged "diluted" in the river at home—and, continues Pound in a 1928 essay, "For fifteen or eighteen years I have cited Williams as sole known American-dwelling author who could be counted on to oppose some sort of barrier to such penetration" (*Literary Essays* 389–90). Williams, then, fully understood the nation's preoccupation with speed and increasing velocity. He took cognizance of Henry Adams's concern about "the acceleration of life" and acknowledged "the time obsession that fills our lives" (*EK* 81, 93). He spoke to a reporter (rather disingenuously) of the "wreck that occurs in a physician's life by the tempo of modern times" (*William Carlos Williams Review* 55). In *Spring and All* Williams satirized that part of America's high-velocity life which he thought mindless, frenzied, and damaging:

> Tomorrow, we rush among our friends congratulating ourselves upon the joy soon to be. Thoughtless of evil we crush out the marrow of those about us with our heavy cars as we go happily from place to place. It seems that there is not time enough in which to speak the full of our exaltation. Only one day is left, one miserable day, before the world comes into its own. Let us hurry! Why bother for this man or that? In the offices of the great newspapers a mad joy reigns as they prepare the final extras. Rushing about, men bump each other into the whirring presses. How funny it seems. All thought of misery has left us. Why should we care? Children laughingly fling themselves under the wheels of the street cars, airplanes crash gaily to earth. Someone has written a poem. (*Imaginations* [*I*] 92)

All the elements of the American engagement in speed and accelerating social rhythms are here: the high-speed machinery of the rotary press and propeller, the nation's mindless equation of motion with progress, the casualties of all that crashing around. Williams, above all, sees rapid motion starved of vitality. There is only action without imagination. "We fly abroad for sensation," he wrote, "anything to escape." "The world of action," he continues, "is a world of stones." And those in it "live in bags" just like the "thousand automatons" who, in *Paterson*, "walk outside their bodies aimlessly." Life buffered from the present is "a cheated existence," but "to do, do, do is still worse" (*In the American Grain* [*AG*] 178, 179; *Paterson* 6; *SE* 14; *EK* 26).

The modernist Williams finds much of the frenzied motion to be a symptom of emptiness within. *Spring and All* speaks to this plight: "Emptiness stares us in the face. . . . Everywhere men look into each other's faces and ask the old unanswerable question: Whither? How? What? Why?" Santayana applauded the Niagara rapids of a high-velocity masculine spirit, but Williams saw instead "the unfathomable mist into which all mankind is plunging" (*I* 96–97).

Williams's readers are struck, nevertheless, by the concluding line of his cheerfully bitter excoriation of frenzied, mobile America. Amid the rush, the crush, the hurry, "Someone has written a poem." Williams affirms a significant apposition of the working poet to the society in frenzied motion. For Williams not only presumes America's high-velocity life but makes that life the context for the poet and his work. He does not envision or urge a separate place for the writer. Even his punctuation is suggestive; neither spacing nor the indentation of a new paragraph separate the poetic act from the cultural context of speed and motion.

Williams apposes the kinetic society to the poet at work and deliberately includes both within a firm context. On the printed page the paragraph must contain them both because they coexist in the larger culture. "Someone has written a poem" in this America of speed and hurry because there exists no valid alternative for the contemporary poet. Quite simply, in the twentieth century there can be no ethos of emotion recollected in tranquillity precisely because there is no tranquillity or, as Eliot would have it, leisure. In Williams's America there are no exits or respites from the kinetic here-and-now. Expatriation is sterile and traditional forms of the past are "empty casings where truth lived yesterday." Worlds imagined elsewhere are but idiotic fantasies of "frail imaginations . . . despoiled of the things under their noses" (*I* 41; *SE* 213; *EK* 143; *I* 131–33; *SE* 15).

From Williams's perspective the poets' challenge—in fact, their necessity—is to discover how the imagination can be vitally consonant with their own age. The era of speed and acceleration requires them to learn, in sum, to engage the imagination instantaneously, to make the poem enact that cognitive speed, and to keep pace, in writing, with the velocity of the culture. "Speak of a flight by plane to Europe," he said (in tones echoing Henry Ford), "[Speak] of the . . . telescope reflector that discovers the nebula . . . travelling at the incredible speed . . . of 2500 miles a second; it is the actual writing that embodies it" (*I* 291).

But the embodiment of speed and instantaneity were difficult. Williams acknowledged this when he called "the immediate" the "first difficulty of modern life" and wrote of "the agonized approach to the moment" (*EK* 114; *I* 89). Williams's *A Novelette* (1932), a work of the late 1920s, reveals and exploits both the difficulty and the agony. For *A Novelette* surrounds the instantaneous poetic act with the American daily life of speed and hurry. Williams, in fact, increases this "tempo of modern times" by setting the work in a late 1920s flu epidemic that accelerated his already-hectic days with round-the-clock house calls throughout Rutherford and its surrounding boroughs. *A Novelette* is an attempt to reveal—even to teach —poetic practice in a culture preoccupied with its own rapid and accelerating rhythms.

A Novelette explicitly ascribes poetic value to cultural conditions of speed and acceleration. These become Williams's instruments to excise inanity and the extraneous in an America of such abundance and plenitude that blockheaded contentment can become the national norm. Because time in the epidemic is now urgent and critical—is literally spare—inanity and the extraneous ("everything that is not seen in detail") vanish. Now "there is no time not to notice." In the "single necessity" of the epidemic, "one worked rapidly" and "values stood out in all fineness . . . because the stresses of life have sharpened the sight." Now "a stress pares off the inanity by force and speed and a sharpness, [and] a closeness of observation comes through." Williams, just prior to these remarks, has instanced that "closeness of observation":

> Where the drop of rain had been, there remained a delicate black stain, the outline of the drop marked clearly on the white paint, in black, within which a shadow, a smoothest tone faded upward between the lines and burst them, thinning out upon the woodwork down which the rain had come. In the tops of the screws the polishing powder could be seen white. (*I* 273)

Close observation, however, is not enough, because the poetic act requires "clarity," the imagination "dynamized into reality." But what is that reality? And how is the mind so "dynamized"? It goes without saying that for Williams haste does not make waste, but poems—provided the poet works efficiently. He explains the efficient poetic moment in terms that are alternately romantic and scientific-technological. On the one hand, it is a state of "imaginative suspense . . . [of] consciousness enlarged by the sympathies," and, on the other, it is "comparable to electricity or steam" (*I* 120). Perhaps these phrases fall short of full definition; but Williams implies that he means, in current terms, an altered state of consciousness, one that is intensely focused, even surreal, with coloration heightened and a holographic vividness of line and detail. It is a cognitive state attainable pharmaceutically through amphetamines, drugs known, appropriately enough, as "speed." Not that Williams used those drugs, but he often worked while overtired, under stress, and sleepless. These are conditions naturally inducive of that "speed" state he learned to use for writing and defined in the literary lexicon available to him, perhaps coming closest in the phrase "the rush that simplifies life" (*I* 175).

The typical poem of that dynamized consciousness is "My Bed Is Narrow," in *The Descent of Winter* (1928), a work begun on shipboard in 1927 as Williams returned from Europe, having left his wife in Geneva with their two sons, who were to attend a Swiss school for a year:

> My bed is narrow
> in a small room
> at sea
>
> The numbers are on
> the wall
> Arabic I

Berth No. 2
was empty above me
the steward

took it apart
and removed
it

only the number
remains

.2.

on an oval disk
of celluloid
tacked

to the whiteenameled
woodwork
with

two bright nails
like stars
beside

the moon (*I* 234–35)

This poem affirms the marriage, the twosome, of the lonely passenger, a poet all at sea in his single cell "apart" from his wife Flossie, whose absence and then presence fill the cabin. The lines are as narrow as the bunk. But the poem is made possible chiefly by the mind alert to the prosaic lettering on the berths. Here is the active perception of the mind "dynamized into reality." The mind that practices efficient observation, that does not fail to notice the polishing powder in the tops of screws, is the mind practiced to see and to seize the enactive moment.

But that hyperconscious state, necessary to the imagination, was no guarantee of poetic success. In *A Novelette* Williams dares to show the intermittent failure of the effort:

Snow changes the aspect of the world—
All this the epidemic bares. The street hydrants are green but the tops are moulded like inverted acorn saucers, red. On the oak leaves the light snow lay encrusted, till the wind turned a leaf over—
No use, no use. The banality wins, is rather increased by the attempt to reduce it. (*I* 274)

Here is the "agonized approach to the moment" and its ultimate failure. The writing is banal. But Williams deliberately leaves the tracings of these failed efforts. He is unwilling to violate the authentic text in order to make a "lying . . . smooth page." Only "piecemeal excellence" is attainable precisely because the poetic effort so often fails. In *A Novelette* Williams leaves failed efforts as a structural scaffolding (*I* 275).

RAPID TRANSIT: THE COMMUTER'S IMAGINATION

By the late 1920s Williams was freely exploring the environment of the modern American writer. *A Novelette* shows this by focusing on the circumstances of writing in an up-tempo America. But the commitment to a kinetic poetics brings up a related issue that critics long ago put aside in their efforts to instate Williams as a serious poet. That outworn image of Dr. Williams jotting at odd moments on prescription blanks needs renewed attention because the vision of Williams scribbling fast on the fly in his car has been misunderstood. It was read inaccurately as the habitual doodling of a mere literary hobbyist, an embarrassing image about an important poet.

A Novelette, on the contrary, suggests that the image of Williams writing en route in his car is an accurate picture of the poetic practice of the serious writer in a high-velocity, twentieth-century America. Williams's was not the only such image. As we noticed, the very idea of the writer's sequestered study—essentially, the idea of "emotion recollected in tranquillity"—was outmoded in the new high-velocity age. The writer's setting and practice had to reflect changed times. Thus in *Exile's Return* Malcolm Cowley describes the writer on a Parisian commuter train "watching the Seine unwind as the train creaked faster, faster; thoughts, verses, situations were flashing into the mind, and there was never any time to write them down" (135). Of course Cowley exaggerates; his book is filled with accounts of prolific writers like the restless Dos Passos who constantly moved about, pausing for intervals of a few weeks or months while drafting *Manhattan Transfer* or *U.S.A.*

Most poets and novelists still worked at desks or tables in rooms. But at least two, Williams and Gertrude Stein, wrote in the very symbol of speed and mobility, the automobile. "Gertrude Stein worked a great deal" in the "restless" postwar years, writes Stein in *The Autobiography of Alice B. Toklas*, "not as in the old days, night after night, but anywhere, in between visits, in the automobile. . . . She was much influenced by the sound of the streets and the movement of the automobiles" (206). The crucial issue here is the propitiousness of circumstance in a high-speed world. For Williams, the poem had to be enacted in writing at the instant of imaginative intensity, which was not always possible. Adverse circumstances often thwarted him. "Try as I will," he says, "the thing comes only when I have one stocking on, the telephone is ringing, my mind is full of difficulties and you [Flossie] have asked me a question. In a flash it comes and is gone" (*I* 294).

Similarly, while "passing hurriedly" in his car to house calls of the flu victims, Williams remarks that "the rush that simplifies life, complicates it," for "there is no time to stop the car to write when only the writing that comes out of an intense simplification would be actual" (*I* 275).

But Williams finds he can sometimes "step up" his "energy" and utilize the car as a mobile private study. "I am alone only while in the car," he says. "What then? Take a pad in the car with me and write while running" (*I* 290). He has already demonstrated this practice. Here he splices his poetic imperative into freshly recollected fragments of vernacular speech and a montage of observed detail:

> I don't know what I'd do if I had six. I'd be in an asylum or the electric chair. I'd kill 'em. *She Regained*. A short novel. Write going. Look to steer. Her ways, serious, alert, WINNING. The wooly back of a little trotting dog, his breath (her breath) standing out before him (her). The breath flittering from the other end of the cars. And now at eleven the sun is warming the air. (*I* 278)

Write going: This passage takes readers directly into the mind of the writer, who acts and enacts while in motion. From a distance we learn, in *Spring and All*, that "someone has written a poem" in a high-velocity America. But *A Novelette* goes further to draw readers directly into the mind of that impersonal "someone" and to show the modern conditions under which the poem is written, as for instance when an opening bridge span literally stops Williams's car:

> As the gates closed and the bridge slowly swung open wasting his time —enforcing a stand-still, he thought again of "Juan Gris," making a path through the ice. That was the name of the approaching tug boat seen through the branches of a bare beech tree. It had a white cabin and a black stack with a broad yellow band around it.
>
> A patch of snow lay on the sand nearby and the ice of the river was behind the green hemlock's very short branches, from a tall tree growing up from below the high bank.
>
> The bridge tender wore spectacles and used a cane. And the rotary movements of the bridge was a good example of simple machinery. Write, said he to himself taking up the yellow pad from the seat of the car and beginning to scratch with— (*I* 284–85)

This passage is explicitly photographic, evocative of Juan Gris and indebted in composition to the photographs of Alfred Stieglitz. But it also demonstrates the literary practice of a writer whose high-speed culture equates inactivity with wastefulness. Williams accepted that cultural outlook: "The thing isn't to find the time [for writing]—we waste hours every day doing absolutely nothing at all" (*Autobiography* 359). Always Williams endorsed writing as kinetic. It "is directed- . . . toward the point where movement is blocked," and the writer must "practice skill in recording the force moving." The crucial issue, presuming the kinetics of writing, is catching "the evasive life of the thing" (*SE* 118; *I* 120; *A* 350). In this context Williams's self-portraits of the writer at work in his car (or, for that matter, in his office amidst patients) are exemplary of the modern.

In *The Embodiment of Knowledge* Williams muses, "This very note I happen to be writing at a cross street where once, in a field, I was seized by the throat, knocked down and kicked by an angry farmer. . . . What is it all about? If I say to my friends: Poetry! they smile and look down. If I say America! they believe me insincere or provincial" (*EK* 46). But of course Dr. Williams was defining America and poetry, not by a nostalgic recollection of a Tom Sawyerish incident in a preindustrial culture, but by the act of writing on-the-move in a state of imaginative intensity. In the previous century Walt Whitman portrayed the American Literatus as a figure in repose. "I loaf and invite my soul," he wrote in *Song of Myself* (1855). "I lean and loafe at my ease" (28). But there was precious little leaning and loafing in the rapid-transit age, and Williams, in apparent response to Whitman, provided the new image. To "write going" or to "write while running" is to be the American writer at work in the twentieth century.

There is another, cognitive issue involved in the contemporary "rapid-transit" experience. For as Williams and others understod, much of twentieth-century life for poet and populace alike was experienced in passing glimpses from the train, from the elevated, from the automobile. All America was in view from vehicles in transit everywhere. For the beholder the experience was qualitatively new. It was at once momentary, fugitive, elusive, incidental. A number of writers besides Williams recognized and incorporated the new moment into literature. Their efforts are worth noticing because comparatively they reveal how radically Williams differs from their aesthetic of the rapid-transit experience.

Young Billy Williams was just seven years old when William Dean Howells published *A Hazard of New Fortunes* (1890), a New York novel featuring a middle-class couple who enjoy riding the Third Avenue elevated at night. She likes "the fleeting intimacy formed with people in second- and third-floor interiors," while he appreciates the homely vignettes (e.g., "a family of workfolk at late tea") which he thinks "better than the theatre." "What drama!" exclaims the husband, his wife pleased by the "domestic intensity mixed with a perfect repose" (66).

The values of Howells's matron were upheld twenty-five years later in Edna Ferber's novel *Personality Plus* (1915). From the train window Ferber's traveling saleswoman glimpses the domestic scenes of "a pig-tailed girl at the piano" or "a family group seated before the table." Ferber's heroine likes "that picture best." Her "keen, imaginative mind could sense the scene" and follow "the trend of the talk." "Just silhouettes as the train flashes by," Ferber remarks, "but very human, very enviable" (110–11).

New York City's elevated trains provided the English visitor, Arnold Bennett, an enticing glimpse of "straitened middle-class life." In *Your United States* (1912) Bennett, riding the "El," is struck by the urban uniformity of "similar faces mysteriously peering in the same posture between the same curtains through the same windows," varied only by intermittent caged canaries and "enfeebled" potted plants. To live such a life, Bennett feels, would be to experience New York as its average citizens do, to understand the "toxin" of life at the borderline of poverty on a "costly rock" (171–72).

On the uptown "El" the narrator of Ernest Poole's *The Harbor* (1915) is as class-conscious as Bennett, and more critical. He dislikes the "proletarian portrait" (to borrow a caption from Williams) on view from the car: "cave-like" workrooms where girls and men turn out piecework garments and cheap novelties, "tenement kitchens, dirty cooking, unmade beds." He concludes, "these glimpses followed one on the other in a dizzying torrent [that] merged into one moving picture. That picture," writes Poole, "was of crowds, crowds, crowds . . . of people living frowzily" in a "prodigious swamp" of poverty (233).

Frowzy living was in part the subject of F. Scott Fitzgerald's rapid-transit moment. In *The Great Gatsby* Fitzgerald's insider-outsider narrator, Nick Carraway, lingers at a vulgar afternoon party and imagines that "high over the city our line of yellow windows [in the soft twilight] must have contributed their share of human secrecy to the casual watcher in the darkening streets, and I was him too, looking up and wondering. I was within and without" (36, 57). By the mid-1920s Fitzgerald could take for granted the very experience that Howells needed to explicate. Fitzgerald assumes such familiarity with these fugitive glimpses that he can have Nick simply imagine one of them in order to emphasize his narrator's status "within and without" the several worlds of that novel.

To some degree all these writers consider the formal quality of the rapid-transit moment. To Howells it was theatrical, to Bennett photographic, the same print duplicated endlessly down the track. The others sensed a cinematic quality. Ferber's "silhouettes as the train flashed by" remind us of the animator's flip-book, while Poole's "dizzying torrent that merged into one moving picture" makes a clear, if pejorative, statement. (Even Nick Carraway feels the cinematic "satisfaction that the constant flicker of men and machines gives to the restless eye.")

All these writers, nevertheless, forfeit the rapid-transit moment itself. They sacrifice it for other purposes. To Fitzgerald it is a technique for characterization, while Howells, Ferber, Bennett, and Poole use it to strengthen their well-established themes on community, domestic values, poverty. For all of them, the scene glimpsed is mere transit to other matters. At best it is a picture invested with anecdotal possibility—which proves to be its very limitation in these works. Nick Carraway proclaims "the inexhaustible variety of life" to be on view through lighted window glass, but in fact the a priori values of all these writers inhibit a variety of experience. From sweatshop to home-sweet-home these rapid-transit scenes become, after all, only thematic stock-in-trade of literary realism. For these writers the moment is, finally, only an illustration and not an experience.

Williams's rapid-transit moment is radically different. In and of itself, it is the experience intact. The poet's opportunity is not to describe the scene á la Howells and the others but to give it form and thus enact it:

The elevated, New York (Courtesy Library of Congress)

View from the New York elevated (Courtesy Library of Congress)

In passing with my mind
on nothing in the world

but the right of way
I enjoy on the road by

virtue of the law—
I saw

an elderly man who
smiled and looked away

to the north past a house—
a woman in blue

who was laughing and
leaning forward to look up

into the man's half
averted face

and a boy of eight who was
looking at the middle of

the man's belly
at a watchchain— (*I* 119–20)

In these lines from *Spring and All* there is no anecdotal value vis-à-vis the poet and the figures he observes. Readers participate as Williams forms the composition, for it is the composing eye rather than the polemical voice that engages us. Williams is extremely careful not to jeopardize the integrity of his composition. No surprising, diverting images follow to eclipse it. Readers anticipating an anecdote are immediately thwarted:

The supreme importance
of this nameless spectacle

sped me by them
without a word—

So much for narrative possibility; nothing is going to "happen" with the threesome while our motorist-poet plays recording secretary to the action. There is not even a title or caption for this "nameless spectacle," which is nonetheless of such "supreme importance" that even as we move forward in the poem, we are impelled to return to the beginning for another look. If this minimalist composition (one that risks and barely escapes banality) is supremely important, we must go back in order to "revalue [the] experience," as Williams urges us to do in the theoretical statements that precede this poem (*I* 116).

Postcard view of New York elevated

But in what terms can we "revalue" the experience of this and similar poems? A comment by Hart Crane seems especially helpful. Crane commended Stieglitz's vitality of "apprehension" in photography in terms directly applicable to Williams. "Speed is at the bottom of it all," Crane wrote, "—the hundredth of a second caught so precisely that the motion is continued from the picture indefinitely: the moment made [as Williams himself wrote] eternal." As if with Williams in mind, Crane added that "this baffling capture is an end in itself" (*Letters* 132).

Williams concludes "The Right of Way" (as the poem was later titled) without really ending it. More precisely, he concludes by beginning the poem anew:

> Why bother where I went?
> for I went spinning on the
>
> four wheels of my car
> along the wet road until
>
> I saw a girl with one leg
> over the rail of a balcony.

We know better than to ask the girl's intention. To ask, Will she jump?—is to miss the point. For the girl, rail, leg, and balcony are elements in a composition which, this poem argues, can endlessly be rediscovered in kind and given form by the poet in transit. Williams arrests and encodes what otherwise would be lost in the slurry of a high-speed day. Speeding and spinning, Williams successfully resists the aesthetic peril of contemporary life even as he exploits its tempo and rhythm. In praise of locality John Dewey could scorn those merely in transit, those in a commuter's limbo without place. But Williams felt otherwise. From adolescence he spent untold hours commuting, at first as a student by train, ferry, and "El," and later, as a physician, by automobile. In large part these hours formed the time of his life, and the rapid-transit experience thus became critical as "an end in itself."

One important source of Williams's rapid-transit poetics is his medical school education. Some documents characterizing the medical student and physician of the early twentieth century suggests that kinetic values in medicine were germane to Williams's development as a writer. The conception of the physician, during the years of Williams's American schooling (1902–6) was undergoing radical change. His own medical school at the University of Pennsylvania was in the forefront of the transformation. Through the 1890s the new emphasis on specialization and research and clinical science was changing both teaching methods and medical practice.

The notion of the passive rote-learning student or practitioner had begun to yield to that of the scientifically questing activist. The didactic lecture, for instance, to an amphitheater of students charged with memorization of data regurgitated in "quiz-compends" was gradually halted. It was replaced by emphasis instead on small groups of students guided by a professor or preceptor in participatory demonstrations or case studies in the laboratory or at the bedside. The hospital, accordingly, was no longer solely a hospice wherein the sick could be nursed by the healer's art, but rather a clinical laboratory in which the bedridden figure could be made to yield scientific information utilized in research and prerequisite to his treatment. It is this quality to which Williams referred when he wrote, "They say the science of medicine is humane. It is not so—but most inhuman in its conception" (*EK* 83).

One document, *Medical Education in the United States and Canada* (1910), codified this conception of the modern medical student and doctor as activists in a fast-changing field. It is a text especially relevant to Williams. The report, so named for its author, the layman-educator Abraham Flexner, is a landmark in the history of modern medicine. The president of the Carnegie Foundation had commissioned Flexner to survey the state of American medical education and to make specific recommendations for change. Flexner, following a grueling schedule, traveled throughout the United States and Canada during 1908–9. His report, once implemented by funds from the Rockefeller Foundation, instigated momentous change in the nation's medical schools, the establishment of the modern medical curriculum, and the complete integration of medicine into university structures.

The Flexner report is relevant to Williams's poetics because of its delineation of the modern medical student and practitioner. Flexner's argument for national reform is based largely on the exemplary model of a handful of leading American medical schools, including Williams's own. The figure of the student and the doctor revealed in the report necessarily reflects the thinking of the most advanced

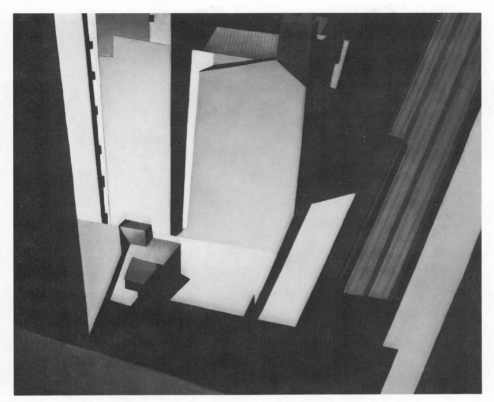

Charles Sheeler, Church Street El *(Courtesy Cleveland Museum of Art, purchase Mr. and Mrs. William H. Marlatt Fund)*

faculty members at these institutions. These men, such as William Osler and William Welch, provided their students the most recent available information on research and treatment. They also instilled in them a sense of their roles, even of their identity, as physicians. The language of a document like the Flexner report is valuable to the study of Williams's poetics because it indicates how Williams was taught to think of himself as he prepared to become a physician. The rhetoric of the report suggests that medical school enabled Williams to adapt to the cultural speed and efficiency, and to the instantaneity of thought that the poet later learned to exploit in literature.

Flexner's text argues that medicine, like other areas of American life, is deliberately moving with increasing rapidity. Rote learning and "mystical and empirical vagaries" would have no future in an applied science moving along "biological and chemical lines" with a "beneficent rapidity." How then could the "fresh young graduate[s] of five and twenty years keep abreast of its progress"?—by transformation from "passive learners" to activists. "[M]odern medicine . . . is characterized by activity. The student no longer merely watches, listens, memorizes;

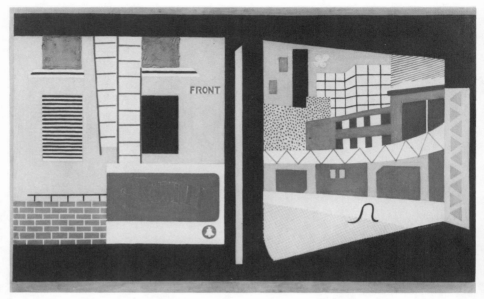

Stuart Davis, House and Street, *1931. Oil on canvas. 26 × 42¼ inches
(Courtesy Collection of Whitney Museum of American Art)*

Stuart Davis, Windshield Mirror, *1932 (Courtesy Philadelphia Museum of Art,
Given by Mrs. Edith Halpert)*

he *does*." As doctors these students will confront "a definite situation" in which observed facts "suggest a line of action." The doctor "constructs a hypothesis" on which "he acts." Between "theory and practice," says the report, "his mind flies like a shuttle." And this split-second cognitive action is as valid for the practitioner of medicine as for the researcher, in fact more so: "If we differentiate investigator and practitioner, it is because in the former case action is leisurely and indirect, in the latter case, immediate and anxious" (63, 25, 53, 55, 56).

One physician, the renowned Osler, cited in the Flexner report (and quoted earlier in this discussion), was principally responsible for bringing the modern methods of clinical science to the University of Pennsylvania, where he taught from 1884 to 1889 before accepting a position at Johns Hopkins. Osler left Penn some thirteen years before Williams arrived to begin his studies, but he remained directly influential on the Philadelphia campus. His younger protégés continued on the faculty, and his textbook, *The Principles and Practice of Modern Medicine* (which Williams is certain to have used), was internationally circulated in nine editions between 1892 and 1916. Osler's biographer reports that he returned intermittently from Baltimore to convene with his medical colleagues in Philadelphia. As a legendary figure he returned, moreover, in April 1905 to deliver the valedictory to the medical students at Penn. Osler's speech, "The Student Life," was subsequently widely published and, like the Flexner report, resounds with a medical ethos that Williams adapted to imaginative literature a dozen years later.

Osler not only defined the age as one of "hurry and bustle," but he also urged students to meet it by developing, for their medical expertise, the very practice Williams adapted to the writing of his poems and prose. "Carry a small note-book which will fit into your waistcoat pocket," Osler told the Penn students. "After the examination . . . two minutes will suffice to record the essentials in the daily progress." "Routine and system when once made a habit, facilitate work," he said, "and the busier you are the more time you will have to make observations after examining a patient. Jot a comment at the end of the notes" (183). Williams, of course, applied Osler's lesson to his literary life, first with the now-reprinted 1914 Little Red Notebook that mixes medical notes with poetic entries, then with the tablet on the seat of the Ford (*William Carlos Williams Review* 1–34).

Osler's other directives to the students pertain as well to Williams's poetics—for instance, his call for that student who, along with a broad outlook and sense of history, "has yet a powerful vision for the minutiae of life." As doctors, he asserts, these students will become "kitchen and backstair men . . . , who know the subject in hand in all possible relationships." Osler tells them: "[N]othing will sustain you more potently than the power to recognize in your humdrum routine . . . the true poetry of life—the poetry of the commonplace." Osler clearly preferred romantic poetry (with the notable exception of Whitman) (174, 177, 183, 186). Yet his call for the vernacular, for the poetry of the commonplace, is exactly the call Williams began to heed some years after Osler delivered "The Student Life." *The Descent of Winter* with its "hero" Dolores Marie Pischak is the "poetry of the commonplace" by a "kitchen and backstair" man.

In poetics Williams seems also to have heeded the kind of warning Osler issued against professional obsolescence in medicine that now moved with "beneficent rapidity." Return every fifth year to the laboratory or hospital for a "quintennial brain-dusting," Osler advised. "Backstair" men especially require such "renovation, rehabilitation, reintegration, resuscitation." To fail in these four Rs meant to fall behind as the medical field of action advanced. The young doctor Williams knew this. He commuted weekly to New York clinics through the 1920s and, during his 1927 European sojourn, attended the Vienna clinics so well described in *A Voyage to Pagany* (1928). Williams felt kindred anxieties about obsolescence in his writing of poetry and prose. He imagined the writer who, while still alive, "will see his own work grow older and begin to die" and who "may even live to see it completely dead." But in the sustenance of "rehabilitation" or "resuscitation" Williams sees "no reason for halting," since "it is in fact the beginning he wants," the very beginning that scholars have proven to be central to Williams's writings. It was in medicine that Williams first learned the lesson by which he rejected Wallace Stevens's argument that "incessant new beginnings lead to sterility" (*EK* 105; *SE* 12). In medical school Williams had learned otherwise. His deliberate, lifelong career of literary innovation suggests that he took voices like Osler's seriously because he found them valid both in medicine and in a society of rapid, accelerating social change.

This is not to say with certainty that Williams read the Flexner report, though there is ample evidence of his familiarity with Osler's work. According to Emily Wallace, Williams's son, Dr. William Eric Williams, reports that his father told him several times that he went to hear Osler at Penn, and in a letter dated April 27, 1906, William George Williams wrote to his son: "I mailed you yesterday what I think you will find a good book, consisting of extracts from Dr. Osler's writings. . . . I hope you will find it helpful and inspiring" (*William Carlos Williams Review* 72, n. 42). Apparently Williams did find it so, for his library included a copy of Osler's *A Way of Life* (1932). Such texts as those of Osler and Flexner are important because they reveal the activist ethos of the modern medical student and practitioner of Williams's time. It is the modern doctor whose mind "flies like a shuttle" in thought that is "immediate and anxious." It is the modern physician for whom "two minutes will suffice to record the essentials" in a life whose very busyness opens up additional time for yet more effort. These qualities, which Williams no doubt internalized in his socialization as a physician, became the very ones integral to his poetics when, in the late 1910s, he emerged from the "mystical vagaries" of Georgian verse in *Al Que Quiere* (1917) and went on to formulate the efficient, kinetic basis for the American modern poem. In this light it seems that medicine was a fundamental part of the "long foreground" of Williams's poetics of high-speed America, and the poet as well as the doctor learned to "write going."

MEDICINE, MOONLIGHT, AND THE EFFICIENT MOMENT

In 1906 in Philadelphia the University of Pennsylvania awarded doctorates to two men. One was the efficiency engineer, Frederick W. Taylor, the other a young graduate in medicine named William Carlos Williams. Their paths did not cross. On the autumn day when the efficiency engineer came to the university to collect his honorary Doctor of Science, young Dr. Williams, a June graduate, was probably in New York City's French Hospital "stinking of ether" as an intern and looking forward to the weekend when he could resume work on his "great poem" (*A* 71).

Safe to say, Williams knew nothing of Taylor in 1906. This young physician, already a college friend of Ezra Pound, planned to live a divided life, earning his living practicing medicine and nourishing his soul by writing poetry. Poetry, he believed, was a sacred trust of moral idealism and noble purpose. Ideas on efficiency, waste, or for that matter on engineers, machines, or structures formed no part of his artistic plan. Poetically speaking, they were beyond the pale. The young doctor's ideas on poetry had taken shape from the Romantic tradition he had imbibed since boyhood in Francis Palgrave's anthology of English lyrics, *The Golden Treasury*. In tribute to the great Romantics, Keats, Wordsworth, Shelley, and Byron, Williams occupied his poetic hours writing genteel, earnest romantic echoes like this:

> Elvira, by love's grace
> There goeth before you
> A clear radiance
> Which maketh all vain souls
> Candles when noon is.
> (*Collected Earlier Poems* [*CEP*] 18)

By the late 1910s, however, Williams had stopped writing his "bad Keats" and "bad Whitman too." Eventually he would denounce these poems for their inverted phrasing, inaccurate rhymes, and stereotypical form (*A* 107). Instead, Williams had begun to write the precise, hard-edged lyrics for which he has been honored. The transformation owed much to the cultural climate that engendered the Taylorist Efficiency Movement. In it Williams discovered a poetics of efficiency and learned to regard the poem as a construction formed of component parts—"an organization of materials" (*I* 73).

As we shall see, Williams came to consider the poem a machine made of words, and he also brought engineering values into poems containing no direct reference to machines or structures. In addition, he designed poems free of redundant word-parts and therefore was able to incorporate values of precision and speed in the hundreds of short lyrics he wrote through the 1920s and intermittently for the rest of his life.

For even in 1906 Williams had more in common with Frederick Taylor's way of thinking than he realized. In medical school he had absorbed values of productive speed. The medical curriculum, moreover, required Williams to perceive the body as a complex machine comprised of component parts. In fact, medical school provided the basis for the poetics Williams developed in artistic maturity, when he learned that the poem could incorporate and enact intense momentary experience from daily life. Williams, in short, was able to produce his lyric machines once he applied both clinical and Taylorist thinking to his poetic life.

This is the story of that application, which deserves a discussion all of its own. In fact, Williams makes an excellent case study of the poetics of the gear-and-girder world first and foremost because he was a poet. Committed to that very genre, poetry, Williams could excel in this world of machines and structures. Of all arts of the written word, poetry claims the concision, the compression, the terseness congruent with the values of efficient machine and structural design. The power of a poem, like that of a machine or structure, could be viewed as a function of the efficient operation of its integrated components, all designed to work for maximal strength and energy output. Some writers understood this. Not by chance did Hemingway call himself a poet. Not by chance did Williams say that "prose may carry a load of ill-defined matter like a ship," but that "poetry is the machine that drives it, pruned to a perfect economy" (*SE* 256–57). If John Dos Passos's monumental, inclusive novels were ships brimming with sociocultural cargo, Williams's poems were purely the machinery of propulsion. In Williams, we see what Frank Lloyd Wright meant when he spoke of "the engineer in the poet."

Williams is especially arresting for another, additional reason. More than any other writer of the gear-and-girder world, he left the biographical record of his struggle to enact that world in written form. He, more clearly than others, documented his battle to become a twentieth-century man, a man of the era of "trees, animals, engines." His essays, poems, and fiction chart his escape route from the archaic romanticism of the late nineteenth century. They map Williams's struggle to find the forms and the practice of a writer of the contemporary moment. His texts show Williams's personal fight to depart the world of Alexander's bridge, into which he had been born, and to immigrate to the country of Frank Lloyd Wright's blocks.

Williams (1883–1963) was a second-generation American, the son of an Englishman and a Puerto Rican mother of French and Spanish descent. The family lived in the northern New Jersey suburb of Rutherford, and Spanish and French were spoken at home, where Williams and his brother absorbed ideas on art from their mother, a former student of painting in the Beaux Arts French tradition. Williams's father regularly read aloud from Shakespeare and insisted that the boys' education include a year in European schools and secondary schooling at New York City's rigorous Horace Mann High School.

Growing up in the 1880s and 1890s in Rutherford, Williams of course experienced the rapid technological change occurring throughout the United States. Looking back at mid-century, he was stunned to recall the conditions of his boyhood. "Imagine! No sewers, no water supply, no gas, even. Certainly no electricity, no telephone, not even a trolley car" (*A* 279–80). He remembered wood-plank sidewalks, outhouses, rainwater collected in a cistern and hand-pumped into an attic holding tank. ("Ed and I got a dime apiece for an hour's pumping when it was needed.") He recalls houses lighted by kerosene lamps ("Am I *that* old?") and streets constantly ripped up "for water, for sewers, for gas." One of the "finest sights" of his boyhood was a local mansion radiant with gaslight for a family wedding. It is no wonder that Williams's mature poems celebrate household technology. "The house is yours," begins the poem "The House," a tour of 9 Ridge Road, the young doctor's gift to his wife:

> This is the kitchen—
> We have a new
> hotwater heater and a new
> gas stove to please you. (*CEP* 70)

For all the new machines and technological systems in American daily life, it was medical school (1902–6) that brought Williams face to face with the gear-and-girder world. There he learned to see the body—and by extension the material world—as a congeries of mechanisms and structures comprised of component parts. Medical school was, in effect, the prep school for Williams's modernist poems. The education he received there essentially indoctrinated him into the material world of constructed reality.

Until the late 1910s Williams, however, did not know—consciously know—how he had learned to see the world. He knew his medicine, of course, and undertook postgraduate work in a German university to increase his expertise. He had no inkling, however, that the perceptual values reinforced daily in medical school and practice could be relevant to imaginative literature. Upon graduation he interned in New York City, spent the year studying pediatrics in Leipzig, and in 1910 began medical practice in Rutherford, marrying Florence Herman ("Flossie") in 1912 and fathering two sons.

All the while Williams lived his divided life. He worked at medicine in the component-part world of Wright's blocks; and he wrote poetry in the organically seamless romantic world of Alexander's bridge. His first volume, the privately printed *Poems* (1909), has not survived. But many poems from *The Tempers* (1913), his second book, show the young poet self-identified as a singer of songs. Here, for instance, are two stanzas of "First Praise" from *The Tempers*:

> Lady of dusk-wood fastnesses,
>   Thou art my Lady.
> I have known the crisp, splintering leaf-tread
>   with thee on before,
> White, slender through the green saplings;
> I have lain by thee on the brown forest floor
>   Beside thee, my Lady. (*CEP* 17)

The voice is the romantic troubadour's. Its world is that of romantic effusion, all gossamer, indistinct, vaguely idealistic. These stanzas are virtually interchangeable with those of Bliss Carman and Richard Hovey, two very popular versifiers of fin de siècle America. The romantic poesy of the world of Alexander's bridge was abundant and in good repute in early twentieth-century America, and Williams took part in it. He gave it every moment he could spare from the gear-and-girder world of his medical practice.

By 1917, however, Williams had spurned that romantic world and was writing poems of hard-edged component parts. At last, the world of Wright's blocks and the world of contemporary medicine had become the world of the poet. He was no longer a singer of ineffably spiritual songs but a designer of a poem-construction:

> In the brilliant gas light
> I turn the kitchen spigot
> and watch the water plash
> into the clean white sink.
> On the grooved drain-board
> to one side is
> a glass filled with parsley—
> crisped green.
>   Waiting
> for the water to freshen—
> I glance at the spotless floor—:
> a pair of rubber sandals
> lie side by side
> under the wall-table
> all is in order for the night. (*CEP* 145)

These stanzas from "Good Night" (*All Que Quiere* [*To Him Who Wants It*]) (1917) show a very different Williams. The domestic order, achieved through the unacknowledged effort of Williams's wife, pleases the poet appreciative of manufactured things, the spigot, the drain-board, the rubber sandals. Vanished is the songster's idealization of the ineffable; in its place we find the assertion of a designed composition. The edges are sharp; each component is distinctly profiled, from the grooved drain-board to the glass filled with crisping parsley, and the poet himself is redefined. The designer has supplanted the romantic singer. At last Williams was realizing how to apply his medical education to poetry. At last he understood how to exploit the gear-and-girder world in language arts.

The story of Williams's transition is itself complex. It originated in personal crisis. Williams's best-laid plans, he found, were going awry. He could not keep on shuttling between two separate worlds, organic and mechanic. *The Tempers* (1913), published in London with Pound's help, recorded Williams's desperation. Recently married, he had just taken out a mortgage on his house at 9 Ridge Road in Rutherford to continue his medical practice, which included house calls and evening office hours. *The Tempers*, in fact, shows a frustrated Williams struggling unsuccessfully to sustain himself as a poet. The romantic young doctor of "To Wish Myself Courage" pledges to write "of the leaves and the moon in a tree top/. . . . When the stress of youth is put away from me." He goes on:

> How can I ever be written out as men say?
> Surely it is merely an interference with the
> long song—This that I am now doing. (*CEP* 32)

As of 1913 poetry meant moonlight ages away from the stressful present, itself perceived only as an obstruction to his long poetic song. In 1913 the life of the moment or of the day paled before the higher realm of the poetic, which Williams accorded a supernal existence all its own.

We must not fail to appreciate the young poet's powerful reasons for keeping his poetry separate from his experience. At mid-century, he looked back and called his medical practice "food and drink" to his poems and identified the "secret gardens of the self" to which he had privileged entry as a physician. Back during his years of medical training, however, Williams's only garden was Keatsean. Much of the rest of the environment was cadavers, roach-infested laboratories, disease, injury, and endless scenes of childbirth. Faced daily with the enormity of gore and sickness, Williams must have cherished the shelter of safe ersatz Keats, which contained his residual "terror" and which no amount of ironic tough talk in letters to his brother Ed could diminish.

Williams had another good reason to fence poetry off from his life and, therefore, from engagement in the experiential poetic "exact moment." His novel, *The Build-Up* (1952), reveals a strong biographical barrier against a poetics based in daily experience. More than any of Williams's other writings, *The Build-up* shows the stultifying texture of social life in Rutherford during his young manhood. It gives readers one more context in which to appreciate Williams's tenacious hold on blurry post-Victorian "truth" and "beauty" in poetry. In several chapters dealing with the years of his early twenties, Williams shows the stifling social atmosphere of his hometown. The scene, a formal evening party, marks the new social prominence of his mother- and father-in-law, Joe and Gurlie Stecher (in real life, the Hermans):

> Gurlie was conscious of being carefully studied by a dumpy little woman on her left who, as soon as she was brought before her, began to clear her throat and look nervously down at the carpet. "This is Mrs. Stecher," said the hostess. "Mrs. Joseph Stecher." Gurlie couldn't see the other's eyes, could hardly, in fact, hear her say anything more than a mumble, with a smirk. She nodded her own head and moved on around the roughly assembled circle of chairs.
>
> "Who was that? I didn't hear," she managed to ask her introducer as they moved to the next chair.

"Mrs. Fletcher, one of our new members."

"I couldn't hear anything she said," Gurlie observed.

"Oh, she's very shy. But her husband is just the opposite. They are very different. But she is very sincere. They are good members. This is Mrs. Greer. . . ."

"How do you do?" said Gurlie.

The lady put out her hand which Gurlie, not expecting it, took with a firm grip, then let go as fast. "Her husband is the Borough Assessor. Mrs. Greer has a wonderful garden." (*The Build-Up* [*B-Up*] 191)

The whole chapter goes on in this killing dialogue. Williams, like Sherwood Anderson and Sinclair Lewis, is dissecting small-town America (though without their respective pathos or satire). Choosing to represent the Rutherford social scene in documentary realism, Williams wisely spaced passages like this to keep his readers' minds from wandering. But for brief spans the reader enters directly into the scene to experience firsthand the deadly dull language. The spoken lines never once rise above cliché, which at mid-century was still Williams's vivid recollection of Rutherford's middle- and upper-middle-class conversation during his early twenties. Considering the level of speech of the social class to which he had been bred if not born, it is probable that Williams cherished his dreamy poetry of "truth" and "beauty." It pointed to an ineffably higher order of life than anything visible or audible around him. The realm of genteel poetry must have been not only a respite from medical school and the French Hospital but also a sanctuary from Rutherford society at its dull best.

Williams, nonetheless, was in jeopardy of entrapment in the world of his poetic escape. Desperate for stressful youth to pass, yearning to become writer-in-residence in the poetic moonlight, he clung to the waning world of Alexander's bridge even as contemporary values became those of the machine culture, kinetic, efficient, fast-paced. Williams, entering his thirties, needed a way to acclimate himself in this world both as a doctor and as a writer. He needed Frederick Taylor's Efficiency Movement, which finally did free Williams from the world of decayed romanticism and show him how the blank page could be a construction site for poems of the gear-and-girder world.

In fact, it is ironic that Williams's path of escape—and creativity—lay in a social movement of the middle class he found so dull, a movement whose conservative utilitarianism Williams would later objectify critically in the figure of Benjamin Franklin. But in the 1910s it was Taylorism, the middle-class Efficiency Movement, which gave Williams entry to the poetry of the gear-and-girder world. Taylorism became the impetus for Williams's discovery that the immediate experience of the moment is the material for the poem. The Efficiency Movement let Williams redefine the poet and the poem as designer and design. The irony here is that Williams found poetic freedom in a movement preoccupied with the budgeting of time.

As we saw, the Efficiency Movement, or craze, began with the well-publicized Eastern Rate Case which made Frederick Taylor's name virtually a household word in middle-class America. Its values were publicized in journalism as efficiency became a gospel seemingly applicable to every area of life from education to the kitchen. Williams's own response to Taylorism and the Efficiency Movement emerged in "Five Philosophical Essays" (*The Embodiment of Knowledge*). As the editor of the essays remarks, their style and the appearance of the transcript indicate that they were probably written in the 1910s. The essays explore Williams's relation to what he felt were polar concepts (for example, constancy and freedom, faith and knowledge), which he tried to reconcile for himself and which address deeply personal concerns. As a doctor-poet Williams argues the relationship of science to art, and as a married man he examines the relationship of constancy (seemingly in marriage) to personal, that is, sexual, freedom.

These essays also show Williams's engagement with personal efficiency in his life. In "Love and Service" he praises the life of an "actual economy that wastes nothing." He tried to define that life in "Waste and Use," which is an exhortation to himself and a warning. "Waste is the only real danger," he writes, defining it as repression ("passion . . . forced into a saving habit"). Williams begins the essay with caveats: "NATURE'S final command is: 'Do not waste.' Insofar as life is to do, it is: 'Do not waste time.' Insofar as life is to see, it is: 'Do not waste space.'" The apogee of personal attainment is the life of "no waste." Throughout the five essays Williams argues that seeing is the action of life, and in "Waste and Use" he comes to urge a constant seeing as life's economy. "To reach this perfection," he writes, "we must be at it continually, thus not wasting time but looking about completes our endeavour by showing that the thing we perfect is not the perfection but perishable and the more we look the more we become convinced of this." Aphoristically he calls economy "simply using to the full," and he continues the essay with a resolve "to do . . . to the fullest of my power with clear eyes" (*EK* 179, 186, 188).

"Waste and Use" shows a younger man's residual filial-pietistic strivings for perfection. It is probable that the Efficiency Movement appealed to Williams, as to countless others, because it renewed the American ethos of personal progress in moral terms attractive precisely because they posed no ideological challenge to late-nineteenth-century Christian liberalism still powerful in the Progressive era. The young doctor who had bowed since boyhood to parental directives on "goodness" could find the perfectionist morality of the Efficiency Movement to be familiar territory.

He found much more. In two important ways the Efficiency Movement contributed to Williams's discovery of the poetry in the experiential moment. For the young doctor-poet with a growing medical practice, a marriage, a mortgage, a baby (as of 1914), and an unswerving determination to live a full literary life, the Efficiency Movement conveyed the message that there was abundant time and energy for increased personal output. It said that even the busiest people had funds of untapped or misused energy that could be put to new or better uses.

For Williams the movement provided cultural assurance that his poetry need not wait until some future time when "the stress of youth is put away." Rather, it encouraged him to find, for poetry, the interstices of time between his many activities. The Efficiency Movement suggested that the moment itself would suffice, that the instant provides opportunity for utilization. Years later Williams would phrase it succinctly: "Unless I apply myself to the minute, my life escapes me." By 1923, in *Spring and All*, he spoke confidently, explicitly of that moment. No longer did he crave a release from the stress of daily life. No longer did he yearn to dwell in the poetic moonlight. Instead, by 1923, Williams defined the poetic act as a moment of contact in the immediate here-and-now: "The reader knows himself as he was twenty years ago and he has also in mind a vision of what he would be, some day. Oh, some day! But the thing that he never knows and never dares to know is what he is at the exact moment that he is. And this moment is the only thing in which I am interested" (*I* 89).

This commitment to the intense present moment is, in fact, a major part of the poetics of the gear-and-girder world. It is Williams's premise for a poetics of efficiency, in which the moment itself is to be utilized in a state of heightened, kinetic consciousness. (Conversely, the efficiency ethos could—and did—become at times oppressive to Williams in the years ahead, for implicitly "efficiency" could never be achieved perfectly. In theory the opportune moment could always be broken down into some smaller unit and yet more cognitive instants could become available for poetry. Close to 1940, when his literary record was as impressive as his patients were numerous, Williams wrote, "You Have Pissed Your Life," the title being a judgment that the poem finds to be irremediable.)

The "Five Philosophical Essays" also show Williams struggling toward an aesthetic based in direct experience of the perceived moment—an aesthetic that the Efficiency Movement authorized in personal, family, social, and political life. In the 1920s Williams would come to express that aesthetic in the term "clarity." Clear "seeing" was, of course, as much a part of modernist aesthetics as it had been for the Romantics. As Gertrude Stein wrote, "Nothing changes from generation to generation except the thing seen and that makes a composition." But for Williams, seeing was prerequisite to locating that poetic "exact moment." In "Love and Service" he wrote that human beings cannot even begin to know, but "can appreciate [and can] behold and . . . behold more." His enjoyment "is merely to look, to see, to appreciate through occupation or otherwise." The essence of the poet or painter, he says, is "sight in the broad sense," which includes hearing. But Williams had to practice seeing and to learn to value the composition before he could relinquish the blurry romantic by committing himself to the present. Only then could he possess the "back streets" whose yards are "cluttered with old chicken wire, ashes, furniture gone wrong" (*EK* 178–80; *CEP* 121).

"Clarity" thus becomes a major tenet of Williams's theory of the efficient imagination because it represents his achievement in locating and possessing the poetic moment. "Clarity! . . . the unscummed impact of sense and mind" is "life."

Its relevance here lies in its very instantaneity, which Williams emphasizes by calling the writer's mind "a lightning calculator . . . racing at top speed to touch and decipher." In the moment of clarity the poet is a mastermind. Williams's "Clarity!" is the cognitive act achieved in the present moment with utmost efficiency (*EK* 26, 38, 53; *SE* 128, 268–69; *Voyage to Pagany* 116).

In practice, it was neither simple nor easy. At mid-century Williams affirmed that "five minutes, ten minutes can always be found," but repeatedly he recounted the difficulty of catching the "evasive life of the thing," of discovering the language that lifts "stereotype" to "insight" in an environment of "a thousand trivialities" (*A* iii, 359, 361). The poems in *Al Que Quiere* are a record of Williams's purposeful struggle over and over to attain that efficient moment of clarity. This poem, "Pastoral," is one example of the enacted efficient moment:

> When I was younger
> it was plain to me
> I must make something of myself.
> Older now
> I walk back streets
> admiring the houses
> of the very poor:
> roof out of line with sides
> the yards cluttered
> with old chicken wire, ashes,
> furniture gone wrong;
> the fences and outhouses
> built of barrel-staves
> and parts of boxes, all,
> if I am fortunate,
> smeared a bluish green
> that properly weathered
> pleases me best
> of all colors.
>
>   No one
> will believe this
> of vast import to the nation. (*CEP* 121)

Moments like these were tremendously important to Williams. Far removed from public life, uncensored by norms of caste and class, uninhibited by personal ambition, they became the efficient clarifying moments enacted in poems. Each is "an identifiable thing . . . instant and perfect." In sequence it comes, is there, and vanishes. "But I have seen it, clearly. . . . I have been possessed by it" (*A* 289). The Efficiency Movement, in this sense, was Williams's liberation. In fact, the most

Grant Wood, Lilies of the Alley with Shoehorn, *1922–25 (Gift of Harriet Y. and John B. Turner II, Courtesy Cedar Rapids Museum of Art)*

serious question may not have been what price he would pay for a poetics of the efficient moment but what would be the cost should he fail to achieve it.

For Williams's father-in-law, the character Joe Stecher, is a haunting figure for Williams. In the *White Mule* trilogy he typifies the sensitive and active man who dies in life because he defers aesthetic instants until he loses all capacity for them. Over the course of the three novels readers see Stecher, a man who loves the natural world—flowers and trees and fresh air—turn away from all of them in single-minded pursuit of business success. He achieves it at horrendous cost. *The Build-Up* shows him in late midlife as a brooding, restless man who owns a farm with livestock and meadows in which he can take no interest. His son's boyhood death and one daughter's elopement with a notorious Casanova have taken their toll. So too has the decades-long obsession with business. Stecher's final cry is one of despair as he agrees to build a new farmhouse, a monument to his money: "All right then, we'll build a house. We'll build it of stone, the biggest God-damned house we can afford. Tell the architect we want the finest house money can buy. . . . Expense be damned!" (*B-Up* 333, 334). Trapped in the hollow of American success, Stecher is left only with his despair, unable to experience the vivifying instants of perception that define life in hundreds of Williams's short lyrics.

Joe Stecher is Williams's caveat, a bleak alternative to the poetic life of infinite efficient moments. Against his example Williams's remark, "Unless I apply myself to the minute, my life escapes me," acquires meaning beyond the mere budgeting of time. Williams suggests, in discourse and poetic example, that cognitive engagement itself defines life. In full revolution against the romantic ethos of emotion recollected in tranquillity, Williams characterizes contemporary life as one of "constant, disruptive change." As we saw, he determined in his writing to embody the "advantageous jumps, swiftnesses, colors, movements of the day." To do so was to achieve the poetics of the efficient moment and thus to be alive in twentieth-century America.

MACHINES MADE OF WORDS

It has been by paying naked attention first to the thing itself that American plumbing, American shoes, American bridges, indexing systems, locomotives, printing presses, city buildings, farm implements and a thousand other things have become notable in the world. Yet we are timid in believing that in the arts discovery and invention will take the same course. And there is no reason why they should unless our writers have the inventive intelligence of our engineers.

William Carlos Williams, "Yours, O Youth," 1921

To make two bald statements: There's nothing sentimental about a machine, and: A poem is a small (or large) machine made of words. When I say there's nothing sentimental about a poem I mean that there can be no part, as in any other machine, that is redundant.

William Carlos Williams, *The Wedge*, 1944

William Carlos Williams spoke literally when he called the poem a machine made of words. And he spoke sincerely when summoning American writers to show the inventive intelligence of the nation's engineers. In the age of ubiquitous structural and machine technology Williams understood that writers in search of new forms could benefit from the conception of art as a structure with a framework and various fixed and moving parts intended to transmit energy. He understood that the poem was a design or arrangement of prefabricated component parts. Like Frank Lloyd Wright, Williams knew this principle was crucial for the contemporary artist. In fiction Ernest Hemingway and John Dos Passos demonstrated their understanding that component parts were central to the conception of the sentence and the narrative.

On the subject of design components in imaginative literature, however, Williams became the most articulate spokesman. As we shall see, the medical education that prepared him for a poetics of kinetic efficiency also taught him to perceive the world in ways congenial with the values of engineering technology. Williams was able to call the poem "an organization of materials . . . as an automobile or a kitchen stove is an organization of materials" because of his medical background (*Interviews* [*In*] 73). In the era of the art-technology crisis Dr. Williams welcomed the opportunities afforded by technology. In large part he was freed from a decayed romanticism by his machines made of words.

Williams welcomed new technologies of all sorts in his poems and fiction. In *The Great American Novel* (1923) he proudly detailed his "great dexterity" in garaging his car and enjoyed making "a little Ford" his heroine (*I* 169–90). As we know, this poet of the age of "trees, animals, engines" freely intersperses technological figures with those of flora and fauna. Readers encounter images of "the weed-grown / chassis / of a wrecked car," "whirling flywheels," bridge "trestles," "machine shrieks," and "triphammers," along with the flowers and trees for which Williams's poems are well known (*CEP* 96, 251, 194–95, 192, 262). His was a holistic world in which the natural mixed freely with objects of human manufacture.

And of course American culture brought Williams the same consciousness of engineers as was available to much of middle-class America. Popularized in movies and novels, and evidenced everywhere in the structures and machines that covered the landscape and the pages of magazines, engineers found their way into Williams's writings. He mused that invention or creation was a basic mark of intelligence "selecting and rejecting its materials—as it would be in an engineer that turns to the time for his opportunity" (*EK* 22). He regretted communication barriers in a specialists' age ("Is there no conversation . . . between farmers and engineers?"). He fretted that "the knowledge of an engineer" would be likely to lure the man, then entrap him, in science where he would be "limited, segregated" (*EK* 46, 62–63). In the poem "The Red Paper Box" in *Spring and All* Williams writes in sportive tones that "twoinch trays / have engineers / that convey glue / to airplanes" (*I* 124). And when Williams disparages his brother Ed's position in a dialogue on art, saying "nobody gives a whoop in hell for such a viewpoint," Ed retorts, "Nobody but an engineer with a bridge to build," a line Williams recorded word for word (*SE* 182).

But the engineer, like machine and structural technology, was much more than a casual reference in Williams's work. For one thing, the poet was no stranger to the

Costly Parts

War times demand that you protect them from undue wear. Three suggestions.

There is a serious shortage of automobile repair men. You are going to find more and more difficulty in getting repairs made. And you are going to pay more for repair service. Labor charges are up; prices of parts are higher and still on the rise.

Meanwhile many motorists are as unconcerned as ever about their cars. The needless wearing out of engine parts goes on.

Why? Incorrect oil—incorrect use of oil—or both.

Here are three points which should be observed by every motorist:

(1) Get the correct oil. You should use an oil of high quality and of the correct body to suit the lubricating requirements of your car. The use of such an oil is the first and most important step in the protection of your engine parts.

(2) Maintain at all times an adequate supply of oil in the oil reservoir. Lack of attention to this may result in insufficient lubrication, premature wear, and in extreme cases—burned-out bearings.

(3) Drain old oil and replenish at proper intervals. If your instruction book advises fresh oil every 1,000 miles, do not run 1,500 or 2,000 miles before replacing. Oil gathers impurities and thins down in use through condensation of the fuel mixture. Running on such "oil" means premature wear to parts.

It will pay you to send for the booklet, "Correct Lubrication" and read the article beginning on page 3. This book treats this and other subjects with authority and clearness in articles prepared by our Board of Engineers. Address our nearest branch.

GARGOYLE
Mobiloils
A grade for each type of motor.

In buying Gargoyle Mobiloils from your dealer, it is safest to purchase in original packages. Look for the red Gargoyle on the container. If the dealer has not the grade specified for your car, he can easily secure it for you.

VACUUM OIL COMPANY, New York, U.S.A.

Specialists in the manufacture of high-grade lubricants for every class of machinery. Obtainable everywhere in the world

Domestic Branches:	Boston Detroit	Kansas City, Kan. New York	Philadelphia Chicago	Minneapolis Indianapolis	Pittsburgh Des Moines

Vacuum Oil Co. advertisement (Courtesy Mobil Corp.)

machine-age anxieties that Willa Cather, Sherwood Anderson, and for that matter Henry James felt in the face of engineering achievement. Williams understood that the arts and technology made competing claims for the imagination, and he acknowledged the rivalry between the technological and the literary mind, revealing his anxiety in "The Flower" in which he says, it

> makes me ill to see them run up
> a new bridge like that in a few months
>
> and I can't find time even to get
> a book written. They have the power,
>
> that's all, she replied. That's what you all
> want. If you can't get it, acknowledge
>
> at least what it is. And they're not
> going to give it to you. Quite right.
>
> For years I've been tormented by
> that miracle, the buildings all lit up—
>
> unable to say anything much to the point
> though it is the major sight
>
> of this region. But foolish to rhapsodize over
> strings of lights, the blaze of a power
>
> in which I have not the least part. (*CEP* 238–39)

Seen across the New Jersey meadowlands, Manhattan's bridges, its skyscrapers, and its electrification all enter into the poet's complaint that twentieth-century power is objectified in engineering technology, while the slow-paced writer is left behind, tormented and sick at heart.

Williams is both anxious and frustrated. Yet unlike Cather and Anderson, he does not assert the superiority of the writer by condemning engineers, machines, and structures in a cluster of subversive, denigrating images. Instead, "The Flower" plays a game intended to demonstrate the supreme flexibility of the poet's imagination when it, too, builds bridges, for the shape of the arched bridge span suggests a flower petal to Williams, who is free to fling his flower-petal arch over time as well as space:

> One petal goes eight blocks
>
> past two churches and a brick school beyond
> the edge of the park where under trees
>
> leafless now, women having nothing else to do
> sit in summer—to a small house
>
> in which I happen to have been born.

Another petal, we learn, "reaches to San Diego," and a third "into the past, to Puerto Rico / when my mother was a child bathing in a small / river and splashing water up on / the yucca leaves to see them roll back pearls" (*CEP* 237, 238).

Even as he complains that the power of technology eludes him, Williams is showing the imaginative versatility which he presumes to be unavailable to the designer of fixed forms like bridges. The poet, Williams suggests, surpasses the engineer in his ability to imagine. The poet can bridge an entire continent at will. He can span decades, reaching back from the Atlantic seaboard of the present to the Spanish Caribbean of his mother's childhood. The poet can even see the yucca leaves as arched spans flowing with the traffic of water pearls.

There is, Williams suggests, no end to the imaginative possibilities available to the poet, who can be positively stimulated by the engineer's designs. He even mused that the writer must "have a *basis*, a local stanchion, by which to bridge over the gap between present learning and the classical" (*In the American Grain* [*AG*] 231). Williams thus differed from Cather and Anderson—and from Henry James, who shuddered at the bridges and skyscrapers and electrical devices that he felt threatened the repose of the imagination. In *The American Scene* James tried to dismiss the skyscrapers by reducing them to such mere domestic stuff as a snaggle-toothed comb or a jammed pin cushion. But Williams, unlike James, resolves to coexist with them, in fact to incorporate them. The poems of *Spring and All* are a record of that incorporation. Williams's candy box "skyscrapers / filled with nut-chocolates" and his "skyscraper soup" of a composite urban-medical-artistic life encompass the dominating technology (*CEP* 244, 253). The images show Williams laying claim to it. It is domesticized to be welcomed as a familiar and not to be dismissed.

Not uncritically, to be sure. Williams sees New York's tall buildings as "Agonized Spires" and describes Manhattan as a high-rise electrified coral colony of "sweaty kitchens" and "swarming backstreets." Its bridge stanchions are "long / sunburnt fingers" piercing deep down into the ventricular heart of the organism (*CEP* 262–63). But the prose gloss on the poems of *Spring and All* indicates Williams's incorporation of all material objects, including the technological. "The objects of the [poet's] world," says Williams, ostensibly of Shakespeare but essentially of himself, "were real to him because he could use them and use them with understanding to make his inventions" (*I* 122). The bridges, skyscrapers, and electrical circuitry that James experienced as a threat to imaginative literature thus become, in Williams, an opportunity for poetic design.

The dynamo, then, can enter Williams's work as a familiar object, not as a larger-than-life religio-social symbol for the age. In "Paterson" he speaks of "the grace and detail of / a dynamo," and in *The Great American Novel* (1923), his self-styled "travesty on . . . conventional American writing," Williams responds to Henry Adams by making the dynamo just one voice among many in contemporary speech. "I'm new, says the great dynamo. I am progress. I make a word. Listen! UMMMMMMMMMMMM—"

It is not clear whether Williams welcomes or spurns the new monosyllabic hum-word. But he certainly incorporates the dynamo as a comic object. He demystifies it, first in an operatic spoof set in the sickroom: "Ow, ow! Oh help me somebody! said [the woman in distress]. UMMMMMM sang the dynamo in the next street, UMMMM." Williams next domesticates the dynamo, again for incorporation. Williams begins with the awesome, theatrical set of a great misty amphitheater of a power station. It is backlighted from the interior, its doors flung wide open to the night. "In [stately] rows sat the great black machines saying vrummmmmmmmmmmmm." For what purpose?—to light the cellar stairs, to warm the patient's heating pad, to cook supper by and iron her husband's pajamas (*I* 162–63). The dynamo, no quasi-religious symbol for the technological age, figures in Williams as a character in a boffo opera vignette, as a possible source of one new monosyllabic word, and as a backstage functionary in domestic life. It is incorporated as a comic object, just like the Ford car and Mack truck whose romance is also detailed in the novel.

In fact, it is Williams's comic vision, which is to say a vision of social inclusiveness, that enables him to embrace technology and inclines him to use utilitarian, engineering terms when defining culture and the writer's place in it. To be sure, like Ezra Pound he understood the shortcomings of the technical mind at its least imaginative. He regretted the disappearance of the apprentice system of the crafts and condemned the intellectual narrowness of technical education, which he thought made boys lamb to the slaughter ("This is not civilization but stupidity") (*EK* 23; *I* 140). In "The American Background" he deplores the meretricious American money culture, railing against "the unmitigated stupidity, the drab tediousness of the democracy, the overwhelming number of the offensively ignorant" (*SE* 119).

But Williams defines authentic culture and the poet's place in it in optimistic —and utilitarian—terms. "Let the hopeful artist manufacture . . . something . . . which will be an organization of materials on a better basis than it had been before." He continues, "It is the job of the workman-artist to manufacture a better world than he sees." Culture "isn't a thing: it's an act," he says in a characteristically kinetic phrase. "If it stands still, it is dead" (*In* 77–78).

Williams elaborates on his utilitarian conception of cultural progress. The poet's manufacture of a better world begins with a grasp of culture, itself "the realization of the qualities of a place in relation to the life which occupies it, embracing everything involved" including vegetation, minerals, geology, geography, "and the condition of knowledge beyond its borders." Culture, then, is "the act of lifting these things into an ordered and utilized whole." The poet, like the scientist or philosopher, plays his part in it, since the "material manifestations" of the human mind are "of equal value whether in clay, iron, or words" (*EK* 130). Asserting the values of organization and utility, Williams sustains his utilitarian argument with a phrase unsurprising to those aware of the art-technology crisis. He takes Willa Cather's title and inverts its meaning: "The slow, foot-weary ascent goes on . . . this painstaking construction from the ground up, this Alexander's Bridge" (*SE* 159). Borrowing Cather's title for the novel that condemns the engineer's flawed psyche,

Williams argues instead that culture is an act of knowledgeable engineering. But his Alexander's bridge is a multi-part construction.

The mature Williams was able to speak so confidently of culture and technology because of his medical background. The physician's training that prepared him for a "rapid-transit," efficient poetics also helped him appreciate the values of the technical mind. It led him eventually to see the poem as a machine made of component parts. American popular culture, of course, was filled with images of machine and structural components. But Williams's medical schooling focussed his eventual understanding of the poem as a machine or structure. Once again, the Flexner report is invaluable in illuminating Williams's poetics, in this instance because it shows that the medical student of Williams's day was oriented to the material world in ways comparable to those of the engineer.

Abraham Flexner begins his discussion of medical-school education with a comparison to engineering education. "The discipline of the modern engineer equals the discipline of the modern physician," he writes, asserting that the physician must nonetheless deal with far more complicated systems requiring "decisive responsibility" (23). The orientation is mechanistic, as Flexner makes explicit. "Medical education is a technical or professional discipline," and the student of anatomy "views the body not as a mosaic to be broken up, but as a machine to be taken to pieces, the more perfectly to comprehend how it works" (58). Dismantled in anatomy class, the "severed and dissociated elements" of the body must be reconceived in a three-dimensional relation (a "stereoscopic relation") requiring drawing and modeling with the help of charts and cross-sections, all in a hands-on student experience.

Flexner's description of ideal laboratory education continues his mechanistic emphasis. Physiology helps the student focus on "the mechanical properties of tissue" and on the "mechanism of the nervous system" (and of all other mechanistic systems including the circulatory, respiratory, and muscular). The "mechanical standpoint," says Flexner, has richly, indisputably justified itself. At the same time the various systems are so highly complex that the student "who has been successfully trained to regard the body as an infinitely complex machine learns to doubt his capacity to mend it summarily" (63). In his training it is "mainly important," nevertheless, that the student "be brought into immediate and increasingly responsible contact with the disordered machine" (96). Besides making the body-as-machine image graphic, Flexner argues that the modern hospital and school are interlocked and that the student is part of the "efficient and intelligent routine" of the "hospital machine" (100) (a context in which we might recall Henry James's observation of the hospital as a "symphony in white," the very orchestral term indicative of the integrated, dynamic system).

As a medical student Williams doubtless absorbed this mechanistic outlook from the very discourse of his professors. The essays of the renowned Osler published, we remember, in the volume Williams owned, suggest the technologic terms afloat in the clinic and at the bedside in the years of Williams's training. Osler, for instance, branched freely into electrical technology to instruct on the neural system. "Watch that musician playing a difficult piece," he says, "batteries, commutators, multipliers, switches, wires innumerable control those nimble fingers, the machinery of which may be set in motion as automatically as a pianola." Elsewhere, in terms of a coal-fired engine, he diagnosed the problems of youthful boredom or depression caused by a young man's "neglecting his machine, driving it too hard, stoking the engines too much, or not cleaning out the ashes or clinkers" (17, 244). Such language, as we have seen, was commonplace in American culture by the turn of the twentieth century. But Williams, a doctor-in-training, was indoctrinated in it. Its daily use in the discourse of medical mentors conveyed the mechanistic assumptions on which medicine was based.

Williams, then, was taught to see his professional world as a congeries of machines. Having learned to regard the body and its individual systems as comprised of separate but integrated component parts, Williams was prepared to apply that same outlook to imaginative literature. Studying the human body, Williams learned again and again the idea of dynamic systems made up of separate components. Unaware of it at the time, Williams was preparing to look at words and poems in the same way an engineer regarded structural steel and engine parts. Technological thinking was second nature to this poet.

Williams continued his gear-and-girder perceptions both in and out of medicine. He wished that readers of his poems might also appreciate the modern physician's approach to the text of the human body. His "Water, Salts, Fat, etc.," a review of *The Human Body* (1927) by Dr. Logan Clendening, commends to general readers a book incorporating the same mechanistic approach Williams had learned in medical school. *The Human Body* is a book for the general reader on the workings of the body and the history of medical progress. Williams liked it enormously and felt it would benefit his family, wife, brother, and sons. *The Human Body* enforces the same kind of mechanistic outlook ingrained years earlier in the discourse of the Flexner report and Osler's essays. Concluding his prefatory chapter, the author calls the mind and soul "restless pieces of machinery" (4). Throughout his text Clendening relies on machine analogies to explain the workings of the body. The bones of the foot are like "powerful steel springs," and "if they were not there, walking would be like riding in an automobile without springs" (64). Just as the wheels and axles are the essential parts of the automobile, so the bones and muscles are the body's framework, even though the enginery of the viscera is more compelling (71). "The body, remember," he writes, "is a machine for the production of energy. In a heat machine or combustion engine, which is what the body is, oxygen is absolutely essential" (105). The autonomic nervous system turns the stomach "from side to side like an electric washer" (76).

Clendening deploys mechanistic terms as liberally as does Osler. Wryly he calls humankind "mechanically minded monkeys" who must "lift the hood and watch the machinery go round, and try to understand it" (71). He refers to the "mechanism" of the nervous system and to the "mechanical difficulty imposed by high blood pressure," and he cites a medical expert who compares diabetes to a defective gasoline engine, with explicit comparisons to the cylinder, carburator, spark plugs, and exhaust. "Every engine produces some waste products during the period of combustion," says Clendening, and "the body is an engine which is no exception to the rule" (109, 166, 183, 193).

Williams's review makes no overt acknowledgment of the mechanistic premises of *The Human Body*. But his very silence on this point speaks volumes. It indicates that such thinking was not the exception but the norm. Mechanistic thinking presumed "truth." It was not open to self-consciousness, much less to challenge. It was, literally, unremarkable. To read *The Human Body* is to see that in the late 1920s Williams sustained and endorsed the kind of perception inculcated in him from his freshman year of medical school. He even called the poet the voice of the collective components of the human anatomy, for it is "the deeper . . . personality speaking, the middle brain, the nerves, the glands, the very muscles and bones of the body" (*In* 98). The relevant point here, for Williams, is that the mechanistic discourse of medicine reinforced the idea that complex things—animate and, by extension, inanimate things—were functional systems of interdependent component parts. They could be disassembled or dissected in the imagination if not in actual practice. The body, the automobile, the kitchen stove, the poem—all could be seen from this perspective.

Thus in imaginative writing (here, *A Novelette*) we see Williams approaching the woman's body as a structure demanding "constant freshness of praise," which he offers as an anatomist analyzing the separate components:

> Look at her bare feet. You will see the effects of wearing shoes—unless she be used to going barefoot. Sometimes the toenails will be round, sometimes square and at others long. At the foot the ankle is joined to the leg. From here to the knee is usually sixteen inches. The knee is important. Let us describe the thigh of a beautiful woman. Most literature is now silent. The physiognomy of the joint between the torso and the thighs is as various as the faces of dogs. (*I* 282)

We never see the entire figure. Williams offers the portrait of a leg only, an antiportrait emphatically rejecting tradition. There are no luxuriant tresses or Shakespearean "pearls that were [her] eyes," only the pelvic joint seen as a dog's face as Williams moves up from the toes. The antiportrait is characteristic of the modernists' iconoclasm—and fundamentally different from the romantic impulse. In *Children of Adam* we can recall Whitman's cry, "O my body! I dare not desert . . . the parts of you," then his list of "leg-fibres, knee, knee-pan, upper-leg, under-leg, / Ankles, instep, foot-ball, toes, toe-joints, the heel." Whitman's anatomical survey, however, concludes with the assertion that these are really signifiers of the soul, not parts of the body. "O I say now these are the soul!" (100–101). The romantic poet says that

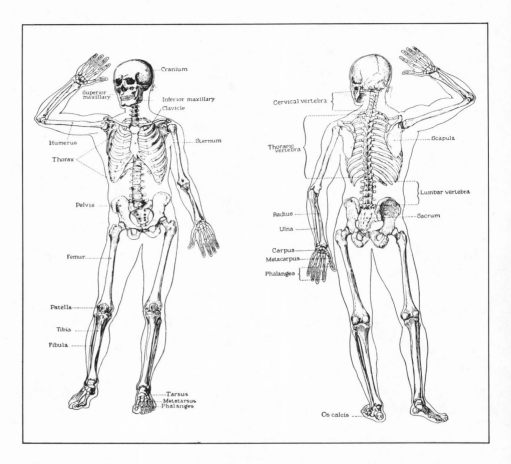

The human skeleton shown in The Human Body *by Logan Clendening, illustrations by W. C. Shepard and Dale Beronius, 1927 (Courtesy Alfred A. Knopf)*

the material, bodily world is essentially a symbol for cosmic spiritual unity. All the anatomical particulars of Whitman's leg signify the realm of the transcendent spirit.

Williams, of course, refers to a very different world. His outlook and method revert to it. The student of anatomy sees the object as a design of separate parts. He responds to it by presenting a study that emphasizes the integrity of its structure part-by-part. The whole is not simply the sum of its parts, but it is a chart of the integrity of those parts in relation to one another.

From there it is just one logical yet momentous step to the poem as a machine or structure comprised of separate but integrated components. The poet, no longer only a student of anatomy, becomes the designer. His design lies in the selection and arrangement of component materials, which may themselves be fabricated elsewhere. Like Dos Passos, Williams often finds his design components in

Skeleton of the Times Building, shown under construction, New York
(Courtesy Library of Congress)

THE NERVOUS SYSTEM AND SIX SENSES

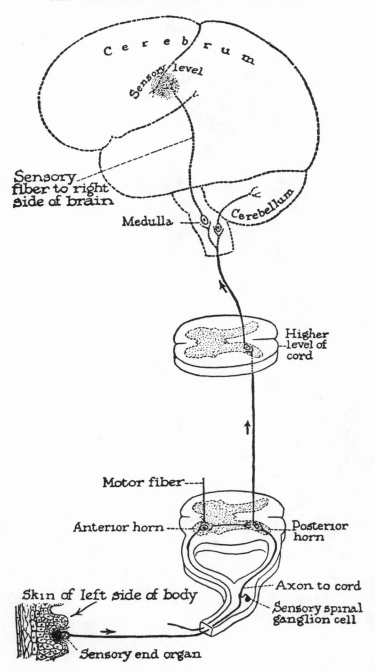

The human nervous system shown in The Human Body *by Logan Clendening,
illustrations by W. C. Shepard and Dale Beronius, 1927
(Courtesy Alfred A. Knopf)*

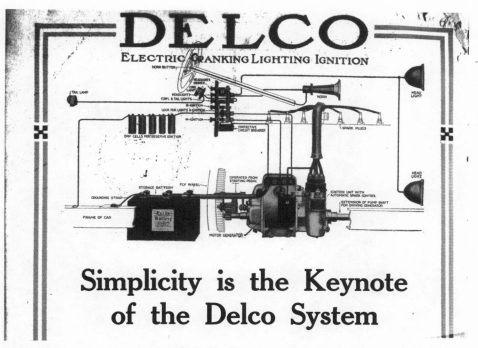

Illustration showing automobile ignition system. Harper's Weekly, 1914
(Courtesy Delco Remy, Division of General Motors Corp.)

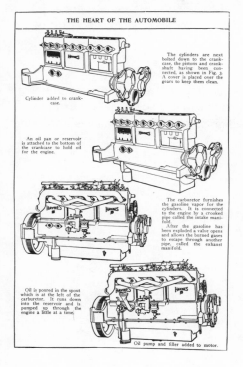

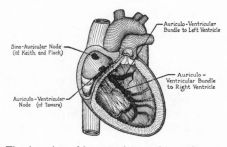

The interior of human heart shown in
The Human Body by Logan Clendening,
illustrations by W. C. Shepard and
Dale Beronius, 1927
(Courtesy Alfred A. Knopf)

The "heart of the automobile," the engine.
The Book of Wonders, 1916

Elsie Driggs, Pittsburgh, *1927. Oil on canvas. 34¼ × 40 inches (Courtesy Collection of Whitney Museum of American Art)*

American popular culture. The poem "Rapid Transit" is a good example of the design formed largely of components manufactured, so to speak, in the word factories of the advertising agencies. Williams, the designer, selects and brings them into arrangement to make the poem:

> Somebody dies every four minutes
> in New York State—
>
> To hell with you and your poetry—
> You will rot and be blown
> through the next solar system
> with the rest of the gases—
>
> What the hell do you know about it?
>
> AXIOMS
>
> Don't get killed

Careful Crossing Campaign
Cross Crossings Cautiously

THE HORSES   black
                        &
PRANCED   white

Outings in New York City

Ho for the open country

Don't stay shut up in hot rooms
Go to one of the Great Parks
Pelham Bay for example

It's on Long Island Sound
with bathing, boating
tennis, baseball, golf, etc.

Acres and acres of green grass
wonderful shade trees, rippling brooks

     Take the Pelham Bay Park Branch
     of the Lexington Ave. (East Side)
     Line and you are there in a few
     minutes

Interborough Rapid Transit Co. (*I* 146–47)

"Rapid Transit" is a poem of the kinetic Williams. It gives a contemporary twist to the "sic transit" motto (*sic transit gloria mundi*—thus passes away the glory of the world). Twentieth-century life is both perilous and fast-paced. Somebody dies in New York every four minutes, so "Don't get killed." Instead, live in the moment. The glory of the world is here and now. As poets see it, the much-vaunted future comes down to decay and solar wind; their opportunity is to make poems immediately. The experience of the poem is the experience of contemporary urban life, fast and disjunctive. Its components include advertising copy, slogans, maxims. All are prefabricated elsewhere and renewed by reformulation in poetic design. Williams remarked that such "common objects" about him have combined with the "seriousness" of his life to make up "an actuality of which I am assembling the parts" (*I* 294). In a state of "clarity" the poet, as designer, chooses those parts that make the most efficient arrangement. Williams said that in considering a poem, he did not care whether it was finished or not: "if it's put down with a good relation to the parts, it becomes a poem. And the meaning of the poem can be grasped by attention to the design" (*In* 53).

Efficient design is ever Williams's objective. From Pound he had learned "the original lesson: Never use two words where one will do" (*In* 81). Given his commitment to poems as arrangements of materials, as efficient machines, we

Charles Demuth, Buildings, Lancaster, *1930. Oil on composition board. 24×20 inches (Courtesy Collection of Whitney Museum of American Art)*

would expect Williams's personal history, *In the American Grain* (1925), to treat Benjamin Franklin sympathetically. Yet the Colonial exponent of American technology and efficiency becomes one of Williams's most contemptible figures, timid, fearful, guarded against passion, defended against experience. "He sensed the power [of lightning] and knew only enough to want to run an engine with it" (*AG* 155). No admirable designer, Franklin figures as a despicable "Poor Richard."

It is Edgar Allan Poe, instead, who emerges as the exemplary American designer,

Paul Outerbridge, photograph, 42nd Street Elevated *(Courtesy Art Institute of Chicago)*

the writer with an algebraic mind whose sentences play with clauses "as with objects." It is Poe who "feels and turns [words] about as if he fitted them to his design with *some* sense of their individual quality." It is Poe, not Franklin, whose efficiency has power ("he wanted a lean style, rapid as a hunter and with an aim as sure"). Williams admired Poe, as readers have noticed, for having achieved the universalizing local that was so important to the New Jersey-based Williams as he prepared *Paterson*. But Poe is equally admirable for his successful "inventions" and for a construction method that "let[s] the real business of composition *show*." Williams especially valued this trait as a doctor trained to let the composition of the human body show and as a citizen of the twentieth century, when the composition of structures and machines was apparent to streetside onlookers as well as to readers of magazines (*AG* 221–22, 227, 230). (In this connection it is worth recalling that the critic of American culture, Van Wyck Brooks, compared Poe with Edison, saying that "the greatest of inventors cannot be called a scientist . . . but a mechanic" and that "Poe is a mechanic of the same sort" [60–61].)

Admiring Poe's feeling for the word-object, Williams reveals his own pleasure in the word, itself a single structural or machine component that gives tactile pleasure just as Frank Lloyd Wright's boyhood blocks did. Williams credits another writer trained in medicine, Gertrude Stein, with using "words as objects out of which you manufacture a little mechanism you call a poem" (*In* 69). (It would, in fact, be interesting to consider Stein's work in this light.) Williams characterized the sentimental poetry around him, poetry of the kind he himself once wrote, as viscous and opaque ("gummy . . . . covered with vain curlicues") (*SE* 111; *I* 320). He couched his praise for Marianne Moore in terms of precision parts pleasing to the eye and to the touch. Cleansed in an acid bath, each word is dried and placed on a clean surface and inspected for nicks or other imperfections. Only those words with perfect edges qualify for assembly into the design (*I* 319–20). The word is "an objective unit in the design—but alive" (*SE* 111). Within the poem the word, the essential unit of design, keeps its identity just as the body part, the machine part, or the structural member does.

Hearing Williams affirm the vitality of poet and poem in the terms "dynamic" and "clarity," we anticipate his remark on component word-objects, vibrant with energy, "shin[ing] in the structural body" of the machines made of words. In *The Great American Novel* the dynamo and the new word hum with powerful currents. Even entropy can be described in these kinetic terms: "words are the reverse motion. . . . Words roll, spin, flare up, rumble, trickle, foam—Slowly they lose momentum. Slowly they cease to stir. At last they break up into their letters" (*I* 160, 162).

Williams's scorn, moreover, for the simile is essentially a rejection of the static adjective, that decorator's tool. The imperative of the writer, on the contrary, "is to learn to employ the verbs in imitation of nature—so that the pieces move naturally." Then, says Williams, "watch, often breathlessly, what they *do*." For authentic writing is "a transit from the adjective . . . to verb." Writing, says Williams, "is an action, a moving process—the verb dominates" (*SE* 302–3, 306).

Williams's emphasis on the primacy of the verb may seem peculiar, considering his preference for word-objects ordinarily classed as nouns and adjectives. The "red wheel / barrow" and "white / chickens" come immediately to mind, as do other figures from Williams's best-known work—the plums, the young housewife, the figure five. There is not a verb among them—unless, of course, one dispenses with the entire system of classification of parts of speech in order to embrace instead a radically different linguistic theory. The theory argues that words in English, like Chinese ideographs, "carry in them *a verbal idea of action*" no matter what their conventional linguistic designation. This, apparently, was what Williams did, for Ernest Fenollosa's theory of language, published as of 1918 through the tireless effort of his literary executor, Pound, came at a propitious time for Williams. Whether he read Fenollosa's "The Chinese Written Character as a Medium for Poetry" in its four installments in the *Little Review* beginning September 1919, or in Pound's *Instigations* (1920), or heard Pound, in correspondence, sketch the argument, Williams must have found Fenollosa's theory to be as permissively liberating as Dewey's remarks on the universalizing local were fortifying when he began to conceive *Paterson*.

Fenollosa offered the poet a theory of language commensurate with the modern moment of speed and machine technology. For Fenollosa's was the perfect linguistic theory for the gear-and-girder world. Echoing Emerson, he said that "the verb must be the primary fact of nature, since motion and change are all we can recognize in her" (rpt. in E. Pound, *Instigations* 374–75). His exposition of the Chinese and Japanese ideograph demonstrated an entirely verbal basis for parts of speech in English. He argues that the color green, for instance, is not adjectival but verbal because "green is only a certain rapidity of vibration." Prepositions "are naturally verbs," and conjunctions, "since they mediate actions, are actions themselves." (Fenollosa, of course, was not alone in exploring this verbal basis of language. In *Principles of Psychology*, William James, discussing the stream of thought, also speculated that conjunctions, prepositions, and adverbial phrases signify experience [1:245–46].)

Within Fenollosa's theory, Williams's "red wheel / barrow" and "white / chickens" become fully active and interactive, as do his other so-called prepositions, adverbs, articles. This idea of the poem constructed as a formal integration of verbal components clearly fit Williams's definition of the poem as "a small (or large) machine made of words." The machine figure asserts energy-producing movement and implicitly warns the poet to rid the poem of inessential verbiage. "The Red Wheelbarrow" demonstrates Fenollosa's language theory and the compatible concept of the efficient machine in which "there can be no part . . . that is redundant":

> so much depends
> upon
>
> a red wheel
> barrow
>
> glazed with rain
> water
>
> beside the white
> chickens. (*CEP* 277)

APPERSON

80 Parts Removed from the 8 Motor

Apperson Automobile Co. advertisement. Collier's, *1918*

Here, "pruned to a perfect economy," is the machine made of words, all of its parts perfectly, formally intergeared (as Williams put it, "undulant") and thus able to achieve its "exact meaning" (*SE* 256). "The Red Wheelbarrow," the kinetic machine, shows the standard of verbal efficiency of operation even as it encodes the rapid-transit, efficient moment.

Rhythmic, undulant word machines like "The Red Wheelbarrow" mesh with another of Williams's preoccupations, the dance. One is reminded of Williams's "Danse Russe" in which the young doctor dances "naked, grotesquely" before the mirror, waving his shirt around his head. Admiring the parts of his body, he is sensuality-in-motion. And in fact it is emotion-in-motion that attracts Williams to the idea of the poem as dance. The rhythms of patterned energy, manifest in machines, form a recurrent theme in his first modernist work, the improvisational *Kora in Hell* (1920). *Kora* commends free-form dance like Isadora Duncan's, describes a tarantella of the *danse macabre*, and even suggests that the medical philosophy of disease is "a stern dance" (*I* 34, 47, 55, 57, 59, 77). Williams admired George Antheil's *Ballet mécanique* (127) and doubtless was aware that the machine age spawned many popular dance productions mimicking machine movement. The choreography of Busby Berkeley's musicals and that of the Rockefeller Center Rockettes, for instance, made the troupes into synchronized dancing machines of the 1930s.

Williams, however, is not interested in these popular representations of machine rhythms because they merely copy or mimic the movement of machinery. Poems in that vein would be lifeless. The poet enmeshes the dance with the "machine made of words" for different reasons. His poem must be a "delicate . . . mechanism" for expression; it is "language charged with emotion"; it is "words, rhythmically organized" (*In* 70, 73). In all these figures Williams suggests that his central concern is a physics of feeling enacted in rhythmic motion. The poem that captures it essentially enacts "an assembly of tides, waves, ripples," meaning "greater and lesser rhythmic particles regularly repeated or destroyed." He cautions that the essence of rhythm is "not sound," not the accented cadences of dactyls, iambs, trochees, and anapests. Instead it is "motion . . . forward and up and down, rapidity of motion and quality of motion" (*In* 67). The dance, encoding feeling in motion, is integral to the poem-as-machine. As Williams said, "If you're writing a love lyric, it's possible that the intensity of a love passion might inspire a certain rhythmic construction which could be called a poem." Without that vital rhythm, there is only mechanical prosody, and thus empty, lifeless form. The vitality of the dance is indispensable to the machine made of words.

Williams never abandoned his poetics of kinetics and efficiency. He became, on the contrary, increasingly explicit about machines made of words in the decades following the 1920s, when, impelled to renewal, he worked in an increasingly wide variety of styles and forms. Late in life in the early 1960s he returned to his "rapid-transit" poems in *Pictures from Brueghel* (1963). The title poems in *Pictures* show the American modernist attracted to an artist he admired for a "living quality of mind," for resourcefulness, alertness, engagement in the workaday world, grim humor, and for eyes that were "driven hard" like Williams's own (3). The poems themselves are unmistakably occasioned by the machine age in which acceleration in the pace of living had become a cultural commonplace and the machine a constant presence in everyday life. "Children's Games II," like all the *Pictures*, is cast in three-line stanzas whose form enacts vigorous motion. The short lines speed along like Williams's "rapid transit" poems of the early 1920s:

> Little girls
> whirling their skirts about
> until they stand out flat
>
> tops pinwheels
> to run in the wind with
> or a toy in three tiers to spin

with a piece
of twine to make it go
blindman's-buff follow the

leader stilts high and low tipcat
jacks
bowls hanging by the knees

standing on your head
run the gauntlet
a dozen on their backs

feet kicking
through which a boy must pass
roll the hoop or a

construction
made of bricks
some mason has abandoned (13)

Here "everything / is motion," as Williams says in the previous poem, demonstrating the point as the toys and children's bodies form an intricate machine set going: "whirling . . . skirts," "tops, pinwheels / to run in the wind with / or a toy in three tiers motion" (12). The twentieth-century American admires the peasant figures "disciplined by the artist / to go round / & round." The interlocked movement is visible, enacted in every component of the poem. From the whirling wheels of the skirts and toys to the pumping pistons of the kicking feet, Williams's *Pictures from Brueghel* is a cluster of twentieth-century machines of visibly moving parts.

SKYSCRAPER

The writers of our generation . . . had one privilege: to write a poem in which all was but order and beauty, a poem rising like a clean tower.

Malcolm Cowley, *Exile's Return*, 1934

o many, modernist America took its characteristic form in the "tower" skyscraper, an urban machine-structure that became a fact of life throughout the United States by the early 1920s. Before the turn of the century Frank Lloyd Wright had proposed a ten-story building of structural steel covered with translucent panels, and in the early 1920s he designed a skyscraper resembling a scaled-up version of his prairie-style houses in the suburban Chicago village of Oak Park. The village reference is not amiss. The title character of Sinclair Lewis's novel, *Babbitt*, spends his workdays in an "austere tower of steel and cement and limestone . . . as fireproof as a rock and as efficient as a typewriter." The skyscraper, says the novelist, is the new American Main Street, and its inhabitants now live in a vertical village (*Babbitt* 5, 29, 30).

The so-called village objectified the new values of a culture shifting gears, for the skyscraper enacted the twentieth-century traits of functionalism, efficiency, and speed. Closely identified with New York City, the skyscraper gave rise to such landmarks as Manhattan's American Radiator Building (1924) and the Chrysler Building (1930) with its white brick tower and stainless-steel arches. The passion for skyscraper height was best instanced in the Empire State Building (1931), which rose 102 stories and 1,250 feet. In the 1980s one architectural critic calls it "an immensely skillful piece of massing—a five-story base, filling out the full site, above which rises a tower with its mass correctly broken by indentations running the full height, and topped off by a crown of setbacks culminating in a gently rounded tower" (Goldberger 49, 58, 84-86). In the early 1930s so politically trenchant a critic as Edmund Wilson conceded, "There is no question that the new Empire State Building is the handsomest skyscraper in New York" (*American Earthquake* 292).

The classic setback skyscraper is the appropriate form with which to conclude this discussion. Visual and kinetic, paradoxically static and soaring, the skyscraper has direct connections with the poems and fiction of Dos Passos,

William F. Lamb, The Empire State Building, *photograph by Irving Browning, 1931 (Courtesy New-York Historical Society)*

Hemingway, and Williams. In crucial ways their texts did enact the values of what Malcolm Cowley called a "clean tower" of modernist poetic privilege. Of course, none of these writers wrote much *about* skyscrapers, not even Dos Passos, whose fiction centered in New York City, or Williams, who saw the skyscraper as a modern candy box ("skyscrapers / filled with nut chocolates" [*I* 99]). Once again, the issue is not mere representation, even though the skyscraper has long lent itself to pictorial treatment.

The connection between literature and skyscraper arises from shared design values. John Dos Passos, for instance, wanted to grasp the life of a modern population within a structure, the novel. He built volume after volume, stopping *U.S.A.* when it became a trilogy—stopping, but not ending. Implicitly the novel-building by the self-styled "architect of history" could go on and on, just as the skyscraper continues its setback masses and invites the eye to see its movement of vertical line beyond its point of termination. Dos Passos's fiction ever pushes for greater length, more windows on contemporary culture, more stories and storeys moving through time and space toward the future.

That swift movement of the eye along the flush planes and vertical thrusts of the skyscraper has implications for literary style. It calls to mind the Hemingway sentence, a direct statement proceeding without digression or qualification. It is the architectural equivalent of the straight line without curves, the column without entablature. "The trunks were straight and brown without branches," writes Hemingway in the mind of the young Nick Adams. He continues, "Around the grove of trees was a bare space. It was brown and soft underfoot as Nick walked on it. . . . The trees had grown tall and the branches moved high. . . . Sharp at the edge of this extension of the forest floor commenced the sweet fern" (*In Our Time* 137). These are direct sentences in observation of the vertical lines and hard edges which the protagonist and the author admire. Both the sentence structure and the semantics support the design values of the "clean tower," the skyscraper. They also point up the irony of Hemingway's relation to nature. He is much identified as a lover of nature, but his prose style insists that his deepest allegiance lies with the geometric forms of twentieth-century urban civilization.

William Carlos Williams's participation in the skyscraper ethos lies in part in his poetic line. He was a miniaturist of the skyscraper form, somewhat like the sculptor John Storrs, whose *Forms in Space* (1924) is small in dimension ($28\frac{1}{2}'' \times 5\frac{1}{2}''$) but formally indebted to the modern skyscraper. In Williams's poetry, the swift thrust of the skyscraper finds its formal counterpart in the emphatically vertical line, here in "Perpetuum Mobile: The City":

There!

There!

There!

John Storrs, Forms in Space, *1924. Aluminum, brass, copper, and wood on a black marble base. 28½ × 5½ × 5½ inches (Courtesy Collection of Whitney Museum of American Art, Gift of Charles Simon)*

> —a dream
> of lights
>   hiding
>
> the iron reason
>   and stone
> a settled
>   cloud—

City (*CEP* 389)

The lines are obviously critical of urban realities, "iron reason" masked by an illusive "dream / of lights." And of course we must read from top to bottom, visually a return voyage from the tower to its base. Williams's lines, however, move with a skyscraper's swiftness. They are as close as possible to a vertical drop. And they are punctuated by the indentations that appear on the page like the sculpted setbacks of the skyscraper form. In fact, on the page Williams's metrics of what he called the "variable foot" move in the pattern of the classic skyscraper setbacks.

Each of these writers built differently, of course. Yet their work consistently elaborates the paradox presented by the skyscraper. It is a fixed form designed to feel like a kinetic one. Rooted in place, it soars, a representative form for the rapid-transit age.

REFERENCES

Aaron, Daniel. *Men of Good Hope: A Story of American Progressives*. New York: Oxford University Press, 1951.

Abodaher, David. *Iacocca: America's Most Dynamic Businessman*. 1982. Reprint. New York: Kensington, 1985.

Adams, Henry. *The Education of Henry Adams*. Edited by Ernest Samuels. 1907. Reprint. Boston: Houghton Mifflin, 1973.

———. *History of the United States of America during the Administration of Thomas Jefferson [and] History of the United States during the Administration of James Madison*. 9 vols. 1888–98. Reprint. New York: Antiquarian Press, 1962.

———. *Letters of Henry Adams*. Edited by Worthington Chauncy Ford. Vol. 1. Boston: Houghton Mifflin, 1938.

———. *The Letters of Henry Adams*. Edited by J. C. Levenson, Ernest Samuels, et al. Vol. 2. Cambridge, Mass.: Harvard University Press, 1982.

———. *Mont St. Michel and Chartres*. 1905. Reprint. Boston: Houghton Mifflin, 1933.

Adams, Samuel Hopkins. *Success*. Boston: Houghton Mifflin, 1921.

Addresses and Discussions at the Conference on Scientific Management Held October 12, 13, 14, Nineteen Hundred and Eleven. Hanover, N.H.: Amos Tuck School of Administration and Finance, 1912.

"America's Arch-Enemy." *Sunset* 38 (June 1917): 20.

Anderson, Sherwood. *Mid-American Chants*. 1918. Reprint. New York: Huebsch, 1923.

———. *Poor White*. 1920. Reprint. New York: Viking, 1966.

———. *Sherwood Anderson's Memoirs: A Critical Edition*. Edited by Ray Lewis White. Chapel Hill: University of North Carolina Press, 1969.

———. *Winesburg, Ohio*. 1919. Reprint. New York: Viking, 1960.

Appleton, Victor. *The Motion-Picture Boys in Earthquake Land*. New York: Grosset and Dunlap, 1913.

———. *Tom Swift and His Air Glider*. New York: Grosset and Dunlap, 1912.

Armytage, W. H. G. *The Rise of the Technocrats*. London: Routledge and Kegan Paul, 1965.

———. *A Social History of Engineering*. 1961. Reprint. Boulder, Colo.: Westview Press, 1976.

Badger, R. Reid. *The Great American Fair: The World's Columbian Exposition and American Culture*. Chicago: Nelson Hall, 1979.

Baker, Carlos. *Ernest Hemingway: A Life Story*. New York: Scribner's, 1969.

Baker, Ray Stannard. *The New Industrial Unrest*. Garden City, N.Y.: Doubleday, 1920.

Baldensberger, H. L. "Salvation by Salvage: The Conservation of Waste Men and Waste Material in a House of Correction." *Survey* 39 (February 2, 1918): 495–96.

Barthes, Roland. *The Eiffel Tower and Other Mythologies*. Translated by Richard Howard. New York: Hill and Wang, 1979.

Beach, Rex. *The Iron Trail: An Alaskan Romance*. New York: Harper and Brothers, 1913.

Beard, Charles, and Mary Beard. *The Rise of American Civilization*. 1927. Reprint. New York: Macmillan, 1953.

Beard, George. *American Nervousness*. 1881. Reprint. New York: Arno, 1972.

Bell, Ian F. A. *Critic as Scientist: The Modernist Poetics of Ezra Pound*. London and New York: Methuen, 1981.

Bellamy, Edward. *Looking Backward 2000–1887*. 1888. Reprint. Introduction by Cecelia Tichi. New York: Penguin, 1982.

Bennett, Arnold. *Your United States*. New York: Harper and Brothers, 1912.

Bercovitch, Sacvan. *Puritan Origins of the American Self*. New Haven: Yale University Press, 1975.

Berthoff, Warner. *The Ferment of Realism:*

American Literature, 1884–1919. New York: Free Press, 1965.

Beyer, O[tto] S. "Engineering." In *Civilization in the United States*, edited by Harold E. Stearns, pp. 417–26. New York: Harcourt, Brace and Co., 1922.

Billington, David P. *The Tower and the Bridge: The New Art of Structural Engineering*. New York: Basic Books, 1983.

Billington, David P., and Robert Mark. "The Cathedral and the Bridge: Structure and Symbol." *Technology and Culture* 25, no. 1 (January 1984): 37–52.

Blackmur, R[ichard] P. *Henry Adams*. Edited by Veronica A. Makowsky. New York: Harcourt Brace Jovanovich, 1980.

Blast: Review of the Great English Vortex. Vols. 1–2. London, 1914–15. Reprint. New York: Kraus Reprints, 1967.

Bodmer, Rudolph J., ed. *The Book of Wonders*. New York: Bureau of Industrial Education, 1916.

Bolter, J. David. *Turing's Man: Western Culture in the Computer Age*. Chapel Hill: University of North Carolina Press, 1984.

Bonner, H. R. "Waste in Education." *National Education Association Addresses and Proceedings* (1921): 795–803.

Bonner, Thomas N. *American Doctors and German Universities: A Chapter in International Intellectual Relations 1870–1914*. Lincoln: University of Nebraska Press, 1963.

Book, William F. *The Intelligence of High School Seniors*. New York: Macmillan, 1922.

———. "You Have Plenty of Energy, But What Do You Do with It?" *American Magazine* 103 (February 1927): 24–25, 189–93.

Boorstin, Daniel J. *The Americans: The Democratic Experience*. New York: Random House, 1973.

Bower, Lahman F. *The Economic Waste of Sin*. New York: Abington, 1924.

Bowman, Sylvia. *The Year 2000: A Critical Biography of Edward Bellamy*. New York: Bookman, 1958.

Breslin, James. *William Carlos Williams: An American Artist*. New York: Oxford University Press, 1970.

Brooks, Van Wyck. *America's Coming of Age*. New York: Huebsch, 1914.

Bruccoli, Matthew, ed. *Ernest Hemingway's Apprenticeship: Oak Park, 1916–1917*. Washington, D.C.: National Cash Register Co., 1971.

Buckingham, B. R. "The Greatest Waste in Education." *School and Society* 24 (November 27, 1926): 653–58.

Byard, A. L. "The Efficient Wife." *Woman's Home Companion* 50 (January 1923): 30–2.

Byrne, Kathleen D., and Richard C. Snyder. *Chrysalis: Willa Cather in Pittsburgh, 1896–1906*. Pittsburgh: Historical Society of Western Pennsylvania, 1980.

Cahan, Abraham. *The Rise of David Levinsky*. 1917. Reprint. New York: Harper and Row, 1966.

Cather, Willa. *Alexander's Bridge*. 1912. Reprint. Lincoln: University of Nebraska Press, 1977.

———. *Collected Short Fiction 1892–1912*. Lincoln: University of Nebraska Press, 1965.

———. *The Song of the Lark*. 1915. Reprint. Boston: Houghton Mifflin, 1983.

Chase, Stuart. *Men and Machines*. New York: Macmillan, 1931.

———. *The Tragedy of Waste*. New York: Macmillan, 1925.

———. *Your Money's Worth: A Study in the Waste of the Consumer Dollar*. New York: Macmillan, 1927.

Child, Georgie B. *Efficient Kitchen*. New York: McBride, 1925.

Clark, John M. "The Empire of Machines." *Yale Review* 12 (October 1922): 133–43.

Clendening, Log. *The Human Body*. New York: Knopf, 1927.

Commager, Henry Steele. *The American Mind*. New Haven: Yale University Press, 1950.

Committee on Elimination of Waste in Industry of the Federated American Engineering Societies. *Waste in Industry*. New York: McGraw-Hill, 1921.

Commons, John R. "Standardizing the Home." *Journal of Home Economics* 2 (February 1910): 23–24.

Conarroe, Joel. *William Carlos Williams's Paterson*. Philadelphia: University of

Pennsylvania Press, 1970.

Condit, Carl W. *The Chicago School of Architecture: A History of Commercial and Public Building in the Chicago Area 1875–1925*. Chicago: University of Chicago Press, 1964.

Copley, Frank B. *Frederick Winslow Taylor, Father of Scientific Management*. 2 vols. 1923. Reprint. New York: Augustus M. Kelley, 1969.

Corner, George W. *Two Centuries of Medicine: A History of the School of Medicine, University of Pennsylvania*. Philadelphia: University of Pennsylvania Press, 1965.

Cowley, Malcolm. *Exile's Return*. 1934. Reprint. New York: Penguin, 1969.

Cox, Harvey. *The Seduction of the Spirit: The Use and Misuse of People's Religion*. New York: Simon and Schuster, 1973.

Crane, Hart. *The Complete Poems and Selected Letters and Prose of Hart Crane*. Edited by Brom Weber. Garden City, N.Y.: Doubleday, 1966.

———. *Letters of Hart Crane 1916–1932*. Edited by Brom Weber. Berkeley and Los Angeles: University of California Press, 1965.

Crane, Stephen. *Great Short Works of Stephen Crane*. New York: Harper and Row, 1968.

Cronau, Rudolf. *Our Wasteful Nation*. New York: Mitchell Kennerley, 1908.

Cushing, Harvey. *The Life of Sir William Osler*. London and New York: Oxford University Press, 1940.

"Cutting Down the Waste." *Literary Digest* 62 (July 12, 1919): 26–27.

Czitrom, Daniel. *Media and the American Mind*. Chapel Hill: University of North Carolina Press, 1982.

Danbom, David B. *The Resisted Revolution: Urban America and the Industrialization of Agriculture, 1900–1930*. Ames: Iowa State University Press, 1979.

Davis, Richard Harding. *Soldiers of Fortune*. 1897. Reprint. New York: Scribner's, 1919.

Davis, Robert H., and Perley P. Sheehan. *Efficiency: A Play in One Act*. New York: George H. Doran, 1917.

"Democracy and Efficiency." *Collier's* 57 (May 20, 1916): 14–15.

Dewey, John. *Characters and Events*. Edited by Joseph Ratner. 2 vols. 1920. Reprint. New York: Octagon, 1970.

Dial 1–4 (September 1840–April 1844).

Dickinson, Lowes. *A Modern Symposium*. New York: Macmillan, 1905.

Dorfman, Joseph. *Thorstein Veblen and His America*. New York: Viking, 1935.

Dos Passos, John. *Manhattan Transfer*. 1925. Reprint. New York: Modern Library, 1932.

———. *Three Soldiers*. 1921. Reprint. Boston: Houghton Mifflin, 1949.

———. *U.S.A.: The 42nd Parallel*. 1930. Reprint. New York: Washington Square Press, 1961.

———. *U.S.A.: 1919*. 1932. Reprint. New York: Washington Square Press, 1961.

———. *U.S.A.: The Big Money*. 1936. Reprint. New York: Washington Square Press, 1961.

Douglas, C[lifford] H[ugh]. *Economic Democracy*. New York: Harcourt, Brace and Howe, 1920.

Douglas, Paul H. "The Economic Wastes of Luxury." *World Tomorrow* 5, no. 6 (June 1911): 165–66.

Drake, Durant. *America Faces the Future*. New York: Macmillan, 1922.

Dreiser, Theodore. *The Financier*. 1912. Reprint. New York: World, 1940.

———. *Jennie Gerhardt*. New York: Harper and Brothers, 1911.

———. *Sister Carrie*. 1900. Reprint. New York: Holt, Rinehart and Winston, 1957.

———. *The Titan*. 1914. Reprint. New York: World, 1925.

Drury, Horace. *Scientific Management: A History and Criticism*. New York: Columbia University Press, 1915.

Dusinberre, William. *Henry Adams: The Myth of Failure*. Charlottesville: University Press of Virginia, 1980.

"Efficiency and Humanity." *Literary Digest* 61 (April 12, 1919): 126.

"Efficiency in Public Service." *Nation* 94 (February 29, 1912): 204–5.

Eliot, C. W. "National Efficiency Best Achieved under Free Governments." *Atlantic* 115 (April 1915): 433–41.

Eliot, T[homas] S[tearns]. *The Complete Poems and Plays 1909–1950*. New York: Harcourt, Brace and World, 1952.

———. *The Waste Land: A Facsimile and Transcript of the Original Drafts Including the Annotations of Ezra Pound*. Edited by Valerie Eliot. New York: Harcourt Brace Jovanovich, 1971.

Emerson, Ralph Waldo. "Compensation." In *Essays: First Series*, edited by Joseph Slater, Alfred Ferguson, and Jean Ferguson Carr, pp. 53–74. Vol. 2 of *The Collected Works of Ralph Waldo Emerson*. Cambridge, Mass.: Harvard University Press, 1979.

———. "The Farmer." In *Society and Solitude*, pp. 139–49. Boston: Fields, Osgood, 1870.

———. *Selections from Ralph Waldo Emerson*. Edited by Stephen E. Whicher. Boston: Houghton Mifflin, 1960.

Faulkner, William. *As I Lay Dying*. 1930. Reprint. New York: Random House, 1957.

Fenton, Charles A. *The Apprenticeship of Ernest Hemingway: The Early Years*. New York: Farrar, Straus, and Young, 1954.

Ferber, Edna. *Emma McChesney & Co*. New York: Grosset and Dunlap, 1915.

———. *Personality Plus*. New York: Grosset and Dunlap, 1914.

———. *Roast Beef, Medium*. New York: Frederick A. Stokes, 1913.

Filene, Edward. *Successful Living in the Machine Age*. New York: Simon and Schuster, 1932.

———. *The Way Out*. Garden City, N.Y.: Doubleday, 1924.

Fitch, James Kip. *Engineering and Western Civilization*. New York: McGraw-Hill, 1951.

———. *The Story of Engineering*. Garden City, N.Y.: Doubleday, 1960.

Fitzgerald, F. Scott. *The Great Gatsby*. 1925. Reprint. New York: Scribner's, 1953.

Fleming, Donald. *William Welch and the Rise of Modern Medicine*. Edited by Oscar Handlin. Boston: Little, Brown, 1954.

Flexner, Abraham. *An Autobiography*. New York: Simon and Schuster, 1960.

———. *Medical Education in the United States and Canada: A Report to the Carnegie Foundation for the Advancement of Teaching*. New York: Carnegie Foundation, 1910.

Florman, Samuel C. *The Existential Pleasures of Engineering*. New York: St. Martin's, 1976.

"Food from Waste Products." *Literary Digest* 46 (January 4, 1913): 15–16.

Ford, Henry, with Samuel Crowther. *My Life and Works*. Garden City, N.Y.: Doubleday, Page, 1922.

———. *Today and Tomorrow*. Garden City, N.Y.: Doubleday, 1926.

Fox, John, Jr. *The Trail of the Lonesome Pine*. New York: Scribner's, 1908.

Frank, Waldo. *The Re-Discovery of America*. New York: Scribner's, 1929.

Frederick, Christine. *Efficient Housekeeping*. Chicago: American School of Home Economics, 1925.

Fuller, Henry Blake. *The Cliff-Dwellers*. 1893. Reprint. Ridgewood, N.J.: Gregg, 1968.

Garland, Hamlin. *Main-Travelled Roads*. 1891. Reprint. New York: New American Library, 1962.

George, Henry. *Progress and Poverty*. 1879. Reprint. New York: Robert Schalkenbach Foundation, 1951.

Giedion, Siegfried. *Mechanization Takes Command*. 1948. Reprint. New York: Norton, 1969.

Gilbert, A[lfred] C., with Marshall McClintock. *The Man Who Lived in Paradise*. New York: Rinehart, 1954.

Goldberger, Paul. *The Skyscraper*. New York: Knopf, 1985.

Grebstein, Sheldon N. *Hemingway's Craft*. Carbondale: Southern Illinois University Press, 1973.

Gregory, Mary H. *Checking the Waste*. Indianapolis: Bobbs-Merrill, 1911.

Grey, Zane. *The U.P. Trail*. 1918. Reprint. New York: Grosset and Dunlap, 1946.

Griscom, Lucy M. "Elimination of Waste in the Household." *Journal of Home Economics* 2 (June 1910): 292–97.

Gropius, Walter. *The New Architecture and the Bauhaus*. Translated from the German by P. Morton Shand. Boston: Charles T. Brandford, n.d.

Haber, Samuel. *Efficiency and Uplift: Scientific Management in the Progressive Era 1890–1920*. Chicago: University of Chicago Press, 1964.

Hackett, Alice Payne. *60 Years of Best Sellers*

1895–1955. New York: Bowker, 1956.

Haller, John S. *American Medicine in Transition 1840–1910*. Champaign-Urbana: University of Illinois Press, 1981.

Hammond, John H. *The Autobiography of John Hays Hammond*. 2 vols. New York: Farrar and Rinehart, 1935.

Hancock, H. Irving. *The Young Engineers in Mexico*. Akron, Ohio: Saalfield, 1913.

———. *The Young Engineers in Nevada*. Philadelphia: Henry Altemus, 1913.

Harbert, Earl N. *The Force So Much Closer Home: Henry Adams and the Adams Family*. New York: New York University Press, 1979.

Hays, Samuel P. *Conservation and the Gospel of Efficiency*. Cambridge, Mass.: Harvard University Press, 1959.

Hemingway, Ernest. *By-line: Ernest Hemingway: Selected Articles and Dispatches of Four Decades*. Edited by William White. New York: Scribner's, 1967.

———. *Ernest Hemingway on Writing*. Edited by Larry W. Phillips. New York: Scribner's, 1984.

———. *In Our Time*. 1925. Reprint. New York: Scribner's, 1970.

———. *The Sun Also Rises*. 1926. Reprint. New York: Scribner's, 1970.

Hermann, Brigette. "An Interview with Genevieve Viollet-le-Duc." In *Eugene Emmanuel Viollet-le-Duc, 1814–1879*, pp. 12–14. London: Academy Editions, 1980.

Herrick, Robert. *Together*. New York: Grosset and Dunlap, 1908.

———. *The Common Lot*. New York: Macmillan, 1904.

———. *Waste*. New York: Harcourt, Brace and Co., 1924.

Hewitt, Abram S. *Selected Writings of Abram S. Hewitt*. Edited by Allan Nevins. New York: Columbia University Press, 1937.

Hitchcock, Embury. *My Fifty Years in Engineering*. Caldwell, Idaho: Caxton, 1930.

Hobson, John A. *Work and Wealth*. New York: Macmillan, 1916.

Hoff-Wilson, Joan. "Herbert Hoover's Agricultural Policies, 1921–1928." In *Herbert Hoover as Secretary of Commerce: Studies in New Era Thought and Practice*, edited by Ellis W. Hawley, pp. 145–56. Iowa City: University of Iowa Press, 1981.

Hook, Andrew, ed. *Dos Passos: A Collection of Critical Essays*. Englewood Cliffs, N.J.: Prentice-Hall, 1974.

Hoover, Herbert. *The Memoirs of Herbert Hoover: Years of Adventure, 1874–1920*. Vol. 2. New York: Macmillan, 1952.

"Hoover: Engineer to the World." *St. Nicholas* 55 (June 1928): 618–23.

"Hoover: Specialist in Public Calamities." *Literary Digest* 97 (April 21, 1928): 40–48.

"Hoover's Fight on Waste." *Literary Digest* 92 (March 19, 1927): 22–23.

Horton, Rod W., and Herbert W. Edwards. *Backgrounds of American Literary Thought*. Englewood Cliffs, N.J.: Prentice-Hall, 1974.

"House of Efficiency." *Craftsman* 29 (October 1915): 103–8.

"Household Engineering." *Good Housekeeping* 66 (March 1918): 59.

"Household Waste and Public Waste." *Journal of Home Economics* 9 (September 1917): 432.

"How Hoover's Forces Fought the Flood." *Literary Digest* 94 (July 30, 1927): 37–42.

Howe, Frederick C. *The High Cost of Living*. New York: Scribner's, 1917.

Howells, William Dean. *A Hazard of New Fortunes*. 1890. Reprint. New York: New American Library, 1965.

———. *Through the Eye of the Needle*. New York: Harper and Brothers, 1907.

Howes, Ethel P. "The Aesthetic Value of Efficiency." *Atlantic* 110 (July 1912): 81–91.

Hughes, Robert. *The Shock of the New*. New York: Knopf, 1980.

Hulme, T. E. *Speculations: Essays on Humanism and the Philosophy of Art*. Edited by Herbert Read. New York: Harcourt, Brace and Co., 1924.

Huneker, James. *New Cosmopolis*. New York: Scribner's, 1915.

Hutchinson, Woods. "Our Human Misfits." *Everybody's Magazine* 25 (October 1911): 519.

Irwin, Will. *Herbert Hoover: A Reminiscent Biography*. New York: Grosset and Dunlap, 1928.

James, Henry. *The American Scene*. 1907. Reprint. Bloomington: Indiana University Press, 1968.

James, William. "The Energies of Men." In *Essays on Faith and Morals*. New York: New American Library, 1962.

————. *Principles of Psychology*. 2 vols. New York: Holt, 1890.

Jewett, Sarah Orne. *The Country of the Pointed Firs and Other Stories*. Garden City, N.Y.: Doubleday, 1956.

Jones, Edith. "Efficient Kitchen." *Country Life* 31 (January 1917): 52–53.

Jordy, William. *American Buildings and Their Architects: Progressive and Academic Ideals at the Turn of the Twentieth Century*. Garden City, N.Y.: Doubleday, 1976.

Josephson, Matthew. "A Sad 'Big' Parade." *Saturday Review of Literature* 9 (March 19, 1932): 600.

Kakar, Sudhir. *Frederick Taylor: A Study in Personality and Innovation*. Cambridge, Mass.: MIT Press, 1970.

Kasson, John. *Civilizing the Machine: Technology and Republican Values in America, 1776–1900*. 1976. Reprint. New York: Penguin, 1977.

Kazin, Alfred. *On Native Ground*. New York: Reynal and Hitchcock, 1942.

Kearns, George. *Guide to Ezra Pound's Selected Cantos*. New Brunswick, N.J.: Rutgers University Press, 1980.

Keefer, Frederick T. *Ernest Poole*. New York: Twayne, 1966.

Kenner, Hugh. *The Pound Era*. Berkeley and Los Angeles: University of California Press, 1971.

Kern, Stephen. *The Culture of Time and Space 1880–1918*. Cambridge, Mass.: Harvard University Press, 1983.

Kimball, Dexter S. *I Remember*. New York: McGraw-Hill, 1953.

King, John Owen, III. "Demonic New World and Wilderness Land." *Prospects: The Annual of American Cultural Studies* 7 (1982): 1–52.

Koestler, F. "Our Stupendous Yearly Waste." *World's Work* 23 (March 1912): 593–95.

Kouwenhoven, John. *The Arts in Modern American Civilization*. 1948. Reprint. New York: Norton, 1967.

————. *Half a Truth Is Better than None: Some Unsystematic Conjectures about Art, Disorder, and American Experience*. Chicago: University of Chicago Press, 1982.

Krause, Sidney J., ed. *Essays in Determinism in American Literature*. Kent, Ohio: Kent State University Press, 1964.

Layton, Edwin T., Jr. *The Revolt of the Engineers: Social Responsibility and the American Engineering Profession*. Cleveland: Case Western University Press, 1971.

————. "Veblen and the Engineers." *American Quarterly* 14 (Spring 1962): 64–72.

Lears, Jackson. *No Place of Grace: Antimodernism and the Transformation of American Culture 1880–1920*. New York: Pantheon, 1981.

Lee, Gerald Stanley. "The Machine-Trainers." *Atlantic Monthly* 111 (January 1913): 198–207.

Levin, David. *History as Romantic Art*. Stanford, Calif.: Stanford University Press, 1959.

Lewis, Sinclair. *Babbitt*. 1922. Reprint. New York: New American Library, 1961.

————. *Dodsworth*. 1929. Reprint. New York: New American Library, 1967.

————. *Main Street*. 1920. Reprint. New York: New American Library, 1980.

————. *Selected Short Stories of Sinclair Lewis*. Garden City, N.Y.: Doubleday, Page, 1935.

Lippmann, Walter. *Drift and Mastery*. New York: Mitchell Kennerly, 1914.

————. "More Brains—Less Sweat." *Everybody's Magazine* 25 (December 1911): 827–28.

Litz, A. Walton, ed. *Eliot in His Time: Essays on the Occasion of the Fiftieth Anniversary of The Waste Land*. Princeton, N.J.: Princeton University Press, 1973.

London, Jack. *The Call of the Wild*. 1903. Reprint. New York: Penguin, 1980.

————. *White Fang*. 1906. Reprint. New York: Penguin, 1980.

Lowell, A. L. "Measurements of Efficiency in College." *Education* 34 (December 1913): 217–24.

Ludington, Townsend. *John Dos Passos: A*

Twentieth-Century Odyssey. New York: Dutton, 1980.

Lynd, Robert, and Helen Merrill Lynd. *Middletown*. 1929. Reprint. New York: Harcourt, Brace and Co., 1956.

Lynde, Francis. *The Quickening*. Indianapolis: Bobbs-Merrill, 1906.

McCullough, David G. *The Johnstown Flood*. New York: Simon and Schuster, 1968.

Maclaurin, Richard C., ed. *The Mechanic Arts*. Vol. 1. Boston: Hall and Locke, 1911.

Maddocks, M. "5000 Homes Are Planned to Make Housework Easy." *Good Housekeeping* 67 (October 1918): 44–45.

———. "The Household Efficient." *Good Housekeeping* 67 (September 1918): 57, 97.

Magny, Claude-Edmonde. *The Age of the American Novel: The Film Aesthetic of Fiction between the Two Wars*. Translated from the French by Eleanor Hochman. 1948. Reprint. New York: Ungar, 1972.

Mariani, Paul. *William Carlos Williams: A New World Naked*. New York: McGraw-Hill, 1981.

———. *William Carlos Williams: The Poet and His Critics*. Chicago: American Library Association, 1975.

Martin, Frederick Townsend. *The Passing of the Idle Rich*. Garden City, N.Y.: Doubleday, 1911.

Martin, Ronald. *American Literature and the Universe of Force*. Durham, N.C.: Duke University Press, 1981.

Marx, Leo. *The Machine in the Garden*. New York: Oxford University Press, 1964.

Maxim, Hudson. *Reminiscences and Comments as Reported by Clifton Johnson*. Garden City, N.Y.: Doubleday, 1924.

———. *The Science of Poetry and the Philosophy of Language*. New York: Funk and Wagnalls, 1910.

Mazzaro, Jerome, ed. *Profile of William Carlos Williams*. Columbus, Ohio: Bobbs-Merrill, 1971.

Meikle, Jeffrey L. *Twentieth-Century Limited: Industrial Design in America, 1925–1939*. Philadelphia: Temple University Press, 1979.

Mencken, H[enry] L[ouis]. *The American Language: An Inquiry into the Development of English in the United States*. 4th ed. New York: Knopf, 1936.

Merritt, Raymond H. *Engineering in American Society 1850–1875*. Lexington: University Press of Kentucky, 1969.

Merz, Charles. *The Great American Bandwagon*. New York: John Day, 1928.

Miller, J. Hillis. *The Disappearance of God: Five Nineteenth-Century Writers*. Cambridge, Mass.: Harvard University Press, 1963.

———. *Poets of Reality: Six Twentieth-Century Writers*. New York: Atheneum, 1966.

———. *William Carlos Williams: A Collection of Critical Essays*. Englewood Cliffs, N.J.: Prentice-Hall, 1966.

Mitchell, S. Weir. *John Sherman, Ironmaster*. New York: Century, 1911.

———. *When All the Woods Are Green*. New York: Century, 1898.

Moers, Ellen. *Two Dreisers*. New York: Viking, 1969.

Monroe, Harriet. *John Wellborn Root: A Study of His Life and Work*. 1896. Reprint. Park Forest, Ill.: Prairie School Press, 1966.

Morison, Samuel Eliot. *One Boy's Boston 1887–1901*. 1962. Reprint. Boston: Northeastern University Press, 1983.

Motoring with a Kodak. Rochester, N.Y.: Eastman Kodak Co., 1914.

Mott, Frank L. *Golden Multitudes: The Story of Best Sellers in the United States*. New York: Macmillan, 1947.

Mowrer, Edgar. *This American World*. New York: J. H. Sears, 1928.

Mumford, Lewis. "The Economics of Contemporary Decoration." *Creative Art* 4 (January 1929): xix–xxii.

———. *My Works and Days*. New York: Harcourt Brace Jovanovich, 1979.

———. *Sticks and Stones: A Study of American Architecture and Civilization*. New York: Norton, 1924.

Munsterberg, Hugo. *The Americans*. London: Williams and Norgate, 1905.

Nash, George H. *The Life of Herbert Hoover: The Engineer, 1874–1914*. New York: Norton, 1983.

"Natural Form and Mechanical Design." *Literary Digest* 17, no. 16 (1898): 463.

Nevius, Blake. *Robert Herrick: The*

Development of a Novelist. Berkeley and Los Angeles: University of California Press, 1962.

The New York Times Film Reviews 1913–1968. Vol. 1. New York: New York Times and Arno Press, 1970.

Noble, David F. *America by Design: Science, Technology, and the Rise of Corporate Capitalism*. New York: Oxford University Press, 1977.

Noble, David W. "The Theology of Thorstein Veblen." In *Thorstein Veblen*, edited by Carlton C. Qualey, pp. 72–105. New York: Columbia University Press, 1968.

Norris, Frank. *McTeague*. 1899. Reprint. New York: New American Library, 1964.

———. *The Octopus* 1901. Reprint. New York: New American Library, 1964.

———. *The Pit*. 1903. Reprint. Edited by James D. Hart. Columbus, Ohio: Merrill, 1970.

"Novel Ways of Saving Your Time, Labor, and Money: Interview with M. Dewey." *American Magazine* 98 (September 1924): 34–35.

O'Brien, Edward J. *The Dance of the Machines*. New York: Macaulay, 1929.

O'Neill, Eugene. *Dynamo*. Vol. 7 of *The Plays of Eugene O'Neill*. New York: Scribner's, 1935.

Osler, William. *Way of Life and Selected Writings*. 1907. Reprint. New York: Dover, 1951.

"Our National Waste." *Scientific American* 116 (May 26, 1917): 535.

Park, Robert Ezra; Ernest W. Burgess; and Roderick D. McKenzie. *The City*. 1925. Reprint. Chicago: University of Chicago Press, 1967.

Pattee, Fred Lewis. *The New American Literature 1890–1930*. New York: Century, 1930.

Petrunkevitch, A. "Wasteful Nature." *Yale Review* 12 (October 1922): 145–58.

Phillips, Camillus. "Running the Home Like a Factory." *Technical World Magazine* 23 (July 1915): 589–92.

Pinchot, Gifford. *The Fight for Conservation*. Garden City, N.Y.: Doubleday, 1910.

Pizer, Donald. *Realism and Naturalism in Nineteenth-Century American Literature*.

Carbondale: Southern Illinois University Press, 1966.

Plowden, David. *Bridges: The Spans of North America*. New York: Viking, 1974.

Poe, Edgar Allan. *Essays and Reviews*. New York: Library of America, 1984.

Poole, Ernest. "Efficiency." *Delineator* 77 (March 1911): 170–71.

———. *The Harbor*. New York: Macmillan, 1926.

Pound, Arthur. *The Iron Man in Industry*. Boston: Atlantic Monthly Press, 1922.

Pound, Ezra. *ABC of Reading*. 1934. Reprint. New York: New Directions, 1960.

———. *Gaudier-Brzeska*. New York: New Directions, 1970.

———. *Instigations of Ezra Pound, Together with an Essay on the Chinese Written Character*. New York: Boni and Liveright, 1920.

———. *Literary Essays*. Edited by T. S. Eliot. New York: New Directions, 1968.

———. *Selected Letters 1907–1941*. 1950. Reprint. New York: New Directions, 1971.

———. *Selected Poems*. New York: New Directions, 1957.

———. *Selected Prose 1909–1965*. New York: New Directions, 1975.

Pupin, Michael. *Romance of the Machine*. New York: Scribner's, 1930.

Purdy, Strother B. "Technopoetics: Seeing What Literature Has to Do with the Machine." *Critical Inquiry* 11 (September 1984): 130–40.

Pyle, W. H. "Educational Waste." *School and Society* 28 (November 10, 1928): 590–91.

Randall, John H. *Our Changing Civilization: How Science and the Machine Are Reconstructing Modern Life*. New York: Frederick Stokes, 1931.

Rapport, Samuel, and Helen Wright, eds. *Engineering*. New York: New York University Press, 1963.

Ratigan, William. *Highways Over Broad Waters: Life and Times of David B. Steinman, Bridgebuilder*. Grand Rapids, Mich.: Eerdmans, 1959.

Redfield, William C. "The Moral Value of Scientific Management." *Atlantic* 110 (August 1912): 411–17.

"The Rise of the Aluminum Piston." *Country*

Life 31 (November 1916): 84.

Rohrkemper, John. *John Dos Passos: A Reference Guide*. Boston: G. K. Hall, 1980.

Roosevelt, Theodore. *The New Nationalism*. New York: Outlook, 1910.

Rorer, S. T. "Wastes in the Kitchen." *Good Housekeeping* 58 (May 1914): 708–10.

Roth, Leland M., ed. *America Builds: Source Documents in American Architecture and Planning*. New York: Harper and Row, 1983.

Rothenberg, Jerome, ed. *Revolution of the Word*. New York: Seabury, 1974.

Rugg, Harold. "The Artist and the Great Transition." In *America and Alfred Stieglitz: A Collective Portrait*, edited by Waldo Frank et al., pp. 91–99. Rev ed. New York: Aperture, 1979.

Salt, Harriet. *Mighty Engineering Feats*. 1937. Reprint. Freeport, N.Y.: Books for Libraries Press, 1962.

Samson, Leon. *The American Mind*. New York: Cape and Smith, 1932.

Samuels, Ernest. *Henry Adams: The Major Phase*. Cambridge, Mass.: Harvard University Press, 1964.

Sanders, David, ed. *Merrill Studies in U.S.A.* Columbus, Ohio: Charles E. Merrill, 1972.

Santayana, George. *The Genteel Tradition: Nine Essays by George Santayana*. Edited by Douglas L. Wilson. Cambridge, Mass.: Harvard University Press, 1967.

Seelye, John. *Prophetic Waters: The River in Early American Life and Literature*. New York: Oxford University Press, 1977.

Shearer, William J. "Elimination of Waste in Education." *National Education Association Addresses and Proceedings* (1920): 513–15.

Shumway, J. "What Is It That I Waste?" *Ladies Home Journal* 34 (July 1917): 28.

Simmel, Georg. *On Individuality and Social Forms: Selected Writings*. Edited by Donald N. Levine. Chicago: University of Chicago Press, n.d.

Sinclair, Upton. *The Jungle*. 1906. Reprint. New York: New American Library, 1980.

Smith, Henry Nash, ed. *Popular Culture and Industrialization 1865–1890*. New York: New York University Press, 1967.

Smith, Rollin E. "The Mighty River of Wheat." *Munsey* 25 (April 1901): 17–30.

Spooner, Henry J. *Wealth from Waste*. 1918. Reprint. Easton, Pa.: Hive Press, 1974.

Stearns, Harold, ed. *Civilization in the United States*. New York: Harcourt Brace and Co., 1922.

Stein, Gertrude. *The Autobiography of Alice B. Toklas*. 1933. Reprint. New York: Random House, 1961.

Stilgoe, John R. *Metropolitan Corridor: Railroads and the American Scene*. New Haven: Yale University Press, 1983.

Strunk, William, Jr., and E. B. White. *Elements of Style*. 3d ed. New York: Macmillan, 1979.

Sullivan, Mark. *Our Times, 1900–1925*. 4 vols., 1926–32. Reprint. New York: Scribner's, 1971.

Supplee, H. "Basic Principles of Efficiency." *Cassier's* 42 (September 1912): 233–38.

Tashjian, Dickran. *Skyscraper Primitives: Dada and the American Avant-Garde 1910–1925*. Middletown, Connecticut: Wesleyan Univ. Press, 1975.

Taylor, Frederick W. *Scientific Management, Comprising Shop Management, The Principles of Scientific Management, Testimony before the House Special Committee*. New York: Harper and Brothers, 1947.

Thoreau, Henry David. "Homer. Ossian. Chaucer." *Dial* 4 (April 1844): 290–305.

Tichi, Cecelia. *New World, New Earth: Environmental Reform in American Literature from the Puritans through Whitman*. New Haven: Yale University Press, 1979.

"To Eliminate Waste by Standardizing." *Literary Digest* 73 (June 24, 1922): 67.

"To Help Us All by Cutting Out Waste." *Literary Digest* 85 (May 2, 1925): 16–17.

Tocqueville, Alexis de. *Democracy in America*. Edited by Thomas Bender. New York: Modern Library, 1981.

Townley, Rod. *The Early Poetry of William Carlos Williams*. Ithaca, N.Y.: Cornell University Press, 1975.

Trachtenberg, Alan. *Brooklyn Bridge: Fact and Symbol*. 1965. Reprint. Chicago: University of Chicago Press, 1979.

———. *The Incorporation of America:*

Culture and Society in the Gilded Age. New York: Hill and Wang, 1982.

"Training the Home Engineer." *Women's Home Companion* 53 (February 1926): 42.

Turner, Frederick Jackson. *The Frontier in American History.* New York: Holt, 1920.

Twain, Mark. *A Connecticut Yankee at King Arthur's Court.* 1889. Reprint. New York: Penguin, 1971.

———. *Letters from the Earth.* Edited by Bernard De Voto. 1942. Reprint. New York: Harper and Row, 1974.

Variety Film Reviews 1907–1980. New York: Garland, 1983.

Vauclain, Samuel M., with Earl May. *Steaming Up!* New York: Brewer and Warren, 1930.

Veblen, Thorstein. *The Engineers and the Price System.* New York: Huebsch, 1921.

———. *The Instinct of Workmanship and the State of the Industrial Arts.* New York: Macmillan, 1914.

———. *The Theory of Business Enterprise.* New York: Scribner's, 1904.

———. *The Theory of the Leisure Class.* 1899. Reprint. Introduction by Robert Lekachman. New York: Penguin, 1979.

Vendler, Helen. *Part of Nature, Part of Us: Modern American Poets.* Cambridge, Mass.: Harvard University Press, 1980.

Viollet-le-Duc, Eugene Emmanuel. *Discourses on Architecture.* Translated from the French by Henry Van Brunt. Boston: Osgood, 1875.

Wagner, Linda. *Dos Passos: Artist as American.* Austin: University of Texas Press, 1979.

———. *Hemingway and Faulkner: Inventors/Masters.* Metuchen, N.J.: Scarecrow Press, 1975.

———. *The Prose of William Carlos Williams.* Middletown, Conn.: Wesleyan University Press, 1970.

Walsh, G. E. "Fortunes in Waste Materials." *Harper's Weekly* 54 (February 5, 1910): 34.

"Waste." *Atlantic* 115 (April 1915): 572–5.

Watson, M. U. "Waste." *Journal of Home Economics* 7 (March 1915): 109–14.

Weiss, George. "Conservation of Waste." *Forum* 57 (February 1917): 241–51.

Wells, H. G. *The Future in America.* New York: Harper and Brothers, 1906.

West, Thomas Reed. *Flesh of Steel: Literature and the Machine in American Culture.* Nashville: Vanderbilt University Press, 1967.

Wharton, Edith. *A Backward Glance.* New York: Appleton-Century, 1934.

———. *The Custom of the Country.* New York: Scribner's, 1913.

———. *Ethan Frome.* 1911. Reprint. New York: Scribner's, 1939.

———. *The Fruit of the Tree.* London: Macmillan, 1907.

———. *The House of Mirth.* 1905. Reprint. New York: New American Library, 1964.

———. *Hudson River Bracketed.* New York: Scribner's, 1929.

———. *Madame de Treymes and Others.* New York: Scribner's, 1970.

———. *The Reef.* New York: Appleton, 1912.

Wharton, Elna H. "Time, a Neglected Commodity." *Delineator* 90 (June 1917): 25.

"What Is Waste?" *Journal of Home Economics* 11 (July 1919): 317–18.

What Was Naturalism? Edited by Edward Stone. New York: Appleton-Century-Crofts, 1959.

Whitaker, Thomas R. *William Carlos Williams.* New York: Twayne, 1968.

White, Martha E. "Aristocracy of Efficiency." *Home Progress* 3 (November 1913): 134–37.

Whitman, Walt. *Leaves of Grass.* Edited by Sculley Bradley and Harold W. Blodgett. New York: Norton, 1973.

"Wicked Food Waste." *Literary Digest* 74 (August 1922): 31.

Wild, Laura. "Training for Social Efficiency." *Education* 32 (December 1911): 226.

Wilkins, Thurman. *Clarence King.* New York: Macmillan, 1958.

Williams, William Carlos. *The Autobiography of William Carlos Williams.* 1951. Reprint. New York: New Directions, 1967.

———. *The Build-Up.* 1952. Reprint. New York: New Directions, 1968.

———. *The Collected Earlier Poems.* New York: New Directions, 1966.

———. *The Collected Later Poems.* New York: New Directions, 1967.

———. *The Embodiment of Knowledge.* New York: New Directions, 1974.

————. *I Wanted to Write a Poem*. Edited by Edith Heal. 1958. Reprint. New York: New Directions, 1967.

————. *Imaginations*. 1970. Reprint. New York: New Directions, 1971.

————. *In the American Grain*. 1933. Reprint. New York: New Directions, 1956.

————. *In the Money*. 1940. Reprint. New York: New Directions, 1967.

————. *Interviews with William Carlos Williams*. Edited by Linda Wagner. New York: New Directions, 1976.

————. *Paterson*. New York: New Directions, 1963.

————. *Pictures from Brueghel and Other Poems*. New York: New Directions, 1962.

————. *Selected Essays*. 1954. Reprint. New York: New Directions, 1969.

————. *Selected Letters*. Edited by John Thirwall. New York: McDowell, Obolensky, 1957.

————. *A Voyage to Pagany*. 1928. Reprint. New York: New Directions, 1970.

————. *White Mule*. New York: New Directions, 1967.

William Carlos Williams Review 9, nos. 1–2 (Fall 1983). Centennial Issue.

Wilson, Carol G. *Herbert Hoover*. New York: Evans, 1968.

Wilson, Edmund. *The American Earthquake: A Documentary of the Twenties and Thirties*. New York: Farrar, Straus and Giroux, 1958.

————. "Dos Passos and the Social Revolution." 1952. Reprint. In *Dos Passos: A Collection of Critical Essays*, edited by Andrew Hook, pp. 34–41. Englewood Cliffs, N.J.: Prentice-Hall, 1974.

Woodruff, Douglas. *This American Republic*. New York: Dutton, 1926.

Wrenn, John H. *John Dos Passos*. New York: Twayne, 1961.

Wright, Frank Lloyd. *An Autobiography*. New York: Duell, Sloan and Pearce, 1943.

————. *A Testament*. New York: Horizon, 1957.

————. *Writings and Buildings*. Edited by Edgar Kaufman and Ben Raeburn. New York: Horizon, 1960.

Wright, Harold Bell. *The Winning of Barbara Worth*. Chicago: Book Supply, 1911.

Yeats, W[illiam] B[utler]. *The Collected Poems of W. B. Yeats*. New York: Macmillan, 1956.

Ziff, Larzer. *The American 1890s: Life and Times of a Lost Generation*. 1966. Reprint. Lincoln: University of Nebraska Press, 1979.

INDEX

Adams, Henry, 42, 43, 70, 99, 180, 181, 235; on efficiency, 75–76, 87, 170; technological values in, 137–68
Adams, Samuel, 221
Aiken, Conrad, 116
Ammann, Othmar, 128
Anderson, Sherwood, 16, 31, 78, 172, 174, 183–94, 219, 262, 270, 271
Antheil, George, 287
Appleton, Victor, 100

Babbitt, Irving, 55
Bancroft, George, 121
Barlow, Joel, 121, 139
Barthes, Roland, 143
Baum, L. Frank, 159
Beach, Rex, 118, 121, 125, 183
Beard, Charles, 234, 240
Beard, George, 51, 235
Beard, Mary, 234, 240
Bellamy, Edward, 63, 74, 75, 87, 90, 98, 121, 134; repudiates instability, 55–58; engineering mentality in *Looking Backward*, 105–16
Bennett, Arnold, 247–48
Berkeley, Busby, 287
Bernays, Edward, 117
Betts, George, 79
Beyer, Otto S., 116
Blackmur, R. P., 153
Bolter, J. David, xii
Book, William, 102
Brooks, Van Wyck, 116, 284
Brown, Charles Brockden, 202
Bryant, William Cullen, 113, 116
Burbank, Luther, 205
Burnham, Daniel, 141, 181
Byard, A. L., 87

Cahan, Abraham, 100
Carman, Bliss, 260
Cather, Willa, 16, 29, 31, 173–80, 270, 271, 272
Channing, William Ellery, 139
Chase, Stuart, 65, 231
Clendening, Logan, 274–75

Commager, Henry Steele, 134
Computer, defining technology of, xi–xii
Comte, Auguste, 43, 113
Condit, Carl, 141
Cooke, Morris L., 135
Cooper, James Fenimore, 200
Cowley, Malcolm, 245, 289
Cox, Harvey, 159
Crane, Hart, ix, 5, 159, 163, 251
Crane, Stephen, 43, 56; themes of instability in, 44

Darwin, Charles, 19, 33, 34, 41, 42, 43
Davis, Richard Harding, 117, 167, 170
Davis, Stuart, 254
Dewey, Melville C., 66
Dickens, Charles, 200
Dickinson, Emily, 29, 163–64
Dodge, Grenville, 123
Donne, John, 33
Donnelly, Ignatius, 54
Dos Passos, John, xi, 16, 37, 56, 58, 76, 78, 90, 91, 136, 172, 173, 194, 195–216, 230, 240, 245, 258, 276, 289, 291
Douglas, Clifford Hugh, 95–96
Dreiser, Theodore, 33, 34, 56, 98, 201; themes of instability in, 44, 45, 49, 51, 98–99
Driggs, Elsie, 280
Driscoll, James R., 100
Dwight, Timothy, 121
Dynamo: as image and symbol, 28, 156–66, 271–72, 284

Eads, James B., 141
Eakins, Thomas, 5, 223
Edison, Thomas Alva, 20, 29, 76, 213, 284
Efficiency, xii; in Bellamy, 55–58; Efficiency Movement, 76, 79–87; as modernist literary value, 79, 87–96; in advertising, 80–86; in Ernest Poole, 88–90; in Ezra Pound, 91–96; in William Carlos Williams, 257–67. *See also* Adams, Henry; Hemingway, Ernest; Taylor, Frederick Winslow; Wright, Frank Lloyd
Eiffel, Gustave, 143